EDL: COMING ~~DOWN THE~~ 'OAD

By BILLY BLAKE

VHC PUBLISHING
By the working class, for the working class

MADE IN ENGLAND

Cover Image courtesy of Rafal Marcinkiewicz ©

Published in Birmingham, England in 2011 by VHC Publishing

ISBN: 978-0-9561302-2-8

They must find it hard to take Truth for Authority who have so long mistaken Authority for Truth."

Gerald Massey 1828-1907

Introduction

Thousands lined the streets to pay tribute to the 2nd Battalion, Royal Anglian Regiment, as it marked its return from the Iraq War with a homecoming parade through Luton town centre. The crowds cheered as the soldiers filed past, some people rushed forward to shake hands with the officers leading the parade, others proudly followed the procession. Some waved flags or held aloft placards saying: '**Welcome Home**' and '**Thank you for your courage**'.

A group of Muslim men had also gathered along the route. As the parade passed them they produced placards that declared '**Anglian soldiers: Butchers of Basra**' and '**Anglian soldiers: Cowards, killers, extremists**'. The men shouted insults such as "**murderers**" and "**cowards**" while gesticulating angrily at the passing soldiers.

One woman nearby moved to stand in front of the protestors. She defiantly waved a small Union Jack, seemingly attempting to shield the soldiers from the vile abuse being levelled at them. Police moved in quickly and surrounded the protestors, but as the parade finished, people nearby reacted angrily and tried to confront them. The police slowly marshalled the Muslim group down a side street, where they could be better protected from the angry mob which had now gathered.

As angry locals remonstrated with police, one officer said: "**Look, they're allowed to protest**". A woman nearby, overcome with anger, replied: "**They have no right to do that, it is disgraceful! How dare you say that!**" Another woman also reacted furiously: "**Our boys have just come back, isn't that disorder?**"

The evening's news broadcasts all carried the story, as did the following day's newspapers. The Muslim protestors were branded as a '**hate-mob**' of '**fanatics**', '**extremists**' and '**cowards**' who had called British soldiers '**pathetic, cowardly, murdering, baby killers**'. The condemnation by the press didn't stop there, the ensuing days papers carried further stories on the radicals with headlines such as '**Britons who hate Britain**' or '**The enemy within?**' The press fully explored and publicised the rantings of the extremists, linking them to al-Qaeda and the Taliban, they informed an already enraged public that the radicals wanted to see '**the black flag of Islam flying over 10 Downing Street**'.

Outrage at the protest reverberated across the nation. The actions of the radicals ignited an explosion of public anger, particularly among the English working class, who for generations had formed the backbone of the Armed Forces. This anger, stoked up by a sensationalist tabloid press, manifested itself mostly on the Internet, particularly social networking sites. On some of these websites, not just anger, hurt and disgust, but coordinated responses to the outrage were discussed.

From this mass outpouring of revulsion, an organised response was devised, leading to the formation of *United People of Luton* (UPL) and *Casuals United*. Local working class lads from Luton led the way, a core group from Luton's Farley Hill estate, plus others from the town who had gone to school or attended football matches together. UPL took to the streets to protest against the extremists.

Mainly using the Internet, alliances were quickly formed and targets identified. The role of the Internet should not be under-estimated, as it has played, and continues to play, a key role in the organisation of the coordinated response to the extremists. United People of Luton and Casuals United were determined to physically oppose the Muslim extremists who, in their eyes, had taken a huge liberty on streets they considered their own. The protest by the radicals was perceived as a direct challenge to the English working class. Their Armed Forces, unable to fight back, had been insulted on streets they considered their own. If the Army couldn't defend themselves, they would have to do it for them.

Up to this point, anyone who had dared to speak out negatively about any aspect of modern multicultural Britain was automatically branded a racist in the press or by anti-fascist groups. This fear factor prevented many from publicly discussing issues which appeared contrary to the diversity dream being promoted. Perhaps it was the level of outrage following the Luton protest, perhaps it was just the straw that broke the camel's back, but led by football hooligans - already considered social pariahs, it could be said they had the least to lose - working class people took to the streets. The social status of the groups which formed is important. Revulsion following the Luton protest wasn't exclusive to the working class, but an active, physical response was.

Although not recognised as such, the English working class is a distinct ethnic group, with its own traditions and culture. It is considered brutal and crude in comparison to the other classes and has always resisted the interference of both. The English working class are traditionally proud people who lead tough lives and operate on a system of core beliefs and values: patriotism, loyalty, a black and white view of right and wrong and an ingrained support of the under-dog (the latter no doubt based on empathy). These beliefs are generally linked to a strong sense of community and localised cultural identity, formed by many small blocks. The family, street, school, pub, local sports team etc are all things which are readily identified with. The prefix 'our' features heavily in working class terminology, 'our kid', 'our street', it is a statement of belonging. The phrase 'our boys' is also widely used when referring to the military, simply because the vast majority of the Armed Forces are the sons and daughters of the working class.

Even though they might not necessarily support a particular war, the English working class will still support the military while they are risking their lives for Queen and Country. Along with family and community history, tales of family involvement with the forces and British military superiority are passed down through family and community networks. With Britain's imperial past, its history is obviously littered with references to the Armed Forces. For this reason, many working class English males, even those with no personal military experience, will feel an affinity with the services.

With this in mind, it's obvious to see how the protest by the radicals in Luton was perceived as a direct challenge by English working class males, who took to the streets believing it was their duty to respond and defend the soldiers. These patriots stepped forward to defend their community, even in spite of the many labels they knew would be thrown at them.

They weren't disappointed, just like the Muslim protestors; they faced the full wrath of the establishment via a coordinated media onslaught. In spite of press guidelines on stereotyping, the groups were described as a collection of drunken, tattooed, balding, potbellied, middle aged men and assigned various agendas, from 'right-wing' and 'racist', to 'fascist' and 'neo-Nazi'. Not once did the media attempt to investigate the reasons they felt compelled to take to the streets (of course to do so would be an admission that modern multicultural Britain wasn't actually working). Not once did they consider their headlines following the Anglian parade might've played a part, instead choosing to fixate on proving the groups had extremist links and repeatedly highlighting the fact football hooligans were taking part. In the eyes of the press and anti-fascist groups, football hooligan involvement proved beyond doubt that right-wing extremists were involved.

The vast majority of British football hooligans share one feature, they are fiercely patriotic. This has led to sustained allegations of far-right links, although these have little basis in fact and have been used more as a stick to beat anyone who had the temerity to be English and proud of their origins. From the riots of Heysel to Dublin, the press have always incorrectly alleged right-wing involvement. In actual fact, both the National Front (NF) in the 70s and 80s and the British National Party (BNP) in the 90s had little success in enlisting football hooligans to their cause.

Like football hooliganism, UPL and Casuals United emerged from working class gang culture, which is based on localised identity. Membership of a gang is a rite of passage for many young working class males, a declaration of allegiance to their community. It is a further statement of identity and belonging.

Gang violence emerged in Britain during the late nineteenth century following the mass migration from the countryside to the towns during the Industrial Revolution. The anonymity of the big towns, the warrens of squalid back-to-back houses, the large factories or the multitude of small indistinctive workshops, polarised the need in young working class men for a defined identity (they had lost the patriarchal order which had reigned in rowdy behaviour of the much smaller villages and with it security and worth). Gangs of youths, bonded by the streets they lived in or the factories where they worked, clashed in towns and cities across England.

As well as excitement, these hooligan gangs gave their members status and identity which had been lost in the migration to the towns. This is relevant to both the UPL/Casuals and the Muslim radicals, as for differing reasons, both groups are struggling to quantify their identity and both have lost their traditional patriarchal order. To emphasise their identity, again relevant to both the EDL and the radicals, the Victorian gangs developed their own fashions to further set them apart from the rest of society. A few gangs literally attained mythical status, even if seemingly some of the most famous and feared, such as Birmingham's Peaky Blinders, or Liverpool's High Rip, didn't actually exist as such. The aura around these gangs was largely created by the creativity of the sensationalist press of the time, little it seems has changed.

The problem of the hooligan gangs was addressed to differing degrees of success with the introduction of Methodist Boys Clubs and the Scout Movement, offering the alternative of organised sports or outdoor pursuits. However, it would be events on the Continent which would ultimately, albeit temporarily, bring an end to urban gang violence.

The First and Second World Wars ripped the heart out of English gang culture. Although gang violence did persist, it wasn't anywhere near pre-war levels and with the martial attitude of the country at the time, if it did occur, it was viewed more as youthful exuberance than criminality. Following the Second World War, with the general feeling of recovery, prosperity and confidence, there was an explosion in both working class youth culture and gang violence. Britain witnessed the rise of the Teddy Boys, Mods, Rockers and the Skinheads; there was also an upsurge in violence at football matches.

Since its foundation, English football has experienced crowd trouble, there have only been two periods - between the wars and the decade following WWII - when violence hasn't been a regular occurrence. Pre-WWI, it was largely restricted to crowds attacking opposing players or officials, but with post-WWII prosperity and affordable travel, young working class men started to travel the country following their local team. Opposing gangs started to clash regularly in and around football grounds, making headline news. This happened as football was being televised for the first time. Televised clashes and sensationalist 'end of civilisation as we know it' newspaper reports, although horrifying the majority of the nation, undoubtedly encouraged more young men to take part (undoubtedly the Anglian protest had a similar effect on some young disenfranchised Muslim men).

The hooligan gangs which formed around each football club gradually became highly organised, not just in respect of their opponents, but also to avoid interference by the police. Fighting at football became so popular amongst young working class men that football hooliganism evolved its own identity and culture. A distinct mode of dress was adopted, as it had amongst their Victorian predecessors, and the thugs became identifiable by their preference for designer clothing and sportswear. This new breed of hooligan referred to themselves as 'dressers' or 'casuals'.

Up until the 1980s, football hooliganism was seen as a British problem. However, again with the onset of cheap travel, this time international, the hooligan gangs started exporting violence to the Continent and beyond. With English fans causing international incidents, the British Government was forced to act and introduced the Football Spectators Act (1989). This legislation included Football Exclusion Orders, banning convicted hooligans from domestic matches. The Football (Disorder) Act 2000 which followed was even more wide ranging, renaming the exclusion orders as Football Banning Orders. Convicted hooligans were now banned from travelling abroad for matches, as well as from domestic games and forced to hand in their passports and sign at their local police station when international fixtures were being played.

As well as the banning orders, the authorities also started to apply for bans in the civil courts (under Anti-Social Behaviour Order legislation). Bans were obtained on some individuals, even when no crime had been committed, but by police alleging association with known hooligans. They got away with such draconian legislation because the press had turned the football hooligans into bogeymen. As a result, it has become perfectly acceptable for the police to treat all football supporters as second class citizens.

Due to these new powers and the police treating fans how they wished, fans in general suffered, but the hooligans began to view opposing gangs less as the enemy and more as people facing the same oppressive laws they were. Gangs still fought, but paid more respect to each other away from football, partly because of the severe consequences they knew they all now faced but also because advances in technology and social networking allowed them more contact, which bred familiarity.

Following initial protests of varying success by United People of Luton and Casuals United, the two groups decided to merge and organise nationally. This national structure needed a name and the *English Defence League* was born. From humble roots, the EDL has become the largest and most effective street army in the UK.

Primarily a single issue group opposed to Islamic extremism, the EDL has also automatically assumed the role of **'defender'** of the traditional English way of life. Its working class supporters believe that as English people, they, their traditions and culture are under attack. This identity crisis and subsequent defensive attitude is a product of multicultural Britain, but was compounded by Scottish, Welsh and Northern Irish devolution in the 1980s and 90s. Up until the 80s, most of the English working class considered themselves British first. In just over a decade, that had changed. Fans following the English national football team are a good example of this. During the 1982 World Cup in Spain, England fans adorned the stadia with Union Jacks, by the 1992 European Championships in Sweden, they carried the English Cross of St George.

Following devolution, as England's neighbours embraced their heritage and culture, it became apparent to many English people that England didn't actually exist as a nation state, certainly not in the way its devolved neighbours now did. They all had their own identity, but English people were still expected to simply consider themselves British. England has no leader, no parliament and no national anthem. The English filled in census forms and found every ethnicity and nationality covered, bar their own. Community leaders from every ethnic group imaginable represented their communities, bar the English. Every patron saints day was promoted, bar St George's Day, every religious festival seemingly celebrated by local authorities, but the indigenous ones played down, or in some cases even renamed.

England was in the grip of a political correctness obsession, the cultures of minority groups were being widely lauded, the host culture ridiculed or ignored. It was middle class intellectual revenge for empire. British, and therefore English, history was widely revised, British-English culture reviled and derided. Attacks on the indigenous community were, and still are, common, but discrimination doesn't enter into the equation because the English are not recognised as a specific ethnic group. We are treated like a deranged family member who is kept locked in a tower and seldom discussed. The refusal to recognise the English thereby denies them the same recognition as other communities. As a result, English people feel excluded from modern multicultural Britain, forced to defend themselves and reassert their culture. This has resulted in English identity becoming polarised for many, leading to a huge resurgence in English nationalism.

Although the EDL includes female (referred to as the EDL Angels), black and Sikh supporters, it is overwhelmingly made up of white, working class men. It is loosely organised locally under the umbrella of an unelected national leadership, supported by an unelected sub-leadership. Respect and status is gained within the movement in a similar fashion to how it is gained in working class culture, length of service (experience), commitment to the cause and ability. Support for the EDL is spread across the UK, but it is strongest in the former blue-collar manufacturing regions abandoned by the ruling elite, such as the midlands and north.

Politicians have allowed UK manufacturing to collapse, even though the words **'Made in Britain'** are still synonymous with quality and there is undoubtedly a worldwide demand for quality goods in emerging economies which now dwarf our own. It was believed that as part of the European Union, Britain could survive on banking and service industries, with unfettered immigration used to supplement the economy.

Following the relaxation of EU borders, the chances of gainful employment for the English working class have lessened further, as economic-migrants from Eastern Europe have flooded into the country. A survey in May 2011 revealed that 81% of new job vacancies are now filled by foreign workers. Every five years or so the government claim there is a lack of skilled workers in the UK, therefore we need to import them. If they reinstated apprenticeships, it would solve the problem, but it's not a problem which they wish to solve domestically. If manufacturing were kick-started again, it would mean working class people would regain influence. They might even become re-politicised and want a say in how the country is run again. No, the ruling classes prefer us in our current compliant, near comatose, state.

British contracts are regularly handed to foreign companies able to outbid British firms, due to EU **'fair competition'** laws. A good example of this is the decision in June 2011, to award a £1.4billion contract to build 1,400 new carriages for the Thameslink rail route to German company Siemens rather than Derby based train-maker Bombardier. As a result 3,000 British workers faced redundancy.

In a time of recession and record public spending cuts, a British government is prepared to give British money, which could've been reinvested in Britain, to foreign workers. Whose side are they on again? If our politicians still had Britain's best interests at heart, that decision, and the many decisions like it, would never be made. They will say protectionism is a bad thing, try telling that to our European neighbours who all fully protect their own workforce. Our politicians will also tell you that reciprocating agreements ensure that Britain will profit in the long run from decisions such as these, but the truth of the matter is they are more allied to their European peers than they are to the majority of the British people.

The loss of employment prospects in many white working class areas has led to less money, which equates to less confidence and political power. These communities are now totally disenfranchised from society and unrepresented politically. Like many working class people, the EDL is outwardly apolitical but is in fact facing up to many political issues the mainstream political parties are unwilling to confront. Therefore, like it or not, the EDL now represents large swathes of the population who don't feel represented by the political drones who the mainstream parties, now indistinguishable from each other and all following the same agenda, offer as representatives.

Since WWII, as well as a wholesale loss of jobs, a lot of working class areas have welcomed large numbers of migrants. For practical reasons, immigrants arriving in Britain have traditionally settled in poorer, working class areas. They have usually quickly integrated, mainly due to close proximity and the subsequent familiarity it breeds, but also because of the shared hardships. Poorer people often have more of a sense of community which overrides ethnicity, as they are all involved in a similar struggle, such as simply putting food on the table. People in poorer areas also tend to look out for each other because they might need the same courtesy repaid one day.

Small Islamic communities have existed in Britain since the 1600s, but large numbers of Muslims started arriving in the UK during the 1960s and 70s. These immigrants from Britain's former imperial colonies settled mostly in the manufacturing regions of the midlands, north and south-east, mainly because these areas offered better employment prospects. The vast majority were from three regions of the sub-continent: Pakistani Punjab, Pakistani Azad (free) Kashmir and Bangladesh. These regions have all suffered long-standing internal conflicts and they have also all spawned fanatical Islamic fundamentalist terror groups.

The new arrivals settled in quickly, worked hard and adopted some Western customs such as dress, although they didn't integrate as fully as other arrivals had. The main reason they didn't integrate wasn't due to their observance of Islam, it was because these communities practised *biraderi* or clan loyalty. Wherever possible they lived, worked and did business only with members of their own extended family or clan. Biraderi ensured that wherever these culturally insular people settled, they built up their own self-sufficient communities, separate from mainstream society. As these communities and the level of self-sufficiency has grown, the level of separation has increased.

The establishment realised in 1970, two years after Enoch Powell's *Birmingham Speech*, that some of the recent arrivals weren't integrating. Powell's public downfall facilitated a pervasive culture of fear within society regarding the discussion of integration. A new policy of multiculturalism was pursued, simply due to the total lack of inclination to acknowledge, let alone confront, any problems with integration. Rather than facilitating social-cohesion, multiculturalism, and its successor diversity, have actually led to division and separation.

A further separation of these Muslim communities occurred following the publication of *The Satanic Verses* by Salman Rushdie in 1988. Many British Muslims considered the book blasphemous and demonstrated, burning copies and attacking bookshops. The book and the response by the British establishment in seemingly condoning its publication, led to the Muslim community feeling victimised. Muslims in Britain suddenly became politicised and several representative groups were formed which would end up wielding considerable influence. Feeling its recently acquired British identity under attack, the Muslim community also looked to the lands it still considered home for comfort and security (nostalgia for its origins played a major part, just as it does with EDL supporters, who also feel marginalised). However, these homelands were culturally and religiously very conservative regions.

As a result, British Muslims became far more religious and more obvious signs of division started appearing. For Muslim men, beards and traditional dress became a more common sight and some Muslim women adopted the face veil (*niqab*). This return to its roots left the Muslim community open to radicalisation from its native lands, where traditionally a more uncompromising brand of Islam was observed. A feeling of victimisation often leads to aggression and radical foreign terrorist networks suddenly found Britain a fertile recruiting ground.

The relaxed immigration policy of the British state allowed terrorist groups to operate freely in a Britain run by a militant liberal political class obsessed with political correctness. These foreign extremists were vocal; they preached a pious observance of Sharia and opposed free speech. Their views were attractive to some in an Islamic community struggling to define itself. Political correctness ensured neither of the issues of extremism or biraderi could be confronted. Therefore, the Muslim community was allowed to further separate from mainstream society and concentrate.

As it has expanded and become more confident, the divisions between the Muslim community and the rest of English society have widened. When problems have been identified, they are ignored, allegedly in the interests of cohesion, but in reality because multiculturalism was being pursued as part of a deliberate but covert agenda to change the social make-up of Britain. Therefore, any public objections to multiculturalism were brutally suppressed.

Working class English people looked on at all of this, startled initially by the opposition to free speech, but also the apparent subjugation of Muslim women within Islam, magnified by the appearance of the veil. They found it hard to believe the UK was dismantling freedoms, that previous generations had fought long and hard for, to accommodate minority groups. The changing nature of Britain's inner cities, due to the Islamic and not British culture which was now being imposed, also worried people. Also, immigrants were still arriving in large numbers and unemployment was still rising. Working class people saw the newcomers arrive and immediately receive benefits, such as social security and NHS treatment, that their forbears had worked hard for years to receive and they had to jump through hoops to obtain.

There was undoubtedly a need for low-skilled workers in Britain in the two decades following the war. But following the industrial decline of the 1970s and 80s, it is hard to justify why large numbers of immigrants were still entering the UK when jobs were so scarce. It was in fact the realisation of a covert social revolution, in effect a class war, which has been surreptitiously waged in the UK for the last 40 years.

Class is still all encompassing in Britain, even after the introduction of the so-called classless society. If anything, over the last twenty years the differences between classes have widened. Now more than ever, class is used as a form of control. Class in Britain is traditionally defined by a complicated range of distinctions including, accent, terminology, education, background and occupation. Accent and terminology are crucial in determining class, but the real distinction, is values.

The middle classes were created by the investment of the upper class and the labour of the working class. They wouldn't exist without either. This has led to a lack of a readily definable identity and has resulted in a long search for meaning. Culturally they are apart from the other two classes, as stated earlier, the middle class identify with their Continental peers more than their working or upper class countrymen and women.

Post-WWII was a period of prosperity for Britain, in which the middle class gained enormous wealth and influence, enabling them to climb socially and politically as never before. The expanding, aggressive new middle classes, bereft of a defined identity, were detached from Britain's established nationalist identity, based on working class and upper class cooperation. The expanding middle class spilled into areas which were considered the preserve of the other two classes. The upper class still largely ruled, but the working class held sway in Britain, mainly because of the demand for manufactured goods. As a result, working class culture and its products such as music, film and fashion were widely celebrated. As they gradually usurped power, the expanding middle classes infiltrated the institutions of both opposing classes and slowly started to assert control, first educationally, starting with a policy of widespread revisionism.

Communism became popular in British universities, especially Oxbridge, during the 1930s. The rise of fascism was seen by many intellectuals as a threat to liberal democracy and following the Nazi invasion of Russia, the struggle of the communist USSR against fascism became romanticised. As well as providing Soviet intelligence with a very productive spy-ring, generations of middle class graduates who passed through university were tutored by communist academics. I am not suggesting everyone was turned into a rabid communist, but a socialist mindset was and still is undoubtedly instilled (lecturers will ask students for a Marxist or feminist perspective, but never a British one). After leaving university many graduates go on to work in public institutions such as the Civil Service, local government, education or even the church.

Britain's proud imperial history (therefore the success of the other two classes) became taboo and has slowly been erased from the nation's school text books. Any positives are dismissed or ignored and any negative aspects of British imperialism emphasised. Education was also markedly dumbed down. Disguised as progress, tried and tested methods of education were abandoned, as was discipline in the classroom (and society in general) and generations of children left school poorly educated. Why would they do this? Simply to pacify the masses, because better educated people have broader horizons, they rightly expect more from society and realise they can actually change things they don't like. They are more likely to become politicised and have opinions on how the country is run or even foreign policy.

In the late 1960s, Britain and the US witnessed an upsurge in protest and civil disorder over issues such as civil rights, nuclear disarmament and the Vietnam War. In the US, this led to concerns that the government did not have enough troops to send to south-east Asia and at the same time contain the growing unrest against at home. Because of sustained public pressure, and against its wishes, the US administration was forced to end the war in Vietnam. In a subsequent report by the influential Tri-Lateral Commission, public participation and resulting influence on government policy was judged to be a '**crisis of democracy**'. The masses were not expected to voice their opinions on national policy or strategy, doing so put too much pressure on the system. The report claimed the public should be more '**passive**' and declared that the '**institutions of indoctrination**', i.e. schools and universities, were not doing their job (they certainly are now, or more to the point aren't).

For this reason, although there is undoubtedly a reactionary nature to the EDL, it shouldn't mean their concerns are any less valid. If individuals are unable to express the undoubted isolation and demonisation they as white, working-class people feel, it doesn't mean they are incorrect and those things aren't happening, it means the education system has failed. The weekend socialists of the left-wing jump on the inability of some of the English working class to explain their feelings adequately, it is used as confirmation of their superiority over the uneducated, lower orders.

Following the attack educationally, a cultural insurgency took place. New middle class graduates were gradually taking over from the old guard in institutions such as the media. Other cultures were promoted widely, and English, particularly working class, traditions were lampooned. It became increasingly unfashionable to be English. Any display of pride in being English was automatically condemned as racist or jingoistic, yet laudable in any other nationality. It is punishment for empire by the self-hating middle class, even though the English working class were the last to profit from it. The slaves of the dark satanic mills are the only ones yet to receive an apology from our current self-hating establishment.

As American left-winger Saul Alinsky once said, '**Ridicule is man's most potent weapon**' and this assertion was fully employed as a whole army of left-wing alternative comedians emerged from university and began to attack all working and upper class institutions (their battle for control with working class comedians has been referred to as a '**civil war**' by alternative comedian Arthur Smith). It is only now we have realised that these pretentious class warriors were laughing at us, not with us. If you want proof, look where those rebels who '**pushed the boundaries**' have all ended up. They've all sold out, they're all on Radio4, as mainstream as the people they once mocked.

It wasn't an overt attack at first, caricatures such as '**Loadsamoney**' or metaphors such as '**Sun readers**' were used (*The Sun*, like *The Mirror* were popular working class newspapers which could be picked up quickly while a tea-break was taken). Seemingly thinking the working class beaten, they have now moved up a social scale and '**Daily Mail readers**' or '**Little Englanders**' are the target. These discriminatory are widely used; class discrimination is the last truly socially acceptable form of prejudice. We see the word '**chav**' or '**ned**' employed to callously stereotype a whole section of the working class. We still see caricatures such as '**Vicky Pollard**' used by university educated neurotic middle class millionaires to portray, vilify and mock whole abandoned communities. Hardly Charles Dickens is it? They stereotype and label, so the lower orders can be bracketed, mocked and their concerns more easily dismissed.

English working class people had no one credible to support them, as the institutions which traditionally defended them had also been targeted, infiltrated and destroyed. In the 70s and 80s, admittedly drunk on the power gained by being in the social ascendancy, the working class took on successive governments. The lions of the working class were led into the gutter by hardcore communist donkeys caring more for the politics of revolution than for the welfare of their members. As a result, Britain became an international laughing stock and there was an excuse for wholesale social change.

The unity of the working class never fully recovered from the draconian clampdown to curb union power that followed. The relationship between the working class and trade unions was never the same again. Union membership and influence plummeted and the working class lost its main voice.

Another traditional voice of the working class, the Labour Party, was brought to its knees at the same time as the unions. Again like the trade unions, the implosion followed infiltration by left-wing extremists. Into the resulting vacuum created in the party walked the polished, media savvy and power-hungry, but bereft of life experience, sons and daughters of the expanding middle classes. Straight out of university, these newcomers cared little for Labour Party founding principles, the party was merely seen as an alternative route to power and re-branded '**New Labour**'. The traditional working class philosophy of the party became unfashionable, a new direction aimed at middle class voters was taken (the dumbed down working class were beginning to become depoliticised).

As a result, working class people no longer felt represented politically. They now see politics as something remote from their lives, simply because there is less chance for them, or people like them, to become involved. Real socialists such as Bessie Braddock or Dave Nellist, drawing only the salary of an average working man in his constituency, are a thing of the past. There are no more Percy Shurmers, rising from trade union and local politics to represent communities they had lived in all of their lives. Try finding any true representatives of the working class in the House of Commons (a laughable title these days due to the lack of commoners); there are no true working class heroes anymore.

Another traditional supporter of the common people, the Church of England, has also deserted the English common people. When was the last time you heard a representative of the Church of England talk about English working class communities and the problems they face? Its representatives are now more bothered about issues of diversity than the people they once purported to represent. These churchmen would be better served surveying their empty pews and reflecting on the reasons that the Church of England has become irrelevant to the majority of its supposed target audience.

Only two individuals in the church have spoken out about the marginalisation and desertion of the English working class, ironically, neither is British born. Archbishop of York, John Sentamu, has warned that the current trend of multiculturalism ignores the essence of what it means to be English. The Ugandan has predicted that if England fails to rediscover its culture there will be more political extremism. Former Bishop of Rochester, Pakistani born Michael Nazir-Ali has said that there have been attempts to impose an '**Islamic character**' on certain areas and the policy of integration which was being pursued had no moral (not really surprising as along with discipline, morality was something which held the old status quo together, therefore surplus to requirements in the new middle class socialist utopia being constructed) or spiritual vision.

When New Labour was elected, the party pursued an aggressive neo-socialist agenda. It was an ethos which had been instilled at university and, with the trend of youth above age and experience and no credible old guard to temper its implementation, it was pursued ruthlessly. The aim was to change the social make-up of Britain. To achieve this, a policy of unfettered immigration was introduced, even though unemployment was rising and manufacturing output was falling at record levels, faster than anywhere else in the West. In fact, under the last Labour government, supposedly the party of the working class, manufacturing fell from 18% of GDP to 12%. They did this simply to engineer social change.

There can be no doubt that Muslim communities form political blocs. In the main these communities vote with biraderi in mind. These inner-city blocs were all important to the Labour plan. An urbanised area often contains a number of seats; miles of less populous or rural areas are often covered by just one. It was a purely political move to supplant one urban community, the now depoliticised ethnic English, who had traditionally been problematic, with one which was newly politicised with no attachment to traditional culture.

The top echelon of the English working class which was equipped to fight back was bought off with the classless society and the right-to-buy council housing sell-off. They were absorbed into the lower middle class. Depoliticised and with no-one to speak for them, ordinary working class people and their concerns, such as housing, welfare, employment and education were ignored by successive governments. With Britain in economic decline and few employment prospects, these abandoned working class people have been left to rot on abandoned council estates. A benefits culture was promoted. Relatively young people with minor ailments were written off, consigned to years of state dependency; simply so real unemployment figures wouldn't be disclosed and they could still justify the high levels of immigration. Whole communities have been pacified with a ready supply of flat-screen televisions, illegal or prescription drugs and cheap supermarket alcohol, which leads us to another traditional English institution under attack, the pub.

The pub has always played an intrinsic role in English culture, they are places where social pretensions are discarded. It is one of the few places it is considered perfectly acceptable by the socially reserved English to converse with a total stranger. Pubs facilitate bonding, they are places where nicknames are gained and friendships are made, communities are built around them. English pubs have complicated rules on etiquette; they also have a patriarchal system which a community surrounding the pub will subscribe to. England is losing pubs at a record rate. Small independent backstreet pubs, some with a community of hundreds around them, are being forced to close by unfair government taxes on beer and a universally unpopular smoking ban. They also face competition from faceless high street chains, the type you see youngsters staggering out of every weekend, where, without the traditional patriarchal system of the traditional pub's tempering behaviour, anything goes.

Hand in hand with the loss of pub culture, England is also losing a lot of its high streets and small traders at record rates. Of course, progress has played some part, the Internet provides many small traders with a low overheads medium to trade through. But like the pub trade, big supermarkets and multinational concerns are taking over, frequently preferring anonymous out of town locations based on the American model. Again, this has undoubtedly produced negative social factors, ignored in the pursuit of profit, turning some town centres into ghost towns, removing the interaction of the high streets and destroying the communities built around them. They say it is because of changing tastes, is it any wonder? We are being bombarded with propaganda 24/7. Control of the media ensures that middle class culture and values are pushed and promoted as the shining path, anything else is deemed crude or vulgar.

They believe these enforced cultural changes will have no negative consequences, unfortunately we are seeing them already. Young Englishmen, feeling no attachment to the contrived middle class modern British culture which is being foisted upon them, and since the destruction of working class culture having no positive working class role models (like some young Muslims), look abroad for inspiration. Certain traditional working class controls for extreme behaviour, such as the ridicule or opinion of respected men within the community, are simply no longer there. As we see English working class culture disappear, we see our youth taking their lead from other more extreme foreign youth cultures. Thanks to the abandonment of education, they are also more susceptible to foreign extremist ideologies.

As English communities the length and breadth of the country have disappeared, any longing for community, or inherent need to participate in wider society is placated by reality TV and sport, particularly talent or 'reality' shows and the English Premiership. These programmes are promoted like a cult, when they aren't on, other shows are discussing them. Viewers are brainwashed into believing their vote matters, "**Remember folks, your vote counts**", it's a shame they don't put as much effort into getting people to vote in elections. More English working class people probably now vote in reality TV shows than participate in elections. On the day of the Premiership transfer deadline in 2011, millions was squandered on overpaid footballers. Meanwhile, the government announced cuts to services not seen since the 1920s and no-one batted an eyelid.

That is where we are today, the English working class are ignored, disregarded and unrepresented. They have faced a concerted covert assault, brainwashed into acting like docile sheep. That is the main reason why the EDL exists, it is nothing to do with racism, but it does concern discrimination. The English working class have been sidelined, supplanted but not quite defeated yet. A number of them now wish to be heard. They are people from communities which are in distress; they fear for their future and that of their children. They don't want any manufactured new England, they want to preserve the land and the culture that their ancestors fought and died for.

Militant Islam was only the spark, a symptom of a disease in our society which has been allowed to develop. The English people wish to preserve their way of life, their culture and its traditions. To achieve this, they are doing the only thing which is left to them; they are taking to the streets.

Outrage

Luton is a large industrial town, thirty miles north of London, with a population of around 200,000. Although situated in the affluent county of Bedfordshire, Luton is a working class town. Even with its close proximity to the capital, Luton is more associated with midlands manufacturing; historically hat making, but latterly light-engineering, especially car and van production.

Following WWII, the town was widely redeveloped. Bomb damage was cleared and Luton's remaining slums were also demolished. Many new council estates, such as Farley Hill, Stopsley, Limbury and Leagrave sprang up as the town expanded in response to the post-war production boom. The town centre was redeveloped (in effect vandalised like many towns and cities up and down the country), but many locals claim that Luton lost its charm, and was left with an unfriendly one-way traffic system and the Arndale Shopping Centre, considered an eyesore by many local people.

Because of its diverse range of industry, Luton didn't suffer as much as other parts of the country during the great industrial decline of the 1980s and 90s. However, as with other similarly diverse manufacturing regions in Britain, it merely delayed the inevitable and Luton has been hard hit since the turn of the century. In 2002, General Motors closed its Vauxhall plant in the town - which at its peak employed 28,000 people. Further job cuts in the van production which remained in the town were announced in 2009. The loss of the majority of the town's manufacturing - the nearby airport is now the largest single source of employment - means that unemployment in Luton is higher than the UK average.

Luton has a history of welcoming migrants, in the early 1900s people from Scotland and Ireland settled in the town. They were followed by people from the West Indies and the Indian sub-continent following WWII and latterly Africans and eastern Europeans.

A large number of the newcomers from the sub-continent were Muslims from Azad Kashmir, a troubled region which borders India and Pakistan with a history of ethnic/religious strife. Pakistani Kashmiri's follow a conservative brand of Islam and are insular by nature. One in five of Luton's population is now Muslim and the majority live in the Bury Park area of the town. Bury Park's Muslim community has long been accused of isolating itself from wider society.

This isolation has become magnified since the introduction of Islamic schools or *madrasah* to the area, which means that a large number of Muslim children in Luton no longer mix with children of other cultures in the mainstream education system. When schools are divided, it breeds division in society at large, but if children mix with children of different backgrounds then they build an understanding of each other from an early age. The self-imposed isolation of Luton's Kashmiri's has led to other negative social factors; whilst the jobless rate in the town as a whole is around 9%, among the Muslim community it is estimated to be as high as 25%.

As a result, there are defined white and Asian areas in Luton and as the Islamic community has expanded, tension has occurred as white Lutonians have seen Asian families moving into areas they considered their own. The town is described by the local council as a '**vibrant multicultural community**', although in reality, it has recently been more associated with division.

Unfortunately, in recent times Luton has also become synonymous with Islamic extremism. In the mid-90s, radical cleric Omar Bakri Mohammed founded a branch of his group al-Muhajiroun in the town. In fact both Bakri and fellow radical Abu Hamza regularly preached at a mosque on Leagrave Road. Following the 9/11 attacks on the USA on 11 September 2001, local Muslim al-Muhajiroun activists pasted inflammatory posters around Luton, mocking the attacks and proclaiming the terrorists as the '**Magnificent 19**'. A month after 9/11, two men from Luton were identified amongst those killed in US bombing raids on Taliban positions in Afghanistan. Afzal Munir and Aftab Manzoor, both 25, had allegedly travelled to Kabul to fight against the Western allies. One Muslim elder from Luton told *BBC News* that the men had been influenced by extremists from London.

Following the news, tensions increased in the town. There were reports of Muslims being taunted in the street and a number of threatening calls were made to Islamic centres. Bedfordshire Police warned local businesses that local football hooligan gang, Men in Gear (MiGs), was planning trouble in Bury Park, but when the backlash did come, it wasn't from local hooligans. A year later, hooligans attached to Plymouth Argyle, in town for their club's match against Luton, clashed with local Muslim youths after drinking in a pub in Bury Park. In a confrontation outside a shop, one man from Plymouth was stabbed in the chest and a number of others were arrested.

In 2004, Luton man Salahuddin Amin was convicted of involvement in a terrorist plot involving a fertiliser bomb, linked to al-Muhajiroun. Although born in London, Amin grew up in Pakistan before moving to Luton when he was sixteen. He returned to Pakistan in 1999 and became radicalised. When he returned to the UK he became involved in an al-Muhajiroun network which established contact with foreign terrorist organisations. Another Luton man, referred to as 'Q' during the fertiliser trial but later named as Mohammed Quayyum Khan, was said to have been a **'facilitator'** with links to al-Qaeda.

After the Luton link to the fertiliser plot was revealed, a response was organised by a small group of local people who demonstrated in the town centre with a banner which read **'Ban the Luton Taliban'**.

In 2005 a website, **'Holy War – al-Qaeda's Luton & Dunstable war front'** declared the Bedfordshire town a frontline in the war against Britain.

In 2008, a leaked intelligence report identified Luton as home to one of the main concentrations of Muslim extremists in the country. As a result of the constant links to terror, seven Muslim centres in the town were chosen to receive Home Office funding under a **'Preventing Violent Extremism'** initiative. However, this only had a limited affect, as some local Muslims still claim that they are regularly intimidated and threatened by local radicals.

10 March 2009: Luton

Following a second tour of duty in war-torn Iraq, 200 members of the 2nd Battalion, Royal Anglian Regiment marked their homecoming with a parade through Luton town centre. Thousands lined the streets to pay tribute to the returning troops, who, led by a brass-band and clad in desert fatigues, proudly filed through the town. Local people applauded and cheered the soldiers, some rushed forward to shake hands with the officers leading the parade, others held aloft placards saying **'Thank you for your courage'**.

A small group of Muslim men had placed themselves on the route. As the soldiers passed by, they suddenly started shouting abuse, holding aloft placards proclaiming **'Anglian soldiers: Butchers of Basra'** and **'Anglian soldiers: Cowards, killers, extremists'**. One woman moved to stand in front of them, defiantly waving a small Union Jack, seemingly attempting to shield the soldiers from the vile taunts. As the realisation of what was happening spread, people reacted furiously. The extremists were quickly hemmed in at the side of the road by police. The parade continued with the Muslim group chanting **"British soldiers go to hell"**. As soon as the troops passed, people rushed forward to confront the radicals. These people weren't young thugs, one was a middle-aged man in a trilby, and others were middle-aged females. Police prevented any physical confrontation and arrested two men. One of them, Kevin Carroll, who was taking pictures of the event, later told the BBC:

> **"I saw them through the camera. I heard the commotion, but I thought it was cheering at first. Then I realised, no, something's not right. When the penny's dropped, I look up and there's the banners, rapists, butchers of Basra, murderers, terrorists, British government go to hell. And then all of a sudden, there was a massive surge, and the**

atmosphere was just so charged. We were trying to get round the back, trying to get into them. We just ran at them, we were going, you fucking wankers, you scum, scum, scum, you know, there was a murderous atmosphere. There were men, women, different colours, creeds, young, old, there was nothing racist about it. Nothing racist about anything, it was just pure rage, outrage. I mean it was just a good old fashioned British punch on the nose if you like. Not that we're condoning going round punching people on the nose, but you know, for such an offence, that would've been sufficient justice, straight on the nose, you know that's just how people felt on the day."

The police marshalled the Islamic group down a side street where they could be better contained and protected, but were followed by angry locals. The Muslim protesters were held at the end of the road as other officers formed a line to prevent people from confronting them. The two groups traded insults at each other, chants of "**Allahu Akbar!**" (God is great) were met with cat-calls and chants of "**scum**" and "**we pay your benefits**".

One elderly man, gesturing towards the Muslims, asked a police officer why they were protecting them. The officer replied that they were just preventing disorder and that they weren't taking sides. An elderly woman stood in front of the line of police, a dignified smile on her face, proudly waving a small Union Flag in defiance. As angry locals remonstrated with the police, one officer said: "**Look, they're allowed to protest**". A woman nearby, overcome with anger, shouted: "**They have no right to do that, it is disgraceful! How dare you say that!**" Another woman also reacted furiously: "**Our boys have just come back, isn't that disorder?**"

Following the parade, Superintendent Andy Martin of Bedfordshire Police, told *Sky News* that a small number of people had caused a disturbance during the parade but it had been quickly contained by officers. Martin confirmed that two men had been arrested and said that both were members of the general public, not participants in what was termed an anti-war demonstration. Defence Secretary John Hutton condemned the '**tiny minority who used the parade as an opportunity to make utterly ridiculous and insulting comments**'. Justice Minister, Shahid Malik, said that all decent people, irrespective of religion, would be sickened by the antics of the extremists. Prime Minister Gordon Brown said the whole country was proud of its brave servicemen and women and that it was disappointing that a tiny minority had disrupted the event. A statement from Luton Central Mosque referred to the group as idiots who should not have been allowed to protest.

The following day, the Royal Anglian Regiment marched through nearby Watford to the cheers of thousands of people. This time there was no protest, but it was obvious more people had attended as a result of the previous day's scenes in Luton.

Abu Omar, one of the Luton protestors, was unapologetic. He told *The Independent* that there had been nothing illegal about the group's placards or chants and claimed they had broken no laws. He was asked if he thought the demonstration would increase tensions in the town and replied that the protest had not been against the people of Luton, it had been against '**soldiers who voluntarily went and fought in an illegal war and killed Muslims**'. Omar said it wasn't their fault if tensions were stirred up and told the paper: '**They have lost men but while they were there many innocent Iraqis lost their lives. I am outraged that these soldiers paraded through the streets. They are nothing more than hired mercenaries, war criminals, terrorists. I was simply voicing my anger, in a lawful, peaceful way, against the Nazi British Army and the war. I do not regret that.**'

The Telegraph claimed some of the men were also members of Ahlus Sunnah wal Jamaah, a group which included former members of banned groups The Saviour Sect and al-Ghurabaa, both spin-offs of al-Muhajiroun. *The Times* also claimed the group was a branch of al-Muhajiroun, called Islam4UK. On the group's website it stated: '**Islam4UK has been established by sincere Muslims as a platform to propagate the supreme Islamic ideology within the UK as a divine alternative to man-made law. The world has witnessed the tyranny of man-made law, whether that be from the apostate rulers in Muslim lands or the disbelieving leaders in the West**'

Anjem Choudary told the *Daily Star* that the group was planning further demonstrations, if they could '**get the numbers**' (the press would undoubtedly help them with that). One of the group's leaders was 31 year old Sayful Islam, real name Ishtiaq Alamgir. He told *The Telegraph* '**they have killed, maimed and raped thousands of innocent people. They can't come here and parade where there is such a Muslim community**'. British born Islam was said to be a keen follower of Omar Bakri Mohammed. University educated, he was said to have been totally uninterested in politics until he met the radical preacher. Islam is unemployed and married with two children. In 2004, he had told the *Evening Standard* that although he was able-bodied, he preferred not to work; instead he devoted his time to the furtherance of Islam. After the protest, the *News of the World* claimed he lived in a £200,000 house and had '**raked in thousands in benefits**'. Another protestor, Jalal Ahmed, who had been pictured carrying a placard which read '**British Government terrorist government**', was suspended from his job as a baggage handler at Luton Airport following the protest. *The Daily Star* alleged that twelve months earlier, Ahmed had been investigated by his employer, after he was seen taking pictures of aircraft.

Although the establishment were keen to paint the protestors as a minority within a minority, the radicals did have some local support. One local shop owner, named only as Abdullah, told *The Independent* that he had been aware of leaflets advertising the protest weeks earlier, had been too busy to attend. His friend Muhammad told the paper: '**They could have marched through somewhere like St Albans, where there are hardly any Muslims, but they chose Luton. It was a very provocative act. Luton's Muslims are not radical but they do feel strongly about the war in Iraq. So why shit on their doorsteps and antagonise them like that?**'

13 April 2009: Luton

In Luton, some people had already set about organising a response to the outrage. Local ex-soldier James Yeomans organised a peaceful '**Respect Our Troops**' march for 28 March, but it soon became evident that the high level of disgust and anger was bringing what the press termed '**darker forces**' into play. Referring to the march, messages such as '**bring your tools**' and '**it's gonna be messy**' started appearing on social networking websites. On 26 March 2009 the *Luton and Dunstable Herald and Post* claimed '**Fascists Stealing a March**' and said that '**right-wing troublemakers**' were trying to hijack the event. Local anti-fascists also claimed the BNP was trying to gain political capital from the march and that the Internet was being used to encourage football hooligans from as far away as Chester and Portsmouth to attend.

It began to dawn on organiser Yeomans that, judging by the response and now the alleged participation of far-right groups, things might be spiralling out of control. He cancelled the march and attacked the extremists who he said were hoping that the event escalated into violence. Even so, many people were still defiant and insisted they would still travel to Luton on the day of the protest. Anti-fascist group, Hope Not Hate, announced it would be holding its own demonstration in the town on the same day.

Following the cancellation of Yeomans march, a man from nearby Dunstable, Paul Ray, applied to police for permission to hold an anti Muslim extremist march in Luton, on 23 April, St George's Day. If Ray's application was on behalf of a group, he was possibly, in hindsight, the wrong person to apply. He was still on bail after being arrested in 2008 for inciting racial hatred through an Internet blog he wrote under the pseudonym '*Lionheart*'. A group of locals, mainly from the Farley Hill estate, including the two men who had been arrested at the Anglian parade, were also organising their own protest. They decided their protest group needed a name which encompassed everyone in the local community and came up with the name United People of Luton (UPL). They contacted Ray, who put them in touch with the webmaster of a group called the United British Alliance (UBA), who created a website for the fledgling group.

On 9 April, *The Herald & Post* reported that the request by Ray had been rejected by Luton Borough Council because he had '**provided scant information about the organisation of the event**'. UPL issued a statement following the rejection, announcing a '**Ban the terrorists march**' in Luton on 13 April 2009:

> '**Save Luton! The whole country witnessed the hate filled scum that gate crashed the soldiers homecoming! Two of their regiment died in Iraq and they should have met a heroes welcome when returning to there [sic] home town. Luton Borough Council and the Bedfordshire Police gave permission to these Muslim fanatics to protest. Our Council and Police force need to decide if they back this disbanded terrorist group Al-Muhajiroun or they back the local residents of Luton! The people of Luton are calling for all the scum that turned out that day to dishonour our armed forces to be given an ASBO that bans them from our town centre 24 hours a day and 7 days a week! This same extremist group stand outside Don Miller's bakery every Saturday and Luton 6th Form College every Tuesday recruiting and trying to convert people for their Jihad. Luton Police and the council allow this - WE WILL NOT!**
>
> **Cut the politically correct tape tying everyone's hands and do something about this Terrorist group who hate everything our great county stands for. We must stress that this is a very small number of Muslim fanatics and not the wider Muslim community so people of Luton lets unite against these people who hate everything our country stands for and turn out in our numbers be that Muslim, Hindu, Catholic, Christian, Jewish, White, Black or Asian. Turn out in your numbers so the whole country can see the residents of Luton are fed up and are having no more of it! Luton Borough Council have recently agreed to a parade for the death of Mohammed, anti Israel parades, Gaza war etc yet turned down an application for a St Georges Day parade on the 23 April. This smacks of double standards. This demonstration has no political links and is not related to any right wing organisations. This is a UPL demonstration. United People of Luton! There is no point sitting in your armchair and shouting at the TV. The only way to get the message across is to take it to the streets. This is a chance to show the police and the Council the power of public opinion. The entire country is behind us!**'

On Bank Holiday Monday, 13 April 2009, around 500 people gathered in Luton town centre for the '**Reclaim our streets**' demonstration. They planned to march from Debenhams in the town centre to the Town Hall, some carried placards which read '**Shame on you Luton Borough Council**' and '**Ban all preachers of hate**'. Police reinforcements were drafted in from neighbouring forces and around 100 officers, some on horseback, held the protestors in George Street. As a police helicopter hovered overhead, the crowd repeatedly sang "**Let us March!**"

A high proportion of the group were young white working class males and Luton Town football songs could be heard amongst the chants, but other marchers had travelled from as far as Birmingham, Portsmouth and London to join in. As police reinforcements arrived, officers shepherded the demonstrators out of the town centre to disperse them, but there were sporadic incidents of disorder reported across Luton throughout the rest of the day.

Following the protest, UPL announced a further demonstration on 24 May 2009, which it called '**Phase II**'. Speaking on his website, *Lionheart*, Paul Ray said that United People of Luton and its supporters from around the country would not give up on demonstrating against local Islamic militants, until Bedfordshire Police enforced the rule of law upon the radicals. Ray also claimed that over the preceding few days, police had conducted dawn raids on several members of UPL, arresting some and bailing them on condition they did not enter Luton town centre for a period of 4 weeks.

These bail terms obviously ruled them out of the next demonstration on 24 May and Ray warned that it was understood that police also intended to arrest 50 more of the '**Reclaim our Streets**' demonstrators, to also prevent them from entering Luton town centre on the 24th May. Ray said: '**the police are paid with tax payers money to uphold law and order and protect the community but it seems that when it comes to Islamic militants, for some reason they are unable or unwilling to do their jobs and protect the public and preserve the 'peace and harmony' of the community. How can that be right for those innocent people who need protecting from these Moslem monsters? This is the reason why people from around the Country will be uniting with the people of Luton on 24th May. We have all had enough of militant Islam within our homeland!!!**'

Weeks later, the Al Ghurabaa Mosque on Bury Park Road was hit by an arson attack. At midnight on 4 May 2009, two men poured petrol through a side window of the mosque and set light to it before making their getaway in a stolen BMW. The fire was discovered and extinguished by someone staying in the building. Following the attack, the mosque issued a statement saying it had previously strongly condemned the provocative protest by the '**small group of extremists**' and revealed the mosque had received a series of threats prior to the attack.

Spokesman, Farasat Latif, told *The Times*: '**We have noticed a lot of ill-feeling among non-Muslims since the Muhajiroun protest. The media played a role in massively exaggerating the support that these guys have and not making clear that we had nothing to do with it. At the da'wah (Islamic outreach) stall in the town centre we have had quite a few people be abusive towards us, but when we explain to them that we were just as appalled as they were by the actions of the protesters they visibly changed in their attitude towards us. I don't accept that many of these people are racists, but they have been misled by what they have read and by what they have been shown.**'

24 May 2009: Luton

Two days before the protest, the *Luton News* reported '**Far right warned off joining protest march**' and said anti-fascists were worried that the march would attract football hooligans and racists. The paper said that worrying messages had also been posted on Facebook, indicating that right-wing groups might be planning to attend. One of the organisers, Mikey Birch, 22, told the paper: '**We want to warn any right-wing organisations they won't be welcome at the march. They won't be allowed to come in with us**'.

The group March for England (MfE) had initially been granted permission by Luton Borough Council to hold the protest, but had pulled out, therefore the council said the event did not now have an official go-ahead. A council spokeswoman told the *Luton News*: '**the police and the council are aware that a march is still going ahead, culminating in the submission of a petition to the council. Both the police and the council have not sanctioned this march and we would urge all those participating to have regard to the safety of others and to the need to comply with the law. Anyone wearing bomber jackets or skinheads will be turned away. They're not part of Luton and we don't want them to turn up thinking they can take part. If you're a racist, don't turn up**'.

On the day of the protest, a large group of protestors gathered in the Manor Park area of Luton. Escorted by police, they marched from the Manor Road recreation ground, through the town centre along George Street. Some carried placards which read '**No Sharia law in the UK**', some wore balaclavas; others wore masks bearing the face of Sayful Islam, with horns added to the head.

As the protest entered George Street, around 500 people broke away and went on a rampage in which an Asian man was assaulted, the windows of an Asian owned business were smashed and cars were damaged. In Stuart Street, police in riot gear and mounted officers tried to control the situation but clashed with the breakaway mob who hurled stones at them. When the main body of marchers arrived at Luton Town Hall, fronted by young men who had covered their faces in balaclavas, they held a short protest before dispersing.

A police spokesman said nine people had been arrested for offences including criminal damage and assault. They would eventually arrest sixteen men in connection with the disturbances. *BBC News* reported that a large number of marchers had made their way into Bury Park where a number of shops and cars were damaged. *The Times* reported '**Trouble flares as Luton residents protest over Muslim extremists**' and said that police officers had fought running battles with protesters after the some of mob '**bolted and began attacking Asian residents**'.

The *Daily Mail* claimed '**Nine arrested after masked mob's march against Muslim extremists turns violent**'. Using the pseudonym Wayne King, Stephen Lennon told the paper that many people were concerned that the Muslim community in Luton had not taken steps to deal with the extremists. Claiming that his community had been racially attacked for years and that churches in Luton were regularly being vandalised by Muslim extremists, Lennon said UPL simply wanted new laws to stop preachers of hate operating in Luton. The *Daily Telegraph* reported that '**Nine rioters arrested after Luton protest turned violent**', Lennon, again speaking as Wayne King, told the paper '**We decided enough was enough after the soldiers got heckled as they marched through the town centre by the Muslim extremists**'.

Lennon had assumed the role of spokesman for UPL. He was born in Luton in November 1982. According to *The Times*, he is the son of Irish immigrant parents, who split up when he was 11. Brought up on a Bedford housing estate and a lapsed Catholic; Lennon attended Putteridge High School in Luton. After leaving school, he had trained as an aircraft engineer, but eventually became a carpenter. Lennon also owns a tanning salon in Luton. His interest in politics began in 2004 when he joined the BNP. Lennon would later tell *BBC News* "**I don't claim to have ever been an angel, nor a politician who wears a suit - we're normal people from the towns and cities of this country**".

Anti-fascist group (and front for the Socialist Workers Party), Unite Against Fascism (UAF), had spotted an opportunity to get involved. UAF joint secretary, Weyman Bennett, claimed the disturbances bore '**all the hallmarks of the far-right**'. One local anti-fascist relayed his version of events on the UAF website: '**I walked out of my front door to be greeted by around a hundred protesters running across the dual carriageway at the top of my road. Some of them had their faces covered with masks or wore black balaclavas. Their placards read 'No Sharia Law' and they were chanting 'Terrorists Out'. They went on to enter a residential street and later returned to the centre of town, where they attempted to break past police on several occasions. Onlookers of all ages and groups in the town centre at that time were running for cover. It was very intimidating. They were banging on Asian shopkeepers' windows…. They were almost all white and male. They said they had come from as far away as Cornwall, Bournemouth and London.**'

Following the second protest and the arson attack, leaders of the al-Ghurabaa Mosque led a 300 strong band of supporters to Dunstable Road, where supporters of al-Muhajiroun regularly sold extremist literature. Several local shopkeepers, apparently annoyed that the extremists were putting people off visiting the area and affecting their trade, joined the group. The extremists were confronted and initially stood their ground, but eventually were forced, by sheer weight of numbers, to pack up their stall and leave.

When news broke of the incident, Stephen Lennon told *The Independent* that as it appeared that members of the local Muslim community were finally confronting al-Muhajiroun, UPL would consider calling off a forthcoming bank holiday march. But behind the scenes the group was working hard communicating with people across the country, determined to form a coordinated response to ensure such an outrageous offence wouldn't go unopposed on British streets again.

Radical Influences

To even begin to try and understand the Muslim radicals, firstly we need to understand at least some aspects of Islam, the religion which drives them.

Islam is not just a religious belief. Islamic doctrine is a complete instruction for followers on how they must live their lives. It serves not only personal spiritual aspirations, but drives politics, economics and the law, science and medicine.

Muslims believe that Allah revealed the universal laws, which form the *Qur'an* – the Final Revelation or Testament – to the Prophet Mohammed. The Qur'an, along with the *Hadith* (the words and actions of Mohammed) and the *Sira* (the biography of Mohammed) form what is known as *The Trilogy*. Muslims believe that the word of Allah, the source of all powers and laws, is sovereign, and above all governments.

There are five obligatory commitments for Muslims, known as The Pillars of Islam:

The *Shahadah*, which means to bear witness or testify, is the Islamic statement of belief in one God and the acceptance that Mohammed was His last prophet. The first words a Muslim child will hear are the Shahadah, the first human name that of Mohammed, recited to them by their father as soon as they are born. A public recital of the Shahadah in Arabic is all that is required for a person to become a Muslim: **There is no god but God, and Mohammed is the messenger of God**.

Salat is to connect with God through daily prayers. Muslims are required to pray five times a day, at dawn, noon, afternoon, sunset and evening. When praying, followers of Islam are required to face in the direction known as the *qiblah*, aligned with the *Kaaba*, a building housed in the al-Haram mosque in Mecca, the holiest site in the Islamic faith.

Sawm is to fast. Muslims are required to abstain from food and drink from dawn to dusk during the holy month of Ramadhan (Ramzan in Urdu the language of many British Muslims). It was during Ramadhan, the ninth month of the Islamic calendar, that Muslims believe that God revealed the first verses of the Qur'an to Mohammed.

Zakat is the giving of alms. Muslims are required to give a percentage of their wealth to the poor or charitable causes. In some Muslim countries, Zakat is compulsory and collected by the state, in others it is voluntary, collected and distributed locally.

Hajj is the pilgrimage to Mecca that able-bodied Muslims who can afford to do so are expected to undertake at least once in their lifetime. To take the Hajj is to follow in the footsteps of the Prophet Mohammed.

The word Islam means surrender, derived from the Arabic word *salaam* which means peace. Therefore, being a Muslim means total surrender or submission to Allah before all else, superseding any man made laws or cultural influences, no matter where in the world they happen to live. Islam has no notion of patriotism or national loyalties. It is this aspect of the totality of Islam as interpreted by extremist radicals that is referred to here.

Islam divides mankind into two distinct groups, Muslim and non-Muslim (*kafir/kuffar*). Irrespective of race or geography, all Muslims in the world form one worldwide community, the *Ummah Wahida*. This notion or brotherhood is essential to Muslims, even non-practising ones. This sense of belonging is instilled in them, culturally as well as religiously, from an early age and stays an intrinsic component of their identity even if faith is lost. In a 2006 poll by Pew, 81% of British Muslims considered themselves Muslim first and British second. This was a higher percentage than in majority Muslim countries such as Jordan or Egypt, however in Pakistan, the homeland of many British Muslims, the figure was higher, 87%.

Islamic law or *Sharia*, is a legal and social code giving believers guidance on most issues which affect them. Sharia was formulated around two centuries after Mohammed's death, it is derived from the *Sunnah* - the actions of Mohammed, and the Qur'an. Under Sharia, all human actions are divided into five categories: obligatory, recommended, permitted (*halal*), disliked or forbidden (*haram*). Certain offences under Sharia, such as unlawful sexual intercourse outside of marriage (including homosexuality), referred to as *hadd*, are punishable by specific penalties which are considered regressive in the West. There is no one authoritative figure to translate Sharia for Muslims, so rulings in Sharia courts differ from region to region, largely based on cultural traditions. Countries, such as Saudi Arabia or Iran enforce the severest penalties for hadd, such as stoning or beheading, but the majority of the Muslim world doesn't.

In contrast with Western culture, under Sharia, women are required to accept that they have a different role to that of men. Again, this is interpreted to differing degrees across the Muslim world. Women must be obedient to men unless the instructions given contravene Sharia. Under Sharia, a woman's testimony is only worth half that of a man's and a man can divorce his wife by simply announcing it but a woman must give justification. Once divorced, the custody of any children transfers to the father at a certain age and if the woman remarries, she automatically loses custody.

Muslims are expected to dress modestly and cover their body when out in public. Again this is interpreted to differing degrees. Women are required to cover their head, and in some cases their face, in more conservative regions, although this is cultural rather than a religious requirement (covering the face is not a Qur'anic obligation). In these countries, a *hijab*, a headscarf which covers the head and neck, or a *jilbab* (a long, loose-fitting outer-garment which covers everything bar the hands and face). A niqab or a *burqa* (a loose fitting outer garment which covers the face, head and body) can also be worn. Also, in these conservative regions the sexes are also fully segregated in public, again a cultural tradition, justified by a stricter interpretation of Islamic doctrine.

A majority Muslim country run in observance with Sharia is considered *Dar al-Islam*, or an abode of Islam. *Dar al-Amn* or an abode of safety, is when Muslims live at peace with non-Muslim hosts according to a Covenant of Security (a set of agreements, one of which states that in return for safety and freedom, Muslims do not attack the nation which they have made their home). The Covenant of Security is theoretical and something which is repeatedly referred to by Muslim radicals in the UK, who believe it has been broken by Britain's role in the War on Terror. It is something that many people in the West, including more importantly those in government, seem to have been oblivious to.

If Islam is suppressed in a country, it is considered *Dar al-Harb*, or an abode of war. *Jihad* is considered an obligation for Muslims. Arabic for struggle, jihad is used in three main contexts: the personal struggle to maintain one's faith, the struggle to improve Islamic society and the struggle of a holy war. Mohammed increased the influence of Islam in the Middle East through conquest; therefore jihad is mentioned frequently in Islamic text, but not all of Mohammed's gains were through violence. Extremists in the anti-jihad movement dismiss Mohammed as a bloodthirsty warrior, but that severely under-estimates both the man and the faith he inspired. It is true to say that the spread of Islam throughout the Middle East sometimes involved violence. But, Mohammed's greatest conquests were brought about by shrewd, non-violent means.

Someone engaged in jihad, or in defence of the Ummah Wahida, is called a *Mujahid*. The idea of jihad as a holy war had been relatively ignored in the Muslim world for years. It was revived in the 1980s by the Americans, who were backing rebel fighters during the Russian occupation of Afghanistan (an organisation set up to recruit foreign jihad fighters, Maktab al-Khidimat (MAK), still had offices in Detroit and Brooklyn up until the 1980s).

A young Saudi called Osama bin Laden, whose family had extensive contacts in the US, would play a key role for the Americans in training the new arrivals in Pakistan before sending them to Afghanistan. Just before the Russian withdrawal, it appears that bin Laden left MAK, forming his own militant Islamic faction, al-Qaeda. Muslims from around the world were encouraged to travel to Afghanistan to join the jihad against the Soviets. Unfortunately it would prove a Pandora's Box, which once opened proved impossible to close. There are now currently over 40 conflicts between Muslims and non-Muslims being waged across the world.

Muslims obtain political guidance from the Qur'an, the Sunnah and Islamic history. In majority Muslim countries, the influence of Islam in politics varies. Some states are run along semi-secular lines, others as caliphates or imamates where the rulings of religious rulers take precedence. Many have experienced long power struggles between fundamentalists and secularists, as the radicals seek to assert and expand the influence of Islam. This expansionist aspect of political Islam, referred to as Islamism, can be identified by four core beliefs:

Islam is a system of divine governance laid down by God.
All Muslims must form one influential political bloc.
In non-Islamic countries, the Muslim community should attempt to form an Islamic caliphate.
All states must be governed by Sharia.

The birth of Islamism can be traced to the aftermath of WWI. Following the fall of the Turkish Ottoman Empire, the Middle East, the traditional homeland of Islam, became fragmented. Some Muslims in the region, worried by the increasing influence and colonisation of the Western powers, formed the Muslim Brotherhood. The aim of the movement was to reunify the former Ottoman states as one Islamic nation. Officially, the movement espouses non-violent means, but has spawned violent breakaway groups. The movement is now thought to have up to 70 offshoot organisations throughout the world and forms the main political opposition in many Muslim states.

It is Islamism that drives Muslim radicals in the UK. These Islamists or Mujahideen seek to topple the status quo, and replace the system of democratic government and secularism with an Islamic political system based on Sharia. To achieve this, they first need to build a power base within the Muslim community. They build barriers between their community and the rest of society by highlighting anything which appears to be the persecution of Muslims or the suppression of Islam. They are aided in the West by liberalism and an obsession with political correctness, diversity and positive discrimination which prevent any problems or issues being discussed. The Islamists feed on division, and Britain's Muslim community is a fertile recruiting ground as a large proportion has already been allowed to separate from mainstream society.

The Islamists take every chance to highlight clashes in culture. In 2003, a Luton schoolgirl, Shabina Begum, took local Denbigh High School to court after she was sent home for wearing a jilbab. The modern jilbab dates back to the 1970s, when Egyptian women wore the garment as a statement of their membership of the Muslim Brotherhood and of their separation from secular Egyptian society. It is possible of course, with the sudden rise in the number of Muslim women in Britain adopting the jilbab or niqab, that a similar statement of separation is being made. Begum initially won the case but the decision was overturned in the House of Lords. Afterwards, it emerged that the girl had been supported by Islamist group Hizb ut Tahrir, obviously keen to promote the issue as an example of the repression Islam faced in the UK.

There are now well over 1 million Muslims of Pakistani origin in the UK and over 70% of those have links to Azad Kashmir, a disputed region split between India and Pakistan which has experienced three wars and a protracted insurgency on the Indian side. The conflict is viewed as a jihad by combatants on the Pakistani side and that has instilled a strong sense of Islamic identity amongst Kashmiri's. As stated earlier, Muslims from Pakistan are culturally conservative, they follow a stricter interpretation of Islam and also adhere to the practice of biraderi. This cultural preference for self-segregation and sufficiency has led to insular, tight-knit communities that have little reason to integrate outside their own community.

Isolation and polarisation of ex-pat communities is not uncommon if they are allowed to separate from mainstream society. British ex-pats on the Spanish Costas are often accused by their hosts of being isolated from Spanish society. Ghettos have formed in some areas, possibly ignored by the authorities due to the income British people bring. British flags are a far more common sight, the cultural identity of the ex-pats seemingly far more important, than it possibly would be if they still lived in the UK.

Again, drawing an analogy with ex-pat Brits on the Costas, when large numbers of one ethnicity settle in a particular area and become self-sufficient, they have less practical need to learn the host language. An estimated 40% of marriages within the British Pakistani community involve relatives from abroad; this has resulted in men and especially women of Pakistani/Kashmiri origin in the UK being less likely to be fluent in English than any other minority group. In fact, around 10,000 foreign spouses arrive in the UK every year and because of this, a lot of second and third generation British Pakistani children will still have one parent who does not speak English.

The isolation from wider society means that some values from the homelands of British Muslims are retained, unaffected by Western influences. Biraderi engenders a strong sense of family honour amongst Kashmiri communities, resulting in around twelve *honour killings* a year in the UK. An honour killing is the murder of a person adjudged to have brought shame on a family or clan through their actions. Shame can be felt for many reasons, including refusing to marry, an illicit relationship, adultery or even in some cases adopting Western culture.

The publication of *The Satanic Verses* by Salman Rushdie in 1988 was a pivotal moment in the forging of modern British Muslim identity. The appearance of the book also heralded the awakening of political Islam in the UK and instilled a '**them and us**' attitude in many British Muslims. With their identity polarised by the perceived attack on their religion and culture, many, already detached through biraderi, separated even further from mainstream British society and sought refuge in their Islamic identity.

People born to immigrant families in the UK have traditionally become less religious than their parents. However, a survey in 2006 by NOP suggested that British Muslims were going in the opposite direction, becoming more devout and less liberal. A third said they would prefer to live under Sharia and even moderate Muslims now claim British and Western values are '**antithetical to Islam**'.

Following the Rushdie Affair, aspects of Western culture adopted by some British Muslims were suddenly frowned upon as being un-Islamic. A pious and more importantly visible, observance of Sharia was endorsed as the only way to be a true Muslim. More traditional, conservative branches of the faith became popular. A new extreme brand of '**pure Islam**' was promoted by a number of firebrand Islamist preachers and it appealed to many newly insecure British Muslims. The Islamists offered puritanical forms of Islam, based on the south-east Asian *Deobandi*, *Barelvi* or Saudi *Wahhabi* interpretations.

Half of Britain's existing mosques belong to the Deobandi branch of the Islamic Sunni Hanafi faith. Originating in northern India, it is a popular in large parts of Pakistan. The belief has faced criticism for its austerity and a failure to realign with the modern world, illustrated by a series of controversial fatwas or religious rulings by Deobandi clerics. Over 80% of imams trained in Britain are Deobandis. The other dominant branch of Islam in the UK is the conservative Barelvi faith, which the vast majority of Muslims in Pakistan and India adhere to. The two branches have clashed repeatedly over the control of mosques in Pakistan since the turn of the century, resulting in numerous deaths and assassinations. A large number of al-Muhajiroun activists were Barelvi's; however in Pakistan the Barelvi faith has opposed the creeping influence of the Taliban.

Wahhabism is a branch of Sunni Islam, which was exported by Saudi Arabia when it was awash with oil revenues. During the 80s and 90s, books, videos and imams trained at Wahhabi theological universities, started arriving in the UK. Many mosques and Islamic schools in the West were financed and supplied by the Saudi regime. The aim of this flood of propaganda was to increase the influence of Wahhabism in the West, as the belief competes with other branches of Sunni Islam and condemns both Sufi and Shia denominations. A number of publications which have been discovered being used in some Wahhabi schools informed students that it was a religious obligation for Muslims to hate Christians and Jews. The literature also condemned democracy as un-Islamic, some of it suggested that the duty of a Muslim living in a land of the kafir was to acquire new knowledge and make money to be later employed in jihad against their hosts. Other publications claimed that it would be lawful to kill and rob homosexuals, people who committed adultery or renounced Islam.

Osama bin Laden is often credited as being a follower of Wahhabi Islam, but in fact, was a follower of Sayyid Qutb, an Egyptian intellectual and member of the Muslim Brotherhood. Qutb was famed for his total opposition to Western society, fellow Egyptian and current leader of al-Qaeda, Ayman Zawahiri, is also a follower.

There isn't one authoritative Muslim leader to interpret Islamic doctrine for British Muslims, therefore individuals interpret it themselves, as their imams instruct them or through other sources, such as the Internet. Considering the insular upbringing of many Muslims in the UK, this can leave them naive and vulnerable to radicalisation from abroad. A lack of Westernised British imams is also a problem, as nine out of ten imams operating in British mosques are from the sub-continent, bringing with them old fashioned and uncompromising views from a very conservative region. They tend to be largely ignorant of Western culture and the problems facing many young British Muslims.

In response to the *Satanic Verses*, the UK Action Committee on Islamic Affairs was formed, followed by the Muslim Parliament in 1992. Both groups were established because Muslims didn't feel represented in British politics. However, far from encouraging Muslims to play an active role in the electoral process, the Muslim Parliament set about discouraging them from voting, effectively isolating the community even further from mainstream British society. In opposition to promotion of the policy of non-engagement, the Muslim Council of Britain was established in 1997, seeking to encourage Muslims to fully engage in British politics.

The war in the Balkans followed both the Rushdie Affair and the Russian withdrawal from Afghanistan. The West didn't want a strong, pro-Russia Serbia in the middle of Eastern Europe so, when the Serbs started winning the civil war, a flood of anti-Serbian propaganda filled Western news programmes. The conflict in Yugoslavia was widely covered in Britain and British Muslims saw fellow Muslims in Bosnia being attacked by their Christian Serb neighbours, as the West apparently stood by, doing little to help. Many Muslims viewed the conflict as an attack on Islam and some travelled to Bosnia to help fight the jihad (again, according to ex-Cabinet Minister Michael Meacher, Mujahideen volunteers were aided by British and US intelligence agencies intent of destablising Serbia).

The war in the Balkans was quickly followed by unrest involving Albanian Muslims in Kosovo, Serbia, and also in Chechnya, where Russian authorities were clamping down on a separatist campaign involving mainly Muslim insurgents. It had got to the stage where as one conflict finished, the Muslim fighters simply changed location to fight a new one.

Around the same time as the emergence of international jihad, Britain witnessed an influx of Islamic immigrants from the Middle East and North Africa. Some of these new arrivals to Britain were veteran jihad fighters and trained killers. A number of them were also exiled from their countries of birth (a clue for the British authorities if ever there was one), because they had been identified as Islamist agitators. Many of them exploited the traditional British custom of offering refuge or political asylum to people fleeing persecution. However, it would soon become readily apparent why they had faced persecution.

Britain, and particularly London, became the capital of worldwide jihad. Impressionable young British Muslims came into contact with people who were not just risking their lives for Islam but very often fighting in places which many young Muslims considered their homelands. To second and third generation British Muslims, uncomfortable with their parents' culture and not feeling part of Western society, the radicals seemed to supply a lot of answers and most importantly to people searching for a defined identity, a sense of belonging. They became radicalised for similar reasons to the many British youths who join gangs, identity and status. Militant Islam was a gang, a big and very powerful gang for true Muslims.

The establishment attitude was that these Mujahideen journeyman could somehow be embraced by multicultural Britain and turned away from radicalism by being exposed to the core British values of free speech and democracy. Driven by political correctness, this multicultural utopian idiocy was pursued to the point of detriment, not just to the national interests, but to the physical safety of the British public. As a result of the lax and irresponsible attitude, Britain has produced more homegrown Muslim suicide bombers than the rest of Europe combined.

Like other fanatics who use religion to justify acts of violence against innocent people, Muslim extremists evoke certain verses of the Qur'an, know as the sword verses, as justification for acts of aggression against non-Muslims. The sword verses deal with war and violence, but they are also from a time when Mohammed and Muslims were being persecuted. Even so, The Prophet did not justify suicide or the killing of innocents, but extremists justify it by claiming that by voting, the general public is complicit in the aggression of its government in Muslim countries.

The vast majority of the young British Mujahideen were inspired by a handful of firebrand Islamist preachers who toured Britain promoting separation, division and involvement in a '**West versus Islam**' jihad.

Syrian Omar Bakri Mohammed fled Syria for Beirut in 1977 because of his involvement with the outlawed Muslim Brotherhood. He joined the group Hizb-ut-Tahrir, and in 1979 moved to Egypt. From there he moved to Saudi Arabia where he formed al-Muhajiroun (the Emigrants). In December 1985, Hizb-ut-Tahrir was banned in Saudi Arabia and Bakri was expelled. He moved to the UK, was given indefinite leave to remain and settled in Tottenham, North London. Bakri was vocal fro the outset, his regular outlandish statements gained him nationwide notoriety and made him a favourite of the tabloids, who mockingly labelled him the '**Tottenham Ayatollah**'.

On slow news days the tabloid press would nip round to Bakri's and he would willingly oblige them with outlandish statements, which were then publicised. The impact of publicising the ranting of a very small minority, within a minority, should not be underestimated. Bakri's message was made available to a wider audience with little realisation or scant regard for the consequences. He may have been a figure of fun to the press, but not everybody was laughing. A comedic caricature, the quintessential '**mad mullah**', Bakri was in fact a deadly and proficient practitioner of radicalisation. Nineteen convicted British terrorists would eventually be linked to Bakri and/or al-Muhajiroun.

Mustafa Kamel entered the country on a student visa in 1979 and later gained citizenship through marriage. He became radicalised after meeting Mujahideen fighters who were in Britain for private (paid for by Saudi sources) medical treatment during the Soviet invasion of Afghanistan and changed his name to Abu Hamza al-Masri. Hamza was another favourite of the tabloid press and not just because of his outlandish statements. He had lost both of his hands and one of his eyes in a mine-clearing incident in Afghanistan. Replacing his hands with two hooks, Hamza fitted the image of the bogeyman perfectly, but to some young British Muslims he was a hero, a proven committed veteran of jihad.

With help from local Algerians in north London, many of them veterans of the Groupe Islamique Armé (GIA - an armed group which bombed the Paris Metro in 1995), Hamza took over Finsbury Park Mosque. He soon established it as a drop-in centre for Mujahideen from across the world where he raised funds for international terrorism and established a network of terrorist training camps across the UK. The camps were designed to toughen up volunteers, in readiness for travelling abroad to participate in jihad.

All the time this was going on, Hamza was in contact with British security services. They seemed to view him as a useful idiot who, as long as they didn't interfere, wouldn't bite the hand that fed him. They took this attitude even though the French and other nations were warning that Hamza was extremely dangerous. Obviously while Britain and the US were using globetrotting Mujahideen for their own agenda, Hamza was viewed as a tool of the state, who would indirectly do the bidding of the West. In return, Hamza viewed the inactivity by British security services as permission to carry on and even expand his activities.

Abu Qatada, later dubbed the '**spiritual leader of al-Qaeda in Europe**', was another influential radical. The Jordanian Palestinian entered Britain on a forged passport in 1993, claiming asylum for himself and his family, alleging he had been tortured in Jordan. However, by 1995 Qatada was reportedly co-ordinating fundraising for Mujahideen fighting in Chechnya. Again like Hamza, Qatada carried out his activities under the nose of British security services. The Four Feathers Community Centre in Baker Street, London was used as a base and from there Qatada issued a series of inflammatory statements. He also forged links with Islamic terrorist groups such as al-Qaeda, Egyptian Islamic Jihad, Algeria's GIA and other similar organisations in Iraq, Indonesia, Libya, Morocco and Tunisia. In 2000, a Jordanian court sentenced Qatada to life imprisonment in his absence, for involvement in a plot to bomb foreign tourists.

Jamaican-born Muslim convert, Abdullah el-Faisal - real name Trevor William Forrest - came to Britain in 1991. Although Jamaican, el-Faisal came to Britain from Saudi Arabia, where he had studied at a university in Riyadh. Although already married, when el-Faisal came to Britain he took another bride which gave him the right to permanently reside in the UK. He became Imam at Brixton Mosque, but was removed by mosque elders who were concerned about the extreme nature of his sermons. Following his expulsion, el-Faisal moved to Tower Hamlets, where he set up an Islamic study centre. He then toured the country issuing sermons in which he called on Muslim mothers to raise their children to be Mujahideen and described Britain as an enemy of Islam.

As well as radicalism, another thing these preachers of hatred and division shared was that they and their families claimed state benefits. They were, in effect, using state funds to finance their crusade to topple the very state that supported them and in the West, governments hamstrung by political correctness and liberalism (and covert political agendas) allowed them to do it. Following 9/11, it seemed there was a definite strategy by Islamists, to use liberal Western values to defeat liberal Western values. Kheir Sajer, a radical Muslim leader in Norway, told Norwegian Muslims that Sharia gave them the right to abuse the non-believers' system. They were told to view the benefits they receive as *jizya* - a tax non-Muslims in Muslim countries are obliged to pay.

The *Daily Mail* has claimed that Bakri Mohammed and his extended family claimed benefits amounting to at least £300,000 from when he arrived in the UK, and also that he lived rent free in a £200,000 house in north London. *The Express* has revealed Abu Hamza was in receipt of three kinds of disability benefits, Income Support, Housing Benefit and help with fuel bills. Unbeknown to the authorities, Hamza had also secretly taken advantage of the right-to-buy scheme to purchase a council flat in Hammersmith, west London for £100,000 in 1999, selling it five years later for £228,000. Also, while a treasury order apparently froze his assets, he had allegedly used a relatives name to buy a house in Greenford, west London, which he rented out, while his family lived in a £600,000 house funded by the taxpayer. The cost doesn't stop there, it is reported that Hamza's legal bill in his fight to stay in the UK has so far cost the British tax-payer over half a million pounds.

Abu Qatada received £8000 a year in Incapacity Benefit for an alleged back condition, while he and his family lived in an £800,000 four-bedroom semi-detached house in Acton, west London. The *Daily Mail* claimed that Qatada and his family received more than £50,000 a year in state benefits including Child Benefit, Income Support, Housing Benefit and Council Tax Credit. When the assets of people suspected of '**committing or providing material support for acts of terrorism**' were frozen by the Government, £180,000 was discovered in a bank account held by Qatada.

When you compare the amounts handed out to these radicals, with the average pay of a soldier, risking their life for the country on basic pay of just £16,500 a year, it is hardly surprising a lot of ordinary hard-working British people get angry. In the words of one long forgotten speech, '**we must be mad, literally mad**'.

Following the Soviet withdrawal from Afghanistan, Osama bin Laden returned home to Saudi Arabia. He was expelled, following criticism of the Saudi regime for allowing US and British forces into the country during the Gulf War. In 1992, while living in Sudan, bin Laden and his group al-Qaeda claimed responsibility for an attack on US troops in Somalia and also an attempted attack on US forces in Yemen. In 1993, a truck bomb was detonated below the North Tower of the World Trade Centre in New York, killing seven people and injuring thousands.

In February 1998, a fatwa was issued by bin Laden and his associates instructing Muslims to '**kill the Americans and their allies - civilians and military**.' The United States occupying lands in the

Arabian Peninsula and the sanctions imposed on Iraq following the liberation of Kuwait were given as reasons for the edict (bin Laden claimed the aim of US policy in the area was to support Israel and to divert attention from the occupation of Jerusalem by destroying its strongest Arab neighbour Iraq). Six months after the fatwa was issued, American embassies in Dar es Salaam, Tanzania and Nairobi, Kenya were targeted with trucks laden with explosives, killing 258 people and leaving over 5000 injured. The United States replied by launching Cruise missile attacks on a terrorist training camp in Afghanistan and a pharmaceutical plant in Sudan, claiming both were funded by bin Laden.

It appeared that all the radical imams operating in the UK at that time were under the impression that the British authorities were observing the Covenant of Security. They believed this gave them free reign, as long as Britain was not attacked. Bakri was now claiming to be the '**mouth, eyes and ears of Osama bin Laden**' and insisted that MI5 knew exactly who he was and who he represented. Bakri claimed he had met with the security services many times and he had a deal which gave him immunity from prosecution: '**I work here in accordance with the covenant of peace which I made with the British Government when I got asylum. We respect the terms of this bond, as Allah orders us to do.**'

In March 1999, Abu Hamza was arrested in connection with a terrorist plot in Yemen. His house was searched, and a large number of recordings of his sermons were seized. Three confiscated videotapes which were ignored at the time contained sermons which seven years later a court would conclude amounted to soliciting murder. In one of the recordings, Hamza told his followers that "**no drop of liquid is loved by Allah, more than the liquid of blood**". The Metropolitan Police passed a file on Hamza to the Crown Prosecution Service (CPS), but it was adjudged as containing insufficient evidence. The following August, eight Britons and two Algerians accused of involvement in the plot went on trial in Yemen. One of the accused, jailed for three years, was Hamza's eldest son, another who was jailed for seven years, was his stepson. The court heard that Hamza had sent the men to Yemen to carry out terrorist attacks.

In December 1999, the British Government introduced the Terrorism Act 2000. Despite repeated warnings from the continent that Islamic terrorism was a growing concern, it was still not considered a threat by the Government. Prior to the attacks on America, counter-terrorism in the UK was still directed at dissident Irish republican terrorist groups, such as the Real IRA. In the year preceding 9/11, the Real IRA launched Soviet RPG-22 anti-tank rocket at the MI6 building in London and detonated bombs in Shepherd's Bush, Colindale and Ealing. British security forces were focusing most of their attention to the threat from over the Irish Sea and also, more importantly, the Irish weren't as politically sensitive a group as Muslims. The new act outlawed certain groups and widened the definition of terrorism from '**violence for political ends**' to '**action, used or threatened, for the purpose of advancing any political, religious or ideological cause**'. The act also gave police the power to hold suspects for up to 48 hours; extended to seven days should a judge deem it necessary. It gave police the power to '**stop and search**' suspects they had grounds to believe were involved in terrorism (these powers would later be declared illegal by the European Court of Human Rights).

The seeds planted by the Islamic radicals slowly grew and started to bear fruit. On Christmas Day 2000, Mohammed Bilal, a 24 year old student from Birmingham, drove a car laden with explosives into an Indian Army base in Srinagar, Kashmir, killing ten people. Bilal, who was believed to have been a member of the Pakistani militant group, Jaish-e-Mohammed and al-Muhajiroun, was Britain's first known suicide bomber.

Following the attack, Omar Bakri Mohammed said: '**I am not surprised by his actions. He becomes a martyr and that is the wish of every Muslim in order to go to paradise**'. Three months later, the British Government would announce a ban on over 20 terrorist groups, including al-Qaeda and the Pakistani/Kashmiri militant groups Lashkar-e-Toiba, Harkat ul-Mujahedeen, and Jaish-e-Mohammed. However, it appeared it was too little too late.

The day before Bilal's attack, al-Qaeda and Indonesian Islamist terrorist group Jemaah Islamiyah, were responsible for a series of explosions in Indonesia. The attacks, which were on churches in the capital Jakarta and eight other cities, killed eighteen people and injured many others.

11 September 2001: New York, 9/11

On 11 September 2001, two passenger planes slammed into New York's World Trade Centre. The Pentagon building in Washington was also hit. Close to three thousand people perished in the attacks which were carried out by nineteen hijackers. Even though he had no previous record of doing anything on such a scale, bin Laden's al-Qaeda was immediately blamed. Bin laden strongly denied the accusation, blaming the attacks on an American-Zionist plot and claiming that the US Government was controlled by American Jews **'whose first priority is Israel, not the United States'**.

Strangely, when questioned as to why there was no mention of 9/11 on bin Laden's FBI **'Most Wanted'** profile, Rex Tomb, Chief of Investigative Publicity for the FBI would later reply that it was because they had **'no hard evidence'** to connect him to 9/11. Even so, the US Government issued a series of demands to the Taliban regime in Afghanistan, where bin Laden was believed to be hiding. They insisted that all terrorist training camps be closed and that the Taliban handed over bin Laden and the other leaders of al-Qaeda. The Taliban refused, replying they would only comply if the US presented evidence linking bin Laden with 9/11. As a response to the Taliban's non-compliance, the USA and UK embarked on the War on Terror.

While his al-Muhajiroun group distributed leaflets mocking 9/11 as **'a Towering Day in World History'**, Omar Bakri told the BBC the attacks on the US were a direct consequence of the evil foreign policy of America and payback for US atrocities against Muslims. He warned the public they should take the threat of Islamic terrorism seriously. Muslim radicals would claim the Covenant of Security had been broken by the actions of Britain and the USA in Afghanistan. A poll commissioned by the BBC in December 2002, indicated that many British Muslims agreed with them; 72% didn't believe claims made by George Bush and Tony Blair that the War on Terror was not a war on Islam. Speaking in 2004, Luton radical Sayful Islam told the *Evening Standard*: **'When I watched those planes go into the Twin Towers, I felt elated. That magnificent action split the world into two camps: you were either with Islam and al-Qaeda or with the enemy. I decided to quit my job and commit myself full-time to al-Muhajiroun. I give my allegiance only to Allah.'**

In December 2001, Briton Richard Reid, tried to blow up American Airlines Flight 63, on route from Paris to Miami, using explosives concealed in his shoes. Labelled the **'shoe-bomber'**, Reid had attended several al-Muhajiroun meetings prior to his attempt at mass murder. He had also attended Finsbury Park Mosque when Hamza had been in control and had been present on various occasions at Brixton Mosque, when Abdullah el-Faisal had preached there. *The Times* reported that Reid had also been **'inspired by Abu Qatada'**.

On 1 February 2002, kidnapped American journalist, Daniel Pearl was beheaded by his al-Qaeda captors. Working for the *Wall Street Journal*, Pearl had been kidnapped in Pakistan while investigating links between Richard Reid and al-Qaeda. Omar Sheikh, a British-born militant from north London who studied at the London School of Economics, was convicted and sentenced to death for his involvement in the kidnap and murder of Pearl. He is currently held in Pakistan and appealing against his sentence. In his book, *In the Line of Fire*, former President of Pakistan, Pervez Musharraf, claims that Omar Sheikh was originally recruited by British intelligence while studying at the London School of Economics to assist its operations in the Balkans. Musharraf believes that at some point (seemingly like many other Mujahideen recruited by the West) Sheikh later became a rogue or double agent.

Around the same time as Pearl's murder, a number of Abu Qatada's videos were found in the Hamburg flat of Mohammed Atta, one of the alleged 9/11 terrorists. The Government was finally forced to act and three months after 9/11, passed legislation allowing police to detain terror suspects without charge or trial. Qatada went into hiding. He was finally traced to a south London council house and arrested on 18 February 2002. Detained at Belmarsh prison, he has since been involved in a protracted legal battle over his detention and deportation to face trial on terror charges in Jordan. In 2009, a European Court of Human Rights ruled that Qatada's detention without charge following 9/11 was illegal and awarded him £2500 in compensation.

Abdullah el-Faisal was also arrested on 18 February 2002. He would later be convicted of soliciting murder and inciting hatred after a court heard he had tried to recruit British schoolboys for terrorist training camps. Assistant Commissioner, Peter Clarke, from Scotland Yard's Anti Terrorist Unit said that el-Faisal had been actively urging young people to commit murder. Sentenced to nine years in prison, el-Faisal served four before being deported back to Jamaica.

Two months after the arrests of Qatada and el-Faisal, Hamza was suspended as imam of Finsbury Park Mosque by the Charities Commission. Police eventually raided the mosque nine months later, on 20 January 2003, as part of an investigation into an alleged terrorist plot involving the poison, Ricin. Following the raid, police sealed the building and eventually handed it back to the trustees Hamza had seized it from. Undeterred, a defiant Hamza held prayer services in the street outside the mosque, under the full glare of the British media.

On 12 October 2002, three bombs exploded outside two nightclubs and the US Embassy on the island of Bali, Indonesia. The attacks killed over 200 people and injured 240. Members of the radical Indonesian Islamist group Jemaah Islamiyah, were accused and convicted of the bombings, with three sentenced to death. A week after the attacks *Al-Jazeera* broadcast a recording alleged to be of Osama bin Laden, which said the Bali bombings were in retaliation for Australia's support of the War on Terror and its interference in East Timor: **"You will be killed just as you kill, and will be bombed just as you bomb. Expect more that will further distress you"**.

On 11 February 2003, over 400 soldiers were deployed to provide extra security at Heathrow Airport to combat a suspected terrorist threat to the capital. Scotland Yard told *The Guardian* that the move was a precautionary measure linked to fears that al-Qaeda was possibly planning to use the Muslim festival of Eid al-Adha as a trigger for attacks. The move, approved by Prime Minister Tony Blair, but later criticised by Home Secretary David Blunkett, was seen as a cynical attempt to use public fear to gain support for draconian terrorism laws and also for the forthcoming invasion of Iraq.

On 20 March 2003, British forces and their American allies took part in the invasion of Iraq. Bakri warned there was frustration at the UK's foreign policy and role in the War on Terror and claimed there were many people abroad who wanted to attack Britain. A month later, two British citizens attempted to bomb a cafe in Tel Aviv, Israel. Asif Hanif from Hounslow and Omar Sharif from Derby are believed to have been Britain's second suicide bombers. Both men had lived in Britain for most of their lives. Sharif was an ex-public schoolboy and had attended a mosque in Derby where Bakri and al-Muhajiroun were known to have been active. Both of the bombers were also known to have attended Finsbury Park Mosque.

Five months later, the JW Marriott Hotel in South Jakarta, Indonesia, was hit by a suicide bomber. The attack killed twelve people and injured 150. The majority of people who died were Indonesian, but two Europeans lost their lives in the attack. A year later, a one-tonne car bomb, was detonated by a suicide bomber outside the Australian embassy in South Jakarta. Nine people were killed in the attack and 150 injured.

On the 11 March 2004, ten bombs exploded on four crowded commuter trains in Madrid, Spain. The attacks killed 191 people and injured over 1800. Bakri said that the bombings were '**an eye for an eye**', revenge for Western attacks on Muslim lands. A month later, at a protest organised by al-Muhajiroun, Abdulrahman Saleem warned British Prime Minister Tony Blair that if he didn't pull British troops out of Iraq and Afghanistan, there would be bloodshed on the streets of London. Bakri also warned that a very well-organised group based in London, al-Qaeda Europe, was on the verge of launching a big operation in the UK.

Two weeks later, Osama bin Laden offered Europe a truce; on condition all European troops left Muslim lands. The British Government immediately rejected the offer. Six months later, Ayman al-Zawahiri, al-Qaeda second-in-command, urged Muslims to mount a worldwide resistance to America and its allies, giving a list of American allies, including Britain, to be targeted.

On 16 September 2004, British civil engineer Kenneth Bigley was kidnapped in Iraq, by members of the Islamic extremist group, Tawhid and Jihad. The group was led by Abu Musab al-Zarqawi, a

Jordanian militant Islamist who, before the Iraq War, had ran a paramilitary training camp in Afghanistan. The Muslim Council of Britain, which sent a two-man delegation to Iraq to try and secure Bigley's release, called the kidnapping '**contrary to the teachings of the Qur'an**'. On 7 October 2004, Bigley's captors beheaded him, releasing the film of his murder on Islamist websites.

In March 2005, Britain introduced Control Orders, designed to restrict the liberty of people identified as posing a terrorist risk. Under the legislation, a number of restrictions could be placed on someone suspected of being implicated in terrorism, including travel restrictions, a curfew and electronic tagging. By this time, Bakri had begun making nightly broadcasts on the Internet. In one, he said that Britain had become Dar al Harb and the covenant between the UK and its Muslim citizens had been '**violated**', due to the introduction of the Control Orders.

In London, a meeting held at Regent's Park Mosque by the Muslim Council of Britain to launch its strategy for the General Election was stormed by masked members of al-Muhajiroun. One of the men shouted: "**The MCB is the mouthpiece for Tony Blair. The MCB can go to hell. Anyone who votes is kafir!**" One radical threw a punch at MCB Secretary General Iqbal Sacranie as he denounced the protest.

7 July 2005: London, 7/7

During the morning rush-hour on 7 July 2005, four coordinated suicide attacks took place on London's public transport system. Fifty-two people lost their lives and over 700 were injured.

Four Muslim men were responsible, three of Pakistani descent from Yorkshire, Mohammad Sidique Khan from Dewsbury, Shehzad Tanweer, Hasib Hussain both from Leeds and British-Jamaican convert Germaine Lindsay from Aylesbury in Buckinghamshire. Lindsay and Khan were reportedly followers of Abdullah el-Faisal. On a video made prior to the attacks, Khan said: "**Until we feel security you will be our targets and until you stop the bombing, gassing, imprisonment and torture of my people, we will not stop this fight. We are at war and I am a soldier**".

The bombers claimed their actions were vindicated by Islamic teachings and they had performed their duty in response to Western interference in Islamic countries. It appeared that other British Muslims shared their view. In a poll following the attacks, one in four of Muslims said the 7/7 bombings were justified as a result of Britain's support for the War on Terror. Three days after the attack, British counter-terrorism officials estimated that between 10,000 and 15,000 Muslims living in Britain were supporters of al-Qaeda and that up to 600 had attended training camps abroad connected to the group.

Two weeks after 7/7, in an almost identical attack, four more terrorists unsuccessfully attempted to bomb London on 21 July. All four bombs failed to go off and an abandoned fifth bomb was discovered two days later. In the hunt for the four bombers, innocent Brazilian electrician, Jean Charles de Menezes, was gunned down in Stockwell tube station on July 22 by armed police who mistook him for one of the suspects, Hussain Osman.

Four men, Muktar Ibrahim, Yassin Omar, Ramzi Mohammed, and Hussain Osman were arrested and found guilty of conspiracy to murder; each was sentenced to a minimum of 40 years imprisonment. A fifth man, Manfo Kwaku Asiedu, who abandoned his bomb, pleaded guilty to a charge of conspiracy to cause explosions. Ghanaian, Asiedu was sentenced to 33 years in prison, with a recommendation that he be deported to Ghana on release. It later emerged that Muktar Ibrahim and 7/7 bomber Shezad Tanzeer had both trained at the same terrorist training camp in Pakistan. The wife of Hussain Osman, Yeshi Girma, along with two others, would later be found guilty of failing to disclose information about terrorism in connection to the attacks and was jailed for fifteen years.

Ayman al-Zawahiri said the attacks were '**volcanoes of wrath**' and a consequence of Britain rejecting the truce offer from bin Laden, adding that the policies of Tony Blair would only bring more destruction to Britain. Anjem Choudary, emerging as a spokesman for al-Muhajiroun, said that he would not inform the police if he knew a terror attack was being planned and urged Muslims to 'defend themselves against attacks by whatever means they have at their disposal'.

A qualified solicitor, although no longer practicing, British born Choudary and his family reportedly live on state benefits. He was apparently a normal teenager at university and only showed signs of his Islamic heritage following the Rushdie Affair. He subsequently met Omar Bakri Mohammed and became involved with al-Muhajiroun.

As a response to the attacks, the Government promised to look at deporting foreign nationals who preached extremism and introduced the 'PREVENT' initiative as part of 'CONTEST' (Counter Terrorism Strategy). PREVENT was one part of four initiatives designed to counter terrorism in the UK; the others were PURSUE (to directly stop terrorist attacks), PROTECT (to strengthen protection against terrorist attacks) and PREPARE (to lessen the effect of attacks which cannot be prevented). Mosques and Islamic groups across the country were given money under PREVENT to run anti-radicalisation programmes. In 2010, £140 million was spent in the battle to win the hearts and minds of young British Muslims.

The initial task of PREVENT was to challenge violent extremist ideology, disrupt those who pursued or promoted it and to increase the resilience of communities susceptible to extremism. However, the moderate and secular Muslim organisation The Quilliam Foundation criticised the scheme, claiming that the people engaged in running such government programmes actually have little knowledge of Islam.

On 20 July 2005, Haroon Rasheed Aswad, from Dewsbury, West Yorkshire, was arrested at a religious school in Pakistan. He was said to be a member of al-Muhajiroun and was found with a suicide bomb belt, explosives and £13,000 in his possession. Aswad's telephone number was said to have been on the mobile phones of all four 7/7 bombers and had made a phone call to one of them only hours before the attacks on London. Around the same time, another British Muslim with links to al-Muhajiroun, Londoner Mobeen Muneef, was picked up by US marines on patrol in Ramadi, Iraq, allegedly attempting to supply weapons to insurgents.

As a result of these persistent links to worldwide Jihad, the Home Office announced it intended to ban al-Muhajiroun. However, before the Government could act, Bakri shut down the organisation and formed two new groups, the Saviour Sect and al-Ghurabaa, both of which soon gained notoriety. The Saviour Sect by bursting into a General Election rally on 20 April 2005, where they threatened speaker George Galloway and declared that any Muslim who took part in the electoral process was an apostate (punishable by death under Sharia). Reporting the incident in its usual reserved fashion the *Daily Star* declared '**Muslim loonies hijack election: Fundamentalists won't stop until UK is an Islamic state**'. The website of the other al-Muhajiroun splinter group, al-Ghurabaa, was found to have links to websites that justified terrorism.

Following a trip to Beirut to visit his Mother in August 2005, Omar Bakri Mohammed was barred from re-entering Britain. Home Secretary Charles Clarke said that his presence in the country was '**not conducive to the public good**'.

On 1 October 2005, Bali, Indonesia was again targeted with by three bombs. Twenty people were killed and over 100 injured in the attacks on the Jimbaran Beach Resort and the town of Kuta. Indonesian police said they believed three suicide bombers carried out the attacks, presidential spokesman Dino Djalal said police had found "**six legs and three heads but no middle bodies, and that's the strong sign of suicide bombers**".

Early in 2006, Danish newspaper *Jyllands-Posten* published a series of twelve cartoons depicting the Prophet Mohammed. The paper claimed it was an attempt to contribute to the debate regarding censorship and criticism of Islam. Following publication, there was uproar across the Muslim world against what was considered blasphemy. Muslims believe it is blasphemous to depict the face of The Prophet, as it is the message of Mohammed which is all important. The Danish embassy in Pakistan was bombed and its embassies in Syria, Lebanon and Iran were torched. The cartoons were reprinted in a number of publications across Europe. In Britain, Labour minister Jack Straw said the decision by some newspapers to print the cartoons was '**disrespectful**' adding that freedom of speech did not mean an open season on religious taboos.

Protests were organised outside the Danish Embassy in London by al-Ghurabaa and the Saviour Sect on 3 and 4 February 2006. Police estimated there were 450 protestors on the first day and the following day estimated that over 3500 were present. One Muslim demonstrator dressed as a suicide bomber, others burned flags or chanted slogans such as "**UK, you will pay, bin-Laden is on his way!**" Some carried placards proclaiming '**Europe, your 9/11 will come**', '**Behead the one who insults the prophet,**' '**Massacre those who insult Islam**' and '**Free speech go to hell**'.

One protester, Umran Javed from Birmingham, later described as a major organiser for al-Muhajiroun, led the protest with chants of "**Bomb, bomb Denmark, bomb, bomb USA!**" Another, Mizanur Rahman, from Palmers Green, north London, called for British soldiers in Iraq to come home in body bags: "**We want to see the Mujahideen shoot down their planes the way we shoot down birds. We want to see their tanks burn in the way we burn their flags**"

Following the protest, the police received over 100 complaints about the conduct of the demonstrators. Over the next year, a number of protestors were arrested and convicted of a range of offences from soliciting murder to stirring up racial hatred. Abdul Mahid, Umran Javed and Mizanur Rahman were jailed for six years for soliciting murder. The court heard that organiser Mahid had distributed literature encouraging Muslims to '**Annihilate those who insult Islam**'.

Five years later, a Somali man, Mohamed Geele, who broke into the home of cartoonist Kurt Westergaard, was found guilty of attempted murder and terrorism. Westergaard's cartoon of a turban bomb was one of the twelve cartoons published in *Jyllands-Posten*. The cartoonist escaped injury by sheltering in a specially built panic room. Geele claimed he was only trying to frighten Westergaard, but the court heard he had broken into the house in Aarhus, Denmark by smashing the door down and once inside, armed with an axe and a knife, had screamed "**You must die!**" and "**You are going to Hell!**" According to the Danish intelligence services, Geele was linked to Al-Shabab, a Somali militant Islamist group.

The Terrorism Act (2006) was introduced in March 2006, making it a criminal offence, to encourage or instigate acts of terrorism. It also prohibited the distribution of terrorist publications and broadened the basis for proscribing organisations to include those that promoted or encouraged terrorism. Both the Saviour Sect and Al-Ghurabaa were banned, but al-Muhajiroun escaped proscription as Bakri had already disbanded it. Four months after proscription, *The Times* reported that members of the two groups had simply formed another group, Ahlus Sunnah wal Jamaah. A journalist who infiltrated the group's website found calls for violent jihad, a declaration that the Queen was an enemy of Islam and recordings of Osama bin Laden. The first outing for Ahlus Sunnah wal Jamaah was a demonstration outside Westminster Cathedral where they pestered worshippers entering the building. Anjem Choudary, who reportedly organised the protest, called for the Pope to face capital punishment.

On 22 June 2006, *BBC News* claimed that an official US Department of Homeland Security report had confirmed an al-Qaeda plot to hijack flights from Heathrow and fly them into the airport and a Canary Wharf skyscraper. The report listed nine attempts, including that of Richard Reid, to target aviation targets worldwide, including the US, Britain, Italy and Australia. However, Australian Attorney-General Philip Ruddock claimed the report was based on flawed US intelligence assessment from three years ago.

On 10 August 2006, Scotland Yard's Anti-Terrorism Unit announced it had arrested 24 people in raids in Birmingham, High Wycombe and London in connection with a suspected terrorist plot to blow up aircraft using liquid explosives. The attacks were allegedly planned by Abu Obaidah al-Masri, a member of al-Qaeda suspected of involvement in the 7/7 London bombings.

The men involved in the plot would all go on trial over the next four years. Ahmed Abdulla Ali, Assad Sarwar and Tanvir Hussain were all found guilty of conspiracy to murder at Woolwich Crown Court. Ali was sentenced to 40 years, Sarwar was told he must serve at least 36 years and Hussain was jailed for 32 years. Another man, Muslim convert Umar Islam, formerly Brian Young, was convicted of conspiracy to murder and sentenced to life imprisonment with a recommendation he serve at least 22 years. Ibrahim Savant, Arafat Khan and Waheed Zaman were found guilty at Woolwich Crown Court and sentenced to life in prison for conspiracy to murder, with a minimum recommendation of 20 years. Adam Khatib was found guilty of plotting to murder persons unknown and jailed for at least 18 years. Another man, Nabeel Hussain, was found guilty of engaging in conduct in preparation to commit acts of terrorism, or assisting another to commit such acts, and was jailed for eight years. White convert, Donald Douglas Stewart-Whyte was found not guilty of conspiracy to murder but was subsequently convicted of possession of a firearm and ammunition found at his address during the raids. He was sentenced to four and a half years in prison but was immediately released due to time served on remand for the original charge. Mohammed Shamim Uddin was jailed for 15 months after being found guilty of possessing information likely to be used to commit or prepare for an act of terrorism. Uddin was found not guilty of two other terrorist charges. He was also given handed a five year, nine month sentence at a separate hearing after pleading guilty to possession of a firearm.

Weeks after the liquid bomb plot was exposed, Home Secretary John Reid was heckled during a visit to Leytonstone, east London. While making a speech, Reid was repeatedly interrupted by Abu Izzadeen, a British-Jamaican convert, who had converted to Islam after hearing Bakri Mohammed preach at Finsbury Park Mosque. Izzadeen, formerly known as Trevor Brooks, told Reid he was in a Muslim area and complained about the state terrorism by British police. He was removed from the meeting by security staff, as police officers present seemed reluctant to act. Izzadeen was among a number of new radicals who were simply stepping up to replace the likes of Bakri, Qatada and Hamza.

On 23 January 2007, police arrested five men in raids across northern England. As a result of the raids, Rizwan Ditta from Halifax was charged with having items for a purpose connected with terrorism or that are likely to be useful to a person committing or preparing an act of terrorism. Mohammad Bilal, also from Halifax, was charged with having items likely to be useful to a person committing an act of terrorism. Both men pleaded guilty, Ditta was sentenced to four years in prison and Bilal two years.

A week later, nine men believed to be involved in a suspected Islamist plot to kidnap torture and behead a British Muslim soldier who had served in Afghanistan were arrested during dawn raids in Birmingham. Eight of the detained men were British of Pakistani descent, one was Pakistani, they were arrested on suspicion of '**the commission, preparation or instigation of acts of terrorism**' under the Terrorism Act 2000. *The Telegraph* reported that the suspects allegedly planned to film the atrocity and post it on the internet as a warning to British Muslims not to help the Armed Forces. The paper also reported that the head of MI5, Dame Eliza Manningham-Buller, had said they were currently monitoring 30 '**Priority One**' plots in Britain and more than 1,600 individuals. Home Secretary, John Reid, called the arrests a major counter- terrorism operation and said they were a reminder of the '**real and serious nature of the threat we face**'.

On 29 June 2007, two days after Gordon Brown replaced Tony Blair as Prime Minister, two car bombs were discovered in London. One was left near the Tiger Tiger nightclub in Haymarket and another in nearby Cockspur Street. Both devices were defused before they could be detonated. *CBS News* reported that a message had appeared on Islamist Internet forum *Al-Hesbah* the day before, which had mentioned the recent knighthood of Salman Rushdie and said '**rejoice, by Allah, London shall be bombed**'.

Two days later, on 30 June 2007, two Muslim men, said to be angry about the Iraq War, drove a Jeep full of petrol and gas canisters into the terminal building at Glasgow Airport. As the Jeep came to a halt after crashing through the entrance, the two men fought with police and passers-by. One of them doused himself with petrol and set himself alight. The man, Kafeel Ahmed, 28, later died in hospital. His accomplice, Bilal Abdulla, 29, from Aylesbury, Buckinghamshire, was a doctor employed at the Royal Alexandra Hospital in Paisley. He had studied medicine in Iraq, returning to Britain after qualifying and lived in Houston, just outside Glasgow.

Abdulla was also convicted of involvement in both the attempted attack on London and the attack on Glasgow, he was jailed for life. Seven other people were also arrested in connection to the London attack, including three doctors. However, only one, Dr Sabeel Ahmed, was convicted. Ahmed was found guilty of withholding information regarding the attack and sentenced to 18 months in prison. He was released after 270 days and deported.

On 19 April 2008, Abu Izzadeen, and five other men, including British born white convert Simon Keeler, were found guilty of inciting terrorism. Izzadeen and Keeler were both sentenced to two and a half years for fundraising for terrorism and four and half years for incitement. Abdul Saleem was jailed for three years, nine months and Ibrahim Hassan, for two years, nine months, both for inciting terrorism. Shah Jilal Hussain and Abdul Mahid, who was already serving a jail term for the Danish Embassy protests, were both sentenced to two years for fundraising for terrorism. The charges were in connection with speeches, referred to as '**a clear call to arms**' which had been made at a central London mosque. Keeler was the first white Muslim to be found guilty of terror charges in Britain.

Following the trial the *Daily Mail* revealed that Izzadeen, his wife and three children lived in a house in Leytonstone, east London, funded by the tax-payer. The *Mail* revealed he received state benefits of £176 a week and that his £100-a-month Council Tax was also paid by the state he sought to overthrow. The paper said Izzadeen had been advertising on the Internet for more wives because he wanted '**more than nine children**'

Polygamy is the practice of marriage to more than one spouse simultaneously and under Sharia men may have up to four wives. Although illegal for the majority of people in the UK, it is tolerated and considered a cultural requirement for some British Muslims. The right of men to claim welfare benefits for each of their multiple wives was endorsed by the Department for Work and Pensions in 2008. This meant that polygamous partnerships in Britain, mainly involving Muslims, were formally recognised by the state but only if the weddings took place in countries where the arrangement is legal.

Izzadeen was released on parole 13 months later, after his sentence was reduced on appeal. However, he was recalled to prison in July 2009, for breaking the terms of his release after he swore at police officers who were checking that he was keeping to his release conditions. On the day of his final release from prison in November 2010, greeted by a crowd of followers including Anjem Choudary, Izzadeen called for Sharia in Britain and a boycott of the poppy. His words were widely broadcast by the media, especially the tabloids, with *The Sun* calling him '**a bile spouting crackpot**'. Lessons from Bakri and Hamza obviously hadn't been learned.

The British links to Islamic terrorism persisted. In April 2007, five Muslim men were jailed for life for a bomb plot linked to al-Qaeda, which targeted the Bluewater Shopping Centre in Kent, the Ministry of Sound nightclub in London and the south-east gas network. Omar Khyam, Waheed Mahmood and Jawad Akbar, from Crawley, Salahuddin Amin, from Luton and Anthony Garcia from east London, were all found guilty of conspiring to cause explosions likely to endanger life between 1 January 2003 and 31 March 2004.

In February 2008, Mohammed Hamid, a Tanzanian born Muslim, who had dubbed himself '**Osama bin London**', was found guilty of encouraging his followers to murder non-Muslims and organising terrorist training camps in Britain. Security services revealed that four of the 21/7 failed suicide bombers had trained at the camps. Jamaican born Muslim convert, Kibley da Costa, Trinidadian convert Mohammed al-Figari, and Somalian Kader Ahmed, all followers of Hamid, were found guilty of attending the camps. Another of the accused, Atilla Ahmet, who became Imam of Finsbury Park Mosque following the arrest of Abu Hamza, had already pleaded guilty to three charges of soliciting murder.

Hamid was jailed indefinitely at Woolwich Crown Court, with a recommendation that he served at least seven and a half years before being considered for release. Ahmet was jailed for 6 years and 11 months for three counts of soliciting murder. The Judge, Mr Justice Pitchers accepted that Ahmet had acted in the fashion he had at public meetings because of his '**love of the limelight**', and he '**probably**' wouldn't have engaged in terrorist acts himself and had always '**found an excuse not to go on any training camp if it involved loss of comfort. However, young, unsophisticated Muslim men might**

easily be taken in by your forceful personality and the fact you were appointed Emir of the group demonstrates this to be so'. *BBC News* reported that the cases of seven other men convicted in connection with the camps were subject to a partial reporting black-out.

Following the case, the *Daily Mail* reported that a BBC documentary crew filmed one training camp, believing it was a paintball weekend for the TV show *Don't Panic I'm Islamic*. The paper alleged that 'senior journalists' later refused to contact the police after Hamid had informed the documentary makers he knew the identities of the 21/7 bombers.

In May the same year, Islamic convert Nicky Reilly tried to blow up the Giraffe restaurant in Exeter. Reilly, who was diagnosed with learning difficulties and Asperger's syndrome, was the only person injured during the failed attack when the bomb went off in his hands in a toilet cubicle in the restaurant. He was jailed for 18 years in January 2009 and is currently being held in Broadmoor high security hospital.

In November 2008, a report compiled by the intelligence branch of the Ministry of Defence, MI5 and Special Branch, leaked by *The Telegraph*, estimated that thousands of extremists were active within the UK. The report said the majority were UK born, mainly of Pakistani origin and aged between 18 and 30. Many were also believed to have attended terrorist training camps abroad. The report also revealed there was a threat from UK based foreign extremists and that radical groups were evenly spread across the nation, with concentrated pockets in Birmingham, London and Luton.

Scotland Yard's counter-terrorist unit had recently foiled a plot to kill the publisher of a novel featuring the Prophet Mohammed. Armed officers arrested three men after a petrol bomb was pushed through the door of the London home of the book's Dutch publisher. Ronald K Noble, Secretary General of Interpol, accused the British Government of failing to properly check people entering the UK against a terrorist database.

Months later, the arrest of 12 people suspected of involvement in an alleged terror bomb plot caused further concerns over Britain's border security. The men were arrested during raids in Manchester, Merseyside and Lancashire. *BBC News* claimed that police had discovered pictures of popular Manchester shopping centres and a nightclub during the raids.

It emerged that 11 of the suspects were Pakistanis, ten of them in the UK on student visas, again sparking fears that controls were too lax.

The fact the men were foreign nationals caused controversy, with critics pointing to deficiencies within the student visa system. According to Home Office figures, 42,000 Pakistani nationals entered the UK on student visas between April 2004 and April 2008. Shadow Home Secretary, Chris Grayling, said the government should tighten background checks on students coming to Britain from countries linked to terror. In response, the Home Office said that the student visa system had already been tightened up and since September 2007, Pakistani nationals who applied for UK student visas have had to pass strict vetting procedures. The Government claimed that the new procedures included fingerprint tests and a check of an applicant's identity against criminal and counter-terrorism databases.

A Casual Response

The scenes from the Anglian Parade in Luton were broadcast across the world and immediately ignited an explosion of outrage amongst the general public in Britain. At the same time as people in Luton were organising a response, nationally people were also picking up the gauntlet. On social networking sites such as Facebook, groups were established to oppose the actions of the extremists. It soon became apparent that many people considered the outrage as not just as an attack on the soldiers, but also as a direct assault on themselves, their culture and way of life.

Also using social networking websites and one in particular called *Firms Reunited*, ex and current football hooligans discussed the Muslim protest and many suggested it was their duty to respond in some way. As far as they saw it, the troops weren't in a position to defend themselves so it was up to them to do it. Alliances, which weeks earlier would have seemed impossible, were discussed and a conclusion arrived at, militant Islam was a national problem and they had to put aside club rivalries to tackle it. Driven by the enthusiasm of Cardiff fan Jeff Marsh, Casuals United was born: '**Uniting the UK's football tribes against the Jihadists, an alliance of British football casuals of various different colours/races who have come together in order to create a massive, but peaceful protest group to force our government to get their act in gear**'.

Marsh was involved with the Soul Crew, a hooligan gang which follows Cardiff City Football Club. He has written two books on his experiences, *'The Trouble with Taffies'* and *'Soul Crew Seasiders'*. Marsh would later tell *The Times*: '**I came up with the idea to unite football fans to forget their petty rivalries and come together in a national movement. There are a lot of people in their forties and fifties who used to be hooligans but went on to settle down. A lot of young football fans want to get involved.**'

It was decided that Casuals United would operate along local football club lines with individual club divisions. Wherever the Muslim extremists protested, they would now be opposed by local patriotic football gangs. People from across the country were pledging their support and a national network was quickly forged. This network has endured and still exists, independent of any subsequent organisations. To the people involved, football has become largely irrelevant in comparison to the fight against militant Islam and the establishment which facilitates its existence.

There were precedents for English football hooligans responding to perceived attacks on their communities. In April 2001, 76 year old pensioner and World War II veteran, Walter Chamberlain, was assaulted by Asian youths in Oldham, Greater Manchester. Two days after the attack, the front page of the *Manchester Evening News* showed a picture of a battered Mr Chamberlain with the headline, '**Get out of our area!**' Mr Chamberlain hadn't used those words in his initial statement, but police said they believed that is what his attackers had said.

The attack came three days after a report on the Radio 4 *Today* programme, which had alleged there were no-go areas for whites in Oldham. There had been racial tensions for a while and like many towns which have welcomed large numbers of people from the sub-continent Oldham is split into distinct white, Pakistani or Bangladeshi areas. In the year before the attack on Mr Chamberlain, 600 racist incidents were recorded by police in Oldham and 60% were attacks on white people. More than 180 of the incidents were violent and the vast majority of these assaults were attacks by Asian youths, usually in gangs of anything from six to twenty, on lone white males.

A week after the attack on Walter Chamberlain, local football team Oldham Athletic were playing host to Stoke City, a club from the midlands with a significant hooligan following. Before the match, pubs around the town were full of football fans, some of them chanting anti-Asian slogans spurred by the attack on Mr Chamberlain. At around 2.00pm, a large group of Stoke fans made their way to the ground. They clashed briefly with Oldham hooligans on Rochdale Road, but police were quickly on the scene. Then, as they made their way to the stadium through the predominantly Bangladeshi area of Westwood, the Stoke firm became involved in clashes with local Asian youths. As well as football, rivalries, what had happened to Mr Chamberlain was fresh in the mind of the Stoke lads and they quickly became involved in running battles with local Asian men. Police intervened again, forcing the football mob towards the stadium.

Once the match was under way both sets of fans sang anti-Asian songs and the Stoke hooligans informed their Oldham counterparts about the clashes with the Asians. It was agreed that following the game, both sets of fans would walk through Westwood together. It was a tenuous alliance; the Oldham lads numbered around 70, Stoke had a massive firm of well over 400 out. There were a tense few minutes when they met, before the Oldham lads realised Stoke meant what they had said. Police escorted the Stoke and Oldham mob back through Westwood. There were some fresh clashes and abuse was chanted by the hooligans as they marched past lines of riot police separating them from large numbers of Asians.

The crowd at the match had been considerably higher than the normal attendance expected for the fixture. This led to claims that the match had been hijacked by racists and far-right elements, but it was simply that English, working class fighting men had attended, for the football and if they could, to seek old fashioned recompense for what had happened to Walter Chamberlain. To these patriotic working class English fighting men, brought up on tales of empire, veterans like Walter Chamberlain were living gods. They had served King and Country and put their lives on the line for Britain and the British way of life. The least the British public could do in return was look after them and ensure they lived the rest of their lives peacefully and safely. In working class eyes, recompense for such a grave offence involved meting out instant rough justice to anyone who dared disrespect, let alone harm one of them.

There were further outbreaks of violence in the north-west that summer. Weeks after the visit of Stoke, hooligans from Oldham, Huddersfield, Shrewsbury and Stockport met in Oldham and clashed with local Asian gangs, precipitating three days of rioting in the town. This was followed by ethnic unrest in Burnley and Bradford.

In Burnley local white football hooligans took to the streets, not as racist agitators as the press were keen to label them, but as they saw it, to defend their community against attacks by Asian gangs. There was widespread disorder over a number of days, with both white and Asian owned businesses attacked. Burnley hooligan, Andrew Porter, was sentenced to three years for his part in the unrest. Commenting on a BRAVO TV documentary and illuminating the shift from British to an English identity for many working class people, Porter said: **"when I got done for the riots, they called me Nazi scum and that I voted BNP, and I had never voted in my life. I don't know where that label has come from, because I'm not British, I'm English"**

Also, following outrage at the burning of British flags at Speakers' Corner in Hyde Park by Muslim radicals around the time of the Iraq War, the '**March for the Flag**' movement, led by football fans, was born. March for the Flag had football hooligan involvement and eventually morphed into '**March for England**' (MfE), which is still a small, but active group.

The **United British Alliance** (UBA) also emerged around this time, mainly as a response to the excesses of Abu Hamza in the press but aiming to confront all terrorist sympathisers in the UK. The UBA, praised by anti-fascist magazine *Searchlight* for its discipline, was a group of predominantly football hooligans, mainly Home Counties based but with some support from the provinces. It was estimated that the UBA, on a good day, could call on up to 100 supporters and the group regularly opposed Abu Hamza outside Finsbury Park Mosque, as he preached in the street following his removal as imam.

The group did have some international links to groups in Holland and the USA. The UBA staged many marches, including the laying of a wreath outside the US embassy on the anniversary of 9/11. At one rally in Trafalgar Square, they forced an al-Muhajiroun protest to leave. The UBA also opposed political correctness and protested outside the law firm of Prime Minister's wife, Cherie Blair, which was defending terror suspects that her husband's government was trying to convict and deport. In 2008, the UBA opposed a pro-Palestinian march in London. As the parade passed their demonstration in Piccadilly, some UBA vaulted fences and scuffled with the marchers. Police intervened and five people were arrested.

Fans of Portsmouth and Tottenham Hotspur were involved with both the UBA and MfE. This factor has meant that the hooligans of certain other London clubs, such as Chelsea or Arsenal, were put off from full association with either group, but hooligans of both clubs have attended UBA events as separate bodies. There has also been friction with right-wing groups, because the UBA allows black members. The UBA was successful for a while but constant harassment by the police, and the fact it was unable to shed its football violence links, eventually caused a decline in numbers.

Of course, both MfE and the UBA have been branded racist, with links to the BNP and the far-right by both the media and anti-fascist groups. This purposely ignores the fact the people involved in these groups are more than likely fully aware of the sacrifice of their forefathers who fought against Nazi and fascist ideologies during WWII. Nazism is alien to them, as is fascism. Their understanding of British history, particularly WWI & II, will not have been instilled in them by the revisionist British education system, full of self-hating middle class liberals following communist doctrine, dumbed down and purposely shunning any mention of Britain's glorious past. It has been passed down word of mouth by the very people who lived it, people such as Mr Walter Chamberlain.

It is also surely obvious, that if these people supported existing extremist groups they wouldn't have had to form their own patriotic groups in the first place. Patriots with nowhere else to go might have investigated or experimented with certain groups such as the BNP, but most of the leadership, of even the moderate nationalist parties, are still tainted by the old days and national socialism. Again, these links will automatically deter most patriots brought up on stories of their family's involvement in the fight against Nazi Germany.

Like the far-left, the media has always been keen to link football hooligans to the far-right. As stated previously, the far-right had had little success in enlisting hooligans to their ranks. Obviously it is the law of averages that small numbers of people have been attracted by far-right parties, these individuals from different clubs have sometimes united when following the English national team abroad, possibly giving the far-right a higher profile to outsiders than it actually warranted.

In 1995, the media jumped on false claims that members of extreme-right-wing group Combat18 had led a riot during a game between the Republic of Ireland and England in Dublin. The riot was in fact more of an English working class reaction to the violence of the IRA over the preceding decades and also to the introduction of the Anglo-Irish Agreement (the agreement gave Ulster a devolved government and the Republic an advisory role in Northern Irish affairs. It was seen as a capitulation by many nationalists). Yet the tabloids jumped on claims that Combat18 had been present in Dublin, just like they had jumped on equally false claims that the NF had been present during the Heysel Disaster in 1985.

In the 90s, with the rise of English nationalism, many football hooligans who didn't want to be associated with the right-wing were attracted to the loyalist culture of Northern Ireland. The unrestrained pride the loyalists of Ulster show in their culture and heritage has long been admired by unrepresented patriots on the mainland. Like the Ulster loyalists, working class patriots on the mainland would probably claim loyalty to the Crown rather than to Parliament, as the Crown represents their identity, culture and traditions more than the political class ever could. After all, the monarchy, unlike the political class, traditionally sends its sons to fight on the same battlefields as the working class.

Following the establishment of UPL and Casuals United, there was a general air of 'someone is finally doing something' amongst working class patriots. Some members of Casuals United, including Jeff Marsh had made contact with members of UPL. On the Internet, dialogue with other groups was taking place, trust and subsequently friendships were forged. It was decided that UPL and Casuals United would merge and operate under one national banner. Jeff Marsh had already formed his own national group for Wales, the Welsh Defence League. An English version was decided upon, and the *English Defence League* was born.

They intended to initially mobilise football hooligans, still under the umbrella of Casuals United and specifically using the Internet, but it was hoped the new name, not associated with football would rally ordinary members of the public to its banner. They were correct, the name has been key to why the EDL was more successful than other preceding groups such as MfE or the UBA. It summed up how many people felt. English people felt their way of life was under attack and it was their duty to defend it. The English psyche has always been more comfortable reacting to aggression than being the aggressor.

Stephen Lennon, who by this time was using another pseudonym, Tommy Robinson, was now acting as spokesman for the EDL. He told *The Guardian* that they had recruited football supporters from clubs including Aston Villa, Cardiff, Chelsea, QPR, Swansea and Wolverhampton Wanderers: '**What does unite the group is a willingness to fight. We feel that only people with that mentality will go [to demonstrate], that's why it's all lads. Your upper class people won't stand there and get attacked, through fear. I am from the mentality that I am not going to back down. It started with what they did to the soldiers, but after that it has been about the two-sided treatment our community get compared to what the Muslim community get from the police and the council. The police hit us with batons and come at them with kid gloves.**'

The real Tommy Robinson was the author of two books, '*MiG Down*' and '*MiG Crew*', charting the adventures of Luton football hooligans Men in Gear. Because of the constant links or references to football hooliganism, anti-fascists claimed that the EDL was using established football hooligan networks to organise. That simply isn't the case, some football hooligans joined the EDL, but the group was viewed with suspicion by many. Most thought that the EDL were insane putting their faces in the spotlight and suspected that the state would clampdown on them very quickly. As the quality of video surveillance and length of banning orders have risen, many football hooligans choose their moments more carefully. To them, it seemed madness to go and poke the establishment unless it was for football reasons. Many with families, homes and jobs at risk shunned the movement, with only a tiny percentage taking part. There was also an elitism aspect, most hooligans believe themselves as fighting men to be the working class elite, they saw the behaviour of the EDL as uncool, the waving of the flags and chanting more akin to the behaviour of normal fans or as they refer to them because of their preference to wear club colours, '**scarfers**'

This is why established hooligan networks were never used by the EDL, it was looked upon as unnecessarily 'heavy'. A lot of football hooligans took part individually or in small groups, their involvement is kept totally separate from their football associations. Some of this separation is out of necessity, as some hooligans involved with the EDL often meet the hooligans of hated rival clubs, something the majority of their peers would never believe could happen. Organisation of the EDL mimics that of football hooliganism, in fact some other aspects of football hooliganism are also copied, such as dress or colloquialisms, but this occurs totally independently of hooligan networks.

A Facebook page entitled English Defence League appeared on 27 June 2009, a website, *www.englishdefenceleague.co.uk* with its own forum soon followed. The EDL stated that it existed due to frustration at the lack of any significant action by the British Government against Muslim preachers of hate and organisations such as Islam4UK and Hizb ut Tahrir. A Scottish Defence League and an Ulster Defence League soon followed. Graphically, the EDL borrows heavily from crusader history; the cross of the crusading soldier-monks of the Knights Templar is widely used, as are other images of crusader knights and shields. EDL members started referring to themselves as infidels, ironically used in crusader times by Christians for their Muslim opponents. Other references to British mythology were utilised, such as Arthurian legend or British Imperial history. A badge was designed, a simple red cross on white shield, and a motto adopted, '**In hoc signo** vinces - with this as your standard you will conquer'. The motto is taken from the coat of arms of Jan Sobieski, commander of the victorious Christian 'Holy League' against the Turks during the Battle of Vienna in 1683.

27 June 2009: Whitechapel

Whitechapel in Tower Hamlets, east London, was chosen as the location of the group's debut on the streets. An inner city district, the borough is one of poorest in Britain and at 40%, has one of the highest Muslim populations in the country, the majority originating from Bangladesh.

Tower Hamlets had been the temporary home of extremist preacher Abdullah el-Faisal and the local East London Mosque had also held a conference featuring Anwar al-Awlaki, who would later be described in the British press as 'the spiritual leader of al-Qaeda in the Arabian Peninsular'. Posters showing New York under attack and the Statue of Liberty engulfed in flames advertised the event. Al-Awlaki has also published guides (in English) on how to assemble explosive devices and is suspected of being behind many al-Qaeda operations. Speaking later on BBC programme *Hard Talk*, Chairman of the mosque, Dr Muhammad Abdul Bari, said the decision to hold the conference was a mistake, but added there was no information suggesting al-Awlaki was involved in terrorism.

The protest in Whitechapel was organised on the *Firms Reunited* website by someone called Dave Shaw. However, as the organiser, Shaw was a notable absentee when the group met on the morning of the demo in a pub near Trafalgar Square. There were mainly football hooligans present, from various clubs such as, Arsenal, Aston Villa, Brentford, Bristol City, Cardiff, Luton, Newcastle, Portsmouth, Queens Park Rangers and Wolverhampton. The police were waiting for them, and with no sign of Shaw, many still en route gave the area a wide berth. The ones who did turn up were told by the police that they could go to Whitechapel, but only with a police escort. The thirty or so present decided to carry on as planned, even with the police in tow.

They made their way to Whitechapel on the tube and got off at Aldgate East, but as they left the station police held, searched, photographed them. They were all issued with a Section 60 Order (Section 60 of the Criminal Justice & Public Order Act 1994 was originally brought in to combat football hooliganism in England. It gives the police the power to stop and search individuals or groups, where there is reasonable cause for them to anticipate violence).

After the searches had been conducted, they were told they were being escorted to Whitechapel tube station. The police could have taken them back to Aldgate East, but for some reason they were marching them through Whitechapel. They marched along the main thoroughfare singing "**Rule Britannia**" and chanting, as astonished shoppers looked on. They were then put on a tube at Whitechapel station and travelled to Charing Cross, where police held them again. This time they were held for three hours, before being issued with a Section 27 Dispersal Order (Section 27 of the Violent Crime Reduction Act 2006 provides the police with a power to direct an individual, aged 16 years or over, who is in a public place to leave the locality. The order prohibits a return to that locality for up to 48 hours). Although the protest wasn't an obvious success, more introductions had been made. A national structure was now fully applied and certain people, some of whom would later form the recognised leadership of the EDL, became organisers in their respective areas.

The EDL now began monitoring radical Islamic websites looking for an opportunity to confront Muslim extremism whenever and wherever they could. In true working class fashion, they now set out to take the fight to their opponents. In the news, it was reported that British forces were increasingly encountering British born Muslims, with English regional accents, on the battlefields of Afghanistan. A military source told the *Daily Mail* that UK troops were fighting a '**surreal mini-civil war**' against men with West Midlands and Yorkshire accents. Also, Anjem Choudary announced that al-Muhajiroun was reforming. He said that it was not an illegal organisation as it hadn't been banned by the Home Office; they had just not been using the name. A video advertising '**The London School of Sharia**', was posted on several Internet sites, Choudary was shown converting an 11 year old white boy to

Islam at an ISLAM4UK road-show in Birmingham in front of a banner which read 'Jesus was a Muslim', Choudary recited sentences in Arabic, which the boy repeated, as Choudary's supporters repeatedly shouted "Allahu Akbar!" When questioned by the *Daily Mail* about the conversion, Choudary said the boy had been genuinely interested in Islam but admitted that his parents hadn't been present.

This outraged the emerging EDL and Birmingham was immediately identified as a hotbed of radical Islam and the venue for the group's next protest.

4 July 2009: Birmingham

Birmingham is Britain's second city, a former industrial powerhouse, once famous throughout the world for high quality goods manufactured by a multitude of craftsmen.

Like Luton, because of the diversity of its manufacturing, Birmingham didn't suffer as much as some areas of the country during the recessions of the 80s and 90s, but since the final collapse of UK manufacturing, the city has suffered considerably. In 2011, Birmingham contained four of the 'top ten' UK unemployment black-spots.

The city has welcomed large numbers of migrants over the years, attracted by the numerous low-skilled factory jobs that were once on offer. Over 14% of Birmingham's population is Muslim and with a population of around a million people, the city has the largest concentration of Muslims in the UK. The vast majority of Birmingham Muslims (possibly 85% or more), have their roots in Azad Kashmir, in fact the city is home to the largest ex-pat Kashmiri community in the world. The city's Central Mosque, built in 1969, was the second purpose-built mosque in the UK. It serves around 4,000 worshippers for Friday prayers and up to 20,000 during festivals.

In July 2007, *The Times* reported that the West Midlands area was one of the UK's 'terror hot-spots' and up to 80 potential terror cells (more than double the number which were under surveillance in London) in the county were being monitored by security services. Casuals United claimed Birmingham had been chosen because most of the Islamist activity in England and probably Europe, originated in parts of the city. The group claimed Birmingham had more no-go areas for non-Muslims than any other city in England. The protest was widely advertised on the Internet and hundreds of people had promised to attend. Speaking for the EDL, Portsmouth activist Trevor Kelway said the group was a peaceful, non-racist organisation and promised that the protest would be 'a great day out for all concerned'.

The protest was a Casuals United demonstration, UPL activists weren't attending; they and others from the south had decided to counter an ISLAM4UK road-show, in Wood Green, London. Casuals United had tried to drum up the support of local football hooligans, but few older, established thugs, worried about the exposure, joined the protest,. The group were more successful with younger males, some of whom were only loosely attached to local hooligan gangs.

The meeting point was the Flapper and Firkin pub on Broad Street in Birmingham. From there the Casuals planned to march into the city centre and protest outside the city's flagship Bullring Shopping Centre. The group was operating on a simple structure which relied on local people organising the protests. Birmingham activists had organised the time, place and date of the meet, then informed others on the day via mobile phone. Following police interference, one group arriving by train was diverted to the other side of the city and plotted up at the Bull Ring Tavern in Digbeth. The group at the Flapper and Firkin, numbering around 50, made their way over to join up with them.

Once united, they numbered around 150, with representatives from across England. They then made their way to the demo site. As they approached the Bullring, the group started chanting and singing songs such as "Rule Britannia" and "No surrender to the Taliban". When they arrived, there were a number of police waiting who quickly surrounded them. As they did this the Casuals started singing "We want our country back!"

The Police who had gathered to contain the demonstration were a collection of ordinary police officers Football Intelligence Officers (FIO), Forward Intelligence Teams (FIT) and Evidence

Gathering Teams (EGT). FIT, identified by blue squares on police standard issue fluorescent jackets, are officers assigned to cover protests. They are often accompanied by EGT teams, identifiable by orange epaulettes, who act as cameramen.

The FIT teams come under the National Public Order Intelligence Unit (NPOIU). NPOIU was established to provide intelligence to police forces regarding people they have identified as domestic extremists. These are individuals, or groups, who seek to bring about political change by direct action against the state or multi-national corporations and include animal rights activists, environmental protestors and political extremists. NPIOU officers attend demonstrations with the intention of gathering intelligence, but also undertake clandestine operations, which include undercover officers and the management of informants. NPIOU has access to various databases operated by police forces throughout the UK, such as the Police National Computer, Crimint or the image database held by CO11 (the Metropolitan Police's own public order unit). Journalist Andrew Gilligan has described the NPIOU as **'a secretive, Scotland Yard-based police taskforce whose role in controlling dissent is central'**.

As well as NPIOU, there is the National Extremism Tactical Co-ordination Unit (NETCU) which advises businesses that are the target of protest campaigns, and the National Domestic Extremism Team (NDET) which carries out investigations into offences committed by political activists. These units come under the National Domestic Extremism Unit (NDEU) and employ hundreds of people, of which two thirds are officers seconded from regional police forces. NDEU is run by the Association of Chief Police Officers (ACPO) and is independent of other forces. Operating on a budget of £8.1 million, these teams are answerable only to the National Co-ordinator for Domestic Extremism, who in turn is only accountable to the ACPO - Terrorism and Allied Matters Committee (which thankfully in the interests of democracy, includes senior government officials).

A FIT officer's main aim is not only to shadow identified targets but also to attain the personal details of other prominent people. This is, more often than not, obtained by carrying out stop and searches on individuals or groups. Section 60 is regularly utilised, allowing police to gather intelligence by stopping people without the need for suspicion. The police have the power under S60 to hold suspects as long as necessary to carry out a search for weapons. It gives police no power to ask the suspect for their name or address, however in reality they regularly interview people whilst performing the search. In law they have no legal power to force people who have committed no crime to disclose their identity (under Article 8 of the UK Human Rights Act 1998, your privacy is assured). Following demonstrations, officers submit written intelligence reports, including names, addresses and descriptions of people. These are entered onto police records.

Within five minutes of the Casuals arrival at the protest site in Birmingham, a group of Asian youths had gathered on the other side of police lines. Casuals United later claimed that these youths started chanting "**kuffar!**" As far as one of them was concerned, they were protesting peacefully under police supervision "**if we had sung anything remotely racist, the police would've arrested us, simple as that, but they seemed to ignore the racist comments coming from the Asians**"

A few coins were thrown by the Asians and the Casuals responded to the provocation, surging towards them and backing the police off a short distance. Police utilised their batons and beat the Casuals back, but the two groups continued to bait each other with chants and songs. After around 45 minutes of protesting, six police vans appeared and started to drive towards the Casuals. Rumours quickly spread that they were all going to be arrested and they pushed against police lines to escape. The police lines between the two groups held but the Casuals flooded in the opposite direction, breaking through police lines and scattering.

The protest was totally ignored by the media, but the EDL later claimed: '**We had to show our solidarity with the local people powerless to stop the spread of militant Islam in the heart of al-Qaeda in England. We are returning on the 8 August due to the popularity of the protest and lack of coverage by the media. We hope this will be another peaceful protest, despite threats from Muslim hate-mongers**'

4 July 2009: Wood Green

Following the announcement of the Birmingham protest on 4 July, Anjem Choudary announced that he was to hold a '**Life under Sharia - Islamic road-show**' in Wood Green, London, on the same day. It was decided that the Birmingham demo should still go ahead, but southern activists would travel to Wood Green to oppose Choudary.

The group met early in the morning at a pub in the Wood Green area. A car containing activists was sent out to locate Choudary but reported that although a small group of Muslims were setting up a stall in the central shopping area, there was no sign of the man himself. In light of this, the group decided that before revealing themselves, they would wait to see if Choudary showed up. A small group of Asian youths had spotted them standing outside the pub and were slowly edging closer. Some of them walked past across the road, shouting insults. Some of the EDL reacted and although others encouraged them not to, it was futile. The Asian youths were chased off and football style chants filled the air.

Suddenly police cars and vans screeched round the corner. The EDL were forcibly corralled and two were arrested. The rest of the group were searched, filmed and questioned. They were informed there was a Section 60 Order in force for Wood Green for the rest of the day; and if they went into the centre they would be arrested. They were then escorted out of the area. It emerged that Police had authorised the Section 60 Order due to the presence of the EDL. As well as the EDL, the order had been used against Choudary, preventing him from setting out his stall in the area. Some in the EDL were adamant that although the police had only used the restrictions because they were present, they had stopped Choudary, by just being there. The EDL had thereby achieved its aim and disrupted the activities of an extremist Muslim group.

Unbeknown to the police, a small number of EDL still remained in Wood Green. When they heard Choudary had set up his road-show in Stratford, east London, they made their way there. They planned to join forces with the UBA, who also planned to confront him. When they arrived, unable to find Choudary, the group stayed in the area. Later that evening, a pub they were in was attacked by a group of over 100 Muslim males, who showered the building with missiles. One of the Casuals was hit by a bus during the incident.

8 August 2009: Birmingham

The EDL was determined to revisit Birmingham. It was thought, that this time if the two groups who had acted separately on 4 July joined forces, and with more people hearing about the protests, they would attract greater numbers.

Prior to the protest, the far-left were busy, distributing leaflets in predominantly Asian areas of the city, encouraging young Asians to take to the streets to defend their communities. UAF issued a statement announcing a counter-demonstration, claiming that both Casuals United and the EDL were linked to the BNP and neo-Nazi groups. Anti-fascists were keen to have the EDL painted as racist and fascist as quickly as possible, simply so they could be dismissed and lose any potential populist support. The strategy was to constantly highlight any possible link with the extreme right, if they said it enough times people might start believing it. As evidence, they pointed to discussions on far-right Internet forums, such as *Blood and Honour*, where the protest was being discussed.

The EDL and Casuals United were appealing for anyone who opposed Islamic extremism to attend their protests. Unfortunately, as well as concerned citizens, some neo-Nazis were also answering the call. It was however, ridiculous to consider everyone who was now taking part as racist. They were mostly from Britain's multicultural urban areas and probably had more experience of living and interacting with other cultures than the middle class communists from leafy suburbs who were attacking them ever could. They had grown up alongside other cultures, but were on the street because integration in modern Britain simply wasn't working. To counter the accusations of racism, the EDL promoted a 'Black and White Unite' agenda, stressing that the fight against militant Islam was not a racial issue. On his website, Luton activist Paul Ray claimed he was worried about far-right infiltration and especially the date of the Birmingham protest. It was being suggested by anti-fascists that the date 8/8, signified HH or 'Heil Hitler'. Ray said that he would not be part of any movement which included neo-Nazis, adding that he had handed over the reins of the EDL to Tommy Robinson a.k.a. Stephen Lennon.

This was news to EDL activists, as Ray had never actually been in charge of the EDL. Up to that point no-one had; Lennon and Kelway had merely been acting as the group's spokesmen. Ray had applied to stage the refused St George's Day protest in Luton and claimed to have been present at the Wood Green counter-demo, but had never been calling any shots. Up to that point it was a democratic process, decided between the people involved from the start. In reality, Ray had clashed with another member, Chris Renton, who along with his brother Rob had day to day involvement in the movement. Anti-fascists had alleged that Chris Renton's name had been on a leaked BNP membership list and were keen to capitalise and produce it as proof that the EDL was merely a front for the BNP. Ray called the two 'pirates', who had 'hijacked' the EDL. He attempted to capitalise on BNP allegations made by anti-fascists and claimed that Renton had, with the backing of football casuals, taken over the movement.

For different reasons to Ray, Jeff Marsh announced he was standing down as leader of Casuals United. Marsh had been arrested during a disturbance following a pre-season match between Cardiff City and Glasgow Celtic. As well as being arrested for affray, Marsh was informed he was also being bailed pending further enquiries on a charge of 'inciting religious hatred'. This charge was apparently due to comments he made following the news that one of the Luton radicals worked airside at Luton Airport.

Marsh announced that he was handing over control to Wayne King a.k.a. Lennon, following what he termed 'police harassment' and advice from his solicitor that he was a serious target for both police and the CPS. Marsh eventually pleaded guilty to the charge of affray and was handed a four months suspended prison sentence, 150 hours Community Service, a five year Football Banning Order and £600 costs. After a year on bail for the inciting religious hatred charge, it was dropped by police.

On the day of the Birmingham demo, hundreds of anti-fascists gathered outside the Bullring Shopping Centre. UAF activist, Sabia Jabeen, told *Channel Islam News* that they were there because the EDL was an organisation of racist thugs connected to the BNP. She said the fact that they had demonstrated unopposed before had given the EDL the confidence to return, but this time she said there were hundreds of UAF to oppose them. Local RESPECT Party councillor Salma Yaqoob addressed the counter-protest. Yaqoob said the EDL were 'fascist thugs' who were 'not wanted in Birmingham' and whipped up the crowd by repeatedly chanting "Whose streets? Our streets!"

The EDL planned to protest outside the Bullring, but at the last minute the police informed them that the site had been chosen by UAF, so they were relocated across the city to Victoria Square. Some EDL met at a pub in the Chinese quarter, but police arrived and immediately issued them with Section 27 Dispersal Orders; forcing them to leave the city centre. It was obvious that after the trouble surrounding the previous protest, West Midlands Police (WMP) simply didn't want them there.

Around 150 EDL met at the Figure of Eight pub on Broad St. At around 2.00pm, shadowed by police, they marched down towards Victoria Square. As they neared the square, they encountered a small group of anti-fascists. The EDL charged, scattering their opponents. Police struggled to regain control, but managed to contain the EDL and escort them the short distance to the demo site.

The demonstration started with chants against Muslim extremists. Anti-fascists and Asian youths appeared nearby and some EDL broke through police lines to confront them. The EDL chased them down New Street, but were prevented from following further by police who had blocked the street with two vans. The EDL took to the back streets, skirted the police and emerged close to the UAF demo, where they were confronted with hundreds of anti-fascists, Asian and Black youths. Held by a thin line of police, the anti-fascists surged towards the EDL. Some of them managed to get through and there was shouting and screaming as the rival factions clashed in the street. Some shoppers found themselves locked in shops as alarms and sirens rang out and riot police struggled to regain control.

WMP spent the rest of the day baton charging and keeping opposing groups apart. A police spokesman said they had made 34 arrests. Assistant Chief Constable, Sharon Rowe, said the force had tried to liaise with the EDL before the demonstration but had been ignored. Local MP, Khalid Mahmood, questioned the wisdom of allowing both protests on the same day. The Internet was awash with videos of mobs of young mostly Asian and Black youths touring the city, assaulting people who they had identified as EDL. One picture carried by national newspapers showed an elderly man clutching a Union Jack, being assaulted by a gang of Asian youths. Another showed a young man, his face a bloodied mess, sinking to his knees as his attackers mercilessly kicked him.

These images were broadcast across the world and the EDL claimed that as a result, its membership had swelled from 400 to over 4000. The group did however admit the turnout had been poor. Some supporters complained that the multicultural '**Black and White Unite**' approach and the message that the BNP and far-right were not welcome were the reasons for the poor turnout and the EDL needed to stop being so politically correct.

The group blamed the violence on Asian youths inflamed by UAF speakers and announced that because of the intimidation they had faced, they would return to the city on the 5 September. In contrast to the last visit to Birmingham, this time the EDL caught the attention of the national press. *The Times* described the group as former football hooligans who were re-grouping under the banner of Casuals United. Calling the group the '**new beast on the far-right**', the article went on to stereotype participants as '**a small army of shirt-sleeved, middle-aged men with beer bellies**'. Obviously, similar stereotypes would not be so readily applied to other minority ethnic groups, but as the Casuals were mainly white and English, they were fair game. Anti-fascists told *The Times* they had correctly predicted the trouble in Birmingham, the EDL were a violent group and the BNP was offering to supply them with people for future demonstrations.

However, the attitude of most EDL members to the BNP was summed up by founder member Davy Cooling, who would later tell *The Guardian* that he had attended BNP events in the past, but had simply not agreed with their policies: '**A few years ago I attended two or three meetings of the BNP in Luton, but I do not agree with their policy of banning black and other ethnic minority groups from membership. It doesn't matter what religion or race you are, everyone is welcome to the EDL**'

The EDL also featured in the August 2009 edition of *Searchlight*. An article implied BNP input, discussing the party's role in the mill town riots of 2001 and leader Nick Griffin's prediction of a coming '**civil war**'. The far-right National Front didn't help the situation by issuing a statement which said that although the EDL and Casuals United had made a number of anti-NF statements, they were standing up for British rights and against the Islamification of Great Britain. The view of the NF was that the EDL was a group of directionless young men and women who were trying to play the anti-racist card whilst at the same time promoting a sort of English/Welsh Nationalism. Claiming they had predicted that groups such as the EDL and Casuals United would emerge, the NF said they were people who needed to be '**educated correctly on the political implications of their actions**'.

On 13 August 2009, *Wales on Sunday* printed a story entitled '**Army made of football hooligans**'. Jeff Marsh told the paper that the Casuals United and the Defence Leagues had around three thousand supporters across the UK. He claimed they were only protesting against the preachers of hate who were actively encouraging young British Muslims to take part in a jihad against the UK. Denying they were intent on violence, Marsh said: '**We do not look for violence but former football hooligans are able to defend themselves against trouble and are not afraid to protest when being pelted with missiles, like what happened in Birmingham. It is not in our interests to go out and cause riots because we will get arrested and hit with ASBOs**'. Gerry Gable of *Searchlight* told the paper they had uncovered links between the EDL and '**other far-right groups**' but didn't elaborate which ones. In response to the accusation, Marsh said that although anti-fascists had identified them as racist, the EDL had black members and they had spoken with some Sikhs who also wanted to join.

The EDL announced a protest in Luton for 19 September 2009, following news that the town had been excluded from an Anglian Regiment Benevolent Fund charity walk. The EDL suspected that the Islamic extremist demonstrators at the Anglian parade had played a part. In response to the announcement, the Home Office issued a three-month ban on any unofficial marches in Luton involving members or supporters of the EDL, Casuals United, MfE or UPL. Chief Superintendent Andy Frost of Bedfordshire Police told the *Luton Herald and Post* that there would be a significant police presence to ensure the ban was observed and claimed the risk to public safety the march posed had left them with no option but to apply for a ban. The EDL was forced to concede defeat and cancelled the march. Luton Town's home game against York City on the same day as the planned protest was postponed due to fears that the EDL might try to use the match to defy the ban.

On the same day the ban on the Luton march was announced, seven Muslim men who had protested against the Anglian Regiment were charged under the Public Order Act. The men, all from Luton, were bailed to appear at Luton Magistrates' Court on 16 September. A further twelve people were charged in connection with the UPL protest on 24 May 2009. They were also bailed to appear in court on 25 September. Following the news, Anjem Choudary made a surprise appeal for dialogue with the EDL. Speaking on the Islam4UK website, Choudary attacked socialist and communist groups who he claimed were **"jumping on the bandwagon"** and exploiting the situation for their own ends. Acknowledging that the EDL came into being after the protest in Luton and his call for Sharia in Birmingham, Choudary said that it was a clear case of Islam against the kuffar and called on people to debate with his group. Choudary said the EDL and Casuals United had a right to oppose and discuss Sharia, but said that people, like UAF, the Labour Party and RESPECT should not be allowed to hijack the discussions.

5 September 2009: Birmingham

The EDL said it was returning to Birmingham because the previous protest in the city had been **'disrupted and deformed by the Government funded UAF'**. The group claimed anti-fascists had told locals that the EDL was really the BNP, but said hopefully everyone now knew that they had no links whatsoever to the party. The EDL said it did not want anyone intent on trouble, or with any agenda other than opposing Islamic extremism to attend the protest as it did not want a repeat of the violence witnessed last time. They appealed to anti-fascists to listen to their message and not to attack them, claiming they too were protesting against fascism, but the fascists they opposed used the banner of Islam to hide behind.

Following the alleged BNP links, the BNP issued a statement in its official party paper, *The British Nationalist*. The party said it was proscribing the EDL, prohibiting any BNP members from associating with EDL supporters or participating in any event organised by the group. The party said the reason for proscription was because they believed the EDL was bringing patriotic and nationalist politics into disrepute. The statement concluded by implying that the EDL was backed by the state.

The demonstration was to be held at Lancaster Circus, on the northern edge of the city centre. It wasn't as high profile a location as the previously, but the EDL said it was confident that the protest would pass off peacefully this time due to the improved communication with WMP. There had been calls for the EDL to be prohibited from protesting, but Birmingham Labour MP Stuart McCabe opposed a ban, saying it would only allow the EDL to claim they were being victimised: **'We can't go around banning things because we don't like them or because of the threat of a reaction from some or other group. It's uncomfortable but our system is built on defending the freedom to express all sorts of opinions'**.

This time Birmingham City Council had followed the advice of Khalid Mahmood and refused permission for a counter-protest. UAF criticised the decision, saying that the council was acting as if racists were welcome in the city. However, anti-fascists were still pledging to travel to the city to oppose the EDL. The police and council had obtained a Section 14 Enforcement Order, giving them the power to arrest anyone who breached set conditions, including the protest location, the maximum number of protestors and the length of the event.

Police told *The Times* they had fully engaged with local mosques and youth workers. WMP claimed they had received assurances from Muslim leaders that local Muslims would be discouraged from attending any counter-protest. However, Dr Mohammed Naseem, chairman of Birmingham Central Mosque, considered the most senior Muslim in the West Midlands, said it was not his place to discourage followers from attending, as it was their right. In fact, Naseem said local Muslims should attend to '**vent their feelings**'.

As well as Muslim extremism, the EDL was now addressing a further concern, Sharia, which it claimed was being covertly implemented in parts of the UK. The group saw the establishment of Sharia tribunals as an example of the Islamification of Britain. The British Government allowed the introduction of Sharia in 2008, when a network of five courts was established in Birmingham, Bradford London, Nuneaton and Manchester, with more proposed for Cardiff, Glasgow and Edinburgh. The official UK Ministry of Justice stance on Sharia in England and Wales is that communities have the option to use religious councils and if there are incompatibilities between English and religious laws, parties still have the option to refer to the family courts.

British Sharia courts or Muslim Arbitration Tribunals are run as charities and participants, in many cases without legal representation, sign an agreement to abide by their decisions. Critics claim there is no independent control or monitoring, proceedings are not recorded, there are no referable legal judgements, nor any real right to appeal. All these things are contrary to the British legal system, basic universal rights such as equality are ignored, simply because of the establishment's obsession with accommodating minority groups. Faisal Aqtab Siddiqi, head of the first Sharia court in Nuneaton, told the *Coventry Evening Telegraph* that Sharia tribunals were merely supplementing English law.

In spite of the many assurances, Former Bishop of Rochester, Dr Michael Nazir Ali, has voiced concerns that some people are coerced into Sharia proceedings. Dr Ali also warned that recognising the tribunals could lead to discrimination, particularly against Muslim women.

On the morning of the protest, EDL supporters assembled in the Figure of Eight pub on Broad Street. There was no obvious police presence, which in light of previous demonstrations in the city, was surprising. At midday, they heard there were disturbances in the city centre and around 60 of them marched towards the main shopping area.

At Victoria Square, they encountered around 30 UAF, surrounding a paste table. As the EDL went to confront them, police seemingly appeared out of nowhere and shepherded them down New Street. Halfway down, they stopped at a pub called the Briar Rose, but staff refused to serve them. They didn't want to go to Lancaster Circus, as other EDL coming by train were still to arrive. Unable to get a drink, the EDL gathered on the street outside, with police at the bottom of the road and anti-fascists on the other side of the police lines, attempting to confront them. Anti-fascists were holding a banner '**Give the EDL the red card**', and chanted "**Nazi scum out of Brum!**"

Some EDL ran up Bennett's Hill intending to come back down an adjacent road towards the counter-demonstrators. As they got to the top of the hill, they encountered a large gang of masked Asian youths carrying large pieces of wood. Some EDL at the front stopped, but others from behind them rushed past and into the Asian gang. Fighting broke out in the shadow of Birmingham Cathedral, as more Asians and a few white anti-fascists arrived on the scene. *The Birmingham Post* reported that numerous people locked themselves in a cafe by the cathedral because they were so scared. One arrested man, sitting handcuffed on the floor, spoke to a BBC journalist: "**I'm from Birmingham mate, I live here. I'm sick of Muslim extremists slagging down our soldiers, thinking they can build up their mosques and call us scum**"

As police arrived, most of the EDL ran into a pub called Bennett's Bar to avoid arrest. Police quickly surrounded the building and there were scuffles at the doors of the pub as the EDL realised they were trapped. The police informed them they would be supplying double-decker buses to transport them to the protest site, but only if they calmed down. Most complied and they waited for the promised transport. Half an hour passed and nothing happened, the EDL inside the pub started to get restless. A small crowd gathered by the entrance, where they were confronted by lines of police with riot shields. A glass was thrown from inside the pub towards police, but it hit and injured an EDL supporter.

While this was going on, a number of EDL left the pub through a fire escape. They walked down an alleyway and emerged onto New Street and confronted the anti-fascists, who scattered. The EDL pursued them a short distance, but as police noticed them, they quickly returned to the pub via the alleyway. Amongst the people who had gathered to watch on New Street, was one elderly gentleman in a tweed suit. He was identified by anti-fascists as "a **local BNP councillor**" (Birmingham has no BNP councillors), but was in fact, local Conservative councillor Peter Douglas-Osborne. He was confronted by anti-fascists, had an egg thrown in his face and received what he called '**a bash on the ear**'.

At 3.00pm a group of 60 Asian men tried to storm Bennett's Bar, but were beaten back by police. One witness told the *Daily Mail* she had to duck into a shop to avoid being caught in the violence. She said she had seen 200 Asian men with bandanas over their faces, running down the street, shouting, screaming and throwing bricks. Another witness told *The Times* it was shocking to see, and that '**some of the protesters just looked like they wanted a ruck.**'

Two buses finally arrived and the EDL guided onto them by police. As they were shepherded onto the buses, they could hear the anti-fascists behind police lines, shouting and throwing missiles. Packed with EDL demonstrators, the buses left Bennett's Hill. The EDL hung flags from the windows, British ones, but also Jamaican and Israeli flags - a deliberate attempt by the group to distance itself from the Nazi allegations. At the top of the road there was a large group of football fans who applauded the buses as they passed. The buses were escorted by police outriders, but a large gap soon appeared between them. Unbeknown to the EDL on the first bus, the second bus was being trashed. The first bus arrived at Lancaster Circus with the second bus nowhere in sight. Police allowed the EDL to leave the bus but herded them down a subway, where they discovered lines of police at the other end, who told them they would be kept there until the second bus arrived.

When the second bus finally arrived, it was wrecked. After a short while, with both groups still separated, another bus arrived to take the EDL from the second bus away. The occupants of the first bus were then told they were not going to be allowed to demonstrate. They were taken to Birmingham International train station in Solihull, where they were released. The other group were taken to a police station in Coventry, where they were held on the bus until 3.00am the next morning, given on-the-spot fines and released.

Commenting afterwards, Dr Mohammed Naseem said the presence of Muslims at the protest was an important stand against '**anti-Islamic fascists**' and showed that the community had a sense of cohesion. He told the *Daily Mail* he had been assured by WMP that opposing protesters would gather in separate locations: '**If it was kept as originally intended, then everybody would have had a chance to give vent to their feelings without coming into contact with each other. And that I will take up with the police**'.

The EDL praised WMP for the way in which they dealt with the trouble and said they believed police had done everything they could on the day to '**implement democracy in Birmingham**'. Describing the streets of Birmingham as being '**over-run with gangs of Muslim Extremists**' the EDL said that the protest being cancelled showed that police could not protect a small number of peaceful protestors, despite drafting in back-up from other forces. The statement said it showed how serious the problem with radical Islam in Birmingham was, but added they wouldn't be returning because they didn't want to see any more innocent people or police officers become the victims of Muslim gangs.

Chief Constable, Chris Simms, said the disturbances had raised a debate over the laws available to police protests balanced with the rights of individuals to safely go about their business. He claimed the EDL had rejected requests to stage a peaceful protest at Lancaster Circus, and instead had sparked a spontaneous and disorganised series of incidents. Simms admitted that local youths had come into the city centre intent on violence and said that both groups would be regarded equally as culpable for the scenes that had unfolded. A team of detectives were currently examining CCTV footage to identify those responsible said Simms, officers were looking for any evidence of incitement and racially or religiously motivated offences and they anticipated adding to the number of people already arrested. Simms added that although the EDL had indicated beforehand that they wanted a peaceful protest, that hadn't been the case and said the group would encounter a far less tolerant approach by police, should they return to the West Midlands. Simms said police would be considering a range of legal measures including injunctions, civil orders and ASBOs.

A total of 90 people were arrested, all men aged between 16 and 39. Eight were charged with violent disorder, and another seven with minor public order offences. More than 80 were issued with on-the-spot fines, most of them passengers on the vandalised bus. Four months later, the *Birmingham Mail* published pictures of 26 men, eighteen wanted in connection with the 8 August demonstration and eight for the 5 September protest. A month after the appeal, WMP announced that they had arrested a further seven men from across the midlands.

The EDL announced that its next demo would be in Manchester on 10 October. The Welsh Defence League also announced its debut on the streets, with a protest in Swansea on 17 October 2009. The WDL was initially founded in Cardiff, but divisions in Swansea, Ebbw Vale, Rhondda, Wrexham and Deeside soon followed. The first target of the group had been a planned Islamic conference at County Hall, Cardiff, where it was rumoured Anjem Choudary would be speaking. Posters advertising the event indicated that sexes would be segregated, so the WDL based their opposition to the event on sexism and rang the venue to complain. The conference was eventually cancelled following concerns over sexual equality.

Following Birmingham, *The Guardian* ran a story which, although predictably claiming that the EDL was recruiting football fans, the involvement of London businessman Alan Lake was mentioned for the first time. *The Guardian* claimed that Lake had recently been advising Swedish nationalists on counter-Jihad, but was now advising the EDL. Lake had told delegates at a conference in Sweden that it was necessary to build a worldwide counter-jihad movement of people who were ready to go out onto the streets to protest. Lake said that he and his friends had already begun to build alliances with football supporters in the UK: '**The thing about the football fans is they go see a match, and then after the match, they're already there on the street, so if you can then bring them off for a demo that works really well. You get the numbers. And they're not scared as well. Everybody else is scared of being beaten up and attacked. They're not scared of that**'

Lake runs anti-jihad website *4freedoms*, a collective of Internet bloggers involved in opposing the spread of Islam but also significantly pro-Israel. These bloggers, many, but not all, of them Jewish, also operate under the umbrella of the International Civil Liberties Alliance (ICLA) in Europe and the Freedom Defence Initiative in the US. These are overtly counter-jihad groups, but also concerned with propagating pro-Israeli support in the Western media and countering any negative stories in the media about the state of Israel.

Groups linked to the powerful and influential American pro-Israel lobby had long realised the power of the Internet and had assembled an army of activists involved in pro-Israeli propaganda. Firstly, a cyber-transformation of the Israel/Palestinian conflict into a battle between the first bastion of the West against the spread of militant Islam was cultivated. Tel Aviv became the new Vienna. Then they looked for people or groups in the West who would identify or empathise with that scenario. Bizarre as it may seem, they found Europe's far-right, who Jews were traditionally and understandably suspicious of, the most fertile recruiting ground. The pro-Zionist lobby then courted these groups (Lake's flirtation with the Swedish Democrats is an example of this) to water the seeds of empathy they had sown on the Internet.

The aim of all this was to give the actions of the state of Israel perceived public support in the West. Israel and its supporters were worried that Western governments were shifting away from their traditional support, especially in light of the recent blockade of Gaza. People on the streets of the West blatantly supporting Israel would make Western governments think twice about condemning any actions that were taken by the Israelis. The sudden rise of the EDL took the pro-Israel bloggers by surprise. It seems they immediately switched their focus from Europe to Britain, and put their Swedish, Dutch and Danish alliances on the back-burner.

Lake is probably using a pseudonym as he has previously been quoted as saying: '**You've got to have pseudonyms, you've got to have, you know, five email addresses, one for your friends, one for your counter-jihad, one for your really extreme counter-jihad comments, and all the rest of it**'. He would later claim to be from the north of England and the son of a plumber, but would continually be credited as bankrolling the EDL. He would tell Norwegian television news show *TV 2 Nyhetene* in April 2011, '**I have given some money to help some EDL things happen**'. However, Jeff Marsh scoffed at the suggestion, '**The EDL is funded by nobody, all that media shite about Alan Lake? The guy wouldn't buy you a cup of coffee, never mind fund a mass movement**'.

Lake would later tell *The Telegraph* that he had become involved in counter-jihad after developing an interest in Islamic writings, but had become alarmed as certain texts preached racism and fascism. Anti-fascist magazine *Searchlight* has claimed Lake's antipathy to Islam may have developed after he started attending The Kensington Temple in Notting Hill, London, a Protestant evangelical church. In the past some members of the church have courted controversy for their hard-line views on Christianity, homosexuality and Islam.

Lake said militant Islam was a problem that was not going to go away. He claimed people were '**worn out with words**' and action was needed on the streets, because the political class in the UK had caved in to Muslim pressure at the expense of basic freedoms. The paper said Lake was seeking to harness football hooligan gangs by timing protests to coincide with local matches, although he denied that was a strategy employed to cause violence:

'**Football fans are a potential source of support. They are a hoi-polloi that gets off their backsides and travels to a city and they are available before and after matches. These guys are prepared to demonstrate, and they are already there because there is a match. This is a dirty, nasty, difficult struggle and you have to work with what is available. If a dog got kicked, would you expect it [to] bark or lodge an official complaint? You can't expect everybody to be an articulate, middle class intellectual. You have a bunch of people here who are no longer represented by the government. They are ignored and used and abused, and relegated to second class status by an ideology which is racist**'

It went unnoticed at the time, but the '**we have an army of bloggers, but that's not going to get things done**' proved to be an early indication that these pro-Zionist counter-jihad groups had noticed the impact of EDL demonstrations were having. They were now attempting to latch onto the EDL simply because it would provide them with what they didn't have, people on the streets. Just who Lake actually was or who he represented would later be questioned many times by people in the EDL worried about his input and seemingly considerable influence.

11 September 2009: Harrow

Obviously gambling that EDL supporters would now automatically rally to its banner, the European branch of ICLA, Stop the Islamification of Europe (SIOE), announced it would be holding a protest outside Harrow Mosque on the anniversary of the attacks on the USA.

SIOE was formed in 2007 by Dane Anders Gravers and Stephen Gash from Carlisle and is the European wing of the Freedom Defence Initiative. SIOE was based on Gravers Danish group Stop Islamiseringen af Danmark (SIAD), which was founded in 2005 following the cartoons controversy, to save Denmark from '**an Islamic invasion**'.

On 11 September 2008, SOIE held a small demonstration outside Lambeth Palace, the London residence of the Archbishop of Canterbury, but the year before, an SIOE demonstration in Brussels marking the anniversary of 9/11 had been banned following purported links to the far-right. SOIE held demonstrations in Holland and Denmark in March 2008, but again the presence of the far-right led to further demonstrations in both countries being cancelled.

SIOE had been given permission to stage a two hour static protest outside Harrow Mosque, beginning at 5.00pm. The rally was automatically linked to the EDL by the media, but in reality was only loosely supported by the group. UAF issued an appeal for people to '**defend Harrow Mosque against anti-Muslim bigots**' but Imam Ajmal Masroor told his congregation to ignore the protest and not retaliate.

The counter-protest started at lunchtime and by 5.00pm had grown to well over a thousand people. Over 500 officers were drafted in to police the event and combat any potential disorder. Around 6.00pm, SIOE announced that the demonstration had been called off. A statement on the group's website said that organiser Stephen Gash had been arrested and anyone on their way should not to attend as the police couldn't cope with the counter-protest. However, a small group of around 25 demonstrators had already arrived and found themselves surrounded by an angry mob of around 1500 people. They were surrounded by police, but trouble immediately started as hundreds of counter-protestors tried to confront them.

Mosque elders tried in vain to placate the mainly Muslim crowd, as the police faced a barrage of missiles including bricks, bottles and fireworks. Running battles ensued between the mob and police. Eventually, the anti-Islamic protestors were led away from the scene, but even so, the counter-protestors continued to clash with officers, tipping over wheelie bins for weapons. Police faced barrages of missiles and were forced to close roads in the area in order to contain the situation.

Ten people were arrested, nine were detained for possession of offensive weapons, and one man, believed to be Gash, was held to prevent a breach of the peace. A police spokeswoman told *Sky News* that the behaviour of some people had been unacceptable and it would not be tolerated.

Tony McNulty, Labour MP for Harrow said that emotions were running high and that most of the SIOE protesters were not from the area. David Ashton, leader of Harrow Council, said he was saddened and dismayed that groups from outside the borough had caused unrest. Ashton condemned those who either foisted extremist views or used Islam as a cover for causing trouble. UAF released a statement claiming that it had been a victory for anti-fascists. The group claimed that the anti-fascist rally had been peaceful and good natured, blaming the violence on '**racists attempting to get near the mosque**'.

In an interview with *The Times*, government minister John Denham condemned the actions of the EDL and SIOE. Denham compared the EDL to the '**Blackshirts**' of Oswald Mosley's British Union of Fascists and claimed they were using similar tactics to those used by the fascists of the 1930s, in inciting Muslims to violence. He said the violent response by Muslims in Harrow had played into the hands of the anti-Islamic demonstrators and SIOE, aided and abetted by the EDL, knew exactly what they were doing. It was, Denham claimed, a tactic designed to provoke and to get a response and announced the Government was about to bring in a programme to '**target extremism in white, working class communities**'.

The EDL responded to the article by calling Denham's appraisal '**dishonest and Orwellian**'. The group claimed that the EDL was a result of the failure of government to seriously address the issue of Islamic extremism. Denham's comparison of the situation in Harrow with the Blackshirts of Oswald Mosley was farcical said the group. The EDL claimed it was simply intended to legitimise the violent response of Muslim youth and the government sponsored anti-fascists. The EDL said it existed because extremist Muslim groups were allowed to tour the UK unchallenged and said fascism was actually closer to radical Islam than anything else. The statement added that failure to recognise legitimate complaints, and to further demonise the EDL, would only result in further alienation of the people who were flocking to the group's banner.

Following the scenes in Harrow, officers from a number of police forces, Greater Manchester, West Midlands, West Yorkshire, the Metropolitan Police and the National Public Order Intelligence Unit, gathered in Birmingham to discuss how best to deal with the EDL. Chris Simms, Chief Constable of West Midlands Police, which was hosting the summit, said they were witnessing a new national phenomenon. He told *BBC News* it was important that they shared their experiences, to help build a clear view of what they were dealing with.

At the end of the month, the EDL held a news conference in a disused factory in Luton. Proceedings were later broadcast on various news channels including the BBC programme *Newsnight*. A group of journalists were led into the factory and were met with the sight of fifteen balaclava clad men, including Lennon and Kevin Carroll (arrested during the Luton outrage) standing in front of various placards.

Lennon was asked if the balaclavas were meant to be intimidating, he replied that they were just as intimidating as a burqa, and asked the reporters how they thought children felt when they stood next to someone dressed in one. He was asked if there was a militant undertone to the EDL, Lennon replied that there wasn't, but they wouldn't be scared into silence and would continue to peacefully protest. He said that the aim of the EDL was to stand up to Islamic extremists who were recruiting on the streets, in colleges and universities as neither the British Government nor the Muslim community was doing anything about it.

In an attempt to shed their racist tag, the group unfurled a swastika flag, doused it in petrol and set it alight. It burned for a while and was eventually put out with a fire extinguisher. Lennon said the burning of the swastika sent a message that the EDL hated Nazis as much as Islamic radicals.

Whose streets? Our Streets!

There was no sign of the EDL going away. The scenes in Birmingham and Harrow had conversely attracted more people to the movement. UAF was one among several anti-fascist groups who were now openly opposing the EDL. Groups such as *Searchlight* magazine's Hope Not Hate, the Socialist Workers Party (SWP), anarchist groups and even local politicians all saw the chance to further their agendas off the back of the EDL.

In the last 30 years, the far-left, in the form of anti-fascist groups (in reality just fronts to suppress opposition to left-wing policies), have held sway on the streets of Britain. Modern anti-fascism can be traced back to the 1970s, a decade which saw mass immigration, economic decline, social breakdown and the rise of the right-wing National Front.

The Anti-Nazi League (ANL) was launched in 1977 by the far-left SWP. Its aim was to combat the growth of the NF and other far-right groups such as British Movement. The ANL was formed by SWP member Paul Holborow, anti-apartheid campaigner and future Labour Minister Peter Hain and Labour MP Ernie Roberts.

Some ex-SWP members have compared membership of the party to being in a cult. Directives which members are expected to follow to the letter are handed down from the Central Committee (knows as the CC in party circles), but above all the most important task for activists is the sale of the party's paper, *Socialist Worker*.

The SWP has often been accused of entryism, entering other groups, such as Red Front or the Socialist Alliance of England and Wales, for its own agenda. There have also been complaints from members of the Stop the War Coalition, that far from helping the group's aims, SWP activists inside the movement were actually hindering progress. The SWP was accused of dominating the coalition, of being more interested in recruiting members to the party rather than the good of the anti-war movement.

ANL initially undertook a large-scale propaganda campaign and deployed teams of activists who attacked right-wing meetings and confronted NF newspaper sellers on the streets. The ANL had some success in the physical confrontations, mainly because it attracted a number of working class supporters.

Following successful operations against the right-wing, the ANL progressed to staging marches in areas they considered heartlands of NF support. Eventually, support for the NF declined and the party slowly imploded amidst infighting, scandal and defection. The leadership of the SWP decided, mistakenly as it turned out, that due to the success of the ANL (in reality more specifically the Rock against Racism campaign which the ANL ran) that the British public was ready to embrace communism and vote for the party at the ballot box.

In 1981, attempting to make the party respectable, the SWP disbanded the ANL, accusing members of thuggish behaviour or squaddism. The expelled activists in turn condemned the SWP as being run by middle class communists. This resonated to some extent, as the party is overwhelmingly middle class; it even contains an aristocrat, Alex Callinicos, the grandson of the second Lord Acton (up the workers!).

A lot of the newly excluded ANL members formed the group Red Action. The group produced its own newspaper, *Red Action*, and with a working class mindset just like the ANL squads, aimed to physically confront fascism on the streets. In 1995, *The Independent* estimated that the group had between 20 and 30 cells across the country, including London, Manchester, Leeds and Glasgow and that Red Action **'enthusiastically espouses the use of violence'**.

Members of Red Action, along with anarchist groups founded Anti-Fascist Action (AFA) in July 1985, as a working class united front of left-wing groups, fighting a common enemy. From the start, movement was plagued by political disputes between members and the opposing groups which formed the alliance. Differences could not be resolved, so soon after its formation, AFA collapsed.

AFA was re-launched in 1989. It was agreed, that the new group wouldn't form alliances with groups that were part of the problem; such as corrupt councillors or the middle class SWP. AFA was launched as a coalition of groups including Red Action and Class War. The Class War Federation is an anarchist group, which has been highly critical of the British far-left, questioning their leftist credentials and accusing them of being middle class and elitist.

AFA busied itself in the production of propaganda such as pamphlets and a magazine, *Fighting Talk*. It financed these activities with collections at meetings and musical events. Operations were conducted against the NF, which was by now limping along, and right-wing music label Blood and Honour. Leafleting groups for the emerging BNP were also targeted. In September 1991, AFA staged a music event in London which attracted 10,000 people. Two months later, 4000 people attended a demonstration against racist attacks in London's East End.

Noting the popularity of AFA, particularly the group's music events and the funds they generated, middle class socialism moved back into anti-fascism. The SWP re-launched the ANL and a group called Youth Against Racism was launched by the group Militant Tendency (a hardcore Marxist/Trotskyite group that had infiltrated the Labour Party). The Anti Racist Alliance was formed around the same time, by black Labour Party activists. These new movements, along with their superior financial backing and contacts in the media, soon out performed AFA and shattered the working class united front which had been formed. Instead of co-operating these new groups competed against each other for a share of the market, and as a result, AFA virtually disappeared.

In 1997 what was left of AFA issued a statement banning all members from associating with anti-fascist magazine, *Searchlight*. Other anarchist groups questioned *Searchlight's* role in the anti-fascist movement and accused its editor, Gerry Gable, of colluding with the state. Gable retaliated and accused certain members of AFA of being closet fascists.

Founded in 1975, *Searchlight* is a British anti-fascist magazine. Its main target is the British National Party but it also follows other right-wing groups. The magazine is published by Gerry Gable, a Jewish former member of the Communist Party of Great Britain.

It is edited by Nick Lowles, a former member of Yorkshire AFA (Lowles allegedly left AFA after he losing a leadership election and an ensuing dispute over direction). He has written several books on football hooliganism and the far-right. *Searchlight* eventually formed the group Hope Not Hate, which Lowles heads, for street mobilisations against fascists. Also working for the antifascist organisation, is former National Front activist Matthew Collins. In 1990, Collins began passing information to *Searchlight* and in 1993 was involved in the exposure of the far-right group, Combat 18.

In 2001, a new group called No Platform was formed by ex-AFA members but barely made a mark. In 2004, former AFA members formed the group ANTIFA. The group has probably been more successful abroad than in the UK, where it only attracts a handful of middle class student activists. Organisation differs from country to country, but most ANTIFA groups are organised locally and affiliated to a national federation.

In 2003, following gains by the BNP, the Anti-Nazi League and the National Assembly Against Racism (NAAR, an offshoot of the Labour Party's Anti-Racist Alliance which believes that any anti-racist group should only be black-led) formed Unite Against Fascism. UAF describes itself as: **'a national campaign with the aim of alerting British society to the rising threat of the extreme right, in particular the British National Party'**.

UAF chair is former Labour Party Mayor of London, Ken Livingstone. The organisation has two joint secretaries, Weyman Bennett (member of the SWP Central Committee and former national organiser of the ANL) and NAAR activist Sabby Dhalu. Martin Smith (now ex-National Secretary SWP), although not listed as an activist on the UAF website, has often acted as a spokesman for the organisation. Smith also runs Love Music Hate Racism (LMHR), an attempt to emulate the Rock against Racism campaign of the original ANL. *Searchlight* originally had representatives on the UAF steering committee, but left following a dispute in 2005 and what *Searchlight* termed a '**whispering campaign**' by SWP members, accusing them of being Zionists who pandered to the BNP.

In November 2007, UAF organised a demonstration at the Oxford Union where BNP leader Nick Griffin had been invited to appear. The demonstration turned violent with anti-fascists clashing with police.

In June 2009, UAF activists hijacked a conference outside the Houses of Parliament by newly elected BNP Members of the European Parliament, Griffin and Andrew Brons. One anti-fascist was filmed throwing a dart at the BNP entourage. Members of the press were attacked and two members of the public were hospitalised. The following day, UAF activists attacked Griffins car, when he arrived at a venue in Manchester.

UAF staged a counter-protest at a BNP festival in Codnor, Derbyshire in August 2009. Nineteen anti-fascists were arrested following clashes with police. Two months later, hundreds of UAF protestors tried to storm the BBC headquarters in Shepherds Bush, after Griffin was invited to take part in the current affairs show Question Time. Up to 300 police and security officers battled with the crowd, three police officers were injured and six arrests were made. Martin Smith of the SWP was one of those arrested and later convicted of assaulting a police officer.

The old disputes between UAF/SWP and their opponents on the anti-fascist circuit still persist. Cracks appeared following the anti-fascist protest against the BNP's Red, White & Blue annual event in Derbyshire, when anti-fascists accused UAF of colluding with police. The group would also face criticism from anti-fascists following demonstrations against the Scottish Defence League in Edinburgh and Glasgow.

Other anti-fascist groups see UAF as a problem. Although they concede the group attracts genuine people who want to oppose the far-right, they consider the treatment of racial issues by UAF as '**patronising and merely done for self-gratifying purposes**'. Some have questioned whether the group's '**scaremongering, hysteria and disinformation**' tactics play into the hands of its opponents. Anarchists on the anti-fascist side condemn UAF as being: '**predominantly middle class students without a fucking clue unwittingly following a rigid authoritarian leadership**'.

Following the first UAF counter-protest against the EDL in Birmingham, Gerry Gable was critical of the group's tactics: '**we don't think inciting people to burn the Union Jack, like the UAF did, is the right way to go about fighting racism. We want to fight it through a coalition of people from the community, working together to resolve issues**'.

10 October 2009: Manchester

Formerly part of Lancashire, Manchester now sits at the heart of the county of Greater Manchester. The city was a centre of cotton production but also developed many diverse industries from chemicals to locomotives. With the trade that such levels of industry brought, the city also became a centre for banking.

The prosperity of the Manchester was tempered by extreme levels of poverty, resulting in a series of nineteenth century working class '**bread and labour**' riots, which included the infamous Peterloo Massacre. As a result, the city became a symbol for working class resistance. Along with the bread and labour riots, Manchester played a major role in opposition to the Corn Laws, played a key role in the Suffragette and Labour Party movements and was the location of the first Trades Union Congress.

Manchester has some of the highest unemployment levels in the UK and over 60% of its residents live in some of Britain's most deprived areas. Close to 10% of Manchester population are Muslim, and Greater Manchester contains one of the largest concentrated Muslim populations in the country. Prior to the protest, Stephen Lennon explained to *BBC News* why the EDL was targeting another major city: '**There are town centres now that are plagued by Islamic extremists, there are women who don't want to go shopping because there are 20 men in long Islamic dress shouting anti-British stuff, calling for a jihad and stirring up religious and racial hatred. Those are our town centres,** and we want them back. We want them back, not from the Muslims, but from the jihadist extremists that are operating in the Muslim communities. And the Muslim communities need to deal with their extremists. They need to drive them out - we have had enough of it'

The demo was arranged for 5.30pm, deliberately late to attract football fans after local games had been played. It was being held in the Piccadilly Gardens area of the city and was billed as a demonstration opposing radical Islam and Sharia, to include a two minute silence for the British Armed Forces. The meeting place was a JD Wetherspoons pub close to Piccadilly Gardens. Supporters were asked to arrive early 'to aid the Police in facilitating our protest', but in reality to avoid the chances of activists being cut-off should a police kettle occur. A kettle is the police practice of shepherding protesters to a pre-designated spot, where they are surrounded by riot-police, trained in crowd control. Once a kettle is formed the crowd is kept in place, until the police deem it safe to disperse them. The EDL had issued protest guidelines to its members prior to yet another static protest.

In the UK, protesters do not need permission to hold an assembly, as freedom of assembly laws ensure that neither the police nor government have the power to ban a static demonstration in a public place, although certain conditions may be imposed, such as a Section 14 Order. The EDL guidelines also gave advice on what rights activists had when dealing with the police. Activists were told to carry no ID. They were informed that they could be searched under Section 44 of the Terrorism Act (this type of excessive policing, employing terrorism legislation on civilian protestors, initially put many people off joining the protests and still does). If they were stopped, they did not have to give a name, address or date of birth and were told that if asked their racial background, they should reply they were of Eskimo origins, as it disrupted police racial monitoring systems.

Greater Manchester Police (GMP) informed the press they had several hundred officers on duty to combat any disorder. They also announced that their colleagues from WMP had arrested a 39 year old man from the West Midlands. The man, local EDL organiser Richard Price, had been arrested during a dawn raid in Birmingham, on suspicion of distributing racially aggravated material and possession of cocaine. He was believed to have been planning to travel to Manchester.

UAF were counter-protesting and by midday around 200 anti-fascists had gathered, some with red flags bearing the legend 'Revolution'. A sound system was introduced and Bob Marley could be heard drifting across the square, just as 150 students arrived to join the counter-protest.

The EDL started gathering at the local Wetherspoons pub, which was ringed by police. Police were also out in force at Piccadilly train station, questioning small groups of men, some carrying flags of St George. Large numbers of EDL and increasing numbers of UAF protestors started to arrive on either side of police lines. UAF estimated they had over 2000 protestors in the area and said they outnumbered the EDL, ignoring the fact that the EDL protest wasn't due to start for another four hours. UAF started chanting "Scum" and surged against police lines in an attempt go get at the EDL, who beckoned them on. The anti-fascists were driven back by mounted police and dog handlers. The atmosphere was charged and a will to confront each other emanated from both sides. Flashpoints were also erupting across the city and a police helicopter could be seen overhead, as GMP tried to gather as much information as possible on the whereabouts of both sides. There were brief scuffles at the Wetherspoons pub, as anti-fascist campaigners tried to confront the gathering EDL.

The EDL in Piccadilly Gardens started to sing "I'm English till I die!" UAF replied with "If it wasn't for the coppers you'd be dead!" The EDL surged forward to confront the anti-fascists, with police dog handlers forcing them back. Onlookers were scattered as police reinforcements ran in and battled to keep a reasonable gap between the two factions. A double line of police now separated the two groups as they chanted at each other. Many participants on both sides were wearing masks or had their faces covered with scarves. Some EDL broke out of their cordon, pursued by riot police; there were also reports of fresh disturbances in the city centre. It appeared the EDL were having the better of the clashes, the students and middle class left-wingers were no match for the working class street fighters of the EDL.

At 3.00pm, following further clashes in the city, police announced they had arrested eighteen people in total and estimated there were now around 1000 UAF and 600 EDL protestors in the vicinity of

Piccadilly Gardens. Through a megaphone, one UAF protester shouted "**There are many more of us than you**", just as around a hundred EDL protestors made their way down Oldham Street to join the protest. As the approaching reinforcements were spotted, cheers rang out from the EDL already there. Police battled to push UAF further back to make room for the fresh EDL arrivals. An Israeli flag was produced by the EDL, its appearance caused anger amongst the UAF and missiles were exchanged between the two groups. GMP informed the press that their helicopter was now tracking a group of men running through the streets close to the Arndale Shopping Centre and said that trouble had also broken out on Market Street, where one man had been arrested.

With their numbers steadily increasing, at the request of police, the EDL started their demonstration early. They held a two minutes silence for fallen British troops, but it was ignored by UAF, who deliberately made noise throughout. One female anti-fascist constantly hurled abuse as the EDL paid their respects, shouting "**Come on Manchester let's make some noise**", and "**Nazi scum off our streets!**" Annoyed by the heckling of the silence, the EDL surged against police lines once more. A large group of Asian men arrived on UAF side of the gardens and started to taunt the EDL, who responded in kind. At this point, police started to force the EDL out of the area. UAF applauded as the EDL were pushed away, the EDL responded with defiant chants of "**England, England!**" UAF protesters were allowed to disperse slowly in small groups.

A huge snaking column of EDL made its way down Tibb Street, escorted by police. When it reached the High Street there was a brief pause as police cleared the way ahead of anti-fascists. Singing and chanting, the EDL marched past the Urbis Exhibition Centre where there were brief clashes as they encountered small groups of UAF. Every time they spotted anti-fascists the EDL surged forward, but were repeatedly beaten back by police. On arrival at Victoria Station, the EDL were put onto buses to take them to Piccadilly Station. Flags soon emerged from the bus windows and inside the EDL were chanting and singing, banging the windows of the bus. It was clear that the EDL viewed the day's proceedings as a victory.

GMP announced that there had been 48 arrests. Assistant Chief Constable Garry Shewan commended the majority of demonstrators for their behaviour, but said the day had been marred by people who had travelled to Manchester intent on violence. One officer present, posting on police Internet forum, *Police Oracle*, said that there had been a real threat of serious disorder and made an interesting observation about the difference in attitude of the two groups. Whenever an EDL supporter was arrested, the officer claimed there was no fuss and very few of them had put up a fight. There was, the officer said, an almost professional attitude of acceptance by EDL supporters in the way they were policed, possibly gained through experience at football matches. However, when anti-fascists were arrested, the officer claimed there was a complete refusal to believe that they could be detained and most put up a fight. The officer categorised UAF into three distinct groups: Militant left-wing campaigners, white middle class students and what the officer referred to as '**local trouble causing usual suspects who were attempting to stir things up**':

'**When questioned in my cordon on the front line of the Anti Fascist League by a young middle class white female with a ring through her nose and filming me on her i-Phone "why are you here, why are you doing this?" I just simply answered: "look at them, look at you, if we weren't here they would rip you to pieces, we are just here to make sure everyone gets to say what they believe in and go home in one piece." She took one look over my shoulder at the group of EDL who by their appearance had obviously got a fair bit more of a physical presence and she said "fair enough"...**'

The EDL congratulated GMP for its policing of the demonstrations, but claimed that large numbers of supporters had been prevented from joining the protest and that the same restrictions hadn't been applied to UAF. A statement said the EDL was pleased that there was no major Asian turnout and hoped British Asians would realise that the EDL had nothing against them and it wanted above all, to welcome them as fellow Englishmen. The group said troublemakers, such as Salma Yaqoob, were trying to keep Asians from integrating in order to secure themselves a power base. The EDL said that many Asians came to the UK to escape oppressive laws and they hoped in the future they would stand with them against bringing laws which their ancestors had escaped to the UK.

The group concluded, with some justification considering the numbers in attendance, that they had reached a major milestone in Manchester. The EDL said it now hoped that the citizens of the UK, regardless of race or religion, would now join them in their fight against radical Islam. Casuals United released a somewhat blunter statement, declaring a '**Casuals United fatwa**' on the *News of the World* for claiming that only 300 EDL had attended the demo: '**Manchester - a big success! As expected the Manchester demo was the biggest turnout yet, with over 2000 lads and lasses from all over the UK. Football rivalries were forgotten as they stood shoulder to shoulder for their country. Left wing idiots stood screaming abuse at us, and looked pretty pathetic screaming "Nazi scum" at us, even though many of our lads were Black, and they sank to an all time low, and showed that their real agenda is anti British by shouting and screaming to deliberately disrupt our two minute silence for our war dead**"

A few days after the protest, the *Oldham Advertiser* reported that a local woman had received death threats after it was claimed she was the anti-fascist using a megaphone during the two-minute silence. The woman told the paper she had been bombarded with hundreds of emails and phone calls but claimed she was the victim of mistaken identity. She admitted she had attended the counter-demonstration, but denied she was a member of UAF. She said she had gone because she was interested in what was going on and whether it posed any danger to her hometown of Oldham, but claimed she did not speak during the silence because she would never disrespect British troops. The woman had however given an interview to a news channel following the protest, condemning the behaviour of the police. A GMP spokesman said that they were investigating the threats.

17 October 2009: Swansea

Ahead of the Swansea protest, Welsh anti-fascists wrote to the Welsh Football Association and Welsh football clubs regarding purported links between clubs and Casuals United - in particular the group's use of club logos. The football club connection to the movement was also being publicised elsewhere in the UK. An article in *the Sunday Sun* reported that Newcastle United Football Club was taking legal advice after the club crest had been used by the North East Division of the EDL.

At the other end of England, an investigation by the *Southampton Daily Echo* announced that the EDL had launched a recruitment drive to enlist local football fans. The *Daily Echo* revealed that 175 people had signed up to the Southampton FC branch of the EDL. A club spokesman said they had taken steps to ensure that any implied affiliation with Southampton FC was eradicated. Local MP John Denham, who had previously publicly condemned the EDL, said he was confident most fans would have nothing to do with the group.

In Bristol, anti-fascists were also voicing concerns that the EDL were trying to gain ground at Bristol Rovers. One fan described how EDL chants had been heard coming from Rovers supporters during an away match in Swindon. In Kent, anti-fascist Bunny La Roche told *Socialist Worker* that local EDL supporters organised around Gillingham Football Club and had attended protests.

As a result of the football links, anti-fascists would target football grounds, distributing leaflets, although the response from fans was muted and hooligans of some clubs took to the streets and actively opposed them. Football gangs had always been at the forefront of the EDL and anti-fascists would struggle to gain any ground in the working class preserve of English football, that many in the EDL considered their home.

The Swansea protest was intended to highlight '**extreme Islam's strong creeping influence in Wales**' and was to be held in Castle Square at 4.00pm. It was seen as a chance for the WDL to show what level of support it could muster, in comparison to the soaring numbers of its English counterpart.

MP for Neath, Peter Hain, told the BBC the WDL wanted a **"white Wales"** and that they hated Jewish, black and Muslim people. A few weeks before the protest, Swansea City hooligans, the Swansea Jacks, had clashed with local Muslims following taunts about the 9/11 attacks.

On the day of the protest, the WDL met at Yates's Winelodge at the top of Castle Square in Swansea city centre. Shortly after 3.30pm, they left Yates's and headed for Castle Square. Some were hastier than others and were quickly surrounded by the police. Seeing this, anti-fascists who had gathered in the area moved onto the main road in front of the WDL. There was a line of police preventing any confrontation but, despite police attempts to move them, the anti-fascists refused to budge and prevented the WDL from getting onto the square.

The WDL were outnumbered by around three to one, but they chanted from behind police lines, surrounded by press. Photographers were shoving cameras in the faces of the WDL supporters, some quickly lost their temper. One shouted **"is this what you want is it?"** and made a Nazi salute to photographers hungry for a right-wing slant, others started chanting **"BNP!"** Some of the WDL produced a flag, which appeared to be a swastika, and proceeded to burn it to the cheers of their comrades. It was in fact an anti-fascist flag with a cross through a swastika. The pictures of that and the Nazi salute would be used by anti-fascists to back up the assertion of the **'real face'** of the Defence Leagues. The tense stand-off lasted for around an hour. South Wales Police eventually dispersed both groups, escorting the WDL to the railway station. When the WDL arrived at the station they were surrounded and held. Some of the group unsuccessfully tried to break out and one arrest was made. Eventually some were allowed to get onto trains and the rest were allowed to disperse in small groups.

Following the protests, Chief Superintendent Mark Mathias told the *South Wales Echo* that he was pleased with the police operation, which allowed the protests to pass off peacefully. Warning that more arrests on both sides could follow, Mathias told the paper that they would be reviewing CCTV to see if there were further offences that could be identified. Tahar Idris, of Swansea Bay Racial Equality Council, claimed the WDL had been **'sent packing with their tails between their legs, and I hope they get the message that they are not wanted here.'** WDL organiser, Simon Daborn, told the *Echo* that the protest had been hijacked by **'racist idiots'** intent on causing trouble:

> "If I had any idea that there would be Nazis there I would not have been involved. We are against extreme Islam, which is even driving out moderate Muslims. There are problems with more mosques being built, the introduction of sharia law, and terrorists who think it is okay to abuse our soldiers and make threats to kill. But on the day of the rally a load of idiots turned up and started screaming 'BNP' and anti-Muslim stuff which was completely wrong. My grandparents fought the Nazis in the World War II. My great grandmother died in the Blitz on Exeter. I would never do anything to insult their memories. As far as I am concerned skin colour, sexuality or religion doesn't matter. But the rally was hijacked by a mix of racists and people who just turned up hoping for a brawl. I was ashamed and embarrassed to be in their company"

Following the protest, the WDL called off a proposed demo in Newport, scheduled for the following Saturday. A statement issued on the Casuals United website said the demonstration in Swansea had been **'hijacked by Nazis'** and that the WDL members who were there were unable to stop the extremists chanting **'BNP'** or making Nazi salutes. The statement claimed that infiltrators had attended with the sole intent of ruining the protest. It was obvious from Nazi websites said Casuals United, that right-wing extremists despised the Defence Leagues because they allowed people of other races to march with them. The Nazi association was something which the WDL would find extremely hard to shed. As a result of the protest, several activists from Swansea were told they were not welcome at future WDL protests.

Days later, the *Luton and Dunstable Express* revealed that Muslim extremists were trying to recruit students outside the University of Bedfordshire and claimed police were powerless to stop them. The paper said that around fifteen radicals, some of whom had abused the Royal Anglian Regiment, had set up a stall outside the Luton campus of the university, handing out leaflets to students as they passed through the main entrance. University officials contacted the police, but when officers arrived they said no laws were being broken. The paper revealed the group had also turned up outside the university's Business School, the previous Friday. The University of Bedfordshire said it was aware of the group, but they were on a public highway and they were not aware of any official complaint regarding their presence.

A police spokeswoman told the *Express* that officers had spoken to the group, they were not causing an obstruction and there was no breach of the peace, so no action was taken. Police said they were aware of the content of the leaflets, as the group handed them out on a regular basis. One of the radicals, Abu Safiyya, a veteran of the Anglian parade, told the paper: **'We are giving out leaflets, talking to students, calling people to Islam. It is not extremism. I was there accusing the soldiers of crimes. They went in to fight and kill for war. It is not justified. You don't want to believe in freedoms. Our whole argument is that Islam is superior. Every person is responsible for their own actions. They make their own decisions'.**

31 October 2009: Leeds, West Yorkshire

Leeds was targeted because of the city's links to the 7/7 suicide-bombers. It was a former manufacturing area, known for its heavy industry and also, along with the surrounding area, as being a centre of textile production. Along with the rest of the country, manufacturing in Leeds and West Yorkshire has collapsed and the biggest employers in the region now are banks and call-centres.

In the weeks before the demonstration, a parliamentary Early Day Motion concerning the EDL was submitted by Bradford West MP Marsha Singh. The MP said the EDL was trying to spread fear, violence, and hatred against the Muslim community and that the demonstration in Leeds was likely to threaten race relations and community cohesion, especially in an area which in the past had been blighted by riots inspired by racism. The area was indeed no stranger to racial unrest. The Chapeltown area of Leeds had witnessed riots by the Afro-Caribbean community in 1975, 1981 and 1987. In 2001, the Harehills area was rocked by six hours of rioting by Asian youths, following the arrest of a Bengali man by police.

Although the Asian population of Leeds is around the national average, the percentage of Muslims is considerably higher in the surrounding areas. To the west of Leeds is Bradford, which has a large Muslim population of around 19%. Eight miles away is Dewsbury, where some areas of the town are 97-98% Muslim.

There was a pro-Sharia march by Islam4UK in London on the day of the Leeds protest, but the EDL was still pursuing the Leeds demo in favour of a London counter-protest as it was unclear whether the Islam4UK demonstration was something that has been planned for months or was a reaction to the success of the EDL. The Leeds event had been planned for a long time and the EDL said it should not be distracted from its mission by events organised by its opponents. The group claimed that if EDL resources were diverted to London, it demonstrated to the radicals that the EDL could be made to change its plans in response to their initiatives. However, any supporters who couldn't get to Leeds were asked to counter-protest against the Islam4UK rally.

The EDL was demonstrating in the City Square area of Leeds and again issued guidelines to supporters, asking them to obey police instructions, as the group said they were there to protect the EDL from the hatred and violence of UAF. Activists were also reminded that racism was wrong and went against the core values of the EDL. Members were asked to disassociate themselves from anyone they saw committing a racist act and to be careful when making gestures with their arms, as anti-fascists and the press would use anything which resembled a Nazi salute as evidence the group was racist or right-wing. The press and anti-fascist groups had made much of some pictures of EDL supporters with their arms aloft, and every single picture was touted as proof that the group were Nazi's.

UAF appealed for activists to '**celebrate and defend multicultural Leeds against the racist EDL**' and had been allotted a section of Victoria Gardens to stage their counter-protest.

West Yorkshire Police issued a statement saying they expected little disruption to the city, as both protests were well away from the main shopping areas. Divisional Commander Chief Superintendent Mark Milsom said they had been involved in discussions with both groups and the aim of the police was to facilitate peaceful protest with minimum disruption. Milsom said they expected some disorder, given the events at previous demonstrations, but had plans in place should trouble occur. He appealed to members of the local Muslim community who were tempted to attend the counter-protest not to, claiming it would potentially play into the hands of both groups.

Around 300 to 400 anti-fascists gathered in Victoria Gardens just after midday on the day of the protest. At the same time, around 300 EDL supporters were being escorted to City Square by police. Hundreds of police officers in bright yellow luminous jackets were employed around both demonstration sites. A police helicopter hovered overhead, as more people made their way through Leeds city centre to the protest sites. One anti-fascist activist claimed: '**the tension in and around Leeds city centre was toxic, I have lived here for more than 15 years and I have never seen Leeds in this state - helicopters overhead, hundreds of police lining the streets, police dogs, mounted police. They clearly were expecting serious trouble**'

The protest sites were in sight of each other and missiles were thrown by both sides as they gathered, some individuals even spat at each other. Police lines swayed with the pressure and a red flare lit by one of the protestors was grabbed and extinguished by officers. The EDL demonstrators chanted "**Muslim bombers off our streets**" and "**We want our country back**". UAF, awash with placards, replied with chants of "**Fascist scum, off our streets!**"

At 3.00pm, police reported that the number of UAF at Victoria Gardens had decreased significantly. They said they were still monitoring the EDL demonstration, which they estimated now numbered around 900 people. More scuffles broke out and officers had to link arms to keep the two sides apart. An EDL infiltrator was discovered in the middle of the UAF demo and was ejected by stewards and police.

Around 300 anti-fascists broke away and ran through nearby Park Square, in an attempt to confront the EDL. Police managed to contain the breakaway group, forcing them back to Victoria Gardens. EDL protesters tried to break through police ranks twice but officers managed, albeit with some difficulty, to stop them. Eventually a group of EDL did break away and surged towards Briggate, the main shopping area of Leeds. Police rushed to contain them and they were eventually stopped, but not before they had confronted anti-fascists and caused severe disruption. The anti-fascists were no match for the EDL in the confrontations and were continually scattered. Back in City Square, an Israeli flag became visible on the EDL side; inflaming anti-fascists. Stephen Lennon, his face covered, made a speech to the crowd:

> "**We gather again to push back the Islamic forces which demand sharia law for every man, woman and child in this country, for Muslims and non-Muslims alike. We raise our voices today in protest here in Leeds and also in London. We raise our voices to wake up our brothers and sisters in this country to the threat of Islamic domination that will only grow stronger day by day unless more people join the counter-jihad and counter-sharia movements. We raise our voices to send a signal to the Government and demand that they take our concerns seriously and stop accommodating and giving money to these forces of sharia. And if you are awake to this threat but still on the sidelines, we raise our voices in order to increase your confidence and courage to take action in some fashion sometime soon.**
>
> **Our soldiers are fighting, suffering and dying in Afghanistan and previously in Iraq. They do so as part of this great democracy but ironically both countries are committed to sharia. Let us remind ourselves what sharia means on freedom of speech, conscience, and**

protest. All we need do is look at a few examples from other countries.

In Pakistan, the Criminal Code articles 295 and 298 have shut down any freedom of speech as regards Islam. The blaspheme laws are a rod to beat down and kill the non-Muslim population. In Saudi Arabia, in 2007 the religious police beat little school girls back into their burning building because they were not properly covered. In Egypt, converts from Islam have to either flee the country or go into hiding. In Iran, protesters are gunned down in the street for declaring their lack of confidence in and support for the recent presidential elections.

And in this country we are apparently not allowed to have an opinion that can be in anyway construed as being negative about Islam. Publishers are threatened if they reprint cartoons of Mohammed or a story about Mohammed's first wife, Aisha. The Organisation of Islamic Conference is pushing to declare that criticism of religion is against the law. By religion they really mean, of course, Islam. In a court case coming up in December a couple are charged with a 'religiously aggravated offence' for supposedly making critical comments in the presence of a Muslim woman. The couple are alleged to have said that Mohammed, the founder of Islam, was a warlord and that Muslim dress for women was a form of bondage.

For those who say we are racists, we ask: What race is Islam? What race are Muslims? Sharia – the rule by a so-called Allah means the domination of non-Muslims. It is a central teaching of Islam and rooted in the Qur'an and the example of Mohammed, the founder of Islam.

But the English Defence League stands here today and in London to say that we will not be a slave to Allah and Allah's representatives here on earth. We will not submit. We are free men and women today, tomorrow and forever"

As Lennon finished, the crowd roared their approval. After his speech, EDL supporters were allowed to leave the site. Witnesses claimed there were claps and cheers from local drinkers as the EDL passed local pubs. There were several clashes around the city centre well into the evening, as groups of EDL clashed with gangs of anti-fascists and Asian youths.

West Yorkshire Police said they were pleased with a **'very successful policing operation'**. Assistant Chief Constable Mark Gilmore said over 2000 people had taken part in the two protests, but admitted there had been a number of minor scuffles and eight arrests. Leader of Leeds City Council, Richard Brett, said that he was pleased the protests had passed without serious incident and praised the planning of the police.

A statement was issued by Casuals United, claiming that well over a thousand people had attended the demo. The group conceded that it hadn't been as good a turnout as Manchester and blamed UAF for the several incidents of disorder. The EDL said as they grew in numbers, the voice of the British people would only get stronger and claimed that the rapid growth of the movement was testament not only to how concerned the British public was about radical Islam, but also how many people felt abandoned by politicians. The group also thanked West Yorkshire Police for making sure they were allowed to demonstrate peacefully without **'Unite Against Freedom'** causing too much trouble. The EDL claimed anti-fascists had repeatedly attempted to attack them, but the police had contained these situations. The group said it looked forward to working as harmoniously with other police forces as they had with West Yorkshire Police.

Anti-fascists didn't seem to share the euphoria of the EDL. One, a veteran activist summed up the mood:

> **'I've never known an atmosphere like the one I experienced this afternoon. There were hundreds of right-wing thugs (complete with obligatory poppies) roaming around the city centre in groups of 20-30. Some were heavily hemmed in by police but others seemed**

to be able to move around the main shopping streets unchallenged. I went with a group of 100-150 anti-fascists to try to get to the EDL demo in City Square from the west but we were stopped by the Police. To be honest, it felt a bit half-hearted. I think the wiser ones among us realised that we were no match for the football hooligans that the EDL seems to be able to turn out in increasing numbers.
Something is going badly wrong. The fascists have lost their fear. In the old days they would never have dared to parade around the centre of a major British city in racist t-shirts whereas today small groups of them stood just across the road from the UAF counter-demo shouting abuse and were only finally chased off by the Police after about a hundred anti-fascists surged across the road towards them (but STILL didn't seem willing to attack). There's a Catch 22 here. Either we mobilise Muslim youth to even up the odds but risk providing the EDL with the propaganda (and ruck) they want or we keep it largely middle class/student and effectively rely on the Police to protect us. Fascists have held a major demo in Leeds and were not challenged. All in all, a depressing day'.

Leeds was a moment of realisation for the anti-fascist movement. The, mainly middle class, communists and students were no match for the experienced street-fighters and football hooligans of the EDL. This would lead to a change in tactics, and a conscious attempt to inflame and mobilise British Muslim youth.

The Islam4UK march in London on the same day as Leeds was called off following 'concerns about safety'. The group had planned to walk from the Houses of Parliament to Trafalgar Square, but Anjem Choudary claimed there were rumours of a 'right wing bomb plot' and cancelled the event. Sixty EDL had turned up to counter-protest and joined other anti-Islamist demonstrators in Piccadilly. According to Casuals United, the protest was peaceful due to the non-attendance of UAF, who were 'busy attacking the police in Leeds'.

Casuals United did however admit that after the demonstration, a clash occurred between the EDL and a small group of right-wingers in the Lord Moon of the Mall public house in Whitehall.

The neo-Nazis, said to be members of Combat 18, had entered a pub in which the EDL were drinking. Combat 18 is a neo-Nazi organisation associated with the Blood and Honour record label. The 18 stands for the initials of Adolf Hitler and the group attained widespread notoriety in Britain during the 1990s following a number of violent street confrontations with the far-left and the publication of several magazines, including Redwatch. Following the murder of one C18 activist and the jailing of two others for his murder the group imploded in the late 90s, with several offshoot organisations being formed by former members.

Words were exchanged between the two groups and a confrontation took place. One of the neo-Nazis was seriously injured when he ran into traffic during the incident. Casuals released a statement regarding the clash: 'Our London divisions tonight had to deal with a situation where Nazi skinheads of Combat 18 turned up, accused the EDL of being cu**s and in the ensuing brawl C18 have taken a serious slap. The enemies of White Britain pile into us every day, calling us racist/fascist/Nazi yet we have to fight our own people because they are as extreme as Choudary and his bunch of cu**s. In only 5 months the defence leagues have grown massively, if you REALLY care about your country, drop the Nazi shit and join us, or you're just as bad as Choudary. No show by Adolf Choudary in London, 100 Casuals turned out to counter him but he cancelled, grizzling about a right wing bomb threat'

One anti-fascist, commenting on the clash on left-wing website Indymedia, said: 'if it is true that the EDL battered C18/Blood&Honour then hats off because that's more militant antifascism than the UAF have ever done!!'

Day-Return Intimidation

Glasgow, like Scotland as a whole, has a relatively small Muslim community and therefore was not thought of as a home of militant Islam. On 30 June 2007 however, two Muslim men, said to be angry about the Iraq War, had driven a Jeep full of petrol and gas canisters into the terminal building at Glasgow Airport.

One case that was pointed to as justification for the SDL protest in Glasgow, was that of Kris Donald from Pollokshields, who was fifteen when he was kidnapped, tortured and murdered in 2004 by a local Pakistani gang. The five-man gang was led by Imran Shahid and the kidnapping was revenge for an attack on Shahid at a Glasgow nightclub the night before by a local white gang. Donald, who had no connection to gangs or the nightclub incident, was chosen simply because he was a 'white boy from the McCulloch Street area' where Shahid's attackers were suspected of being from. After being kidnapped, Kris Donald was held and stabbed thirteen times, doused in petrol, set on fire and left to die. Three of the accused went on the run to Pakistan, but were eventually captured and extradited back to the UK. Four men were eventually convicted of the abduction and racially motivated murder, a fifth man was convicted of abduction.

The case received little coverage on the national news, the BBC admitted it had got it wrong but refuted accusations the lack of coverage was a result of Donald being white and his attackers Asian. In the wake of the murder, *The Scotsman* reported that six months earlier, Strathclyde Police had abandoned an investigation to clamp down on the rise of Asian gangs in Glasgow's south side, after the operation was deemed to be politically incorrect. In 2006, *The Guardian* reported that nearly half of all victims of racially motivated murders in the preceding decade had been white. Senior police officers told the paper that political correctness and the fear of discussing the issue meant that race crime against white people was under-reported. The Chief Constable of Cheshire, Peter Fahy, said it was harder to get the media interested where murder victims were young white men and a lot of police officers were worried about even discussing the subject in case they '**said the wrong thing**'.

In August 2010, the *Daily Record* reported that a few streets away from the spot where Kris Donald was abducted, an Asian gang had attempted to abduct a fourteen year old schoolboy, telling him: '**You're the next Kris Donald! We're going to murder you!**' The gang dragged the terrified boy towards their car but he managed to free himself. Locals claimed that after the Donald murder, there had been a visible police presence in the area, but since the police had scaled down their presence, ethnic tensions were re-emerging.

14 November 2009: Glasgow, Scotland

The Glasgow demonstration was called by the Scottish Defence League, which appeared to be getting off to a slow start. The protest was to be held in Glasgow city centre, close to Scotland's biggest mosque. Just as the EDL were automatically linked to the far-right in England, north of the border, the SDL were automatically linked with sectarianism.

In the weeks preceding the protest, in the alarmist fashion driven by political agenda which was now a regular pre-protest feature, the *Scottish Sunday Mail* reported that a mob of English racists and neo-Nazis linked to the BNP were travelling from Birmingham, Luton, London and Carlisle to '**bring terror to the streets of Scotland**'. The paper said that police officers and politicians were concerned about the possibility of potential confrontations with Muslims. Speaking for the EDL, Leisha Brookes told the *Sunday Mail* that they would be demonstrating the strength of their support in Glasgow, which she claimed was growing at a rate of almost 1000 a month. Brookes estimated the group would have several hundred supporters in Scotland, with most coming from Glasgow and Edinburgh.

A spokesman for Glasgow City Council said there would not be a licensed procession, as a proper application had not been submitted. He said an email applying for permission to march had been sent to the council by a man calling himself Donald but had been turned down as he had refused to disclose details of the organisers, stewarding or the route. A group calling itself the Scottish Defence League had then made an official application to stage a march on November 14, but the submission did not comply with council procedure and the matter did not go any further. If people still turned up, the spokesman said it would be a policing matter. Behind the scenes however, the SDL had been organising a static protest, which technically they didn't need permission for.

On the day of the protest, hundreds of police surrounded a group of SDL who had gathered in the Cambridge Bar in Glasgow. A police helicopter hovered overhead, monitoring proceedings. At noon, the SDL protestors left the bar singing "**Rule Britannia**" and headed into the city centre. They were soon confronted by a group of around 30 anti-fascists, but police managed to keep the two groups apart. Officers also attended an altercation in Gordon Street, where another group of SDL had clashed with anti-fascists. Police surrounded the SDL and held them.

A counter-protest, Scotland United, which had been organised by Aamer Anwar, a Scottish-Pakistani human-rights lawyer, started at Glasgow Green. Speaking to a 1500-strong crowd, Deputy First Minister of Scotland, Nicola Sturgeon, said the SDL had no right to be heard and that ordinary, decent citizens should not to have to listen to the "**vile hatred spouted by these people. Our message to them is clear we will not have it in Glasgow and we will send you packing from every corner of Scotland**".

Police eventually provided coaches to take the SDL supporters away from the city and said that five men had been arrested at different locations for alleged breaches of the peace. The SDL issued a statement criticising Sturgeon for her remarks, calling her a '**rabid anti English bigot**' and '**a chancer who jumps on any bandwagon that suits her**'.

Although the counter-demo was seen as a success, UAF received criticism for its running of the counter-protest. Some anti-fascists claimed they were diverted away from the city and the SDL, not by police but by UAF: '**We were forced to endure the inane ramblings of all manner of middle class 'liberals' and 'socialists' whos [sic] party lines and rhetoric bore no relation to what the vast majority of us thought and in the meantime the police were herding the SDL onto coaches out of town. When we questioned this decision and the choice of speakers UAF stewards threatened to have us arrested**'.

A month after the demonstration, on the 13 December 2009, Scottish newspaper the *Sunday Herald* ran a story, '**Revealed: the secret links between the Scottish Defence League and the BNP**'. The paper claimed to have spoken to an anonymous SDL supporter who informed the *Herald* that the BNP and the SDL shared many members, the threat of expulsion by the BNP was '**a publicity thing**' designed to placate the media and although the SDL wasn't formed by the BNP, party members were amongst its earliest supporters.

Nick Griffin dismissed the claims, saying that he didn't believe for a moment that a genuine BNP member would support the SDL, as the two groups had very little in common. Griffin claimed the SDL was doing something the BNP had abandoned years ago and his party didn't '**want to spend time stomping up the street making a nuisance of ourselves**'.

21 November 2009: Wrexham

Following the Swansea debacle, the WDL was trying again, with Wrexham in North Wales as the venue this time.

Wrexham was once one of the most industrialised areas in Wales, but is now seemingly in terminal decline since the almost total collapse of the region's coal, tannery and steel industries. The town has one of the largest industrial estates in the UK, so factory work has played a prominent role, but larger employers such as Firestone, Dow Corning, Duracell and Tetra Pak have long relocated production to more economically viable regions abroad.

Wrexham had witnessed racial unrest in 2003, when the Caia Park Estate erupted into three days of race riots between local youths and Iraqi Kurdish refugees. The disturbances saw fourteen arrests, with injuries to four policemen and a member of the press. The refugees were eventually moved out to Stoke on Trent.

In the week before the protest, Shahid Malik, government minister responsible for preventing extremism and encouraging cohesion, denounced the EDL. However, Malik said he still believed the group should be allowed to voice its opinion and criticised the counter-demonstrators who had opposed the EDL in Birmingham, saying they had let themselves be provoked.

Ian Titherington, secretary of Searchlight Wales, told local newspaper *The Leader* that the WDL didn't really exist as an organisation and the group was really just a handful of football hooligans. As before, prior to the Swansea and Glasgow protests, racist anti-English terminology was utilised freely by anti-fascists using racism to bolster opposition to the Defence Leagues. Titherington claimed the WDL was bussing people in from England and there would be more support for the Wrexham demonstration than the Swansea protest, as it was closer to Manchester and Birmingham (hint-hint). He said Wrexham would witness '**day-return intimidation**', where English people turned up, intimidated the local community and then left.

On the day of the protest, WDL supporters were instructed to gather at a Wetherspoons pub called The Elihu Yale in Wrexham town centre. It was a cold day and raining heavily. There was a visible police presence around the town and officers from five different forces had been drafted in for the protest (the bill for policing was eventually estimated at £217,000). The demo was to take place at 3.00pm and by noon the pub was fairly full. There was a mixture of local drinkers and WDL inside, outside stood a number of police officers. As the afternoon progressed, the number of WDL slowly but steadily increased.

Around 2.00pm, a group of EDL from Bolton arrived, some entered the pub but the rest stood outside, unfurling a flag and chanting. Attracted by the commotion outside, the WDL spilled out of the pub and onto the street. There were scuffles with police as they were contained by officers. There were shouts and jeers from the other side of the road as a small group of anti-fascists, along with some eastern European skinheads (Wrexham has a large eastern European community), unfurled a Palestinian flag and taunted the WDL. The WDL made a surge towards them but the police line held firm. They were prevented from re-entering the pub as the doors had been locked by staff.

The police swept the pub for any remaining WDL; one was roughly dragged out of the pub by his hair. The police held the WDL outside then moved them down the road, towards the railway station. With very few anti-fascists present to complicate things, it was a relatively straightforward manoeuvre for the police. The WDL were held in the rain at the station and eventually dispersed.

Police said there had been four arrests for public order offences. Deputy Chief Constable, Ian Shannon, was pleased with the police operation and thanked local people for their patience and understanding. Ian Titherington, again playing the anti-English race card, said the day had been a humiliation for the WDL, claiming the only way they could hold the event was to bus people in from Bolton. Obviously forgetting Wales was still part of the UK, he said the WDL did not '**sell any local links**' by singing the National Anthem.

As in Swansea, the turn out for Wrexham was relatively poor and there were criticisms from English activists who questioned whether it was really worth holding protests in Scotland and Wales. Four months after the protest, *North Wales Daily Post* reported police were investigating an anti-Muslim Facebook page called '**No to the Super Mosque in Wrexham**'. The website reportedly claimed that permission had been given by the local council for a mosque at the site of the old Miners Institute in the town. Police told the *Daily Post* they were investigating the matter and liaising with members of the local community.

Nine days after Wrexham, Baroness Warsi of the Conservative Party was attacked by Muslim radicals in Luton as she accompanied a local Conservative parliamentary candidate on a tour of Bury Park. The extremists pelted the Baroness with eggs and she was forced to seek refuge in a nearby shop.

Some of the men were connected to the same group that had abused the Anglian soldiers. One of them was Sayful Islam, he told the *Luton Herald and Post*: "**Baroness Warsi purports to be a Muslim but really she's just pushing a government agenda. She should be received with condemnation. She is clearly in opposition to Sharia**"

There were more ugly scenes later the same day when Warsi was confronted a second time at the Beech Hill Conservative Club in Leagrave Road, Luton. Protected by police officers, Warsi offered to debate with the radicals. Luton man, Gavin Reid, was later convicted under the Public Order Act over the incident and sentenced to six weeks imprisonment at Westminster Magistrates' Court.

5 December 2009: Nottingham

Nottingham is has always been regarded as a textile city, traditionally specialising in lace. Post-WWII, the industry fell into decline, all but disappearing and the city's industry diversified into light engineering. Nottingham was the home of famed British bicycle manufacturers Raleigh and Sturmey Archer, both now relocated abroad due to cheaper labour costs.

The EDL chose Nottingham because the Mercian Regiment was parading through the city following a six-month tour of duty in the Helmand Province of Afghanistan, where it had lost five soldiers. It promised to be a busy day, as along with the parade, there was a football match between Nottingham Forest and local rivals Leicester City. Nottingham City Council leader Jon Collins told the *Nottingham Evening Post* it would cost around £170,000 to police all the events. Calling the EDL 'a **small bunch of fascists**', Collins said its aim was to promote trouble and urged people not to counter-demonstrate.

The EDL had been allocated a spot close to Nottingham Castle for the demonstration, only a short walk from The Company Inn, on Castle Wharf, where they would assemble at 2.00pm. A UAF counter-protest was assembling at the same time on Maid Marian Way. Officers would then lead both groups to their respective demonstration sites. Another rally, unconnected to UAF, was being staged by Nottinghamshire Stop the BNP, illuminating the divisions between anti-fascist groups.

Prior to the protest, the EDL again issued guidelines, stating that they would not tolerate any racist behaviour and asking activists to be aware when raising their arms in a way which could be construed as a Nazi salute. Anti-fascists were still jumping on pictures of EDL activists with their arms raised, they were usually merely people singing but stills of people with their arms in the air were labelled as Nazi gestures by press and left-wing groups alike. The group correctly claimed the press and anti-fascists would have photographers, specifically looking for the opportunity to catch people out in this way.

UAF activists had been busy during the run up to the demo, claiming they had phoned The Company Inn, asking if they understood the potential political and cultural significance (they were apparently serious) of allowing the EDL to assemble on their premises. The telephone number of owners J.D. Wetherspoons was posted on the Internet with a message begging anti-fascists to '**ring them please!!**' One activist said they had spoken to a Wetherspoons customer services manager, who had assured them they would not allow anyone '**even vaguely**' looking like they were part of the EDL protest into their premises. It was hardly the militancy anti-fascists had always preached, but losing the battle on the streets, they were desperate for any small victory.

On the day of the demo, the city centre was full of shoppers, army families and member of the British Legion. The traditional German market was in place and also a temporary ice-rink in the Old Market Square. A Salvation Army band played carols, while steel barriers were set in place for the parade by council workers. Nottinghamshire Police had deployed more than 700 officers, drafted in from Derbyshire, Humberside, Lincolnshire, Leicestershire, Northamptonshire, South Yorkshire, West Midlands and West Yorkshire.

UAF met early in Market Square, numbers were small until the Nottingham Stop the BNP rally joined them. One anti-fascist told *The Guardian* they were counter-protesting because they believed the EDL was a racist organisation. They admitted there had been calls for people not to counter-demonstrate, but said if they didn't, it would give the EDL the confidence to do what they wanted.

As the morning wore on, small groups of antifascists and Asian youths repeatedly clashed with small groups of EDL around the city centre. The counter-demo started, numbers bolstered by trade unionists and students from Nottingham's two universities. Anti-fascists chanted "**Nazi scum off our streets!**" as they marched round the castle, closed for the day; the statue of Robin Hood outside encased in a protective wooden shield. The anti-fascists were stopped by a line of police on Maid Marion Way, just around the corner from the EDL demo site, where they chanted "**Whose streets? Our streets!**"

Thousands gathered to watch the homecoming parade. They cheered and waved flags as 600 troops marched proudly past. As the soldiers marched, a small group of EDL emerged from a nearby pub, carrying flags. They scuffled briefly with a gang of Asian youths, forcing police to intervene. With the police keeping them apart, the two groups hurled insults and missiles at each other. Meanwhile, a couple of elderly women carrying shopping bags, oblivious to what was going on, walked casually between the opposing groups.

The Company Inn was packed with EDL, with more gathered outside in the winter sun, singing and chanting. Some of the group waved placards proclaiming '**Protect Women**', '**No to sharia**' and '**No Surrender to Radical Islam**'. One member of the EDL, a serving soldier, told *The Guardian*: '**We came here to support our lads and the UAF and other militants have turned up. I think it's disgusting. I look at their protest and there's a Pakistani flag flying with a Muslim symbol**'

As police escorted the EDL, many with their faces covered with scarves, from The Company Inn to the demo site, they sang "**we want our country back**" and chanted "**Muslim bombers off our streets!**" It was a good turnout, with well over 700 present. Police halted them at the bottom of Castle Boulevard as a small group of anti-fascists were spotted. Some of the EDL, emboldened with alcohol, attempted to break through police lines to confront '**the reds**'. Officers responded by beating the EDL back with their batons. The EDL at the front clashed with police, as their comrades, massed behind them, pushed forward eager to reach the protest site. Mounted officers were called to restore order. As they were held back a chant of "**E, E, EDL!**" filled the air, the noise reverberating off nearby buildings. Police, concerned things might escalate ushered anti-fascists, press and members of the public well away from the area. Some EDL supporters were dragged from the crowd and wrested to the ground by officers.

At the demo, there was a speech by an ex-soldier, proudly wearing his regimental beret. He was surrounded by placards which read '**Do not bow to Islam**' and '**One law for all – No sharia law in the UK**'. As he spoke through a hand-held megaphone some activists started to heckle police officers who were watching proceedings from a bridge overlooking the site. Then, the crowd suddenly started chanting "**wanker, wanker**" in unison at someone else on the bridge who had obviously caught their attention. It appeared to be Councillor Jon Collins, who had made derogatory comments about the EDL in the run up to the protest.

As the protest came to an end, EDL supporters found they were penned in at both ends of the street by police. A group of around 30 tried to leave at the bottom of the street but they were forced back by officers. They went to the opposite end of the road and attempted to leave again. This time they charged at police lines and officers struggled to prevent them from breaking out. Police eventually escorted the EDL out of the bottom end of the street, past the castle. As they marched, the column a mass of flags and placards, the EDL sang "**I'm English till I die**". A march by the EDL was now a sight to behold, the dark clothes of participants contrasting with the bright colours of their swirling flags and banners. As the police escorted the EDL away, there were sporadic scuffles between them and officers. One EDL member was beaten to the floor by police and tasered when he resisted arrest.

There was trouble outside The Bank pub in the Old Market Square, where a large group of EDL faced a sizeable gang of Asian youths, with police standing in between. The Asian youths, some waving Pakistani flags, were standing on market stalls shouting obscenities at the EDL, who replied in kind with songs and chants. The confrontation carried on for some time, police then deployed mounted officers to push the EDL back. A lot of them were forced into The Bank pub, with the police ordering the doormen to lock the doors.

The main body of EDL was escorted back through the city centre to their trains and coaches at Nottingham station. As darkness fell, groups of anti-fascists, Asian youths and EDL roamed the city centre looking to confront each other. There were still EDL in various pubs, from which they emerged from time to time to clash with small gangs of Asian youths. These skirmishes carried on around the city's pubs well into the evening. Following the protest, Nottinghamshire Police said eleven men had been arrested, all on suspicion of public order offences, and one police officer had sustained an arm injury.

Three weeks later, on Christmas Day 2009, Umar Farouk Abdulmutallab, a Nigerian who had studied at University College London (UCL), attempted to detonate explosives concealed in his underwear on a flight from Amsterdam to Detroit. Abdulmutallab was linked to radical cleric Anwar al-Awlaki, who he was suspected to have met in Yemen before the attack. If convicted, the failed suicide bomber faces a life sentence and is currently (2011) in custody awaiting trial.

Abdulmutallab had studied for a degree in Mechanical Engineering at UCL. He was also President of the university's Islamic society. He was the fourth president of a London student society to face terrorism charges in three years, proof that there was a worrying trend of extremism emerging in some universities. The Federation of Student Islamic Societies claims there is no substantial evidence to suggest that radicalisation is taking place on campuses and a spokesman told *BBC News* that students were more likely to be radicalised by '**watching the bombs fall on Iraq**'. However, the Quilliam Foundation has said that universities have been recognised as key places where Islamist ideologies can spread.

In 2006, Sheikh Musa Admani, Imam at London Metropolitan University, pleaded with both the Home Office and academics to supervise and control university Islamic societies, which he claimed were being run by radicals. He warned that vulnerable, friendless first-year Muslim students, confused about the conflict between Islam and secular values, were natural prey for extremists. In 2010, Higher Education Minister, David Lammy, told *BBC News* that the Government had identified universities at risk from extremist groups and those establishments were being encouraged to work with Special Branch to combat radical elements.

Universities continue to invite controversial radical preachers to address students and there is a very good reason for that. In March 2011, *The Telegraph* reported that British universities had been in receipt of hundreds of millions of pounds from Saudi Arabia and other Islamic sources. Up until 2008, eight universities, Oxford, Cambridge, Durham, City University, UCL, London School of Economics, Exeter and Dundee received more than £233.5 million from Muslim countries and individuals who claimed they wanted to promote a better understanding of Islam.

Donations such as these are now believed to be the biggest source of income for British universities. Professor Anthony Glees, who compiled the funding data, said the real agenda was to promote the extremist Wahhabi branch of Islam. His study revealed that 70% of lectures at one university were '**implacably hostile to the West and Israel**'. Another report by the Centre for Social Cohesion entitled '**A degree of influence**' concluded that British universities were now '**effectively up for sale to the highest bidder**'.

Even with the persistent British links to real terrorism, the press were still keen to paint the EDL as an extremist organisation. On 2 January 2010, a feature in the *Daily Mail* supplement announced '**This is England: Masked like terrorists, members of Britain's newest and fastest - growing protest group intimidate a Muslim woman on a train en route to a violent demo**'. Setting its stall out straight away, the report claimed the men involved were '**some of the most violent football hooligans in Britain**' and claimed that a Muslim woman in a hijab had appeared intimidated by the presence of the EDL when the reporter had followed the group on a train from Bolton to Manchester.

Journalist Billy Briggs claimed there was evidence that neo-Nazis from Combat 18 and other far-right groups had attended EDL demonstrations and published a picture of WDL activists burning the anti-Nazi flag in Swansea to prove the point. For further evidence of involvement with the far-right,

Briggs said that '**self-proclaimed leader**', Tommy Robinson a.k.a. Stephen Lennon had self-admittedly attended BNP meetings in the past, that another prominent member, Davy Cooling, was a BNP member and Sean Walsh, an EDL activist from Luton was a member of the BNP's Bedfordshire Facebook group.

Briggs said Lennon could '**barely conceal his anger**' as he explained what had spurred him to take to the streets: '**For more than a decade now there's been tension in Luton between Muslim youths and Whites. We all get on fine - Black, White, Indian, Chinese... Everyone does, in fact, apart from these Muslim youths who've become extremely radicalised since the first Gulf War. This is because preachers of hate live in Luton and have been recruiting for radical Islamist groups for years. Our government does nothing about them so we decided that we'd start protesting. We have nothing against Muslims, only those who preach hatred. They are traitors who should be hanged and we'll keep taking to the streets until the Government kicks them out.**'

Briggs also met with two '**alarmingly astute**' people he claimed were orchestrating the EDL, it was Alan Lake again, this time with another activist referred to as 'Kinana'. Kinana is closely linked to Lake, he helps with the running of *4freedoms* and organises monthly anti- jihad meetings in London. He is American, works in the City of London and can be seen on some EDL demonstrations carrying an American flag.

Lake was described as a 45-year-old computer expert from London. Lake told Briggs he had contacted the EDL offering to both fund (Lennon would later claim on the BBC programme Newsnight that Lake had '**never given the EDL a penny**') and advise them in an effort to unite '**the thinkers**' and '**those prepared to take to the streets**'. Describing it as '**the perfect storm coming together**', Lake said that although street violence was not desirable it was sometimes inevitable as there were '**issues when you are dealing with football thugs but what can we do?**'

Lake told Briggs he would only support the EDL as long as it didn't associate with the BNP. Intimating he was in control in some way, he claimed there were different extremist groups infiltrating and trying to cause rifts or trying to waylay the agenda (he was right there, his group was one of them), but they intended to exclude those influences.

Briggs said Lake and Kinana were outwardly intelligent and concluded that their political nous, combined with a street army consisting of football hooligans, made the EDL a quasi-political force. Professor Matthew Goodwin, a Home Office advisor on far-right organisations, told Briggs that the EDL should be taken seriously as it was now '**well-organised and not just a minor irritant. It has become a rallying point for a number of different groups and to have them marching through sensitive areas is a major concern**'.

10 January 2010: Wootton Bassett

The town of Wootton Basset in Wiltshire, now granted the prefix Royal, is synonymous with the funeral cortèges of fallen servicemen and women returning from Iraq and Afghanistan. Members of the public would regularly assemble along the route, often joined by members of bereaved families, as coffins bearing the fallen passed through the town on their way from RAF Lyneham to the John Radcliffe Hospital in Oxford.

In 2011, it was announced that repatriation ceremonies would move from RAF Lyneham to RAF Brize Norton in Oxfordshire. Repatriation originally took place at RAF Brize Norton, but to allow for redevelopment of the airfield had been moved to RAF Lyneham in 2007. Even so, the move faced criticism from some people who claimed that the funeral corteges would now leave through a side entrance and purposely avoiding the nearby town of Carterton, where people could possibly assemble to pay their respects as they had in Wootton Basset.

On 2 January 2010, the newspapers reported that Islam4UK was planning to march through Wootton Bassett, to protest against the war in Afghanistan. The group said the planned march would not coincide with a repatriation ceremony, but they felt it was totally unacceptable to honour servicemen who had contributed directly or indirectly to the deaths of well over 100,000 Muslims in Afghanistan. As a result, Islam4UK had decided to launch the **'Wootton Bassett March'** to highlight **'the real casualties of this brutal Crusade'**.

The tabloid media frenzy was instant. *The Daily Mail* called it an outrage that the group was planning to march through the **'war heroes' town'**. *The Mirror* alleged Choudary had compared British troops in Afghanistan to Nazis. *The Daily Record* claimed Choudary planned the march to honour Afghanistan's **'real war dead'** and claimed that 500 members of Islam4UK (there was no evidence to suggest the group could pull such numbers) were planning to carry coffins through the town. Calling the group **'fanatics'** *The Sun* said it was an outrage that Islam4UK was planning to march through a town which had become **'a symbol of our war dead'** and mentioned the plan to carry 500 coffins. *The Daily Star* called Choudary a **'hate-preacher'** weighing in with the headline **'Sick taunts at families'** and also claimed 500 coffins would be carried by Islam4UK.

These headlines, like the ones the previous March after the Anglian parade, obviously raised the ante considerably with the general public. Groups opposing the plans sprang up on social networking site Facebook, one group opposing the march gained more than 220,000 members in a matter of days. A spokeswoman for Wiltshire Police told the BBC that under the Public Order Act, the organiser of any march must inform police of the date, time and route of any proposed procession. She said that there had been no contact from Islam4UK or any other group wishing to arrange a march in Wootton Bassett.

Prime Minister Gordon Brown branded the plans **'abhorrent and offensive'**. Liberal Democrat MP, Chris Huhne, said that the extremists should be grateful they lived in a country which valued freedom of speech and did not lock up protesters, as was the case in many Islamic countries. Huhne correctly claimed the media furore was playing right into the hands of **'shameless self-publicist Anjem Choudary'**, who he said he hoped, would realise how much pain his plans would cause the families of fallen servicemen and abandon them. Huhne was correct, it was about publicity. Choudary was a student of Omar Bakri Mohammed, an accomplished and proven practitioner of press-assisted radicalisation. Yes, the plan would abhor the majority of British people, but some in the Muslim community, faced with Choudary's argument regarding the civilian casualties in Afghanistan, would possibly be swayed and begin to empathise with the radicals. That is the modus operandi of radicals such as Omar Bakri Mohammed or Anjem Choudary and the press acting almost as a willing partner.

Dr Shaaz Mahboob, of the group British Muslims for Secular Democracy (BMSD), said they were alarmed and disappointed to hear about the planned march and believed it would cause unnecessary distress to the friends and relatives of fallen British service personnel. If Islam4UK persisted with its plans, Dr Mahboob warned Anjem Choudary that BMSD and their associates would counter-demonstrate with Union Jacks. He said they wanted to show the public that the vast majority of British Muslims did not agree with such tactics and were happy to publicly oppose the radicals.

The EDL issued a statement calling the plan the **'most heinous idea yet by Islam4UK'**. The group said that although Choudary repeatedly highlighted how hundreds of thousands of innocent Afghani-Muslims were being **'murdered'** by coalition troops, he never mentioned how many innocent Muslims were being killed by the Taliban or by suicide bombers in Afghanistan. The EDL said that it was Choudary's democratic right to despise the UK, no matter how disgusted people might be by his views. The group said it was offering an **'olive branch'** to Choudary, an offer to pay all his expenses should he choose to relocate to a country, such as Saudi Arabia, which observed Sharia. By moving to Saudi Arabia, the EDL said Choudary would prove just how genuine he was about wishing to live under Sharia. The group said the offer was also open to any other members of Islam4UK who were sick of Britain, the only stipulation being, that they gave up their right to a British passport and citizenship.

A week later Choudary issued an appeal for an **'honest dialogue'** with the families of British soldiers, claiming the announcement had been successful in highlighting many important issues. He said despite the fact that he had only declared a desire to march, without having spoken to the police or local authorities, the media had used it to divert everyone's attention away from the truth about Afghanistan, its true cost and its real purpose. Choudary denied that there had ever been a plan to carry 500 coffins through the town, and claimed that had been fabricated by the media (he did seemingly have a point there).

On Sunday 10 January 2010, the newspapers carried stories that the Government was planning to proscribe Islam4UK under the Terrorism Act. Proscription would make it an offence to belong to the group in question and failure to comply could carry a sentence of up to ten years imprisonment. The Terrorism Act allowed the authorities to shut down websites and prohibit proscribed organisations from raising funds.

Having achieved his objective, with the newspapers foaming at the mouth, and now with the threat of proscription, Choudary released a statement cancelling the Wootton Bassett march. A statement said that after successfully highlighting the plight of Muslims in Afghanistan, and following consultation with Omar Bakri Mohammed (ping!), it had been decided that no more could be achieved even if a procession were to take place. The cancellation didn't mean that Islam4UK would remain silent on the atrocities being committed in Afghanistan under the guise of fighting for freedom and democracy said Choudary. It also didn't mean that Islam4UK would stop highlighting the true cost of 'this war against Islam and Muslims'.

Aside from the issue of Afghanistan, Choudary said the mere idea of a procession had opened up many people's eyes as to how the government really viewed the concept of freedom and democracy, which it was supposedly sending its citizens to die for. Even if al-Muhajiroun and Islam4UK were proscribed said Choudary, another platform with a new name would simply appear and continue to call for Sharia. He said neither group had called for any violent or military activities and were ideological and political groups that believed that Muslims lived in the UK under the Covenant of Security. In addition, Choudary said claims that they were inciting racial hatred were absurd, since Islam transcended the boundaries of race and ethnicity. He said they had the right to deem their belief superior to others and advocate it as a better alternative.

On Sunday 10 January 2010, as the newspapers revealed the plans for proscription, rumours circulating amongst EDL activists suggested that the Islam4UK march was going ahead that day. Around midday, supporters were told that four coaches of radicals had been seen leaving London, apparently headed for Wootton Bassett. This was followed by another message that said Wiltshire Police had confirmed that Choudary was on his way to the town. Any EDL who could get there were instructed to do so straight away.

By 2.30pm, there were over 150 EDL on the streets of Wootton Bassett, ready, willing and very able to physically oppose Islam4UK. Local people were directing operations on the ground via the Internet. They warned that police had blockaded the town and were telling any EDL to head for two pubs in the town centre. Fresh rumours started circulating, that coaches carrying radicals had arrived at the Sainsbury's car-park in Wootton Bassett. The majority of EDL headed to the War Memorial, to defend it from any attempted march past and to also hold a two minutes silence. Others, including members of Casuals United made their way over to the Sainsbury's store, to directly confront the radicals, in the words of one Casual, they intended to 'steam into them, no messing about'.

An estimated 200 EDL were now on the streets of Wootton Bassett. Dozens of police officers patrolled the high street as the EDL moved between different pubs during the afternoon. The *Wiltshire Gazette and Herald* reported that locals had reacted angrily to the rumours that the march was to take place. Wiltshire councillor, Allison Bucknell, told the paper that there had been a rumour something was going to happen so the police had decided to have a visible presence, but it had all come to nothing, costing the taxpayer a lot of money.

One of the EDL told *The Herald* they were there because they had heard through social networking sites that Islam4UK was marching. He said although it may have been a wasted journey, they would be there again the next time they heard that it was taking place. A female EDL member told the *Daily Telegraph* that she had heard that Choudary would go to the war memorial and start shouting about the war. She said he had no right to claim benefits off the state and then think he could go to Wootton

Bassett and 'call **our heroes murderers**'. The paper said the '**right-wing extremists**' had travelled from as far as Wolverhampton and Nottingham.

Wiltshire Police issued a statement denying it had been contacted regarding any march and said it would seek a banning order if the correct procedures were not adhered to. Police said they were aware of refreshed reports that a march organised by Islam4UK was due to take place, but there was clear legislation in place, contained in the 1986 Public Order Act, which dictated the process to be undertaken before any march could take place. Following consultation earlier in the week, police said they had been assured by Choudary that the required seven days notice would be forthcoming before any march took place.

Even though Islam4UK didn't appear, whether it was yet another publicity stunt or maybe just the rumour mill going into overdrive was unclear, EDL members were jubilant at the speed and effectiveness of their mobilisation. One supporter on the EDL website said: '**Wherever these anti-British extremists appear, one thing they can now be sure of is that every time they crawl from under their stones, patriots in numbers will be there to oppose them**'.

The next day, Monday 11 January 2010, five of seven Muslim men were found guilty of using threatening, abusive or insulting words or behaviour at the Anglian homecoming parade in Luton at town's Magistrates' Court. When the case had opened, the seven defendants had refused, as is the custom, to stand for the judge, claiming that their religion forbade them to stand for anyone but Allah. Instead of charging the men with contempt of court, District Judge Carolyn Mellanby set a precedent by allowing the men a special dispensation to enter the court after her. Again this was an example of the establishment pandering to a minority, illuminating a two-tier legal system, which, totally ignoring the anger the defendants actions had ignited, was now propagating more resentment by giving them special dispensation ordinary people would not receive.

Solicitors defending the men argued that prior to the protest; their clients had discussed their plans with Bedfordshire Police, who had not objected to the plans or their placards, therefore the prosecution was retrospective. Finding the five men, Munim Abdul, 28, Jalal Ahmed, 21, Yousaf Bashir, 29, Shajjadar Choudhury, 31, and Ziaur Rahman, 32, guilty the judge said: '**I find that a criminal prosecution and conviction of five of the seven defendants is a proportionate response to the legitimate aim of protection of society and maintenance of public order, not only for the future but to ensure there is sufficient public confidence and support in the peace-keeping responsibilities of the police and the courts. I have no doubt it is abusive and insulting to tell soldiers to 'Go to Hell', to call soldiers murderers, rapists and baby killers. It is not just insulting to the soldiers but to the citizens of Luton who were out on the streets that day to welcome soldiers home**'

The defendants faced a maximum fine of £1,000 but were instead handed two-year conditional discharges and each ordered to pay £500 costs. Outside court following the verdict, the defendants reacted defiantly. Under a banner which read: '**Islam will dominate the world - Freedom can go to Hell**', one of the defendant's, Shajjadar Choudhury said that the trial had showed the failure of freedom of speech and democracy.

The following day, the Home Secretary, Alan Johnson, announced that from Thursday 14 January 2010, Islam4UK would become a proscribed organisation, making it a criminal offence to be a member. Johnson said that the group had tried to escape previous proscription by changing its name, but an updated prohibition order would extend to the group's more recent titles which included: Call to Submission, Islam4UK, Islamic Path, and London School of Sharia. The Home Secretary said that proscription was a tough, but necessary power which he didn't take lightly. He said they could not permit any group which propagated the views of banned international preachers of hate and organised hate-filled public protests to operate in Britain.

Islam4UK reacted with a statement announcing that they were closing down all operations, but added that the struggle for a UK caliphate would still continue. The statement said that the announcement by the '**Brown regime**' proscribing al-Muhajiroun and Islam4UK was a victory for

Islam and Muslims. The majority of the organisations that had been proscribed were Muslim and therefore automatically construed as terrorist said the statement. Islam4UK accused the British Government of terrorism via its foreign policy and support for the War on Terror and claimed the banning of ideological and political movements was an evident failure of democracy and freedom. In reference to the Covenant of Security, the group called the proscription an attack against Islam and Muslims, adding that they were '**following in the footsteps of Muslim martyrs**', who had been subject to arrests, torture, murder, and banning.

The Muslim Council of Britain said that banning Islam4UK would not serve long term interests, and described the group as a '**tiny band of misfits**' which the overwhelming majority of Britons, including Muslims, wanted nothing to do with. An MCB spokesman said that the Government's overriding concern should be for the public safety of citizens, irrespective of their backgrounds. He added they were concerned that groups such as the EDL were still free to cause people to fear for their safety in violation of the law, yet non-violent groups were being '**banned for political expediency**'. Maajid Nawaz, director of The Quilliam Foundation, supported the ban on the grounds that Islam4UK had repeatedly encouraged and endorsed terrorism. Nawaz said the ban was necessary and that at least 20 of the group's former members and supporters had been convicted of serious offences such as planning terrorist acts, fundraising for terrorism and inciting murder and hatred.

The EDL issued a statement claiming credit for the ban and said the Government had realised that the people of Britain wanted something done about Islamic extremists who abused British freedoms to spread their message of hate. The statement added that as welcome as the ban was, it was already clear that it would be ineffective, as the Government had only banned a series of names under which the group may operate, rather than banning the advocacy of Sharia that formed the core of the group's activities.

The EDL warned there were other groups still operating unchecked in the UK and asked how long it would be before the same people appeared again under a new name as they had done before. It was looked upon as a victory, but the EDL was right, Islam4UK merely changed its name, and employed new front men. Militant Islam was not going to go away quietly.

Rise of the Infidels

The next destination for the EDL was Stoke on Trent. The city is situated in the heart of the Potteries area of north Staffordshire, once of worldwide renown for high-quality ceramics and mass produced tableware. The 1980s and 90s saw the rise of cheaper foreign pottery production and many factories closed. Some of the remainder, although retaining bases in the area, opened factories abroad where the production costs are much less.

Steelworking and mining were also major industries in the area, but the last deep mine was closed in 1998 and the Shelton Bar Steelworks followed suit in 2000. In a couple of decades, the area had lost most of its manufacturing and experienced a rapid rise in unemployment. Therefore, Stoke on Trent was seen as somewhere the EDL could yield considerable local support.

The population of Stoke is around 240,000, and the city has a large white working class population. Fewer than 7 % of residents are from ethnic minorities and the largest single minority group are of Pakistani origin. One in five people in Stoke are unemployed, the highest level of unemployment in the midlands. The region was granted £7million from the Regional Development Fund in 2009 to help ease the jobless figures. However, this money did little to regenerate the flat-lining manufacturing industry.

The EDL claimed that radical Islamist groups were still operating unchallenged across the UK and the demonstration was to exercise the right to peacefully protest and raise public awareness of the growing danger of militant Islam. The group said it had assured the authorities that they would conduct themselves in an orderly manner and cause as little disruption to the city as possible. The EDL did however voice concerns over rumours that Staffordshire Police officers had been telling local residents they were associated with the BNP and stressed they were apolitical and did not endorse any political party. Activists from Luton and Birmingham had leafleted the area in the weeks preceding the protest, including the Britannia Stadium, home of Stoke City FC (where they were moved on by police).

The group planned to have two speakers at the demo; Guramit Singh, a Sikh from Nottingham who had contacted the group following the protest in the city and an unnamed black member of the EDL from Luton. The group said the presence of the two men showed that ethnic minorities were now playing an active role in the EDL and would hopefully be an integral part of the future leadership. The statement claimed that some Sikhs had come forward and promised that '**other components of modern Britain**' would soon also declare their support. It is true that there are Sikhs involved with the EDL, Singh and a handful of others, but not in any great numbers.

Fast tracking minorities was designed to counter left-wing claims that the EDL was racist. It was futile, as any person from a minority group in the EDL is immediately branded a '**token**', or in Singh's case, a '**poster-boy**', by anti-fascists. It also alienated other EDL supporters, who viewed it as similar to the '**positive discrimination society**' they were supposedly opposing. The role and prominence of other minorities, such as LGBT or Jewish activists, who seemed to be constantly favoured and promoted above ordinary white working class members, would cause much debate within the movement.

A joint counter-protest was called by UAF and the North Staffordshire Campaign against Racism & Fascism (Norscarf), supported by Stoke-on-Trent TUC. Jason Hill, president of North Staffordshire TUC, told *Socialist Worker* that they were expecting a good turnout, coaches of anti-fascists were coming from across the country and students from Staffordshire University were also organising a march. Just by way of a change, a UAF statement accused the EDL of being football hooligans with links to the BNP.

It was true that on early demonstrations, when the police response was still inconsistent, football lads had been the main protagonists. Although they still featured, the hooligans started to find themselves in the minority to young men with no football links who had also rallied to the banner of the EDL. They had taken their lead from the football thugs, developing a similar network of EDL firms or in their case, divisions. Some of these groups have taken part in autonomous activism locally. As with football hooligan gangs, they have a focus, a group of likeminded people they can identify with, pursuing a common, and in their eyes, a just cause. They can go and feel part of something they feel is worthwhile, even honourable and vent their frustrations. However, unlike the tribal football firms, these EDL groups are politically and patriotically motivated.

The day before the Stoke protest, the EDL complained about the suggestive terminology being employed by the press to report on EDL protests. The group claimed that the media only '**cherry-picked**' certain events to paint them in a bad light. National Union of Journalists (NUJ) banners are often at the forefront of anti-fascist counter-protests, in fact the NUJ now has its own left-wing pressure group, NUJ-Left. Therefore, the EDL being identified as racist by the press wasn't surprising; it did however question the reality of the UK's supposedly free press.

Reporting guidelines in the UK are defined by the NUJ, its members i.e. most of the national press, have to abide by these guidelines. Editors are instructed to avoid racial stereotypes and not to allow articles, letters, columns or phone-in shows to be used to further the message of groups which the NUJ has identified as racist.

The blatant opposition of the press resulted in some journalists following the EDL receiving threats. One claimed he had received a threat following the Leeds protest. He was sent an email entitled '**Fatwa**' from someone he called '**a prominent EDL & WDL organiser**'. The email allegedly told him to enjoy any money he had made from the EDL, as he would be '**fed up**' if he was spotted at future protests. A photographer who also followed the EDL also received an alleged death threat. The NUJ issued a statement denouncing intimidation and violence against the press, and called on the police to take '**tough and urgent action**'.

23 January 2010: Stoke on Trent

On the morning of the protest, those arriving at Stoke-on-Trent train station were met by large numbers of police. Earlier that morning EDL graffiti was daubed on the Gilani Noor Mosque in the Normacot area of the city, although the EDL claimed the culprits were in fact anti-fascist agent provocateurs.

Double-decker buses ferried the EDL to the protest site and others started arriving at the Reginald Mitchell pub (named after the designer of that iconic symbol of British defiance, the Spitfire) in the centre of Hanley shortly after noon. As the EDL assembled, supporters sang "**I'm English 'til I die**" and "**Muslim bombers, off our streets!**" Black EDL shirts were clearly visible amongst the crowd, each one emblazoned with the division or part of the country the owner represented. Merchandising seemed to be proving the EDL's main way of generating funds, regardless what the press said about Alan Lake. The chartered buses took nearly half-an-hour to ferry all the EDL to the pub from the train station. There was a brief scuffle inside the pub over football loyalties, it didn't last long however and was broken up by other EDL supporters.

Around 400 anti-fascists were taking part in the counter-demonstration. At 2.00pm they marched, escorted by police, to their demo site on Albion Street, outside Hanley Town Hall. As the counter demonstration was spotted, the EDL in the Reginald Mitchell left and made their way to their protest site, also escorted by police. When the EDL arrived outside the Town Hall, they saw UAF and surged towards them, but found their way barred by a line of police. The EDL turnout of around 1500 dwarfed the UAF counter-protest. It was a mixed crowd, one participant, former local councillor Jenny Holdcroft, told local paper *The Sentinel*, '**People have to come out and be strong and stand together because if not, we are going to lose this country**'.

The two groups baited each other and the EDL repeatedly surged forward trying to break through police lines. A few of the police holding them back had their helmets wrestled from their heads. These were then tossed around as trophies by the cheering crowd. The leadership pleaded with the EDL to calm down and listen to the speakers. It was possibly the largest EDL turnout to date and contained a local turnout previously not witnessed. Three speakers were scheduled to address the crowd. An anonymous black activist was first to take the microphone and was roundly applauded. The agenda was still to dismiss the claims of racism against the movement and he addressed that issue straight away:

"As a black man I stand here to say that the English Defence League is not a racist organisation. I have known many of these people for years and have participated in previous demonstrations. Racism is simply not part of their policy or reflected by their membership. My presence here gives lie to the accusation by many media outlets and anti-racist organisations that the EDL is a front for racist organisations in this country. I would not be here if it was.
The EDL is supportive of my interests in promoting harmony between races and people of colour. I see the EDL as defending my interests as a black man to live in a society where skin colour does not play a part in how society functions. As Martin Luther King Junior said many years ago in his famous 'I have a dream' speech: 'one day our children will live in a nation where they will not be judged by the colour of their skin, but by the content of their character. The EDL's stand against sharia law and radical Islam is a stand against a supremacist ideology masquerading as a religion which says that Muslims are better than non-Muslims and that Muslim men are the best of the lot. This distinction based on what a person believes is no less evil than a distinction based on colour. My conscience, that is what I choose to believe, is as much a part of me as the colour of my skin. If I choose not to embrace Islam I am no less a man because of it. And from what I understand of Islam I would say I am much better off if I do NOT submit to Allah!"

The speech was applauded by the people surrounding the speakers, although in the background EDL supporters continued to clash with police. Next it was the turn of Guramit Singh to address the crowd:

"For nearly a year now the EDL have been fighting against the threat of militant Islam, Sharia law being introduced, and supporting our soldiers abroad. I think the Government have forgotten just how much of a threat militant Islam is, have they forgot about 9/11, have they forgot about 7/7, have they forgot about the hostage situation in Russia in 2004 where 1200 were kept hostage for 3 days and 300 were murdered, nearly 200 of which were children, all done in the name of Islam.
Although I don't believe the introduction of Sharia law to be an immediate threat it is a worry we have to face now, the enemy is knocking at our door but this Government refuses to answer due to its politically correct madness, I don't want a future where my children or grandchildren will have to bow before Islam.
I don't want a future for my children where I have to worry if a Muslim man would be able to have sex with my daughter when she is a minor and him having a legal right to do so, I don't want to see the grandmothers, mothers, daughters, and sisters of this great land suppressed by Islam, I don't want to have to worry if they are beaten, hanged, stoned, raped, or even circumcised due to the freedom they enjoy, the Suffragettes suffered and fought for women's rights in this country, I don't want this country to go back in time.
For close to a year the EDL have been marching making the public and government aware of these threats to this country, one issue we have highlighted time and time again is our concerns about ISLAM4UK, which is led by hate cleric Anjem Choudary and his team of militant cowardly goons, the same person that spits on this country and its people and then has the audacity to claim benefits from it to support himself and his family, the same organisation which praises the terrorists attacks I highlighted earlier and fully supports them.

Only recently the Government banned his farce of an organisation Islam4UK after their proposed march on Wootton Bassett. Too late Mr Gordon Brown, the damage has been done, we ask you to listen to our plea now, we have proven our theories are correct. Already Anjem Choudary and his team of rats is starting a new organisation. Your ban on Islam4UK has not deterred them. Let's start with banning his and all of his organisation's benefits. They're trying so hard to disrupt this Country I find it quite frankly impossible they are actively seeking work to be in legal receipt of them. From there start putting them on the watch list and infiltrate any areas of concern, from there start deporting them to foreign countries such as Afghanistan they are so clearly concerned about. The public needs to wake up and start putting pressure on the Government to start doing something about this."

As Singh spoke, EDL supporters started to hurl missiles at the police. Some jumped on top of a bus stop opposite the protest site. Two more youths climbed on the roof of an arcade, taunting police with one of the captured police helmets. As officers attempted to detain them, the crowd surged forward to prevent arrests being made.

Things were rapidly spiralling out of control, EDL protestors were showing a level of anger not seen before. Of course, the trouble would be blamed on football hooligans, alcohol or the presence of anti-fascists, when in fact it was pure frustration. This was a former proud manufacturing area, now lying in ruins. Robbed of the prospect of employment, young men of the area had turned out to demand, in their own way, that they be listened to. Staffordshire Police were forced to bar the exit from the square with police vehicles, as they hadn't the manpower to contain a crowd the size of the one they were facing.

Demonstrators tried to tip over a yellow police van; one of them jumped on the bonnet and repeatedly kicked the windscreen until it smashed. Another jumped onto the roof of another van and mocked officers. A number of police vehicles were damaged during the disturbance. As police battled to keep the EDL in the square, the crowd repeatedly surged against them and at 4,00pm an EDL speaker appealed to the crowd: **"You are going to get us banned. The EDL do not want trouble!"**

The EDL asked supporters to board the buses back to the train station or make their way home and police gradually allowed the EDL to slowly disperse. After the demonstration had finished there were reports of clashes between demonstrators and police in the Cobridge, Northwood and Central Forest Park areas of the city. Paul Walker, of the EDL Stoke on Trent Division, told *The Sentinel* he was upset by the trouble, but claimed the EDL had been antagonised, due to the police allowing anti-fascists so close.

Staffordshire Police announced that seventeen men connected to the EDL had been detained for a variety of offences. Superintendent Dave Mellor told *Sky News* that the vast majority of demonstrators had expressed their views peacefully, but the actions of a small minority had been totally unacceptable. He said officers would be reviewing CCTV to pursue those identified as committing offences. Forty police officers were injured, two required hospital treatment; one was punched in the face and the other suffered serious arm injuries.

Eight officers drafted in from West Mercia Police would later claim compensation for injuries sustained during the demonstration. Two of them were knocked unconscious when they and six colleagues were in a van which was attacked in Parliament Row. Andy Adams of the Police Federation told *The Sentinel* that lots of other officers had been assaulted and pushed around but what had happened to the West Mercia officers could have been fatal. Deputy Chief Constable of Staffordshire, Douglas Paxton, said that the demonstration had been challenging and they had deployed trained, equipped and appropriately protected officers. Paxton admitted however, that risk could not be completely eliminated as operations had to be **'dynamic and fluid'**.

Local Labour MP Mark Fisher said that it was regrettable people had been injured and arrested. He said it was not good for the city to host such events, but he was pleased that political parties had stayed out of it. Fellow Labour MP Rob Flello said the EDL had behaved like thugs and the riot was exactly what he had feared would happen. He said the police had done a fantastic job and that the EDL had shown their true colours. Council Chief Executive, John van de Laarschot said that Stoke-on-Trent was a strong, multicultural city and although some protesters chose to cause trouble, the protest was handled effectively and fairly by the Police.

Following the Stoke protest, Stephen Lennon featured on *Pits and Pots* - an independent news and discussion website based in Stoke. Lennon, under the pseudonym Tommy Robinson, was quizzed about the disruption the protest caused. Lennon said the frustration of people who were angry with the Islamification of their country needed to be channelled. He said the police bore some responsibility for the trouble, as they had allowed UAF to march to within ten metres of the EDL and wave a Pakistani flag. It was that, said Lennon, which had caused the eruption of violence.

Internet activist Paul Ray was again trying to ferment unrest. Ray was making references to the Crusades, and the Knights Templar, and was now referring to himself as '**Grandmaster Ray**' the '**spiritual leader of the EDL**'. Ray had now teamed up with German ex-neo-Nazi Nick Greger, or Nasty Nick as he preferred to be called. Greger, the former head of a Nazi group from Dresden, Germany, renounced National Socialism and now has a Star of David tattooed on his wrist. They are both now (2011) thought to be residing in Malta.

Ray's main gripe was still Chris Renton's involvement with the EDL, although Renton didn't seem to be figuring much by this point. Ray claimed that the leadership of the EDL had '**crossed the line of any form of decency**' by refusing to acknowledge what needed to be done. He said he had told the leadership they needed to remove Chris Renton, but they had refused and turned on him instead. Because of his high profile as a victimised patriot in the early days of the EDL, Ray did have some sympathisers. In response, the EDL dismissed the allegations as lies and urged supporters to avoid all contact with Ray or his associates.

Obviously buoyed by the high turnout at Stoke, the EDL immediately announced two more protests, Edinburgh on 20 February, and Bolton on 6 March. The group also issued a statement calling for a UK ban on the face veil. It was an issue recently raised by Nigel Farage of the UK Independence Party (UKIP) and the EDL said they viewed the garment as a significant threat to national security, as anyone could wear one without being identified. British people could not wear balaclavas when entering a bank, said the EDL, so Muslims shouldn't be permitted to wear clothing such as a niqab or burqa, the same rules should apply to all.

In 2006, then Leader of the House of Commons, Jack Straw said the veil was a '**visible statement of separation and of difference**' and that he asked women visiting his surgery to consider removing it. Straw said he feared that wearing the full veil made relations between communities difficult. Many British people agree with him, believing the veil is a regressive step in sexual equality, subjugates and isolates women. Backing this assertion, in 2010 a poll by You Gov revealed 69% believed Islam encouraged the repression of women. This obviously results in negative social factors. BBC has reported that only one in five Pakistani and Bangladeshi women are active in the UK job market, compared with seven in ten black and white women. A further poll by You Gov in July 2010 revealed that 67% of British people interviewed agreed with banning the veil. This attitude is also shared in Europe, as Belgium, Italy and Spain all have legislation in place to ban the veil, with France introducing a public ban on 11 April 2011. Nevertheless, British Immigration Minister, Damien Green, said a UK ban would be '**un-British**' and '**contrary to a tolerant and mutually respectful society**'.

The EDL also called for the immediate halting of the construction of all new mosques in Britain. The group said the request was based on the fact that the Government had no idea who was living in the country. The EDL urged the Government to launch an urgent investigation into the source of funding for new mosques, as they believed they were funded by Saudi Arabia to promote Wahhabi Islam.

A week after the Bolton protest was announced; it was suddenly cancelled. It had emerged that there was to be a Hindu religious festival in the town on the same day. In a statement, the EDL said that due to the respect they had for the **'peace loving Hindu community'**, they had decided to cancel the protest, claiming anti-fascists were planning to attack the Hindu festival dressed in EDL clothing. The group stressed that the cancellation showed that it was not against all foreigners as anti-fascists led people to believe. Behind the scenes however, people had been worried that some supporters would see the Hindus and mistake them for Muslims.

UAF claimed that the protest had been cancelled because the EDL knew its **'crew of hooligans and Nazis'** would go on the rampage and attack Hindus. Stoke had highlighted a problem for the EDL. The protest had been a success with the numbers in attendance exceeding their wildest dreams, the varying estimates of between 1500-1800 was its highest turnout to date. However, the group realised that due to the make-up of its support, it couldn't always guarantee it could be controlled. The main troublemakers in Stoke had been angry locals, young white working class males, frustrated, ignored and isolated from mainstream society. They weren't committed supporters, but had attended as the EDL was in town and many of them used it as an excuse to air their frustrations. To try and combat this, the EDL announced that it would employ its own stewards to help police future protests.

On 8 February 2010, the BBC ran the first of a series of programmes entitled *Generation Jihad* which investigated the terrorist threat from young British Muslim extremists radicalised by the Internet. The first programme featured extremists who had come from West Yorkshire, in particular Bradford and Dewsbury. It was obviously of interest to the EDL and Casuals United, with many activists thinking it would highlight and justify their cause. The programme gave the EDL just enough information with which to act and with twelve minutes of the programme still to run, people were already talking about a Bradford protest.

Bradford would be raising the ante considerably. Close to 20% of the city's population was from the sub-continent and 78% of those were of Pakistani/Kashmiri origin. Because of this, the city was nicknamed **'Bradistan'** and has suffered numerous incidents of racially linked, disorder. The EDL issued an official statement confirming the protest, which was to be based on the *Generation Jihad* programme. The group said it intended to march through Bradford on 30 May 2010, to urge the Government to address the deteriorating situation on the streets of Britain, before the whole situation got out of hand.

The group also announced another demonstration in Aylesbury, Buckinghamshire, on 2 May 2010, but that went almost unnoticed; all anyone wanted to talk about was Bradford. Some EDL questioned the wisdom of choosing Bradford; warning that the Government wouldn't allow it to happen, that it was asking to have the EDL proscribed like Islam4UK had been. These dissenting voices were drowned out by others who claimed that there shouldn't be any no-go areas in the UK. As far as they were concerned, it was a British city which was a hub of anti-British Islamic activity.

20 February 2010: Edinburgh

Ahead of the Edinburgh protest by the SDL, the *Sunday Herald* claimed that leaders of the Defence Leagues had admitted that they had lost control over their supporters. The article concentrated on the Stoke demonstration, calling it a **'pogrom against Muslims'** and suggesting that the proposed Edinburgh demo could descend into chaos. Jeff Marsh told the paper: **'Stoke was horrendous. It went mental. Hundreds of BNP members turned up. You can't go around rioting like that, because eventually they'll ban the movement. The people that came don't care about the EDL; they just turn up for the riots. We're not conspiring to cause riots. Yes, we have a lot of criminals attaching themselves to us and people that come along to kick off, but we're trying to deal with that'**

The article did carry some positives for the EDL, estimating the numbers in Stoke at more than 1500 and adding that they had easily outnumbered the anti-fascists. Marsh was jubilant and said the Defence Leagues had gone from 30 or 40 people when they had started, to turnouts of thousands in under a year. Aamer Anwar, organiser of one of Edinburgh's two planned anti-fascist rallies, Scotland United, urged the police to come down hard on the SDL if they misbehaved. Anwar said he hoped he wouldn't see a repeat of the scenes in Stoke and the fact that the EDL put some 1500 'thugs' onto the streets should set off alarm bells. It was proof that anti-fascists had been shaken by the imbalance of the numbers in Stoke.

Left-wing activists had been busy in the weeks before the protest, the Edinburgh Anti-Fascist Alliance (a front for the Scottish Socialist Party), wrote to over 300 local pubs warning landlords they might encounter problems when renewing their licence or face a boycott should they allow the SDL to meet on their premises. An SDL spokesman told the *Sunday Herald* that the Defence Leagues assembled in public houses for safety reasons. He said SDL supporters were better off inside a pub when there were anti-fascists on the streets who wanted to attack them, and questioned on what basis a pub could bar SDL members. He said the pubs were scared of the anti-fascists, because they would turn up after the protest at pubs they hadn't managed to intimidate into closure.

As the EDL had traditionally used Wetherspoons premises in the past, the company's bar in George Street arranged for extra security on the day of the protest. A spokesman for J.D. Wetherspoons told *The Herald* they would allow anyone in, as long as there was no trouble and added that people couldn't be banned from pubs because of their views, as they would have empty pubs. The spokesman said that although they didn't agree with the EDL or SDL, if supporters of either group entered one of their pubs and didn't cause trouble, they wouldn't be barred.

The day of the protest began with police raiding the houses of people they believed were key figures in the SDL. Edinburgh Council couldn't stop a static protest but the SDL hadn't given proper notice, so the police believed they were acting within the margins of the law. Stephen Lennon was at Luton Airport early that morning, waiting to catch a flight to Edinburgh. He and a companion were suddenly surrounded by armed police and detained. While this was taking place, Lennon's house was raided and searched by armed officers. He was told he was being detained on suspicion of causing criminal damage to a hotel he had stayed at in Leeds. Lennon was taken to a police station in Sheffield for questioning.

The Welsh contingent, which included leading figures in Casuals United, flew direct to Edinburgh from Cardiff. When they arrived in Edinburgh Airport, they were also detained by police. A lot of the English contingent had travelled up by train. They were also detained when they arrived at Edinburgh's Waverley train station and held for the duration of the protest.

The whole of the Royal Mile in Edinburgh had been closed by the Lothian and Borders Police and the fluorescent jackets of officers could be seen dotted along its entire length. There were around 700 police on duty; with officers drafted in from neighbouring forces. By 10:30am, 200 anti-fascists had gathered on Princes Mall and The Mound. The two groups, Scotland United and Edinburgh Anti-Fascist Alliance formed an awkward coalition.

At around 11.00am, rumours spread that the SDL had appeared on the Royal Mile. The majority of anti-fascists headed straight there, but UAF stewards, although largely ignored, desperately tried to stop them from marching off. Many anti-fascists were angry at the behaviour of UAF, one later claimed: 'Aamer Anwar and Weyman Bennett's little double act as the march starting [sic] going up The Mound, with their pathetic, hysterical pleas to turn round, as apparently "the SDL haven't got permission to march so we don't need to go" (Anwar), "It's only Hibs casuals in that pub", "the SDL are in Haymarket" & "150 fascists are going to attack the Scotland United demo" (all Bennett. predictably, all made up shite.). Congratulations to Edinburgh Anti-Fascist Alliance for a hugely successful day, despite the outrageous, sectarian behaviour of 'Unite Against Fascism', who succeeded in splitting the march and turning it into a farcical faction fight'

Around 60 SDL/EDL had met at a pub called Jenny Ha's opposite the Scottish Parliament. Police quickly sealed off the street. The EDL would later claim that up to 250 supporters were held at train stations across Scotland by police and prevented from attending the protest. At 1.00pm, the SDL assembled by the exit of the pub, waiting for the police to lead them to the protest site. Nothing happened and people began to ask what the hold up was. News gradually spread that the police were not allowing the protest. The SDL attempted to leave but were pushed back by police at the entrance.

SDL protestations that their freedom of speech was being denied were ignored. Police informed them their demonstration was over and that buses would be provided to take them out of the area. The SDL reacted angrily to this news and blockaded themselves inside the pub, piling tables up against the main entrance and securing other doors. After a short stand-off the SDL decided they would leave after all, filing slowly out and searched by police as they left. Accompanied by officers on board, they were driven off on the buses, past jeering and cheering anti-fascists lining the street. The convoy of buses made its way to Linlithgow, around 20 miles from Edinburgh. When they arrived, the police released the SDL, telling them they were free to go.

It wasn't a successful day for the SDL. The EDL had taken off in England but the SDL was struggling for numbers. A few weeks later, the *Sunday Herald* suggested sectarianism between Protestants and Catholics was to blame for the failure of the SDL. The paper declared that the SDL was in '**meltdown**', it only had 25 members and that hooligans who followed Hibernian and Celtic football clubs had planned to attack the group in Edinburgh because it contained mainly Glasgow Rangers and Heart of Midlothian supporters. Jeff Marsh told the paper that the Scottish lads seemed unable to forget their differences and could not get past the sectarian divide. He said they were speaking to various Scottish firms, trying to unite them, and they wouldn't give up.

The EDL wasn't long in accusing the police in Edinburgh of falsely arresting its activists and preventing their right to freedom of speech. The group claimed some supporters had been detained without cause and others who arrived at the train station had been forced onto trains heading away from Edinburgh. The group claimed that anti-fascists were allowed to wander the streets and had attacked a number of EDL and SDL supporters while nearby police officers turned a blind eye. The statement said it was clear that the actions of the police were politically motivated and that the police as a whole could no longer be considered as neutral. The EDL said this view was reinforced by the comments of Scottish Justice Minister, Kenny MacAskill, who following the protest had said that the fact that the SDL didn't make it out of Waverley Station was testament to good policing. The EDL said the police operation was a travesty for democracy and they couldn't stand idly by while the forces of fascism took over the country. Pledging to return in greater numbers, the statement said their ancestors had fought for their liberties and they would do the same.

Stephen Lennon was bailed the following day. A quickly put together statement and video was released, in which a clearly angry Lennon recounted what had happened. He said the Bradford demo was now cancelled, in what the EDL leader described as a small concession to the authorities. It emerged that police had arranged for him to answer bail at the Sheffield police station on the day of the planned Bradford protest, now instead of travelling to Bradford, the EDL were asked to assemble in Sheffield to support him. In a statement the EDL issued what it dramatically called, '**a call to mobilisation**' and said it needed '**every single person who supports the EDL to stand up and be counted and when required we need you to take to the streets in a peaceful and law abiding manner to support the leadership**'.

The EDL said it would not be bullied into silence by the establishment and the struggle against militant Islam would continue. As predicted by some activists, it appeared that Bradford had been a step too far, too soon. The EDL also announced a rally outside the Houses of Parliament in London, on Friday 5 March, in support of Dutch MP, Geert Wilders, who was visiting the UK to promote his controversial film *Fitna*, which explored the links between Islam and terrorism.

5 March 2010: London

Geert Wilders was invited to the Houses of Parliament by Lord Pearson and Baroness Cox of UKIP. It was rumoured that Alan Lake, who was now undoubtedly guiding the EDL, hoped UKIP could be the political wing of the anti-jihad movement in Britain, especially since under Lord Pearson the party was taking a more anti-Islamic stance. Pearson regularly spoke out against Islam and former leader Nigel Farage had recently addressed the issue of the burqa in British society. Lake was rumoured to be a friend of UKIP MEP Gerard Batten and also Magnus Nielsen, a UKIP candidate Lake had claimed was prepared to speak at EDL rallies. Lake told *The Guardian* that there was '**some synergy**' between the EDL and UKIP.

Wilders, like assassinated Dutch MP Pim Fortuyn, was campaigning to have the first article removed from the Dutch constitution, which covers discrimination. The Dutchman, who was facing prosecution in Holland for '**inciting hatred**' with his film *Fitna,* had previously been invited to the UK in January 2009. Muslim radicals had responded to the news by protesting in London. The Home Secretary, Jacqui Smith, told Wilders his visit would threaten community harmony and public security, and barred him from entering the UK. Wilders ignored the ban and flew to London regardless but was detained on arrival by UK Border Agency officials and returned to the Netherlands on the next available flight. He lodged an appeal and the decision to bar him was overturned by an Asylum and Immigration Tribunal in October 2009.

The EDL claimed the Wilders had been harassed, threatened and litigated against because of his views, and whether people agreed or not, as an elected representative of his country, he should be heard. The group was using volunteer stewards for the first time, drawn from the group's supporters, to assist in crowd control. The leadership claimed their presence would make it easier for the EDL to obtain a fairer hearing in the press. Also, for the first time in a history of unlicensed marches to static protest sites, the EDL was being allowed by police to march an agreed route. Activists were told the demonstration would take longer than usual but because of this the EDL believed the exposure along the route would be much greater.

It was obvious, especially following the Edinburgh arrests that the EDL wanted to be seen to be cooperating, but the fact they were being allowed to march also showed some accommodation by the establishment. The EDL also stressed that racism and violence would not be tolerated and certain chants involving Allah were now banned. EDL activists had long been hostile to the press, because of what they saw as biased reporting, but now they were asked to be respectful to any members of the media. It was an obvious attempt to change perceptions. If they couldn't yet make the movement respectable, then they would try and make it at least more acceptable.

On the morning of the Wilders march a small group of EDL turned up at Luton Magistrates' Court to support the two men on trial for public order offences connected to the Royal Anglian Regiment parade in Luton. In court, the prosecution alleged that Brian Kelso and Kevin Carroll had been among a crowd of around 30 '**hardcore protestors**' who had shouted at the Muslim demonstrators. Just how spontaneous objectors to a perceived outrage could be termed hardcore protestors wasn't explained. It appeared the prosecution may have been utilising terms which had begun to appear in the press and other media, as at the time of the homecoming parade in Luton, there was no UPL, no Casuals United or EDL.

Kelso told police the Muslim protesters were abusing people he considered heroes and his only intention had been "**to give them a piece of my mind**". The men's actions had been captured by *BBC News* cameras. Kelso, 27, and Carroll, 40, both from Luton, were found guilty of using threatening words, or behaviour likely to cause harassment, alarm, or distress. Both men received a nine-month conditional discharge and ordered to pay costs of £175. Both said they intended to appeal. Neither Kelso nor Carroll, who was related to Lennon, had been obviously involved with the EDL up to this point. Now the trial was over Carroll made it clear that he was an active member of the group. .

In Westminster, Wilders showed his film to 60 invited guests and afterwards made a speech. He told an ensuing press conference that he was calling for an end to further immigration from Islamic countries, but added that Muslims already resident in the West would be welcome to stay. Lady Cox said the visit had been a victory for free speech, saying it was important to debate such issues sensibly in a responsible and democratic way.

As Wilders spoke to the press, the EDL marched. In the footsteps of their ancestors, the common people of England were marching again on Parliament, stirred by perceived injustice. Before beginning the march, the EDL assembled at the Tate Britain, just down river from Parliament. There they were addressed by Guramit Singh, who called on all religions to oppose radical Islam, finishing his speech with the words "**God bless the Christians, Jews, Sikhs, even God bless the Muslims, they'll need it when they're burning in fucking hell**". Singh would later claim that the word '**militant**' had been accidentally omitted from the speech, but if it had been, it was a mistake which would be used by the left-wing media to accuse Singh and the EDL of racism.

The EDL set off, some activists carried placards proclaiming '**England needs a Geert**', '**We will never submit to Islam**' and '**Geert Wilders England salutes you**'. The marchers, flanked by police, encountered small groups of anti-fascists along the way. Insults were traded between the groups but, thanks to the police presence, proceedings remained largely peaceful.

UAF had been slow off the mark, releasing hurried appeals for anti-fascists to attend an '**emergency protest**' against the EDL (with the obligatory references to football hooliganism and the BNP) only days before. They had assembled outside the Houses of Parliament to try and prevent the EDL from marching past. They had been surrounded by police outside St Stephen's Gate since 11.00am and were addressed by MP, Jeremy Corbyn. The anti-fascists staged a sit-in on Abingdon Street, attempting to stop the EDL from marching through. As they sat on the floor the anti-fascists chanted "**EDL go to hell! Take your fascist mates as well!**" Police moved in and arrested approximately 50 of them, eventually holding the rest by the Jewel Tower at the southern end of the Parliament buildings. The EDL arrived, and police guided them into College Green. Both sides faced each other across the road and after allowing the groups to trade insults for a while, the police finally led the EDL away and dispersed the anti-fascists.

The march didn't receive much coverage in the press, possibly because the majority of the arrests had been anti-fascists. *BBC News* reported that '**Dutch MP Geert Wilders' anti-Islam film sparks protests**'. Under the headline '**God bless the Muslims. They'll need it when they're burning in effing hell**' Daniel Trilling of the left-of-centre *New Statesman*, after making the usual obligatory, irrelevant and increasingly boring references to the BNP, said that the Wilders demo should show anyone in any doubt the character of the EDL. Quoting Peter Hain, who was of the opinion that the group represented a '**racist and fascist threat**', Trilling said that had been illustrated by the behaviour of some EDL supporters but made no mention of anti-fascist arrests.

The EDL viewed the day as a massive success, celebrating the fact that so many UAF had been arrested. Anti-fascists complained about police tactics, such as '**illegal headlocks**'. With only a couple of arrests, the EDL was claiming the moral high-ground, contemplating the possibility of being perceived as almost law abiding. This delusion wasn't to last long.

A week later, on Sunday 14 March 2010, the *News of the World* claimed '**Patriotic EDL exposed as racist, violent thugs! The repulsive race-hate face of the English Defence League is unveiled today by the News of the World. A three-month probe by our undercover investigators exposes the TRUE nature of the organisation that claims to be patriotic, non-violent and non-racist**'. The article claimed the EDL was backed by '**bigots, football thugs, and BNP defectors**' who were intent on starting a race war. Two undercover reporters had infiltrated the group and claimed they had witnessed '**sickening booze and drug-fuelled behaviour**'. The article claimed the reporters had observed abuse directed at Asian and black members of the public and had also '**unmasked a leading figure declaring his hatred of Pakis.**' The investigators had filmed Guramit Singh saying '**I fucking hate the Pakis. India needs to go to war with Pakistan.**' The paper claimed that Singh had also told a reporter he could, '**sort any problems he was having with local Muslims**'.

Approached for a comment, Singh insisted he wasn't racist and said the comment had been made '**in the heat of the moment**'. The paper also reported that there had been a '**rapid growth of football hooligans in the EDL**' which was hardly newsworthy, as the EDL had never hidden the fact that it was started by ex-football hooligans. The *NOTW* claimed that one hooligan, 18 year old Joel Titus, was recruited by Casuals United's Jeff Marsh, described as '**a thug who served two years in jail for stabbing two Manchester United fans**'. Journalists had also filmed EDL members on a coach before the Stoke protest drinking and boasting of using cocaine. The report mentioned Geert Wilders visit to the Houses of Parliament where it claimed scuffles had broken out between the EDL and UAF, resulting in 50 arrests. This obviously wasn't true, as there were no clashes apart from between the police and anti-fascists. The report obviously omitted the fact that 48 of the 50 arrests involved anti-fascists attached to UAF.

Responding to the story, the EDL claimed the article was a contortion of the truth and that the movement could handle being portrayed as '**racist yobs**' as long as it stayed true to its cause. The group claimed the article was misleading and that the reporters were '**freelance mercenary journalists after a sensationalist story to sell to the highest bidder**'. They also claimed that the Government was worried about the growing numbers of the Defence Leagues and suggested the article had political origins as the Government had been pressurised by the Muslim Council of Great Britain into attempting to silence the EDL: '**These claims won't be taken seriously by the EDL as this paper is not even fit to wrap fish and chips! Had the NOTW forgotten that we streamed the whole event live? Did they not see our non-White and Jewish support? Did they not read that out of 50 arrests 48 were from UAF? And we are still the 'violent racist thugs' who embrace anyone no matter of their nationality, their skin colour, their religion, their creed, or sexual orientation. Shame the same can't be said of the government funded anti-gay, anti-Semitic UAF**'.

Jeff Marsh was more vociferous in his condemnation of the article. Marsh said the *NOTW* had attempted to paint him as some sort of Fagin character and denied recruiting Titus to the movement. He said that the message of Casuals United was for hooligans to stop fighting over football and therefore asked why it was continually being labelled as a hooligan group. Marsh maintained the dossier that the *NOTW* claimed to have was '**made up of stuff that's been on the Internet for six months. This is pure lazy journalism and a desperate attempt to stop the fastest growing patriot movement ever. If a teenage kid in school was given half an hour on Google to research the EDL that is what they would have written**'.

On 16 March 2010, the police investigation into criminal damage involving Stephen Lennon at the Leeds hotel was suddenly dropped. Lennon was to answer bail in Sheffield, but a statement issued by the EDL announced all charges against him had been dropped and said Lennon was now considering what action to take. Following the arrest of 48 anti-fascists and the seemingly soft approach to the EDL by the Metropolitan Police at the Wilders march, anti-fascists lost no time implying a deal had been struck. They claimed that Lennon had informed on other EDL members but these claims were immediately rubbished by Marsh:

'**They feel a silly rumour of 'grassing' on the Internet will cause division in the EDL. The reason the authorities are terrified of the EDL is that they know the organisers of football supporters in the UK are intelligent. We have tight networks formed by 20 years of knowing each other via casual culture (fighting each other - has now been declared over) so infiltration at medium level is nigh on impossible. We aren't criminals so what can they grass us for? There is no membership scheme in the EDL/SDL/UDL/WDL so many of these people just turn up with their mates and don't have to give names and addresses to anyone to be published online like the BNP fools. Infiltration is impossible, as if you claim to support a football team, a few phone calls can establish your background as most lads grew up together and if no-one knows you, your cover is blown and these checks are ongoing. Divisions work on a cell structure - Tommy deals with only a handful of people and no one person is in a position to grass up numerous others - addresses are not exchanged and un-registered 'pay-as-you-go' SIM cards for mobile phones are the norm. If EDL members kick off and attack police they will be arrested, but most members are peaceful unless attacked. There is no one person in a position to do any grassing as that's the culture here – there is no membership and there never will be. Nearly every leader has been nicked and had houses searched and not one has yet been charged – why? As this is not a conspiracy to cause violence, it is an attempt to stop violence, by uniting all the football lads**'

Marsh was right, most football hooligans in the country were linked in some way, someone knew someone who knew someone, and this was even more the case since the adoption of the Internet. Everyone who claimed to be football coming into the EDL could be verified quickly in some way. The left would also imply Lennon had given the police information on the travelling arrangements of known football hooligans for the forthcoming World Cup in South Africa. In reality the thugs of one club would very rarely know the plans of another firm, so the allegations fell on stony ground. One noticeable factor following the Edinburgh arrest was the apparent change in attitude by the police. Conspiracy theories abounded, but other factors such as the police later claiming the EDL was not extremist, suggests that Lennon was investigated and raided for extremism but police found he didn't actually fit the bill.

Following the Wilders march, the LGBT (Lesbian, Gay, Bisexual and Transgender – labelled the BLT Division by some EDL activists) Division of the EDL was founded. The LGBT community possibly had the most to fear from Sharia and Islamification, and the idea had come from the Wilders demo as founder 'Ray Britannia' explained: **'I was at the demo in London on the 5th and some of the opposition we shouting "We're black, we're Asian, we're Jewish and we're Gay!" and if I had a megaphone I would have shouted "What the fuck do you think I am then?" The EDL is all about different kinds of people coming together to fight a common threat, that includes gay people as well'.**

The LGBT Division contradicted the perception that the EDL were all racist football hooligans and their rainbow flag and the pink triangles were soon a common sight at EDL protests. However, along with other minority groups, extremists would use them to join the movement and cause considerable discontent amongst some ordinary rank and file members. In the case of the LGBT Division, a small minority would try to claim the EDL was now a gay-rights pressure group and attempt to force their opinions on people, using a leadership keen to embrace, and more importantly being seen to embrace, minority groups. This attitude did gay activists no favours among the movement's white working class supporters, many of whom believed such favouritism simply mirrored the two-tier system they opposed.

20 March 2010: Bolton

Bolton is a former mill town, once part of Lancashire, now part of Greater Manchester. The town was once a centre for textile production, specialising in cotton and wool and also engineering. Following World War Two, Bolton gradually lost most of its industry, now less than 20% of the town's jobs are found in manufacturing.

Also following WWII, a number of Muslim migrants made their home in Bolton, settling in the Deane and Derby areas. The majority of these newcomers originated from India and came to work in the town's textile mills. The Muslim population of Bolton is now around 15%.

The EDL's rescheduled visit faced opposition from the local council, which appealed to the Home Office to ban the protest. Home Secretary Alan Johnson responded to the concerns saying that the Government supported the right of people to peacefully express their views in public under the principles of free speech. Johnson said all relevant laws had been examined and he had no power to prohibit a static protest. Bolton councillor Cliff Morris said they were disappointed that the Home Secretary was unable to ban the protest. Morris said the council had been working with the police and local community groups and urged local people not to take part in any counter-demonstration.

The *Bolton News* reported that amid fears the day would end in violence, many shops and bars were boarding up their premises, most local pubs had decided to close and many local businesses had also chosen not to open. UAF planned to counter-demonstrate and had set about mobilising anti-fascists. The group claimed to have 37 coaches travelling to Bolton from all over England.

The day before the protest, two Muslim brothers from nearby Blackburn, who had filmed each other on **'terrorist training exercises'** crawling through the undergrowth of a local park were jailed. The two men, who had dubbed themselves the **'Blackburn Resistance'**, were also said to have stockpiled weapons. Abbas Iqbal was sentenced to two years in prison for dissemination of terrorist material and one year for preparing for acts of terrorism. His brother, Ilyas Iqbal, was sentenced to 18 months for possession of a document likely to be useful for terrorism. Ilyas had attended the College of Islamic Guidance and Knowledge in Blackburn, where an accomplice of shoe-bomber Richard Reid, Sajid Badat, was also a student.

On the day of the protest, early arrivals to a cold, wet and largely deserted Bolton town centre found what the *Bolton News* referred to as a '**ring of steel**', a series of steel barriers erected by council workmen. Victoria Square in the town where the protest and counter-demo were to take place was divided into two halves with a neutral section in the middle, populated only by police and Bolton's large war memorial.

By midday, UAF activists started arriving. James Haywood of the National Union of Students told *Socialist Worker* that students should play a leading role in the '**anti-fascist struggle**' and they needed to '**smash the EDL**'. As more and more UAF arrived, a small number of EDL also made an appearance on the opposing side of the barriers. Seeing this, some UAF attempted to break through and confront them, but were held by police. Other anti-fascists tried to leave the site but their exit was also barred by the police, who obviously didn't want them roaming round town confronting any approaching EDL. Police struggled to calm the situation and reinforcements were summoned. Another large body of UAF arrived and were immediately aggressive towards police. They were pushed back by officers, as small groups of EDL looked on, motionless. Mounted police prepared their horses to charge the anti-fascist crowd, as snatch-squads clad in dark blue riot gear rushed in, dragging people out. Most of the anti-fascists were resisting arrest and struggling with police.

Most UAF were now at the demo site; most of the EDL however, were still en route in local assembly points a.k.a. pubs. There were reports of clashes between rival gangs around the town.

There were around 1,000 anti-fascists in Victoria Square, but a number were being steadily led away by police. Weyman Bennett addressed the crowd and bizarrely declared that the police were rioting and out of control. Bennett said that anti-fascism was not a crime and it was about time the police stopped treating it as such. It was obvious to everyone the mood was getting uglier and there were renewed scuffles between anti-fascists and police. UAF chanted "**Whose streets? Our streets!**" as missiles were thrown at the police and some anti-fascists started a fire. A large group again tried to break out of the compound and anti-fascists chanted "**shame on you!**" as police battled to contain them. A smoke bomb was thrown into the neutral section, shrouding the war memorial in smoke. Appeals for calm were made by the police over a public address system.

Assistant Chief Constable Shewan said GMP would use all resources available to them to address the disorder. He urged protestors to work with police, not against them, and warned that as it was no longer a peaceful protest, action would be taken if necessary. GMP told the press they were concerned that anti-fascist '**cheerleaders**' were inflaming the crowd and as Rhetta Moran of Manchester UAF started to address the counter-protest, she was seized by police officers and arrested.

UAF leaders started to chant "**this is not a riot**", through their PA system and told the media they were angry at police heavy handedness. Anti-fascists, some holding '**Stop the BNP**' placards, repeatedly surged forward as police struggled to control them. GMP said that some UAF supporters seemed determined to cause trouble. Anti-fascists taunted the police and small holes appeared in the crowd, where police reacted and deployed dog-handlers. A UAF speaker announced "**the police are trying to instigate a riot**" as yet another police snatch-squad waded into the crowd. An attempt to snatch Weyman Bennett was foiled as anti-fascists wrestled him from the clutches of police.

The Crompton Place Shopping Centre was forced to close its doors as rival groups clashed outside. Again, as in Leeds and Manchester, the working class street-fighters of the EDL were seemingly having the better of the exchanges. It appeared to be a poor turn-out for the EDL, but a large number were now reported to be making their way down Newport Street toward the site. ACC Shewan announced he was pleased with the conduct of the EDL up to that point.

The EDL in Victoria Square suddenly appeared to leave the square. Seeing this, UAF cheered wildly as the EDL seemingly retreated. Anti-fascists started chanting **"No Pasaran!"** They had defeated the Nazis! They were jubilant, celebrating victory and started singing **"We shall not be moved!"**

However, their joy proved somewhat premature, as chants of **"Muslim bombers off our streets!"** could suddenly be heard getting gradually louder. The EDL in the square had merely gone to meet a snaking mass of their comrades who, with a police escort, were slowly making their way to the square. They had been led slowly through the streets of Bolton towards the protest site, a line of stewards and riot police checking their advance and some locals applauding them on their way.

The column stalled briefly before being allowed to enter the square and the chant of **"E, E, EDL!"** filled the air. Finally released by police, the EDL roared like a triumphant army as they entered the arena. The anti-fascists were dumbstruck, as an immense, noisy, flag waving, swarming mass of patriots flooded towards them.

These were the forgotten people, the sons and daughters of old England, here to reclaim their birthright. A mass of coloured flags filled the square, as it was reclaimed in the name of the English people. Here were the descendants of people who built the modern world, their battle flag rich with exotic names from far flung shores. Now more familiar sounding names were being added, Birmingham, Manchester, Leeds, London and now Bolton. There were well over 1500 of them, all chanting in unison and drowning out the chants of the anti-fascists. It was pure, crude and brutal Anglo-Saxon defiance. They had a simple message for their opponents, two fingers. We will not submit.

Bolton's war memorial stood proudly between the two groups, bearing the legend **'Tell ye your children'**. The entrance alone was a victory in itself, the surprise of anti-fascists was palpable. They had severely misjudged the EDL's level of support. As they confronted the anti-fascists the EDL mocked them with chants of **"who are ya, who are ya?"** More EDL were approaching the demo site, some were being escorted down Bradshawgate and police rushed to Newport Street to meet another large group. It was a massive turnout, the biggest to date. Some smaller groups of UAF and Asian youths were trying to prevent the EDL getting to the square, one group in Oxford Street tried to form a physical barrier across the road.

There was scuffling at the foot of the Town Hall steps and riot police pulled out more UAF including, this time, Bennett. UAF press officer, Anindya Bhattacharyya, said a dozen riot police had charged in and grabbed Bennett and Martin Smith had also been arrested. With Smith and Bennett out of action it was left to Paul Holborow to address the crowd. Holborow is a veteran anti-fascist and spoke about **'victory for our side in Bolton'**.

One EDL supporter, speaking to the BBC's Ben Anderson, said: **"I think the UAF are wrong. The way they shout Nazi, Nazi, Nazi scum at us, we're not Nazis, we're English people. There's nothing here for us. The people and the working class, white Englishmen of this country, a lot of us out of work, millions of us out of work, we're not being listened to. The mainstream political parties aren't listening to us, we're poor, we're stuck in poverty, it's a poverty trap. All we want is work, and that's all we want. We've got no voice; the country is dying a death. I don't want to say anymore because I'm getting emotional"**.

EDL stewards clashed with their supporters as they tried to lift a barrier separating them from UAF. Another group broke away from the protest but were stopped by police as they attempted to head down Deansgate. GMP said they now estimated there were 1500 UAF and in excess of 2000 EDL present. There was a confrontation at the railway station, as Asian youths and a small number of anti-fascists took on a group of EDL who hadn't made it to protest site. Problems were also reported around the Market Place, as opposing gangs clashed and trouble also erupted on Deane Road.

Bolton was a battleground. GMP's Garry Shewan said he was determined to identify offenders and bring them to justice. *Socialist Worker* reported that young Asians had been prevented from attending the counter-protest by police. However, around 3.00pm, a large body of Asian men joined the UAF ranks. When the Asians appeared, police in charge on the ground decided it was time to call a halt to the day's proceedings. Officers in riot gear started to force the EDL out of the square. Two men were arrested as the EDL reacted to the rough treatment. The EDL continued to clash with police as they were forced away from the square. Further clashes occurred around the town centre into the evening as groups of EDL encountered roaming gangs of Asian youths.

Following the protest Garry Shewan said police had attempted to facilitate a peaceful protest but some groups of people, predominantly associated with UAF, had engaged in '**violent confrontation**'. It was clear to him he said, that a large number had attended with the sole intention of committing disorder which was wholly unacceptable. He claimed the anti-fascists had turned their anger onto police, acted with extreme violence and their actions had led to injuries to officers, protestors and members of the public. In advertently rubbing salt into the wounds of UAF, Shewan praised the efforts of the EDL stewards, who he said had worked with GMP in the face of some very ugly confrontations.

The BBC announced that Weyman Bennett had been charged with conspiracy to organise violent disorder and that at least 74 other people had also been arrested. Following his release, Bennett insisted he was innocent and had been seized by officers while protesting peacefully. Claiming he had attended over 200 demos and had never been arrested, Bennett said there was no evidence against him and his arrest was not a good sign for democracy. Adding that officers had informed him as soon as he had arrived they would arrest him, Bennett said that GMP were hostile to anti-racists and there should be an investigation, because police neutrality needed to be questioned. Rhetta Moran of UAF, who like Bennett had been arrested on suspicion of inciting violent disorder, was also bailed on the condition she did not attend any EDL or UAF gatherings.

UAF spokesman, Bartley Wilcox said they had not seen anything like it since the 1930s. Back then, he claimed, the police had protected Oswald Mosley and attacked anti-fascists in the same manner they had in Bolton. UAF published video footage of 89 year-old anti-fascist Bertie Lewis, who was allegedly knocked down by police as they made an arrest. In response, GMP released a video of the protest showing UAF attempting to break through barriers. Deputy Chief Constable Simon Byrne said the safety of protestors, police and members of the public had been the primary concern of officers and the incident involving Mr Lewis was regrettable. Byrne stressed that the footage was unclear but would be reviewed as a matter of course, but added that police had been faced with aggression and it was clear a large number of people had gone to Bolton to cause disorder. He strongly refuted allegations that his officers were heavy handed and said had it not been for thorough planning and the bravery of officers, many more people could have been very seriously injured.

Eight months later, it was announced that officers who arrested a UAF protester in Bolton were being investigated by the Independent Police Complaints Commission (IPCC). Charges of threatening behaviour against the man, 63 year old Alan Clough, were dropped after footage emerged which showed police attacking him. IPCC Commissioner Naseem Malik said that the footage of Clough's arrest had been aired in the media and had caused public concern; therefore it was in the public interest that the IPCC investigated the incident. The investigation would examine the level of force used on Clough and the apparent difference between the footage and accounts given by police officers involved.

Chief Superintendent Dave Keller of GMP said they would thoroughly investigate the matter and appropriate action would be taken if any officer was found to have acted inappropriately. In the wake of the collapse of the Clough case, the charges of conspiracy to incite violent disorder against both Weyman Bennett and Rhetta Moran were dropped by Greater Manchester Police.

The EDL had now had two successful, peaceful demonstrations, the stewarding system had seemingly worked well and relations between EDL supporters and police had been largely good. The EDL released a statement claiming UAF must be embarrassed about Bolton, because all anti-fascists had wanted to do was have a punch up. When they had not obliged them, the EDL claimed UAF had started on the police. Milking it for all it was worth, the group claimed that EDL supporters were still socialising in local pubs when they heard news of the UAF charging police lines. The group claimed their reaction was akin to the '**cool and considered response of Sir Francis Drake when he heard about the Spanish Armada. They continued to slowly drink their pints and continue with their conversations**'.

The EDL did, slightly naively, complain about coverage of the demo by the BBC and said the coverage the channel gave the event seemed to be '**conveyed through clenched teeth**' since it did not have anything of substance with which it could criticise the EDL with. The group also announced that it had expelled two members, following what it called a personal attack on Guramit Singh. The EDL claimed that racist comments had been made to Singh and they would not tolerate personal attacks on any EDL members. This was obviously an attempt to weed out racists but the rule forbidding criticism of people in the movement could and would be utilised in the future to suppress dissent regarding certain decisions made by the leadership.

Casuals United announced a WDL demonstration for Cardiff in June, which was planned to coincide with a Welsh international rugby match. It was hoped that large numbers of Welsh rugby fans with painted faces and flags would overwhelm any action by UAF. An EDL demo at Harrow Mosque was also announced by Casuals United, but never intended to happen. Casuals were seemingly enjoying the fact they could announce something and receive an immediate reaction from anti-fascists and the media. Casuals United also announced it would also start to directly target UAF meetings.

The March meeting of the National Union of Journalists, London Photographers Branch (LPB) condemned what it called '**the targeting of journalists**'. The group said that members who regularly covered EDL protests faced threats and violence, claiming several journalists had been physically attacked at the Stoke on Trent protest. The LPB also claimed that threats had been sent by email warning journalists not to document protests, and pictures of photographers had appeared on both EDL and Casuals United websites.

In response, the EDL claimed the pictures were merely intended to make supporters aware of people they believed were deliberately misrepresenting them. It should've been obvious to the media, and soon would be to UAF, that a working class group like the EDL would confront people who were going out of their way to, they believed, unfairly discredit them. It wasn't so much because these people were journalists, supplying the material for anti-EDL articles in the press, it was the simple fact they were considered communists, reds. There was a strong belief within the EDL that even though not ruled directly by the far-left, a covert communist agenda had been surreptitiously introduced and was followed to the letter in a country subsequently paralysed by political correctness. The EDL had started to see the left-wing as the enemy, as much as any Islamist group was. It was hardly surprising, as the left, especially the trade union movement, regularly turned out against them.

Proving the point, at the end of March, the EDL released a statement which said that although they realised that unions had a part to play in protecting workers' rights, they had become too influential and too militant in the political sphere. This, claimed the EDL, was where vested interests infringed upon a democratic political platform, so much so that democracy seemed to be ebbing away and being replaced with communism. Great Britain didn't do communism said the EDL, it never had, yet the communists of the unions were afforded even more influence as the ruling Labour Party looked to fund its upcoming election campaign.

4 April 2010: Dudley

Dudley is a large town close to Birmingham in the West Midlands. The town is part of an area called the Black Country, so called because of the pollution created by the heavy manufacturing which had taken place in the area. From as early as the 1700s, the Black Country became known as a centre for metalwork and eventually became one of the most heavily industrialised regions of the UK.

Along with the other manufacturing regions of the UK, during the 1970s and 80s the area experienced a sharp decline in demand for the goods it produced. Thousands of works and factories, scattered amongst the residential areas which had grown up around them, have slowly disappeared. Even so, locals still feel attached to their industrial heritage, as was shown in 2010, when hundreds of people turned out to see a replica of the anchor of the liner *Titanic* being returned to nearby

Netherton, where the original was made. It was an obvious chance for people to tell their children, **"this is what we did - we really were the best in the world"**.

Following WWII, Dudley welcomed an influx of newcomers from the Commonwealth, including a large number of Pakistani Muslims from Kashmir. They were attracted by the many opportunities of employment Dudley then offered and settled in the Kates Hill and Buffery Park areas of the town.

Dudley witnessed some of Britain's first race riots in July 1962, when dozens of white men rioted in the North Street area of the town where a number of West Indian immigrants had settled. In September 1991, another riot took place in Kates Hill, which saw clashes between white and Asian youths.

In 2003, Dudley Muslim Association (DMA) announced plans for a new mosque on a site in Hall Street in the Kates Hill area of the town, obtained in a land-swap deal with Dudley Council, claiming the existing mosque had outgrown its present home on Castle Hill. Local planners initially rejected the plans on the grounds that the location was prime industrial land and should be set aside to create jobs. Dudley Council turned down further plans in 2007, after a petition opposing the scheme raised 22,000 signatures and demonstrations were staged by local people. The DMA took their fight to a public inquiry and a government planning inspector granted the appeal.

Local opposition to the mosque, set to be built in a prominent location overlooking the town, had been strong. It was felt the ordinary people of Dudley were being ignored, so the EDL decided it should take up their case. Announcing the demonstration, an EDL spokesman told the *Dudley News* that the group was targeting the town because laws had been bypassed to placate one section of the community over the concerns of another.

The proposed demonstration faced the usual opposition from local politicians. Conservative Anne Millward, Labour's David Sparks, Liberal-Democrat Dave Tyler and Malcolm Davis of UKIP all signed a statement, published in the *Black Country Express & Star*, calling on the EDL to abandon its protest. Malcolm Davis, who had been a vocal opponent of the proposed mosque, told the paper that the EDL was not welcome. He said the group had sent him an email, thinking he would support them, but he didn't. Davis said he suspected the group was targeting Dudley because they thought there was a problem, but there wasn't as far as he was concerned. Davis said he still opposed the building of the mosque, but the town was dealing with it in its own way and didn't need '**violent outsiders**'. Adding that he expected trouble, the councillor said he hoped local people kept away from the protest and let the police deal with it. Council leader Millward said that shops in the town would be closed for the day and the council and police would be asking town centre pubs to close. Millward also criticised UAF for organising a counter-protest, calling their plans '**highly irresponsible**'.

UAF, reeling from the EDL's successes in London and Bolton, announced they would not directly oppose the EDL this time and instead, would hold a '**celebration of diversity**' on the other side of town, scheduled to start three hours before the EDL demonstration. UAF spokesman, Martin Lynch, told the *Express and Star* that they didn't think the EDL should be allowed to protest in Dudley, or anywhere else for that matter.

Prior to the demonstration the EDL issued a statement, highlighting the fact that during the last two demonstrations, out of 132 arrests, only 10 of those had been EDL, the remaining 122 were anti-fascists. In a message to members the group reiterated that '**nil arrests**' was the goal: '**Sometimes, the real strength of man is when he holds his temper when faced with an enemy. And the strategy of peaceful protest is working marvellously well. Violence plays into the hands of our enemies, which is why our enemies are trying to goad us**'. The statement added that to ensure a peaceful demonstration took place in Dudley, some sensible systems of crowd control had been agreed with police. There were to be pre-arranged muster points for the demo and activists would walk from these, with a police escort, to the demonstration site. The EDL also announced that if the '**voice of the people**' was ignored they would return to Dudley every four weeks, until the plans for the mosque were scrapped.

Three days before the demo, on Wednesday 31 March, West Midlands Police issued a message to EDL supporters on the force's website. Police said their priority was the safety of the public and protestors, therefore the policing operation would be '**robust and decisive**'. WMP was committed, said the statement, to upholding the democratic right of the EDL to air their beliefs, but only if they did so peacefully. Two days before the protest, anti-Nazi slogans were daubed in and around Dudley town centre. A 16 year-old local UAF activist was arrested. Officers recovered various items from his house including UAF leaflets and SWP membership forms.

On the morning of the protest, Chief Inspector Mark Payne said WMP had made arrests overnight to deal with '**some people who might be placing additional heat on the demonstration**.' Payne said the arrests were an early indication that WMP would not tolerate anything other than a peaceful protest, adding that reports of damage to a local mosque were completely untrue.

The UAF rally was the usual mix of left-wingers and a handful of local Asian people (in some areas of Dudley Asian youths were taken on daytrips organised by the council to prevent them joining the counter-protest). There were a few trade union banners on show, though police had removed the poles and had also confiscated any placards on sticks. As the event got underway, a succession of speakers raised points about alleged police brutality in Bolton. Martin Smith said UAF would not be criminalised and that the EDL were a bunch of "**football hooligans, united only by their vicious hatred of Muslims**". As the speeches were being made, EDL were rumoured to have been spotted nearby, leading to a small number of people breaking away to confront them. UAF Stewards struggled to keep the gathering together, especially when more rumours began to circulate, this time that the EDL were marching to Netherton. The stewards insisted these were lies spread by agent-provocateurs attempting to split the demonstration.

The EDL demo was being held on the Constitution Hill car-park, overlooked by the site of the proposed mosque. Coaches were parked up on a specially closed dual-carriageway half a mile from the site and police held their occupants on the road while they waited for others to arrive. The police were taking a relaxed attitude, some officers told activists that the EDL had assured them that they would be peaceful and if they were, they would have no problems. Once all the coaches had arrived, the march to the demo site began. Around 1000 people, singing and chanting, slowly made their way up the dual-carriageway flanked by police. Activists carried placards with slogans such as '**Open your eyes for your children's sake**', '**Dudley we will not desert you**' and '**No-one wants this mosque**'.

A police officer with a loud hailer informed the EDL that anyone covering their faces would face arrest. As the marchers arrived at the top of the hill, they saw that the site already contained around a thousand people. There was a huge local turnout, some Dudley inhabitants said they had been waiting years for something like this, ordinary people felt they had a voice again. Like Bolton, ordinary people had again turned out in because a movement which finally addressed at least some of their concerns was in town. The marchers from the coaches were absorbed into the crowd at the demo site, which was completely surrounded by temporary metal fencing.

The first speakers took to the stage, one a young Asian woman in her early 20s, the other a young black male with dreadlocks. The female addressed the crowd: "**either we are pro-British or not. If not, it's time for you to leave the country**". She went on to address the issue of first-cousin marriages in Islamic communities and the impact of the call to prayer from some mosques, which she described as "**noise pollution**". The crowd roared its approval and her black companion raised his fist in the air to salute them. Following the speech there was a commotion at the back of the car park where rows of riot police were stationed. Police had been spotted running away from the site and rumours quickly spread that a gang of Asian youths were on their way. Hundreds of people surged to the fences to confront the suspected threat. Speakers from the stage pleaded with the crowd, "**The speeches are here this is where the demonstration is, come back!**" The mood however, had visibly changed.

There were scuffles between the EDL and police, but officers managed to stop them leaving the site and some sort of order was regained. It didn't last long however, the EDL crowd surged again, this time to the opposite corner of the site. A large angry mob bayed at both the police and press stationed behind the barriers. Amid the chaos, a man climbed a lamp-post and attached two EDL placards to it. Suddenly, a group of anti-fascists were spotted running down the dual carriageway towards the site from the direction of Kates Hill. In response to this, the EDL surged towards the fences, pushing and pulling them, while police battled to hold them in place. One of the fences was eventually toppled and people flooded through the gap. Police battled to contain the leak, but the EDL overwhelmed them and flooded through, scattering in all directions. Most headed in pursuit of the anti-fascists, who seeing the EDL surge through the fences were now in full flight. One breakaway group of EDL emerged close to the site of the counter-demo and were confronted by a large number of Muslim youths. The groups clashed, hurling missiles at each other, but were quickly dispersed by riot police.

WMP arrested nine people, five for possession of offensive weapons, two for public order offences and two for criminal damage. Officers were also investigating alleged thefts from local shops and some reports of criminal damage. Police estimated around 2000 EDL supporters had attended the protest and that around 1500 had attended the UAF counter-demo. Assistant Chief Constable Suzette Davenport said that their priority would always be the safety of the public and protesters, whilst ensuring events like this did not 'impact on the stability of Dudley's communities'.

EDL spokesman Steve Simmons said the trouble had started after bricks were thrown into the demo site, which had agitated the crowd and made them surge forward. He claimed people intent on trouble had infiltrated the protest and praised police for the way they had kept the opposing sides apart. Simmons added that although they had spent three days discussing the protest, some things hadn't gone to plan and they needed to address that. Dudley Borough Council announced that both protests had cost around £400,000 to police and said the EDL had caused £150,000 worth of damage. Speaking to the *Sunday Mercury*, Stephen Lennon apologised for the disruption and cost, but said he felt people would thank them in the long run. Lennon said the EDL just wanted their chance to have their objections heard. The paper said that the cost to individual councils for each EDL protest was estimated at £150,000 and the total bill to date for all EDL protests was £1.95million.

In the week following the demonstration, Malcolm Davis, who had originally opposed the visit of the EDL, issued an open letter regarding the protest. In the letter, the councillor admitted he had opposed the EDL, but after, against his wishes, his sons had attended the demonstration, he now defended the group and said the trouble was mere frustration at being herded like animals. However, not everyone shared the view of Davis. During a visit to Dudley during the General Election campaign, Conservative leader David Cameron said if his party won the election he would look at banning groups such as the EDL: 'The EDL are terrible people, we would always keep these groups under review and if we needed to ban them, we would ban them or any groups which incite hatred'.

Rumours of far-right infiltration followed the Dudley protest, with some EDL supporters incorrectly claiming that the trouble had been started by Nazis. The accusations forced the leadership to issue a statement warning EDL supporters of approaches from far-right nationalists who might attempt to recruit them. The statement said that National Socialism was a violent, racist ideology akin to Islam. In fact, claimed the statement, Nazism and Islamism were opposite sides of the same coin; as both were supremacist in nature, ideologically intolerant of people who didn't conform, and both had an inherent hatred of Jews. The group made it clear that it supported Israel's right to exist and welcomed anyone, regardless of race, religion, colour or creed into their ranks as long as they shared the aims of the EDL. They said that Nazis had no place in the EDL and the leadership wanted any exposed and ejected. The statement added that the grandparents of EDL supporters had waged a long war against the Nazis, so people could enjoy the freedoms they enjoyed today. Were it not for the blood sacrifice of their ancestors, said the EDL, people in the UK would now be speaking German.

Two weeks after the protest, Birmingham newspaper, the *Sunday Mercury*, led with the exclusive 'EDL leader Tommy Robinson unmasked'. Accompanying the article was a picture of Lennon, clad in a hood, his face partially revealed. The *Mercury* had interviewed Lennon on the eve of the Dudley protest and after identifying him, had employed a photographer with a zoom lens to photograph him during the demo. It was the first time many people, including many EDL supporters, had actually seen Lennon, as he had hidden his identity up to now by wearing balaclavas or face-masks. When questioned by *BBC News* as to why he hid his identity, Lennon said it was because he lived in a multicultural area and was worried for the safety of his family should his identity become known. Strangely, his unmasking was largely ignored, or even missed, by the rest of the press and the anti-fascist movement.

Days later, the EDL were blamed for hijacking a St George's Day parade in Ruislip, Middlesex, after rioting broke out in the town. Up to 500 people had gathered outside The Bell pub to enjoy a barbecue, live music and the arrival of a parade from RAF Northolt, when trouble began and two groups started fighting. At one point it was estimated between 70 and 80 people were involved. A police officer, who had responded to the incident, said many of the troublemakers were wearing EDL polo shirts. There had not been any violence at the event before and the landlord of the Bell, blamed '**outsiders**' for the disturbance.

Turning the Tables

There was an obvious anti-communist sentiment emerging amongst EDL activists. The various communist groups which attached themselves to the anti-fascist movement were seen as upholding a system which had been covertly imposed on the British people. Rank and file EDL members were keen to diversify the struggle against the reds and it was only a matter of time before anti-fascists were targeted away from demonstrations. It was a favoured tactic of the left-wing but they seemed totally unprepared for it happening to them.

EDL activists were attending SWP/UAF meetings as early as October 2009. Then plans were put in place to picket the UAF AGM in London in February 2010. That provoked some debate within the EDL as some thought UAF was an irrelevance and that the real enemy were the Islamists. Others however, believed that white middle class communism was the real enemy, as they enforced the current two-tier system, which facilitated the existence of militant Islam. Football hooligans involved in the EDL also wanted to give UAF a taste of their own medicine, the fact UAF was claiming to be winning the battle was reason enough. It was a football hooligan mentality, looking for weaknesses, taking your opponent's end, taking liberties, humiliating and defeating them. Because of the working class roots of the EDL, this mindset would be automatically adopted by the majority within the movement.

On Wednesday 17 March 2010, EDL activists targeted a UAF meeting which Weyman Bennett was due to attend in Temple Meads, Bristol. It was intended to build support for the campaign against the EDL. Activists from the south-west infiltrated the gathering, but to their disappointment Bennett had pulled out at the last minute. As the meeting got under way, one of them stood up and announced that he was a member of the EDL. There was an audible gasp from the room as the three letters were uttered. The EDL activist asked the anti-fascists why they were campaigning against the EDL, when they weren't fascists; they were people who simply opposed militant Islam. There was uproar, and as more EDL made themselves known, insults flew between the two groups, with some people angrily facing up to each other.

The EDL activist tried to speak again but each time he did the anti-fascists shouted "**fascist**" and "**Nazi**" at him. The other EDL present objected, asking "**what about free speech?**" The man then informed the meeting that as well as being a member of the EDL, he was also a member of the Armed Forces. After that admission, the anti-fascists refused to let him say another word and the meeting ended in chaos as police officers entered the room. The EDL were told to leave, even though it was a public meeting, as the organisers didn't want them there. As they left, scuffles broke out once more between the two sides. With true dramatic licence, but obviously bearing in mind that people confronting communists with opposing views must be a truly traumatic experience, on the UAF website one anti-fascist claimed '**it was one of the most frightening experiences of my life**'.

Days later, EDL activists attended a UAF meeting in Manchester. The meeting was over and most anti-fascists had left by the time they arrived, but a few remaining in the building were said to have been terrified by the sudden appearance of the EDL, who unsuccessfully tried to gain access to the building. EDL from the north-east also disrupted a UAF meeting in Newcastle, again convened to discuss how to defeat the EDL. Their appearance caused a heated confrontation and the meeting was eventually called off. UAF, like the SWP, advertised its meetings, simply because they wanted as many people as possible to attend and buy newspapers. Unfortunately more EDL and Casuals now wanted to attend the meetings than people interested in Marxism.

A meeting of the far-left Northern Indymedia Collective was also cancelled following phone calls to Leeds University where it was being held. Anti-fascists called the cancellation a '**pathetic cave-in by the university**' but also noted that it was a '**worrying development from the EDL**'.

The EDL also had fast-food giant Kentucky Fried Chicken (KFC) in its sights. KFC had started halal trials in certain areas. Halal means permitted under Sharia, the opposite of haram, which means forbidden. *Dhabihah* is the method of slaughter employed under Sharia, where animals are not pre-stunned and slaughter involves a deep cut to the neck with a sharp knife, whilst religious tracts are recited.

In 2003, the Farm Animal Welfare Council claimed that the manner in which halal (and Jewish kosher) meat was processed caused severe suffering to animals. The Rev Patrick Sookhdeo, head of the Barnabas Fund, which helps for Christians facing persecution, said some extremist Muslims viewed the spread of halal food as a partial success in their efforts to impose Sharia on the West.

In 2007, supermarket giant ASDA announced halal trials in some stores. Two years later, major fast-food chains KFC, Subway and Domino's, made some of their restaurants halal-only. Domino's Pizza was one of the first, with halal-only trials in three of its stores, Birmingham, Bradford and Blackburn. These outlets were targeted by the EDL and activists were urged to phone the store and '**ask them why you can't have pepperoni**'. Another tactic was to enter stores, order food, and then when it arrived ask if it was halal. If the reply was to the affirmative, activists would then say they didn't want it as they considered the associated ritual slaughter as animal cruelty. Casuals United claimed that behind these trials were Muslim companies who wanted to '**secure employment for their people in the halal meat industry**'.

The KFC campaign started in earnest on 6 April 2010. A KFC store in Newport, South Wales was targeted by telephone. The number of the shop was widely distributed and activists were urged to phone them as '**they're getting really annoyed now**'. A week later, on 15 April 2009, EDL activists from the north-west disrupted a KFC managers meeting held at Bewley's Hotel in Manchester Airport. EDL activists from Preston, Blackburn, Middleton and Stockport burst into the meeting to complain about KFC's halal trials. They were met with around fifteen rather bemused members of KFC middle-management. The EDL fired questions at the KFC representatives but were met with a wall of silence. Annoyed by the lack of reaction, one EDL supporter warned the managers: "**We will come to all your meetings. We will find you, no matter where you go.**"

Other actions against the company's stores around the country followed. The EDL Blackburn Division would also stage a demonstration outside a KFC outlet in the town. Police said up to 27 people took part and no arrests were made, but a local newspaper reported that several EDL supporters were kicked off the retail park by security officers for drinking cans of lager. On the same day as the Blackburn protest, a group calling itself Our England Today staged a demonstration outside a KFC restaurant in Deepdale, Preston.

An event by Love Music Hate Racism was organised for 17 April 2010, at a venue called Mozart's in Swansea. EDL activists rang the venue to voice their opposition to the concert. Later that day, it was announced the event had been cancelled because of threats made to the venue should it have gone ahead. EDL and Casuals United activists were overjoyed at the thought of organiser Martin Smith having to refund the money for tickets sold. In what was an unprecedented action against UAF, meetings at O'Neil's in Swansea and Camden Town Hall in London were also targeted and subsequently cancelled during this period.

On 22 April 2010, the city of Bristol hosted the second in a series of televised General Election leaders debates. The EDL announced that activists would be attending '**divisions from across the south-west are mobilising to make our voices heard and let this Government know the British public will no longer stand by and watch the rampant Islamification of our country. Various other groups including the UAF and SWP will be there. Lots of national and local press will also be there. Let's make this a big one. We will never surrender, long live the free!**'

The debate was held at the Arnolfini Centre in Bristol. The communists and anarchists who were also proposing to protest were split over the EDL being in attendance. Some said they would oppose the EDL; others were of the opinion that the group would be a distraction for the police and enhance the chance of their own protest being effective. Around 15-20 EDL met at the Shakespeare Tavern, close to the Arnolfini Centre. They were immediately surrounded by police, and followed whilst they toured the pubs in the area. They were vocal and visible, standing outside the pubs singing, which prompted a few minor clashes with left-wingers. The EDL eventually infiltrated the left-wing protest in Queen Square and immediately clashed with the communists. Police entered the crowd and escorted the EDL out. A number of communists attempted to follow them and there were further scuffles. Although the EDL were outnumbered, the, mainly middle class, communists were wary and wouldn't fully commit to an attack. Mounted police and dog-handlers were deployed to keep the groups apart.

Following the protest, Avon and Somerset Police announced they had arrested nine men in total on suspicion of affray. Ian Bone, of Anarchist group Class War, claimed to have been present. He saw the events as a victory for anti-fascists and a turning point for them on the streets. Bone also claimed some EDL were hospitalised, however, there were no reports of anyone being hospitalised, by either police or press.

1 May 2010: Aylesbury

Aylesbury is an affluent, middle class market town approximately 40 miles from London, with a population of around 65,000. There are approximately 6-7000 Muslims in the town, mainly from Kashmir, Pakistan and Bangladesh. The town has a small but growing Muslim community, it has one mosque, built 25 years ago, which the Muslim community claims is now too small for its requirements. The local Mosque Association has purchased a building which it intends to turn into an Islamic Culture and Community Centre, subject to approval by the local council.

The town has been linked to Islamic militancy in the past. Bilal Abdulla, the doctor who drove the Jeep full of gas canisters and petrol into the Glasgow Airport terminal building was born in Aylesbury. Also, 7/7 bomber Germaine Lindsay was living in the town when he took part on the attack on London.

Prior to the protest, a row erupted at a liaison meeting between the EDL, police and Aylesbury council. To prevent any encounters with counter-demonstrators, council officials had hoped to keep the EDL on the outskirts of town before the rally in Market Square. They also said that the EDL needed a licence to put up a stage and use loud-speakers and would not allow them to carry wooden framed banners to the protest. Following the row, Lennon told the *Bucks Herald* that the EDL was now planning to evade police and instead gather in Vale Park, where the anti-fascist demonstration was being held. Lennon also said that if the demonstration didn't go how they wanted it to, they'd be back in six weeks, adding that no other local authority had tried to block the EDL like Aylesbury had.

On the eve of the demo, a Muslim protester who daubed graffiti on a war memorial in Burton on Trent, proclaiming '**Islam will dominate the world**' walked free from court after it was ruled his actions were not motivated by religion. Tohseef Shah, 21, who had also daubed '**Osama is on his way**' and '**Kill Gordon Brown**' on the walls of the memorial, would have faced a tougher sentence if the court had accepted that the insults were inspired by religious hatred. The Crown Prosecution Service decided not to pursue a conviction for religious hatred because no particular religious or racial group was targeted, but instead prosecuted him for criminal damage. After pleading guilty, Shah was given a two-year conditional discharge and ordered to pay £500 compensation.

Korean War veteran, Roy Whenman, 78, told the *Daily Mail*: '**If what he wrote on the memorial wasn't evidence of racial or religious hatred then what is? The memorial commemorates people of my generation who died for our freedom as well as those fighting in wars today. It's diabolical that someone could deface it in this way.**' Shah, who was believed to be a member of a group called Road to Jannah, refused to speak to the press. A man called Abdullah Ibn Abbas, who described himself as the spiritual leader of the group, told the *Daily Mail*: '**It really doesn't concern us how the British people feel about the graffiti he wrote. The real outrage should be about the thousands of Muslims who are being killed and butchered as a result of British foreign policy.**'

The case highlighted the very reason the EDL were on the streets. There was a total disrespect for British culture, customs and values. The memory of fallen servicemen and women, who had made the ultimate sacrifice in the service of the country (as sacred to English patriots as any religious doctrine) was being openly attacked. This was another in a long line of insults being heaped upon the British people which the establishment did nothing to stop. In fact, they encouraged it by bending backwards to accommodate and excuse the people perpetrating outrage after outrage. It was another example of the two-tier legal system in Britain, as Judge Carolyn Mellanby's decision to ignore accepted procedure had already shown. It was however, impeccable timing for the EDL. It was hoped that the news would add hundreds to the protest.

On the morning of the Aylesbury protest, there were the usual reports of violence. Superintendent Richard List of Thames Valley Police said there had been rumours circulating with regards to people being assaulted in the town, but no such incidents had taken place. List said that it would be a challenging day as a national issue was played out on their local stage. Aylesbury Vale District Council said that local bus services would be cancelled, local taxis were also not operating for a 24-hour period and pubs in the area would be shut throughout day.

By 11.00am, EDL coaches could be seen entering the town and a large police operation began. Officers were drafted in from as far away as Hampshire and South Wales to assist and a police helicopter hovered overhead as mounted officers made their way into town. The first (and last) coach carrying anti-fascists arrived in Vale Park. It contained members of Oxford LMHR and Buckinghamshire UNISON members. Steve Bell of UNISON insisted it was not a counter-protest; and said if the EDL wanted a confrontation they would withdraw.

Police sat waiting in riot vans on Fleet Street and numerous officers guarded the area around the local mosque. All street furniture had been removed and the statues in Market Square protected with hoardings. By 1.00pm, Market Square was closed with members of the public escorted out of the area by police. There were hundreds of EDL already in town, some had bought beer from local supermarkets and wandered the streets drinking. There were EDL in most of the local pubs and a group stood outside the Bricklayers Arms chanting. At 2.15pm, a *Bucks Herald* reporter estimated that the crowd in Market Square now numbered in their thousands, with still more arriving. Police moved quickly to quash rumours that Aylesbury Mosque had been attacked and insisted there had been no serious disorder. By 2.45pm there were around 1800 EDL in Market square, chanting **"where's your famous UAF?"** They had all gone home; the counter-protest had only attracted 75 activists and was well over by this point.

Some EDL protestors climbed on top of a statue in the Square and a Cross of St George was put on Baron Chesham. Another boxed-off statue was utilised as an impromptu stage and an announcer for the EDL, draped in an Israeli flag, declared they would hold a two minutes silence for Britain's war dead. Following the demo, some supporters questioned if the servicemen, and civilians, killed in atrocities during British Mandate Palestine by Jewish terrorists were included in the silence. It was an issue which would continue to rumble on.

Following the silence and speeches, some EDL activists attempted to leave the protest site. Scuffles broke out between them and police outside the Cloisters Shopping Centre. Around 200 protesters then tried to burst through police lines as officers armed with riot shields, batons and dogs battled to contain them. EDL supporters then began fighting amongst themselves, police didn't intervene and the trouble was quelled by other EDL. The crowd then returned their attention to the police and made another concerted effort to break out of the cordon. Finally, the police relaxed their grip and allowed the crowd to leave the square. They were then halted again in a car park area underneath the shopping centre. There were renewed clashes between the police and EDL and police announced they were disappointed the protest wasn't being staged peacefully. A police spokesman later told *The Telegraph* that the EDL had surged against police lines contrary to the wishes of their stewards. Some protestors finally managed to break through and spilled into the car-park of a local supermarket. More broke off down Exchange Street, as the police rapidly lost control. The EDL were left to wander around the town as police said they were now encouraging people to board their coaches and leave the area.

It was needless; the trouble was caused by the intransigence of the police in not being to be flexible enough to let people go home when they wanted to. There was no opposition, there had been no trouble up until that point, but time and time again the police would needlessly abuse the human rights of EDL supporters. It was very similar to the way English football fans are regularly treated by the police, with contempt.

Market Square was deserted, some small groups of EDL still played cat and mouse with police, but most had boarded their coaches for the homeward journey. Police arrested two EDL activists from Birmingham who they identified as being involved in the earlier disturbances. Police announced they had made twelve arrests in all, eight for possession of offensive weapons, three for public order and one for being drunk and disorderly. Thames Valley Police said that they had experienced a few problems and were disappointed that there was some public disorder towards the end of the protest, but there were no reported injuries to police or the public.

It was considered a peaceful demonstration by the EDL, but would be built up by the authorities during later trials of the two arrested Birmingham activists. In fact, there were more people injured (including 10 police officers) outside a clothing sale in Brick Lane on the same day as the Aylesbury demo.

2 May 2010: Dudley

The day after Aylesbury, the EDL suddenly announced that supporters had climbed onto the roof of a disused factory in Dudley, thought to be the site of the proposed mosque. The disused factory building was on former Goodyear Tyres land, next to the site of Alan Nuttall Ltd. The EDL said they were prepared to stay on the roof for a week and were equipped with tents and a public address system from which they would announce an Islamic call to prayer from the building, five times a day: '**Some of our supporters are at present barricaded on the roof of a derelict building near the site of the proposed £18m Mega Mosque in Dudley. They have food and water to last them weeks, and a PA system to give speeches. I believe they even have a Playstation! They will be playing the call to prayer to let those who are not bothered by this mosque know what to look forward to**'.

In the streets surrounding the derelict factory, Islamic music and calls to prayer could be heard coming from the roof. Police arrived and immediately closed all roads in the immediate area. Around 30 EDL had come to support the protest and scuffles broke out between them and local Asian youths who had congregated nearby. The police herded the EDL contingent into a car park outside the factory. Ever-increasing numbers of Asian men made repeated attempts to reach them whilst being repeatedly chased back by police dog handlers. Every time the Asian mob approached, the EDL on the roof played the call to prayer, warning their comrades below of their enemy's advance. This had the effect of inflaming the Asians all the more and they made increasingly frantic attempts to get to the factory. More police were drafted into the area and the Asian mob was finally dispersed. The police then issued the EDL with Section 27 Dispersal Orders, preventing them from returning to the area for 48 hours.

During the night, the activists on the roof were bombarded with missiles, as Asian youths repeatedly attempted to break police lines to get to them. Negotiators had made contact with the men on the roof and police were expressing concerns that the generator they were using was unsafe and '**likely to explode**'. The men ignored the warning and carried on with their protest.

The following morning, West Midlands Police announced they had sealed off an area of Dudley while an ongoing protest by members of the EDL took place. Police said they suspected there were four protestors on the roof, no arrests had been made but one local youth had been taken to hospital for minor injuries. Casuals United issued an update from the scene: '**According to sources on the ground large numbers of Muslims are on the streets and are likely to attack any whites they come across, be careful if attending**'.

Seemingly coincidentally, a story appeared in that day's edition of the *Express and Star*, claiming the plans for the proposed mosque had been scrapped. The paper claimed that the scheme had now been ditched by the DMA. Deputy leader of Dudley Borough Council, Les Jones, said that after months of '**delicate negotiations**' it had been agreed that DMA would redevelop the existing site in Castle Hill instead. Malcolm Davis said he was delighted with the outcome.

At midday, *Sky News* reported that groups of EDL had gathered in Dudley as the protest continued. The *Daily Mail* reported that four men dressed in balaclavas and army fatigues remained on the roof of an old clothing factory and that they had unfurled banners reading **'No to the Burka'** and **'No Mosque'**. Chief Inspector Matt Markham from West Midlands Police told the paper that WMP had always facilitated peaceful protests by the EDL, but they did not welcome this kind of demonstration. Markham said the message to anyone thinking of turning up with the intention of causing disorder, was not to bother, as WMP had resources available to deal with any disturbance **'swiftly and robustly'**.

Later that afternoon, at 3.40pm, the rooftop was stormed by police armed with tasers, who gained entry by smashing their way through the roof. EDL witnesses claimed the activists were assaulted as they were arrested and brought down. A spokesman for the EDL said that if there was any truth in the rumours the police had assaulted the men, then they wouldn't be liaising with them in future.

Following the arrests, the EDL who had gathered at ground level were dispersed by police. Violence then broke out in the town centre, as EDL supporters clashed with local Asian youths. Police were attacked with bricks during the incident and made eight arrests. WMP announced that they had brought a safe and peaceful conclusion to the protest. The force said they had successfully removed two men from the factory roof, who were currently helping them with their enquiries.

In response to the protest, Chairman of DMA, Dr Khurshid Ahmed, accused the EDL of **'un-English behaviour'** and of provoking religious hatred. Ahmed also said the truth about the mosque had been distorted for political ends and misinformation had been spread about the cost and scale of the project: **'This was not a protest – this was wilful incitement to religious hatred by playing that loud call-to-prayer. The people of Dudley have nine mosques and have never experienced a call as loud as that – or anywhere in Britain. Our call to prayer can only be heard within the parameters of the mosque'** The EDL called the doctor's accusations **'fallacious and deceptive rhetoric'** and issued a simple response: **'Don't ignore the will of Dudley people who NEVER wanted this mosque to be built!**

The day after the protest, the EDL claimed that the two arrested men, who they named as Leon from Stockport (who had led the protest at the KFC managers meeting) and Snowy from Yorkshire, had not yet had access to a solicitor. There were still complaints that the men had been roughly treated by police, so an impromptu protest was called. Supporters were told to head for the Bilston Road Police Station in Wolverhampton where the two men were being held. As activists answered the call, Chief Inspector Matt Markham dismissed the claims and said a lot of misinformation had been circulating on social networking sites. Markham confirmed that the two EDL members had been treated in accordance with the law and had been given access to legal advice in accordance with PACE (Police and Criminal Evidence Act).

Nonetheless, around 30 EDL from around the country, including Wolverhampton, Birmingham, Bolton, Derby, Dudley, Leicester, Liverpool and Manchester descended on the police station in the centre of Wolverhampton. Flags were draped over the railings in front of the station, as around eight police officers stood guard at the entrance. The crowd, joined by a few local members of the public, chanted in support of the two men and handed out leaflets to people getting off trams across the road. After about an hour, the police sealed off the road and officers assured the protestors that the men had seen a solicitor. A police EGT appeared, conspicuous by their orange epaulettes and started filming the EDL, some of whom had their faces covered. The protest was generally good-natured, but police did confiscate two cases of beer. At 10.30pm the protestors were informed that the two men would be appearing at Dudley Magistrates' Court the following morning and dispersed, many of them vowed to attend court the next day.

The following morning, in a van accompanied by police motorcycle outriders with sirens blaring, Snowy and Leon left Bilston Street Police Station for their appearance in court. Some EDL, who had mistakenly gone to Wolverhampton instead of Dudley, cheered as the convoy passed. Around 30 EDL gathered outside Dudley Magistrates' Court. Police were in attendance, with a couple of officers inside the court and two sitting in a patrol car over the road. The situation changed around 11.30am, shortly before the defendants were due to appear. Three van loads of police arrived, accompanied by a

Football Surveillance Vehicle equipped with rooftop camera. The police stayed in their vehicles and the observation van filmed the activists who had gathered outside court. Fifteen minutes later, an EDL supporter came out and announced that the two had been remanded in custody. He said they had appeared in a poor state, one with a broken arm while the other had a black eye. The pair would be back in court the following Monday, but this time via video-link from prison, possibly to prevent another EDL turn-out.

The *Dudley News* later named the two men as Leon McCreery, aged 28, from Stockport, Greater Manchester and 39-year-old John Shaw from Knaresborough, Yorkshire. They were accused of burglary and public order offences. The paper said that another man, aged 34, had also appeared before Dudley Magistrates Court the day before and had been bound over for a breach of the peace. Seven other men, aged between 16 and 34, had also been arrested for public order offences and remained on bail. The *Dudley News* also confirmed that plans for the mosque in Hall Street had been scrapped. Council Leader, Anne Millward, told the paper they had worked hard looking for an alternative to the Hall Street site. She claimed the site of the proposed mosque was prime employment land and was important for the creation of jobs.

McCreery and Shaw were quickly labelled the 'Dudley Two' and a fund to pay for their legal costs was established. McCreery issued a statement from prison:

'My EDL brothers and sisters, Snowy and I are being held as political prisoners, prisoners of corruptors and vested interests, we see just how deeply imbued politically correct idiocy reflects in the application of law by those who are supposed to uphold it. I would just like to say this to you my fellow patriots this is very important..... Although tensions are high and passions are flaring I ask you to remain calm in the face of adversity, through thick and thin the EDL must win this battle. Many have come to ruin us, and we say let them come we have nothing to hide or fear. Our enemy is not West Midlands Police it is the top brass who favour or at the very least, capitulate to the aggressive Muslim attitude on a street level. Caving into threats of rioting if we were not brought down from the roof and brought to justice as swiftly as possible. Caving into the political will of Islam. Charges of burglary are laughable as there was nothing in that derelict building worth stealing, it was already stripped out, people were squatting there and yet we have burgled it somehow? I had nothing in my possession that belonged in that building, so why the charge of burglary? I would have thought if they were to try and pin anything on me it would be "attempted burglary" so I'm not sure how these trumped up charges hold up in a court of law. The police for the most part have been very kind to us, they actually sympathise with us and quietly support us even, they know what we are fighting for. I bear no malice towards West Midlands Police as they are only doing what they are told to do.

Some of the prison guards are ex-military so again support for us is there, they know what we are doing, I bear no malice towards them either. The only police officer I can genuinely say I dislike is the one who broke my arm, he beat me when I did not resist arrest, I was not violent I was in fact very passive as I resigned myself to being arrested. It looks like certain individuals want to make me a martyr for this cause, but I still say to them I will never surrender! And finally, NO MORE MOSQUES IN DUDLEY! Time for people to make a stand, its time for the people of Dudley to be heard, no politician or Islamist dirt bag will take that fundamental right away from us, not now, not ever. Amen'

On Monday 17 May, McCreery was released from prison on bail, followed by Shaw a day later. Shaw's release coincided with three demo dates being announced. The EDL would visit Walsall on 19 June, Dudley on 17 July and Bradford on 28 August. A demonstration in Leicester was also announced for September.

The Walsall demo was a contentious issue, as the town's Ahmadi Muslim Association had appealed against the refusal of plans to convert a disused warehouse into a mosque. 800 local people had opposed the application but many of them were Muslim. Ahmadiyya is a variation of Islam in which followers believe there was a further prophet, Hadhrat Mirza Ghulam Ahmad. As a result, both Sunni and Shia faiths consider Ahmadiyya Muslims as heretics.

When it became apparent that there was local orthodox Islamic opposition to the mosque, EDL spokesman Steve Simmons told the *Birmingham Mail* the protest was being postponed to enable research to be carried out into the area's Muslim population. Simmons added that the planned protest for Dudley in July was still going ahead and that the EDL was also looking at returning to Birmingham, possibly with a protest in Alum Rock, sometime in the summer.

A BBC documentary, *Young, Angry and British*, officially sanctioned by the leadership, was aired on Wednesday, 2 June 2010. A reporter had been given access to the EDL and allowed to attend three demonstrations: '**Ben Anderson gets exclusive access to the English Defence League, the movement set up to protest against what it sees as the dangerous spread of militant Islam in Britain. But with their demonstrations often descending into serious violence, he asks what is motivating more and more young men to join up**'

It would soon become apparent that the minds of the programme makers had already been made up about what was motivating young men to join the EDL; racism. Starting with scenes of violence from various protests, with Anderson asking what the movement stood for and asking how potent it was. It featured Kevin Carroll, who admitted to being an active EDL member, and another young EDL supporter, Aaron, who was filmed on the Wilders march. The cameraman filming Anderson during the march had the camera pushed into his face by masked EDL supporters. It showed the problems still faced by the EDL in trying to make the movement more accessible, the vast majority of EDL were very suspicious of the media, and in some cases downright hostile to journalists.

The programme highlighted incidents of racism by EDL supporters, but for balance featured a black member and Abdul, a lapsed Muslim supporter from Glasgow. Guramit Singh's speech at the Wilders demo followed, concentrating on the words, "**and even God bless the Muslims, they'll need it when they're burning in fucking hell!**" Anderson, Carroll and his co-accused, Brian Kelso also toured the site of the original incident in Luton which initiated the movement, meeting up with other Luton EDL members then making their way to the group's HQ, a disused Luton warehouse. As no-one would appear unmasked on camera, Anderson mused what the organisation had to hide, seemingly totally discounting the possibility it being because of genuine fears of repercussions by radicals, not just for the activists but also for their families.

The programme constantly prodded and probed for an explanation to what '**sort**' of racism was in action within the EDL. They had already seemingly decided the EDL was racist but just couldn't ascertain the strain. EDL supporters from Stoke tried to explain the effect of the decline in manufacturing on working class communities, but Anderson was having none of it, questioning whether the men were right to expect British jobs for British workers (as long as you're alright Ben). Anderson said it was becoming clear that the EDL were not a unified group of tolerant people, but a rag-bag of factions, some more racist than others. Therefore, according to Anderson, everyone in the EDL is racist, just to differing degrees. The programme was peppered with close-ups of half-full beer glasses, or proof the group was racist, such as two individuals at the Nottingham demo shouting "**BNP! BNP!**" Guramit Singh was featured, doing research for his next speech. Singh said he was studying how women were suppressed under Sharia. In the next shot viewers saw a calendar on the wall of the house they were sitting in, with a picture of a bikini clad woman on it.

Anderson met Carroll again, this time to question him over claims that he had endorsed a local BNP candidate before an election. Carroll refused to answer at first, asking to make a call before he did. Following the phone call, a young mixed-race woman appeared. Turning to Anderson, Carroll asked "**This is my daughter, how can I be racist?**" Carroll claimed he was the son of immigrants and that he had been hoodwinked into signing the nomination for the BNP candidate. People from the BNP had knocked his door said Carroll, assured him the party wasn't racist and said they were simply sticking up for British interests, such as British jobs for British workers. He claimed when he signed the nomination, he knew nothing about politics or what the BNP stood for. Anderson concluded that Carroll's explanation was unconvincing.

The documentary was condescending in the extreme, at one point claiming a day out with the EDL was a highlight of an activist's social calendar, not contemplating for a minute people felt forced to take to the streets. The programme showed footage of the Dudley demonstration. It showed the violence but omitted the two speakers, an Asian female and a black male. Perhaps these ethnic minority speakers being roundly cheered by the EDL would've ruined the illusion of inherent racism within the movement the programme was trying to portray? Filmed as the Dudley demo was ending in chaos, seemingly tasting the reality of modern Britain, Anderson said, **"This is not part of England I recognise at all, it's all completely segregated. It really is two completely separate communities and today at least, just itching to get at each others throats"**

Welcome to the real world for many people Mr Anderson. The whole focus of the programme seemed to be to prove the EDL was a racist organisation. Whilst various members did their best to prove they weren't, all protestations were dismissed in the voice-over. There was outright dismissal of reasons suggested as to why the EDL existed, such as concerns by mainly white working class supporters over the loss of jobs and the creeping Islamification many of their communities faced. These genuine concerns were something the BBC appeared reluctant to even acknowledge, let alone relay. Could it be if the real reasons were confronted, some uncomfortable truths would also have to be faced, truths which once unearthed, might not easily be swept back under the progressive sofa cushions of the middle class liberal elite?

The Guardian also ran an expose on the EDL. A journalist apparently spent four months secretly following the group. A film accompanied the online article and showed some EDL members making racist comments and also violence which had occurred in Stoke on Trent. It didn't however mention the lack of EDL arrests on the Wilders demo in London or the arrests on the UAF side, but cut to Weyman Bennett, who claimed he had received threats from EDL members. Basically, from hours of investigative journalism the 'expose' found three incidents of racism, which were repeatedly featured.

On 17 May, the EDL website was suddenly shut down and removed from the Internet. Trevor Kelway, now billed as the group's **'International Counter-Jihad Relations Officer'** claimed the site had been suspended because of an article that had described, using verses from the Qur'an, how Islam considered or treated non-believers. The EDL was told that the article contravened UK racism laws and the site was closed. Kelway said if that was the case, then it meant one of two things, that the Qur'an itself contravened UK racism laws or Islam had an exemption from those laws and was being treated as a special case. Since the Qur'an was still available for sale in UK bookshops, Kelway said it must mean that the latter was true. If that was the case, he said it meant that the UK was already under a form of Sharia which demanded that Islam was above criticism and completely outside the realms of discussion. Kelway added that when the Racial and Religious Hatred Act was put before Parliament, the British people were assured that freedom of expression would not be a casualty, but it appeared they had been seriously misled.

Kelway was asserting that under the same legislation used to close the EDL website, the Qur'an itself qualified as 'hate speech', but it appeared that the law only seemed to apply to one side of the argument. This could be compared to verses in The Bible of course, but this wasn't about Sharia, it was about political correctness. It also begged the question, if the authorities could shut down the EDL website, why didn't they do the same with the many Islamist websites, some of which had a track record of radicalising many young British Muslims. The offending sections of the EDL website were removed and it was back online shortly afterwards. Kelway also revealed that the EDL was sending representatives to an International Civil Liberties Alliance conference in Switzerland, the following month.

29 May 2010: Newcastle upon Tyne

In the weeks running up to the Newcastle protest, north-east organiser and police liaison officer, Tony Williamson was frozen out of the EDL. Williamson was viewed as too negative and argumentative by other members of the leadership and as a result, was unceremoniously dropped.

Williamson was friendly with Jon 'Snowy' Shaw and his exclusion led to an angry attack on Facebook by Shaw on the leadership, especially and the media section's Steve Simmons, who Shaw blamed for Williamson's exit. Both Stephen Lennon and Trevor Kelway contacted Shaw to iron things out and the comments were quickly removed. It was suspected Williamson had input into Shaw's statement, but in light of Paul Ray's recent dissent the leadership knew the matter needed clearing up. EDL supporters were asking for an explanation for Snowy's outburst, Shaw was regarded as a hero by many grassroots EDL.

Lennon issued a statement on the EDL website entitled '**In response to Snowy**' in which he said the leadership were shocked to have read a statement full of lies about Steve Simmons and unsubstantiated allegations against him would not be tolerated. Lennon said public attacks were not acceptable, but even so, the EDL would continue to fully support Shaw. He said that when Shaw was in prison, solicitors Freeman and Co, due to the high publicity the case would bring, had agreed to represent both him and McCreery at a cost of £5000. That money was paid while the two were in prison said Lennon, the current donations for the fund stood at £3200, but a member of the leadership team had donated the rest until the fund could repay them. He added that £4000 had been given to Shaw to organise coaches, but to date only £1300 had been returned. Although Lennon said he accepted this was a misunderstanding on behalf of the coach firm, it was relevant when the integrity of the leadership was being questioned.

Lennon then addressed Williamson, who he said had retired from police liaison as he did not want the responsibility. The EDL needed leaders who were capable said Lennon, so Guramit Singh and Steve Simmons had been drafted in to do the job. Snowy had rung them both, said Lennon, annoyed they had replaced Williamson but at no point had he contacted himself, Trevor Kelway, Jack Smith, Jeff Marsh, Richard Price, McCreery, Singh or Joel Titus, naming the broad leadership, about the matter. Lennon added that when Shaw was in custody the decision had been made to change the leadership structure back to the original five of Marsh, Kelway, Price, Titus and himself, as they all had the same opinions and were united.

There were also concerns from some activists about the input of Alan Lake into the movement. A week earlier, on 23 May 2010, Lake posted what opponents would term his '**Final Solution**' on *4freedoms*. Lake said he foresaw a time when the UK would become divided into Islamic and non-Islamic enclaves, which they should send the '**liberal twits**' to.

Lake said that by forcing the liberals into the enclaves, they would be '**sending them to their death at worst, and at best they and their families will be subjected to all the depredations, persecution and abuse that non-Muslims worldwide currently 'enjoy' in countries like Pakistan... It will be great to see them executed or tortured to death**'. Lake asked people to contribute the names of people who they would send to the enclaves and started the list himself by suggesting the Archbishop of Canterbury, Prime Minister David Cameron and Deputy Prime Minister Nick Clegg.

It was the first of a number of controversial statements Lake would make, worrying some moderates in the EDL, especially it now appeared Lake was now organising demonstrations. Lake withdrew the statement after he was challenged by EDL supporters over the wisdom of posting such nonsense, but it was widely publicised on anti-fascist websites and would repeatedly resurface in the future.

Prior to the Newcastle demo, Northumbria Police gave the EDL the opportunity to police itself. A TUC conference was also being held in the city, along with the annual Apprentice Boys of Derry march. Police resources would obviously be stretched, possibly the reason behind the EDL being given the self-policing option. Activists attending the demo were urged to listen to the stewards and follow their directions. The EDL planned to demonstrate at the Bigg Market in Newcastle city centre from

2.00pm to 3.00pm and would assemble on Berwick Street, before marching to the site. UAF planned to counter-protest on Newgate Street.

At noon, there was a reported confrontation between EDL and anti-fascists at the city's Central Train Station, but no arrests were made and both groups were dispersed. Northumbria Police had established a cordon on Grainger Street, between Newgate Street and Bigg Market, to divide the two protests. They announced the policing operation was to facilitate peaceful protests and that the force intended to maintain a neutral stance and would only act to '**preserve the safety of everyone taking part**'. By 12.30pm, around 200 EDL had gathered on Berwick Street and were chanting loudly. Ronnie Burgess of the EDL told the *Newcastle Journal* that if some supporters were in Newcastle for trouble, they would be weeded out. He said the rally was about being proud to be English, not racism against minorities: "**Our people feel like strangers in their own land and now we want to reclaim it**"

Just after 1.30pm, both demonstrations started to make their way to the protest sites. UAF activists chanted "**Nazi scum, off our streets!**" The EDL column, well over a thousand strong and a mass of St George Crosses, had its pace dictated by a few police officers and EDL stewards. The EDL sang "**I'm England till I die**" and "**Rule Britannia**" as they made their way through the city. The larger EDL group took more time than the anti-fascists to arrive on their side of police lines in Bigg Market. The EDL had set up a PA system at their venue and arrivals were met by loud music and a performance by singer Alex, who had released a pro-EDL CD the week before. As they assembled, the EDL were treated to a rendition of '**When Johnny comes marching home again**' by another singer, Anglo-Saxon. This was followed by a minutes silence for British troops fighting in Afghanistan. The end of the silence was greeted with loud cheers and the introduction of Snowy Shaw. As Shaw rose to speak, clad in combat gear and wearing a baseball cap, he led the crowd with a chant of "**E, E, EDL!**"

> "It's so good to be back amongst friends, and if there is any justice in our country we won't have to go away again. We did our protest for the people of Dudley and a great cause. But what you did for us is beyond words. It kept our spirits up and we knew we would never be forgotten. As you know police officers armed with tasers stormed the roof and an armed motorcade escorted us to court and prison. Why? Are we terrorists? Have we hurt anyone? It's a show of strength by the state to scare us all into giving up our fight. Will they not listen? Nothing will stop us, no-one! We can't afford to because this country as we know it will cease to exist.
> We must stop the rise of Sharia and the rise of radical Islam, and we must stop it now! While in prison we staged another peaceful protest against the injustice of our treatment and given no option other than halal meat. Some prison staff believed the UAF commie propaganda about us, but over our short stay, their attitudes to us and the EDL and what we stood for, completely changed. People from all walks of life from every generation are waking up to the injustices the once silent majority have to suffer. We are not silent anymore, we are united as one, we are the EDL. We will never forget what you all did for us, me especially, how you looked after and supported my young family. God bless you all. God save the Queen and no surrender!"

People rushed forward to shake Shaw by the hand - he was treated like a hero by EDL supporters. Guramit Singh was next up, the MC, Alan Lake, apologising for him in advance, joking that he was "**half pissed**". Singh arrived somewhat sheepishly, clad in a blue hoody and pulled some notes from his pocket. He struggled to be heard with a speech which covered a planned mosque on the site of Ground Zero in New York. He constantly stopped, looking unsure. The address system was checked, but still Singh struggled to get his point across. He was stopped midway by Lake, who seemed to be questioning the length of the speech. Singh was allowed to carry on but his speech was mumbled and was unintelligible to the majority of the crowd. Singh stopped again but was encouraged by activists at the front who urged him to "**get it done, come on get it done!**" It was by far Singh's worst performance since he had entered the spotlight. Lake took charge again, Stephen Lennon came into view and was introduced as Tommy Robinson to the cheers of the crowd:

"I am Tommy Robinson. As leader of the English Defence League I stand here today to say happy birthday to all of us! We are one year old next month and continue to spread like a wild fire! We are young but growing in numbers, experience and maturity. Currently there are about 200 EDL divisions in this country. Feel your strength! Take confidence in each other. Know that you are not alone. You are part of a great tidal wave of protest and patriotism that will save this country.

Let me say a word about my disguise. It is a sign that we are not yet free to be free in this country. But someday we will all be able to respect freedom of speech without being the target of violence and threats of violence. As you know, freedom of speech is a sham when it comes to almost any criticism of Islam. For those who criticise our security arrangements I ask them to just think of Theo Van Gogh who was murdered in 2004.

In the early days, in the midst of the abuse from counter demonstrators, the media and politicians (all of which continue today) I asked myself who will defend this country? When push comes to shove, who will actually defend this country? Who will put their life on the line for this country? The answer that came to me was this: It is the people around me, the people here and now, the ordinary people of this country who have risen up and are continuing to stand up to say enough is enough. I include, of course, our brave soldiers who suffer and die in far away lands who then come back to this country having learned a thing or two about Sharia law.

Our society is under threat because our tolerance and our generosity towards those of other countries and cultures are being used by intolerant people, in order to promote intolerance. This is a weakness in our society which can be exploited by them for only so long. Our work is to address that weakness and eliminate it. We celebrate our movement today to free this country from the practice and growth of Sharia law and other manifestations of a foreign ideology.

We say: No to Sharia, no to special privileges based on religion and belief systems, no to special laws to protect almighty Allah from the same scrutiny and even humour that the Christian God and Jewish God receives. The God of the Christians and Jews I believe can take a joke or two, but poor ole Allah and Mohammed need defending from films, jokes and cartoons! How weak and pathetic is that? Ayatollah Khomeini has said there are no jokes in Islam. 'What sort of joker is he,' I thought.

Our message since the beginning is that we are peacefully protesting against militant Islam. We will continue to do just that until the threat from Muslims who wish to impose Sharia law on this green and pleasant land disappear completely. Our children deserve no less from us.

We carry this message on all our marches and, if need be, we will shout it from the rooftops. There is one rooftop in Dudley that has the distinction of becoming a platform for our message and we have Leon and Snowy to thank for that. Thank you Leon and Snowy!

Sometimes I think this country has fallen down a rabbit hole with Alice into Wonderland. Recently a special immigration court said two men were al-Qaeda operatives - but that they could not be deported because they faced torture or death back in their home in Pakistan. I believe that they have forsaken their right to appeal to their human rights when they deny human rights to the people in this country!

On 5 March we went to London to support one of the most courageous politicians in Europe today, Geert Wilders. We hope the Dutch people vote him in as the Dutch Prime minister on 6 June. However, we look in vain for similar courage among our politicians in this country. But we cannot stop and wait for them. We will act and continue to show the people in power that we love this country and will not allow it to be destroyed by militant Islam. Together we will achieve this great victory! May God bless and guide our efforts, God bless the Queen!"

The crowd roared its approval, and following Lennon's speech dispersed quietly with no real problems. Activists were complimentary about the softly-softly approach employed by Northumbria Police.

Four days after Newcastle, Ray and Greger reappeared on You Tube with two videos entitled 'A message to the EDL Parts 1 & 2'. Ray claimed it was he who had formed the EDL and that he had put Tommy Robinson in place as leader. He then contradicted himself by saying he had been deposed as leader and stabbed in the back by Chris Renton and Steve Simmons. Ray said a new leadership was needed and named Tony Williamson as one member of a potential new leadership team. Ray's statement and Williamson's departure had fermented unrest and some in the EDL openly questioned Ray's claims.

Lennon released yet another statement blaming Williamson for the unrest. It emerged that Williamson's exit wasn't as amicable as first portrayed and he was now accused by Lennon of 'lying to cause division within the EDL'. Lennon said Williamson was also implicated in a proposed takeover of the EDL with Ray and Greger. Lennon reiterated that the EDL only had one leadership: himself, Kelway, Marsh, Smith, Titus and Price. These were the earliest founding members, claimed Lennon, adding that although McCreery and Shaw could also be seen as leaders for their bravery and dedication to the cause, anyone else claiming to be leadership would now be considered an infiltrator. Regarding Ray's claims about Chris Renton, Lennon said he was never an EDL leader, and had left the group due to personal issues: 'Let it be known we are in this for the long haul, we wont go away, and if that upsets some highly strung sensitivities then so be it, its a necessary sacrifice for a greater good, no longer will patriots be ignored, no longer will the British Lion be silenced. We have come too far and achieved too much to let some wankers jump on the EDL bandwagon and use it for their own purposes, hijack a legitimate cause and cause friction to divide and conquer. We are aware of the forces working against us, very aware in fact. Snowy will be making a statement about the situation due course, its time for the infighting to stop, its time for unity. It's time to take our country back'.

As well as the public infighting, in the Middle East, the Israeli Defence Force boarded a 'peace flotilla' headed for Gaza. Some pro-Palestinian activists were killed and the event was widely celebrated by the majority of EDL supporters as 'Israel standing up to militant Islam'. A pro-Israel demonstration was organised in London and a few EDL activists went along to join in. The majority of the EDL are probably pro-Israel, some use the term 'my enemy's enemy is my friend' as they identify the Israeli/Palestinian problem as Israel fighting Islamic extremism, rather than it being a land issue. This theory has been propagated by certain pro-Zionist extremists within the movement. Following the pro-Israel demo and the interest shown in the EDL by some young Jews at the protest, there was talk of forming a Jewish Division. The Israeli flags had originally been taken to the later Birmingham protest to prove the movement was not racist or neo-Nazi. It now looked as if it had paid dividends in another way.

On 24 May 2010 the Jewish Division of the EDL was founded: 'For Jewish supporters of the English Defence League and supporters of Jewish people everywhere. This Division of the EDL was formed to give the Jewish members and supporters of the EDL the chance to be heard and to show the country that EDL is not a fascist organisation. The EDL supports Jews who have so much to loss if Sharia ever did rule Britain. The Jewish communities in Britain would no longer exist'

The *Jewish Chronicle* revealed that Jewish organisations had responded with shock at the news. Jon Benjamin of the Jewish Board of Deputies said that the supposed support of the EDL for Israel was empty and duplicitous, built on a foundation of Islamophobia and hatred which they rejected entirely.

Benjamin said they knew what hatred for hatred's sake could cause and the overwhelming majority of Jews would not be drawn in by **'this transparent attempt to manipulate a tense political conflict'**. Mark Gardner of the Jewish Community Security Trust told the paper that the EDL had caused tension and fear, intimidating entire Muslim communities. He said Jews ought to remember that they have long experience of being on the receiving end of bigotry.

However, former CST member Mark Israel had a differing view. He said at first he had thought the EDL was an off-shoot of the BNP but had been investigating them. He said the group was very pro-active, unlike the Board of Deputies.

5 June 2010: Cardiff

The Cardiff demonstration was organised in response to news that a halal slaughterhouse was being opened in nearby Neath. It was also against plans to hold Sharia hearings in Cardiff. Mike Smith of the WDL told the press that the rally would be peaceful and was not racist or anti-Muslim: "**They want to build a new Sharia law court in Cardiff. We say there's one law for everybody in this country. If you come and live in our country, that's fine. But you have to accept our ways and our laws. We don't want you imposing your law on us**".

Shaykh Siddiqi, a representative of the proposed Cardiff tribunal, said that the court was needed as they were trying to give third or fourth generation British Muslims the services necessary to make Britain their home. Saleem Kidwai of the Muslim Council of Wales told *BBC News* that most of the public knew that 99.9% of Muslims were not extremists and claimed the WDL was just using that as an excuse to bring hatred among the community. Kidwai said the response to the protest should be wisdom and not emotion, however, hundreds of Muslim taxi drivers in the city pledged to strike in protest at what they called '**a racist rally**'.

South Wales Police admitted it would be a challenge as the demonstrations, rugby and cricket matches, plus a concert were all due to take place on the same day and they were drafting in 500 police officers in from 21 forces to assist them.

WDL organisers liaised with police and a bar near Queen Street Station was agreed as a meeting point. The night before the protest however, the pub in question withdrew permission for the WDL to meet there. They were relocated to Bar Zinc, also in the city centre, but unfortunately a well known meeting place for Cardiff hooligans, the Soul Crew. The WDL, some of whom were Cardiff fans themselves, had met with the Soul Crew a week or so before and had explained the non-racist nature of the Defence Leagues and that the protests were in support of British soldiers. The Cardiff boys said that at best, they would support the demo, at worst they would not interfere with it, but only on the proviso that no hooligans from hated rivals Swansea City attended. As a result, Swansea WDL agreed to hold a separate rally in Swansea. There were also concerns among the WDL regarding the English who were travelling to the demo. Some WDL claimed they had experienced some problems when travelling to England for demos, so it was anticipated there might be some anti-English feeling in Cardiff. Any EDL travelling to Cardiff were asked not to bring any English flags and at all costs to avoid confrontation with Welsh rugby fans.

On the morning of the protest, around 30 WDL and a handful of EDL from Liverpool met at Bar Zinc. Some of the Soul Crew had also turned up, but there was a good atmosphere and it looked as if it would be a successful day. However, some of the Cardiff hooligans soon started to make anti-English comments. Members of the WDL tried to calm things down but a hostile atmosphere soon prevailed. More EDL arrived at the bar and unfortunately a few of them had ignored the request not to bring English flags. One Cardiff hooligan approached one of the WDL and said: "**I can't believe you've brought these English cunts here**".

As police stood nearby watching proceedings, a group of EDL from Bristol stood drinking outside the bar. Rumours circulated among the Soul Crew that they were abusing passers-by. A couple of Cardiff lads had a word with them and an argument broke out. More WDL turned up, along with more

Cardiff hooligans. Some of the WDL were turned away from the pub by Soul Crew members. Police informed the WDL that a bus was on its way to transport them to the demo site, which was fortunate because the bad feeling in the bar was escalating. The bus arrived and the WDL were taken away to the protest site by police.

After the main body of WDL had left Bar Zinc, a minibus full of EDL from Luton turned up. The minibus was immediately attacked and its windows were smashed. The Luton contingent were confused, they were being attacked by Welsh football lads, not anti-fascists. A group of Asian youths appeared from a nearby park, armed with lumps of wood and some anti-fascists also arrived on the scene. Seeing these, and considerably outnumbered, the Luton lads backed off. As they did, the Asian youths and anti-fascists who had appeared were attacked by the Cardiff hooligans.

At noon, the anti-fascist counter-protest set off from Cardiff Bay, with banners from various trade unions prominent among the marchers. Around 300 anti-fascists chanted "**WDL, go to hell, take your Nazi mates as well**" as they made their way to the demo site outside Cardiff Crown Court. At around 2.00pm, a bus containing the WDL arrived at the demo site. As the WDL got off, they were faced by anti-fascists on the other side of police lines. UAF activists hurled insults at the WDL, who responded in turn by chanting "**you're not British anymore**".

A second bus carrying WDL arrived and some anti-fascists ran to attack it. Police attempted to form a human chain to keep the groups apart, as the counter-protestors battled to breach their lines. Officers managed to hold the anti-fascists and escort the WDL to their demo site. As the two groups faced each other, some anti-fascists hurled missiles. A large bottle of cider, coins, a lighter and a large roll of tape whizzed overhead as the two sides traded insults. Police horses and dogs were called in to maintain order and the police drove the anti-fascists away. A large Wolverhampton Wanderers flag was produced at the front of the WDL protest as they chanted "**UAF, off our streets!**"

Guramit Singh addressed the protest. He said the people of Wales should be massively concerned about the huge slaughterhouse planned for the south of Wales. Singh said although it had been claimed it would create 3000 jobs for people of all cultures that was a lie, because non-Muslims could not be involved in the halal food procedure.

On the UAF side, middle class anti-fascists chanted "**the workers, united, will never be defeated**" as others attempted to sell *Socialist Worker*. Around 3.00pm, police started to force the anti-fascists back, away from view of the WDL. A few minutes later the WDL protestors were escorted out of the square by police. They were escorted towards Central Station, to be put onto trains and coaches. As they marched, Asian and Somali youths appeared from side streets and threw missiles at the WDL. The police did nothing to prevent these youths from following and WDL leaders had a hard job trying to stop people retaliating. The escort finally arrived at Central Station, some of the WDL jumped into their cars and others onto trains. The police had also set about dispersing the anti-fascist campaigners who remained in the square.

Following the protests South Wales Police issued a statement announcing that both events in Cardiff and Swansea had passed off peacefully. The statement said that two men and a woman had been arrested for public order offences in Cardiff, but there were no arrests at the Swansea demonstration.

The following week, EDL renegade Paul Ray and Nick Greger released another two videos. Ray claimed he had been sent threatening text messages, therefore in response he and Greger would expose the type of people running the EDL. Ray claimed that Lennon had threatened to kidnap his mother and that Kevin Carroll was an IRA sympathiser. Obviously hoping it would strike a chord with those in the EDL who were sympathetic to Ulster loyalism, Ray said Luton was a known '**IRA stronghold**' and most of the EDL leadership were Irish Catholics. Ray questioned why English people were following them.

In a second video, Ray said that an "**olive branch**" had been sent to Lennon, but had been rejected. Forgetting he had already claimed to have '**handed over the reins**' in a previous statement, Ray said he was expelling the current leadership. Greger then claimed he had rung Lennon and demanded a statement confirming that Chris Renton had left the EDL. No statement was apparently issued, so therefore Greger said they were expelling Lennon, Singh, Renton and Jack Smith from the leadership. Greger also warned that a **"well-known man will soon appear within the new leadership, a man from Ulster who is also currently in exile"**. That was almost certainly a reference to Greger's friend, prominent loyalist, Johnny Adair. When the *Belfast Telegraph* spoke to Adair about the EDL he refused to comment, but confirmed he had been in touch with Greger and was planning to meet him. In mentioning Adair, Ray was obviously gambling that it would invoke fear or respect EDL members sympathetic to Ulster loyalist cause.

When their threats bore no fruit, a new video was posted showing a balaclava clad Lennon at an early press conference. Bizarrely asking if he thought he was Zorro, the video then showed various unmasked pictures of Lennon under the banner '**Zorro unmasked**'. The video culminated with another picture of Lennon under the caption: '**I'll do anything officer, just don't tell anyone my name**', followed with a picture of a mass grave and a tombstone inscribed with '**RIP**'. The video was met with derision by the majority of EDL. On Facebook, Lennon appeared to admit the photographs were of him: '**Hey at least people can see my hansome [sic] face now**'. Lennon was unmasked again, but unlike the Sunday Mercury expose, his unmasking wouldn't go unnoticed this time.

Our Boys

A conference called 'The Book that shook the world' was planned for 20 June 2010, at the Troxy centre in Tower Hamlets, which included several speakers considered 'hardcore Islamists' by the EDL. Posters advertising the event advised people attending that the sexes would be segregated. On hearing the news, the EDL immediately called a demonstration opposing the conference. In response to the EDL announcement, local anti-fascists set up a counter-protest called United East End.

Although none of the speakers were on the Government banned list, Deputy Council Leader, Josh Peck, told the *East London Advertiser* that the council didn't support the conference and called on the Troxy to cancel it in the interests of safety and cohesion. Peck said that if necessary, the council would review its relationship with the venue. Council Leader, Helal Abbas, urged police to find a way so the conference and the EDL demo didn't coincide, claiming neither was representative of the local community. Councillor Abbas called on the local community to hold its nerve in the face of what he called 'blatant provocation' by the EDL.

Police had given the go-ahead to a day of demonstrations and stressed they had no legal power to ban the Islamic event or any proposed protest against it. However, ten days before the conference was due to be staged; the Troxy announced it was cancelling the event. A spokesman for the venue told the *East London Advertiser* they had recently signed up to the local council's 'No Place for Hate' campaign and felt some of the speakers planned for the conference had the potential to clash with the terms of the pledge. The EDL obviously saw the scrapping of the conference as a victory:

'The English Defence League would like to announce that we have achieved a great victory by putting pressure on Tower Hamlets council to force the cancellation of the controversial conference that was due to take place at the Troxy on Sunday the 20th June 2010. Our behind the scenes P.R. team lobbied the venue and the local council as well as the Met Police until we achieved our aim of having this conference banned because it could stir up religious or racial hatred. Laws apply to everyone otherwise that's discrimination!
We are aware that many people were looking forward to this demo in the very heart of political Islam; however our battle on this occasion has been won. This is just one of many battles in a far reaching war both nationally and internationally. We are declaring a date for a new demo to be held at Wembley on the 26th of this month so don't feel too disappointed!
Why Wembley? Because Zakir Naik a world renowned Islamist charlatan is attending a 'Peace Conference' on Saturday 26th June 2010 at Wembley Arena, London. Topic: Universal Brotherhood
Zakir Naik will be faced with a universal brotherhood of proud Infidels, the EDL ummah! We will protest about this Islamist apologist and his stealth Jihad by preaching under a provision of 'peace' highlighting it to the rest of the world so they too can take direct action and make a difference. We are after all citizens of a worldwide anti Jihad ummah. Can we please make sure all our Divisions pull out all the stops to get a huge turnout for this event in our capital city of London? We need to be out there spreading the word getting good people involved, getting people to understand our message and stand with us against the propagation of Islamism and those who make excuses for it. People why try to justify any form of Islamic misogyny, hatred, intolerance, violence and oppression are not welcome here in the UK end of! We still stand strong, we will never surrender. See you there!'

The *Advertiser* reported that the Metropolitan Police had warned the EDL they would have faced hostile scenes in Tower Hamlets as thousands of people were coming from across London to counter-protest. Lennon told the paper that police had told him if the EDL had protested, it would've been a suicide mission. He claimed that police also suggested the EDL had won simply by forcing the Troxy to cancel, but he questioned why it had taken the threat of an EDL protest to force the cancellation. Lennon said the new target for the EDL was the '**al-Khair Peace Convention 2010**' at Wembley Arena, organised by a Muslim charity, al-Khair Foundation.

Even in the wake of the cancellation, anti-fascist campaigners still planned to march in Tower Hamlets to show '**East End solidarity against the far right**'. Local Labour MP Jim Fitzpatrick accused the organisers of using the EDL to further their own agenda when the danger had passed. He said at best, anti-fascists were causing concern in the community and at worst stirring up fear and anger. It was dangerous, said Fitzpatrick, for anti-fascists to use the EDL to stir up the community.

In the north-west, EDL activists from Bolton and Wigan were also busy. They staged a demonstration outside Astley Bridge Police Station in Bolton. The protest was over the handling of a terror suspect's case. A man from the Bolton area had been arrested by British police on suspicion of involvement in two bomb attacks in India. The suspect was initially remanded in custody whilst extradition proceedings were contemplated but a High Court hearing gave him bail and he was allowed to return home to Bolton. Around 40 EDL demonstrated against the decision outside the station on Saturday 12 June. They handed in a petition to police, requesting that the Secretary of State for Justice reconsider the decision. Paul Lancashire of the EDL told the *Bolton News* '**When defendants are accused of involvement in incidents of serious violence, they should be remanded in custody until their case has been dealt with**'.

The protest was seen as a success, many in the EDL thought it was proof the movement was crossing into the mainstream, but GMP did face criticism from anti-fascists for accepting the petition. Chief Superintendent, Steve Hartley, told *Bolton News* it was not the role of the police to get involved in political arguments and they had been placed in a challenging position. He said a police officer accepted the petition from protesters to pass on to the relevant agency, as they would have done with any other group or section of the community.

15 June 2010: Barking

On 15 June 2010, the Royal Anglian Regiment was given the Freedom of the Borough by Barking & Dagenham Council. The regiment was scheduled to parade through the borough to mark the event and give local people the chance to show their appreciation.

A new Islamist group calling itself Muslims against Crusaders (MAC) said it would oppose the parade. The group referred to the soldiers as '**death squads**' and said they were responsible for '**sadistic crimes which killed thousands of innocent men, women and children during the wars in Iraq and Afghanistan**'. On the group's website, one member, Abu Amanah, said: '**On the 15th of June, in Green Street, the British Army, the kuffar, will be coming back from Afghanistan. They will be parading in the Barking area, where they will be parading about the crimes they have committed. Therefore we will hold a static demonstration where we will be forbidding the evil. Therefore I urge all Muslim brothers and sisters to come out and join us and forbid this evil**'

EDL members became aware of the threat to the parade and, although no official protest was arranged, activists were encouraged to attend, to counter any protest by extremists: '**Well it looks like they have singled out the Anglians again, this time at Barking. It's come to our attention that there will be a Muslim protest against the above, we can't let this happen. Although this isn't an official EDL demo, it is supported by the EDL, and local divisions will be turning out, to support the troops and counter any other demos. Anybody who wishes to join them will be welcomed**'

On the day of the parade, around 40 Muslim protesters bearing black flags and placards arrived at Barking tube station. As they attempted to leave, they were immediately attacked by an angry mob of patriots and police were forced to intervene and hold off their attackers. The placards they carried proclaimed 'British Soldiers go to Hell', 'Hitler's henchmen had the same excuse - we were just doing our job' and 'The Bastards are back'.

At their designated protest site, MAC introduced a public address system, through which one of them shouted, "This is a protest against parading in a Muslim area. We love death the way you love life" MAC, ringed by police, branded the soldiers "despots" and "butchers". Angry locals who had turned out to welcome the troops looked on as the group chanted in Arabic. One local woman told the *Daily Mail* 'I'm here for the army and the British forces. The protesters are entitled to their opinion but they are taking it out on the wrong people. They should be taking it out on the Government'.

Across the road stood around 100 members of the public and EDL, proudly flying Union Jacks and Crosses of St George. The chants of the extremists were met with chants of "We pay your benefits" and "Muslim bombers, off our streets!" The parade was slightly delayed, due to escalating hostility between the two groups. Drinkers at a local pub reportedly started throwing frozen pork sausages and eggs at the radicals.

Seconds after the parade had passed by, three young white men calmly walked past police and into the side of MAC. As soon as they saw entered the crowd of Muslim protestors they shouted and waded into them, scattering them in all directions. As this happened, the people across the road burst through police lines and ran to confront the radicals. Punches were traded between the opposing groups as police desperately struggled to restore order. Police surrounded MAC and one man was wrestled to the ground and arrested. Police held the EDL and forced the radicals back. Eventually the MAC protestors were escorted back to the tube station, flanked by police with bystanders hurling abuse at them. One woman was in tears as she stood on a metal fence repeatedly screaming "scum!" at the extremists. The radicals were escorted onto the tube, but there were reportedly further scuffles at nearby Upton Park station as they were ambushed by young hooligans who followed West Ham United.

That evening, twelve members of EDL Youth travelled to Whitechapel where they were involved in skirmishes with local Muslims. They ended up surrounded by police in the Grave Maurice pub next to Whitechapel tube station. With locals congregating outside, police told the EDL they would have to be escorted out of the area through a corridor of officers. They were taken to the station, while police officers scuffled with Muslim men who were chanting "EDL scum". When the EDL were inside the station, police closed the shutters to prevent anyone else gaining entry. Outside the station, four local anti-fascists who were there to oppose the EDL were turned on and attacked by the Muslim gang.

MAC were roundly criticised in the press more the protest. One witness told the *Daily Express* she had seen a Muslim protester spit in a soldier's face during the parade. Another, an elderly man, told the *London Standard* "our young men are out there fighting for us and they are in our country doing this. If that was a miners' strike the police would be in there with their batons". Barking councillor, Manzour Hussain, told the *Evening Standard* that the MAC group did not represent the vast majority of law abiding, peaceful Muslims, who he said respected Britain's Armed Forces. Barking Council Leader, Liam Smith, told *The Independent* that the march had been unaffected by the protest and he was glad the actions of a vocal minority failed to spoil what was a proud day in the borough's history. He added that the Royal Anglians were Barking's local regiment and the turnout for the parade showed that local people were proud of them and the difficult and dangerous job they did. Smith also wrote to Home Secretary Theresa May asking her to ban Muslims Against Crusades, fearing their inflammatory leaflets could cause violence.

EDL activists on the Internet immediately got to work, bombarding the free website provider that MAC was using with complaints. The site was shut down soon after. Boxing fans had also identified former British light-middleweight boxer Anthony Small as being part of the MAC demonstration. The following Friday, Small issued a statement in *Boxing News*:

'I'm not a member of any particular group. I'm just a Muslim who believes all Muslims stand as one and I stand for the honour of my Muslim brothers and sisters who have been killed around the world. When I see people committing atrocities then coming back and parading medals they've won by killing those brothers and sisters I'm going to stand up and speak out. The spitting is a lie. We didn't get close enough to the soldiers to spit at them. And if anyone finds a placard saying 'return home murderers' inflammatory then how about the ones who have been murdered in Afghanistan - innocent men and children - as the definition of murder is to unlawfully kill someone? People say soldiers are only doing their job-but you can say the same thing about Hitler. The soldiers are young boy's - the one's who come back having to wear nappies and needing sleeping pill's and the mothers and wives who see them come back in bodybags are all victim's of war too'

Three days after the scenes in Barking, Home Secretary Theresa May, announced that Dr Zakir Naik was being barred from entering the UK. He had been due to give a lecture at the Wembley Arena event which the EDL was opposing. May said she had excluded Naik from the UK due to numerous comments he had made which were evidence of his unacceptable behaviour. She added that coming to the UK was a privilege, not a right and she was not willing to allow those who might not be conducive to the public good to enter the country.

Following the announcement, an advisor in the Office of Security and Counter Terrorism (OSCT) was suspended after allegedly criticising the decision to exclude Naik. In a letter to *The Telegraph*, four Conservative MPs said they endorsed the ruling by May, but had been disturbed to learn that some senior civil servants within the OSCT had criticised the decision. Nicholas Boles, Angie Bray, Robert Halfon and Richard Harrington said it was essential that the Home Secretary enjoyed the loyalty of civil servants working for her. It was more evidence of the institutional liberalism which infested the establishment. Even after ten years of home-grown terrorism and subversive elements from abroad radicalising young British Muslims, there were still people in authority who insisted there was no problem.

EDL activists saw May's decision as a victory and speculated whether their planned protest had affected the decision. The group decided it was now pointless staging the Wembley demonstration and switched their attention to Barking instead. The EDL said it wanted to register its disgust at the activities of MAC and show its support for the Armed Forces. Two days after the switch, Barking was cancelled. The leadership claimed they needed to focus all their energies on the Dudley protest, called to oppose the planned mosque and to support McCreery and Shaw, the '**Dudley Two**'.

MAC had promised to demonstrate against every Armed Forces homecoming parade and in response the EDL announced it would be attending all military parades to ensure '**our troops get the respect they deserve**'. The day after the cancellation of Barking, United East End held their protest in Tower Hamlets. The crowd consisted mainly of young Muslim males, many of them concealing their faces with scarves and chanting "**Allahu Akbar!**"

Local Councilor Helal Abbas, who had called for the Islamic conference to be cancelled, spoke but was booed by sections of the crowd. He was followed by controversial ex-MP George Galloway, who, tanned and wearing sunglasses, warned the EDL: "**If you dare, touch the hijab on a Muslim woman's head, if you dare touch the hair on the beard of a Muslim man in Tower Hamlets, you will have to fight your way through ten thousand dead bodies**" Two weeks after the speech, the *Glasgow Sunday Herald* announced that police were investigating Galloway's comments, but no charges would ever be brought.

26 June 2010: Armed Forces Day

Saturday 26th June 2010 was national '**Armed Forces Day**' in the UK and was billed as an opportunity for the nation to show its support for the men and women who make up the Armed Forces. A national event attended by Prince Charles was held in Cardiff, with others staged across the country. The EDL had vowed to attend every parade in case any extremist group turned up to insult the Armed Forces.

The EDL had originally had an Armed Forces Division, but it had folded following concerns that EDL membership could harm the careers of serving soldiers. The participation in political activities is covered by *The Queen's Regulations for the Army*. Soldiers are not allowed to take an active part in the activities of a political party or movement, nor participate in political marches or demonstrations. Although soldiers may attend political meetings, they are not allowed to do so in uniform and they must not take any action which would bring the Army into disrepute. Even though it classes itself as a non-political group, an organisation such as the EDL, which seeks to change laws or government policy, can still be classes as a '**political party or movement**', as referred to in Army regulations.

On the eve of Armed Forces Day, the Yorkshire (Duke of Wellington's) Regiment was parading through Bradford to celebrate being granted the Freedom of the City. The EDL saw this as a key event, Bradford was pencilled in as a future demo and they reasoned that groups such as MAC would have support in the city.

A small group of 30 EDL gathered at The Queen pub in the city centre. They were surrounded a large number of police, but were handing out leaflets to passers-by. A small group of Muslim youths gathered on Sunbridge Road but were quickly dispersed by mounted police.

Proceedings got underway just after 4.00pm, with the Lord Mayor inspecting the parade in Centenary Square. The Yorkshire Regiment then marched through the city. The EDL cheered loudly as they passed and sang "**Rule Britannia**". The EDL followed the soldiers, waving flags and chanting. This led to accusations from some locals that they had hijacked the parade: '**It passed off relatively peacefully apart from the EDL who were determined to provoke a reaction and spoilt the parade by tagging on the end of it shouting EDL slogans. Just like the Muslim extremists should not hijack these events, neither should the EDL and we should support our troops. If there is anything to be said it needs to be directed at the politicians**'

A small number of EDL Youth broke away from the main group and headed towards Ivegate to confront some Asian youths who had gathered there. Police intervened and redirected the EDL away. The main body of EDL were from out of town, so were led by police towards the train station. As they left, groups of Asian youths began to congregate in nearby Centenary Square, but there were no reports of any further trouble.

The next day, the nation paid homage to the Armed Forces and events took place across the country, with the EDL attending many of them. At around 7.00pm, the EDL released and urgent request on its Facebook page: '**George Galloway and 200 radical pro-Palestine supporters are in Wythenshawe Forum now. EDL have started arriving. Can all EDL in Manchester start making their way there!**' EDL activists mobilised, '**Allahway**' as they were now referring to the maverick former-MP, would be a major scalp as it was undoubtedly every EDL supporter's dream to confront him. By 8.40pm, fifteen EDL had arrived at the Wythenshawe Forum. They identified the room the meeting was being held in, but as they entered, immediately clashed with Galloway supporters. One EDL supporter was grabbed and held in a side room until police arrived. The man was arrested and taken to Didsbury Police Station.

The July edition of anti-fascist magazine *Searchlight* was previewed at the end of June, it claimed the real name of EDL leader Tommy Robinson was Stephen Yaxley-Lennon. It also claimed that Lennon was a former BNP member who had also served 12 months in prison for assault. The article mocked the fact that Lennon lived in Wilstead, Bedford and not Luton itself, as he had told *BBC News* that he hid his identity because he lived in a part of Luton with a high number of Islamic extremists and feared for his safety. *Searchlight* now had what it had always been looking for, a link to the BNP. Even though they conceded Lennon was an ex-member, it was still enough to condemn him and the EDL in the eyes of the far-left. *Searchlight* explained the unmasking of Lennon was thanks to Ray and Greger: '**Paul Ray, self-styled spiritual guru of the EDL, has posted a series of messages on his Lionheart blog, in which he and his friend Nick Greger announce their intention to take control of the EDL. It is thought that Ray and Greger were responsible for the appearance of a video on You Tube that unveiled Robinson as Stephen Yaxley along with a series of photographs, following outlandish claims by Ray that the EDL led by Robinson threatened to kidnap and harm members of Ray's family**'.

Following the revelations, the EDL issued a statement saying they were aware of the article and were in the process of looking into its contents. The group promised a statement, which never materialised, but in the meantime, asked supporters to **'treat the article with the contempt it deserves'**.

On 2 July 2010, several EDL websites were hacked and pro-Palestinian and anti-Semitic messages left on them: **'Fuck Zionist Jews! - Boycot israel! [sic] - Fuck the American Government! Message to Admin/Web-master: To have a good site you must have good security and you clearly don't, learn to secure a site before you open one. Defacing is not a crime, it's professional web-design - free of charge! Money will buy you a bed, but not a good night's sleep, a house but not a home, a companion but not a friend - Free Palestine'**.

Anti-fascists, conveniently ignoring the anti-Semitism of the hackers, applauded the disruption to the EDL. Trevor Kelway called the hacking a minor hiccup and said the loss of a few pages would not affect the group. However, he assured supporters they were working to ensure it didn't happen again.

With the protest in Bradford planned for the end of August, Yorkshire Anarchist Federation (YAFED) announced a public meeting for 3 July 2010, at the Swarthmore Education Centre in Leeds. The group called for all **'independent proletarian antifascists'** (yes these people really do still think it's still the 1930s) in the region to work together **'for an antifascist coalition that can win the fight on the streets'**. The announcement ended with the rallying call **'Bash the EDL! Let's get organised!'**

The EDL were always looking for a chance to confront the left-wing away from demos and with details of the YAFED meeting being publicised, it became an obvious target. What the anti-fascists repeatedly failed to comprehend was the working class mentality of the EDL. Ending a statement with **'bash the EDL'** was a red rag to a bull as far as white working class males were concerned; YAFED might as well have sent the EDL an invitation. EDL activists saw something like this as a direct challenge and took it personally.

On the day of the meeting, five EDL activists, including rooftop hero Snowy Shaw, met at a pub near the venue. There was a noticeable police presence in the area and the group were unsure what their chances of getting in were. They pressed a buzzer to gain access. A caretaker answered, let them in and they went upstairs and into the meeting. Around fifteen anti-fascists were present and asked who they were. Shaw replied they were **"class-warriors from Wakefield"** but it was obvious they didn't believe him. One of the EDL asked how the anarchists planned to stop the EDL in Bradford and words were exchanged between the two groups.

The anarchists were obviously intimidated by the presence of the EDL, even outnumbering them four to one. The far-left had been doing this sort of thing for years and seemed shocked it was now happening to them. YAFED had said they would **'Bash the Fash'**, yet the EDL had just breezed into their meeting regardless. Feeling they had made their point, the EDL left. In a message to anti-fascists on the EDL's forum, one activist said: **'We could have destroyed your meeting yesterday in a heartbeat, the lad in the black T-shirt seemed the only one who was 'up for it' but we didn't. There were girls present and student types and we have our morals, I doubt you have or would have done the same. We will oppose you everywhere, any place and anytime and by any means necessary. You are nothing and always will be, you go on about 'controlling the streets' but you control nothing, we 'control the streets' and we do it without smashing up McDonalds'**.

YAFED was widely criticised, one anti-fascist claimed that the group had **'little or no history of antifascist activity'** and had let the EDL **'waltz'** into their meeting. Another claimed it was ridiculous to publicly announce such a meeting, especially since they hadn't invited any of the existing West Yorkshire anti-fascist groups. It was obviously embarrassing for anti-fascists that the EDL were walking into meeting after meeting with apparent impunity. The far-left were forced to face facts (a strange new concept for them), they simply could not match the working class street-fighters of the EDL. It would lead to them to consider a reoccurring suggestion, mobilising British Muslims.

In Lincoln, the local Islamic association had purchased the former St. Matthews Church in Boultham Park Road in 2007, planning to convert it into a mosque and community centre. Over £60,000 had been collected in just a few months to buy the building. Planning permission and listed building consent were obtained in July 2008. A month later the former church was destroyed by fire in a suspected arson attack.

Following the blaze, a further planning application was rejected due to traffic concerns and an appeal was lodged to reverse the decision. Dr Tanweer Ahmed, of the Islamic Association of Lincoln said the Muslim community was angry and frustrated and that they were also proposing to build a community centre that would be open to the public. Bishop of Lincoln, Dr Mike Saxbee, said it was vital that local Muslims found a permanent place of worship and that the people of Lincoln had a moral commitment to help them do so.

On 9 July 2010, Casuals United announced that '**Lincoln Casuals**' had disrupted a meeting to discuss the proposed mosque and had been involved in a confrontation. Casuals United claimed that the Lincoln mosque was being funded by Tablighi Jamaat, a faction which observed the extreme Saudi branch of Wahhabi Islam.

The following day, a dozen EDL attended a Pro-Palestine Festival in Halifax. Six of them occupied a balcony overlooking the event, hanging an Israeli flag over the side of the building, much to the annoyance of the left-wingers at the festival. Police arrived and told the EDL that by occupying the building they were committing an offence. So, accompanied by officers, they marched out chanting "**Muslim bombers off our streets!**"

On the same day, police were called to keep the peace as EDL activists attended an anti-fascist meeting in Bolton. The *Bolton News* claimed that people in EDL clothing had tried to enter the meeting staged by Justice4Bolton, which was calling for charges against UAF counter-demonstrators arrested at the Bolton protest to be dropped. Around twenty EDL, both male and female, were denied entry by police, but argued they were there to debate, not to cause trouble.

Three days later, on the evening of 13 July 2010, the EDL became aware of a planned meeting at the Rutland Arms, Sheffield, by left-wing website Indymedia. The site had been highly critical of Yorkshire Anarchist Federation whose meeting had been disrupted by the EDL, now it was their turn for a visit. Because of the criticism levelled at YAFED by Indymedia, it was thought security would be tight, so the EDL, led by Snowy Shaw, sent scouts in before they committed themselves. There was no security, so the main group was beckoned over and made their way into the meeting. Shaw announced who they were and asked why Indymedia put lives in danger by publishing photographs and details of EDL supporters. They were immediately asked to leave but ignored the request. One anti-fascist told Shaw that he had never attended an anti-EDL event and the two groups entered into a discussion. The Labour Party and the miners' strike of 1984 were discussed; seemingly they shared some common ground, but both sides filmed and photographed each other throughout.

Someone had gone to summon the landlord to remove the EDL. He entered the room, and once he felt the EDL had said their piece, asked them to leave. The EDL left with two communists following them. A further conversation took place on the stairs, with one of the anti-fascists suggested that the EDL was sponsored by the state. Shaw noticed one of them was filming him with a phone, so flicked the phone from his hand. The anti-fascists tried to grab Shaw and a brief scuffle took place.

The EDL had become increasingly cavalier in its approach to anti-fascist meetings. Anti-fascists might chant '**our streets!**' at demos but in reality things were very different. Left-wing events had traditionally been public affairs, because of the desire to attract the very same people they now found attending, the working class. It must have come as a shock to them that the workers finally attending didn't just disagree; they vehemently opposed their left-wing ideals.

The EDL kept up the pressure on the far- left and started to seriously affect their ability to hold meetings. The main purpose was to keep the anti-fascists on their toes, to make them aware that the EDL would turn up anywhere to confront them. The EDL knew that their visits had to be peaceful, any trouble would only reflect badly on the group and all activists were made fully aware of that. The EDL simply didn't respect the mainly middle class anti-fascists, accusing them of lacking courage or '**bottle**'. Small groups of EDL walked into meeting after meeting, regardless of numbers.

The anti-fascist movement reacted with a mix of horror and grudging respect, some even admitted to keenly following the exploits of '**Snowy and the boys**', wondering what they would get up to next. Through this rampant political activism, the EDL were putting the anti-fascist movement to shame. Some anti-fascists complained that the EDL were now far more proactive than any anti-fascist group. It was the sort of activism the far-left dreamed about undertaking, it was a revolution, a cultural insurgency, yet these Bolsheviks found themselves on the side of the establishment which the real social revolutionaries of the EDL were now seeking to topple. Life is full of ironies.

Weeks after the Sheffield, UAF held another meeting in Nottingham to discuss tactics for the forthcoming protest in Bradford. Around 20 East Midlands EDL attended the meeting, but when they arrived at the venue, police were waiting outside. UAF had obviously been tipped off that the EDL planned to attend. This was later blamed on Guramit Singh, who had posted about the plans on Facebook. The EDL tried to gain entry, but were denied by police. They argued that as it was a public meeting, they as members of the public ought to be allowed in. One offered to go in alone and put the EDL side of the argument, but the request was denied. As they stood outside, they could see into the meeting.

The police told the EDL they had to move to a designated area where they could hold a protest, luckily outside a nearby pub. At around 9.30pm a few UAF left the building and walked away in the opposite direction. It emerged that the others who had been inside had left, escorted by police, through a back door. To the amazement of the EDL, a Norwegian film crew suddenly turned up to film them. Presumably they had been tipped off by Alan Lake, who was said to have connections in the Scandinavian media.

17 July 2010: Dudley

Ahead of the return to Dudley, a leaked report compiled by civil servants (feasibly from the same department as the civil servant who had criticised May after the decision to exclude Dr Naik) revealed that they considered al-Muhajiroun and Hizb ut Tahrir '**non-violent groups**' which were not necessarily involved in violent extremism. The report concluded that individuals do not progress from such non-violent extremist groups to terrorist groups and such non-violent extremist groups may actually provide a '**safety valve**' for frustration. They said this, even though nineteen terrorists had clear and proven links to al-Muhajiroun. There was obviously still a staggeringly unreal and dangerous naivety regarding the Islamist issue in the establishment.

The EDL announced structural changes within the organisation. The group said that regional organisers would now control all divisions in their area. The regions nominated were, North-East, North-West, Yorkshire and Humberside, East Midlands, West Midlands, East Anglia, South-West, South-East and the EDL Youth Division. The statement acknowledged some members were aggrieved by the lack of communication with the leadership, but people would now have the chance to have their say through the regional organisers.

The EDL faced criticism returning to Dudley, as the mosque plans had apparently been scrapped. A council spokesman said the group was opposing a former proposal for a mosque and that the DMA had now agreed to pursue an alternative site, making the EDL protest pointless. The group had leafleted the town prior to the protest, as the press seemed reluctant to publicise the event. The EDL said it would not be assembling in a preordained place and the location would only be released at the last minute. Even so, the group added that liaison with West Midlands Police would still take place.

On 2 July the *Birmingham Mail* revealed that Home Secretary, Theresa May, had agreed to meet a delegation from Dudley concerned about the protest. In the House of Commons, Labour MP for Dudley North, Ian Austin, asked May to ensure the EDL didn't cause disruption, claiming recent .demonstrations had seen violence and disorder, with property and people attacked. Margot James, MP for nearby Stourbridge, wrote to the Home Office requesting extended police powers, so they could ban protests on the grounds of public order. James told *The Guardian* she was keen to preserve freedom of expression but the loophole that allowed the EDL to call their activities a rally (static protest) and not a march, escaping a potential ban, should be closed. The EDL responded angrily to James' suggestion: '**Is it just another strange coincidence, that we never heard a peep about such legislation in the last 50 years of socialist street protest dominance? You decide, but it certainly seems as if the hunt is now on for our freedom of association**'.

With eight days to go, *The Guardian* reported the council was terming the protest as a '**waste of taxpayers' money**'. Councillor Anne Millward told the paper that the visits by the EDL cost the taxpayer thousands of pounds and called on the organisers to cancel the protest. The paper also reported that an EDL supporter had appeared in court accused of placing a pig's head on the wall outside Dudley Central Mosque. Kevin Smith, from nearby Brierley Hill, was found guilty of Religiously Aggravated Harassment and sentenced to eight weeks in prison, suspended for twelve months. Dudley Magistrates heard that police believed Smith was on his way to the EDL protest in Newcastle when he placed the head on the wall of the mosque.

On 11 July, the EDL issued a statement complaining about the liaison meetings with West Midlands Police. They had initially met with WMP and Kirk Dawes of The Centre for Conflict Transformation, an organisation which aims to reduce gang violence. The EDL reminded supporters that, prior to the Newcastle demo all arrangements with Northumbria Police had been discussed and agreed within two weeks, which they claimed resulted in a peaceful protest with zero arrests. The group said it was proof that they could protest peacefully when they had the full co-operation and help of police.

The EDL claimed that previous meetings had been positive, but one officer was difficult to deal with. The group claimed that every compromise they offered was rubbished by the officer and it soon became apparent they could no longer discuss matters with him. Asserting they were not making any kind of threat, the EDL said that peaceful protest was something that must be facilitated, as outlined in the Universal Declaration of Human Rights. They also revealed that West Midlands Police had issued everyone at the meeting with a Section 14 Notice. The EDL was angry at this development and rejected the Section 14 as they said they believed there was an attack being waged on the nation, which threatened the continuance of the community. The group said it would not bow to state sponsored intimidation: '**It's about time West Midlands Police actually facilitated a peaceful protest for the EDL. Admitting that they have made some serious errors in previous protests is just not good enough, they are there to do a job and they should be there to help provide a peaceful outcome. The notices served against us MUST be rescinded. We are going to Dudley!**'

To improve the situation, the EDL requested that WMP contact their counterparts in Northumbria who had handled the Newcastle protest, but the request was refused. WMP said they did not require outside advice and would run the operation how they saw fit. The EDL then asked a contact in the Metropolitan Police to get in touch with them, but they were also apparently rebuffed. The EDL speculated that WMP wanted the protest to end in disruption and said that denying people the right to freedom of assembly would add to the frustration and harden the resolve of supporters.

The group claimed that West Midlands Police had a curious track record when it came to opposing hate speech, referring to the force targeting Channel 4 and Hardcash Productions after they had exposed questionable activities in some Birmingham mosques. Assistant Chief Constable Anil Patani had looked to prosecute the programme makers of the programme *Undercover Mosque*. When the CPS advised there were insufficient grounds for a prosecution, Patani reported the programme to OFCOM claiming it had misrepresented the views of the Muslim preachers featured in it. The complaint was rejected by OFCOM who considered the programme '**a legitimate investigation**'. The EDL claimed WMP was discriminating against them '**the English Defence League are bashed for "costing the taxpayer" in policing our events but when Anil Patani costs the taxpayer £100,000 in trumped up racial and religious hatred charges and libel costs for a group of people who have made a FACTUAL documentary, then why should we accept that as another excuse to keep us from demonstrating? In fact is it any surprise that Anil Patani's Counter Terrorism Unit is one of the units assigned to investigate the English Defence League?**'

Dudley Borough Council released a statement on Tuesday 13 July 2010, stating it had explored all options, but, neither they nor the police had the power to ban a static protest. WMP had decided the rally would take place from 1-.30pm to 3.30pm in the town's Stafford Street car-park. The EDL had advertised the protest as a 5.00pm start, so obviously the failure of police liaison had resulted in confusion. Announcing road closures for the day, the council said the town would be open for business as normal and also gave a brief history of the planning applications for the proposed mosque, adding that outline planning approval still stood.

This contradicted recent articles in the local press and previous statements made by councillors, which had stated that the plans for the mosque had been scrapped. Just three weeks later, the *Express and Star* would announce that the plans for Hall Street were back on the table after discussions for an alternative site had broken down. A plan to extend the site of the existing Dudley Central Mosque was ruled out because of technical issues, leaving the site in Hall Street, which the DMA already had permission for, as the only option left. The DMA had in fact also rejected another option of the site of the former Gala Bingo hall on Castle Hill. Khurshid Ahmed, Chairman of Dudley Central Mosque, said he would wait until the council had exhausted all options before going ahead with the Hall Street development, adding that they had little choice but to build there if no acceptable alternative could be identified.

On the day of the protest, In Dudley, heavy showers fell on a deserted town centre. A lot of businesses had boarded up their windows and those which had opened were employing security staff. The usually bustling market stalls were empty and surrounded by security fencing. Rubbish bins had been sealed with white plastic and tape, presumably there were concerns an EDL protest would eventually be targeted by extremists.

EDL coaches were meeting at three pubs in nearby Tipton, The Harrier, The Wagon and Horses, and The Kings Arms. Activists travelling by train were heading for Dudley Port train station where police would bus them to the protest site. EDL who had headed straight for the site gathered at the Three Crowns on the High St. The pub was full, as were the others in Tipton and many activists gathered outside with their flags on show. One man in a '**Tipton EDL**' tee-shirt was taken to one side by two police officers and searched. Around noon, police started clearing the Three Crowns and ushered the EDL towards the protest site. As they did this, EDL coaches started to arrive, cheered by those on the pavement. WMP said there had been no reports of any disorder, they said they were monitoring the EDL as they headed into the town and said anti-fascists were also assembling for their rally outside Dudley Zoo.

The Stafford Street site was sealed by steel screens on all sides bar one, which was contained by a series of low portable steel barriers. Lines of police officers stood behind these barriers facing the EDL. There was a lack of organisation at the site, there were problems with the PA system and it seemed as if no-one was willing to direct proceedings. As a result, the crowd became restless and a large number of people tried to leave the site, clashing with police, who were obviously determined to keep them in.

At 1.40pm, electronic signs flashed a message from WMP announcing that there was a Section 14 Order now in force. The officer in charge could now dictate the number of people taking part in the demo. It was obvious police now judged the EDL at the site too unruly, they were obviously not prepared to bus more participants into an already problematic situation. The EDL claimed police were holding hundreds of supporters at the train station and pubs in Tipton, preventing them attending the protest. One small convoy of EDL coaches was mistakenly taken to the anti-fascist protest by police. As soon as officers realised their mistake, they turned round but it was too late. Some EDL had jumped out and were confronting anti-fascists and Asian youths gathered on Castle Hill.

In other parts of the town, groups of EDL trying to walk to the protest from the pubs in Tipton and station clashed with roaming gangs of Asians. Around 40 were attacked by an Asian gang who hurled missiles at them. They retaliated but police intervened, forcing the EDL towards the town centre, where they clashed with more Asian youths at the bus station.

At the demo site, lines of photographers faced the EDL, some of whom played up to the cameras. Even though activists posed for photographs, a steady stream of insults was traded between them and some members of the press. Some photographers were veterans of protests and extremely disliked, as the EDL claimed they worked in collusion with anti-fascists. Following the arrival of more coaches, a large group of EDL ran over to the rear of the site and started to tear down fencing which bordered local houses. Once the fences started coming down, bricks and pieces of wood began raining down on nearby police. Officers, some in riot gear, managed to stop the EDL leaving the site, however, what was now an uncontrollable mob swept back across the car park. The crowd surged to the right hand side and then back over to the left, eventually running down the hill back to the fences. This time the fences were ripped down, and a number of EDL made their way out and into town.

The protest was late starting due to problems with the sound system and the fact that most of the leadership were stuck in Tipton. Numbers were disappointing compared with the previous Dudley demo, but tempered by the fact that police had prevented some people from attending. At 2.06pm the EDL issued a statement declaring that another visit to Dudley was already being organised. The group said it would not have its members' freedoms restricted by WMP. Half an hour later, the speeches started.

The first speaker was Allan Hetherington-Cleverley from East Sussex, who made a rousing speech to an appreciative crowd. He was followed by Roberta Moore from the EDL Jewish Division. She talked about Sharia and the niqab. Moore was one of a handful of Jews who had attached themselves to the EDL since the Gaza flotilla incident. She claimed to be a Brazilian, who had joined the Israeli Defence Force aged 18, serving in Gaza and Ramallah. She also claims to have served in the TA 'on bomb disposal' when she came to Britain. Moore claimed to be part of another group, *Shayeret 14*, which she told EDL activists, was an organisation with similar objectives to the EDL.

Moore was blunt to the point of condescension, she was also a fanatical Zionist and some EDL would accuse her of putting the interests of Israel above those of England. On Facebook, she had recently called the Jewish terrorists who murdered British servicemen in British Mandate Palestine 'heroes' and their victims 'assholes who had invaded the land', which hadn't been well received by a lot of EDL to say the least. As a result, Moore's speech was booed by some small sections of the crowd.

Once the speeches had finished, the EDL immediately looked for a way out. However, for some reason, the police weren't ready to allow them to leave. The crowd probed police lines as officers hurried in relays to don riot-gear. The crowd surged to the bottom of the site and hurled missiles at police in a bid to escape. Some found an unguarded route through a block of flats and emerged onto surrounding streets where several cars, houses and businesses were attacked. One witness claimed that 200 EDL had carried out a 'frenzied attack' on whatever was at hand.

In the Castle Hill area of the town, close to Dudley Central Mosque, there were clashes between the EDL and Muslim youths. Police managed to get in between the two groups and stop the confrontation from escalating, driving the EDL away. At 3.51pm, police said they were investigating damage to a Hindu temple. The main body of the EDL were still at the protest site. They were now slowly allowed to disperse by police. Some EDL were clashing with officers as they left. WMP were suddenly keen to clear the site and some EDL supporters took exception to what they considered heavy-handed tactics. EDL supporters picked up the metal barriers and hurled them into the police lines. In response lines of riot-police charged them repeatedly. Close to the Three Crowns pub, three people needed treatment for head injuries, sustained in clashes with police.

As the EDL started to head away from the area, six people were injured when they were struck by a car, close to the protest site. At 4.19pm, West Midlands Police revealed that casualties from a collision in King St had been taken to hospital and appealed for witnesses to contact them. Back in Tipton at The Harrier pub, rumours were circulating that the collision had resulted in the death of an EDL supporter. Similar rumours weren't uncommon following demonstrations, but this was being touted by members of the leadership. One man asked for quiet and said that there was some bad news. He announced that an EDL member had been killed and called for a minute's silence.

Some of the EDL started to organise themselves, planning to head back into the town centre for revenge. Luckily, further news started filtering through that there may not have been a fatality after all. A day later, *BBC News* reported that three men had suffered head injuries during the collision. Three others also needed hospital treatment. The driver, who had initially fled the scene, had handed himself in to police shortly afterwards.

In Dudley, small groups of EDL headed towards the bus station. As they arrived, they were attacked by groups of Asian youths. A large group of EDL had made their way to Castle Hill, where they encountered lines of riot-police. A police loud-haler warned the EDL to move back otherwise batons would be used to disperse them.

At 5.00pm, police said they were still working to disperse small pockets of EDL and groups opposed to them, but many had now left the area on coaches. Twenty-one arrests were made in total - seventeen for violent disorder, two for affray, one for a public order offence and one for possession of an offensive weapon. Assistant Chief Constable, Sharon Rowe, told the *Dudley News* she condemned the violence which had erupted at the end of the rally. She said a lot of effort had gone into facilitating a peaceful protest and it was hugely disappointing that there were elements from the EDL and local youth intent on causing disorder. Rowe said every effort would be made to identify and prosecute the people responsible.

The EDL placed the blame for the disturbances squarely on the shoulders of the police. In a statement the group said it had come to the conclusion that every other police force in the country wanted to work with them, apart from WMP and this was why there were problems every time a protest was held in Dudley. Kevin Carroll responded to claims that EDL supporters had attacked a Hindu temple by saying if it was true, then the EDL would pay for any repairs. He apologised to the Hindu community and later revealed that the EDL had visited the temple and carried out repairs to damage which had been sustained on the day of the protest.

On 20 July 2010, anti-fascist website, *1millionunited*, claimed the ex-soldier who had addressed the Dudley protest, Allan Hetherington-Cleverley, used to be called Allan Gallop. The website also claimed that Gallop had been jailed in 2005 for his part in an operation to smuggle Chinese illegal immigrants into Britain. It also referred to a 1991 book, *Blackbird: The Unauthorised Biography of Paul McCartney*, by Geoffrey Giuliano and Dennis Laine, in which claims were made that, in 1983, Gallop had been involved in a plot to kidnap Linda McCartney, the wife of ex-Beatle, Paul.

On *4freedoms*, someone posting as The Grenadier, claiming to be Hetherington-Cleverley said he had made no secret of his criminal past to the EDL. He admitted he had served four years in prison for 'facilitation' of illegal entry into the UK but said he wasn't ashamed of what he had done, as he had done it under duress. Regarding the McCartney allegations The Grenadier said until now he had known nothing about the book and its accusations, but would now seek legal advice, adding that he had never been arrested for attempting or conspiring with others to kidnap Linda McCartney or anyone else for that matter.

On the 21 July 2010, over a hundred EDL activists gathered in Luton, for Kevin Carroll's appeal against his pubic order conviction. Judge Christopher Compston dismissed the appeal and ordered that Carroll pay further costs of £330. Following the hearing, Carroll made a brief speech outside the court: **"I'm not against Muslims, I'm against extremist ideology. This was causing massive disruption in this town. I would do it again no matter what it cost, even if it costs me my living. Thank you patriots, and people of our great democracy, for supporting me. God Bless our Troops, God save the Queen"**

The EDL then headed towards the White House public house on Bridge Street. A police cordon on George Street initially barred their way, but they were eventually allowed through, followed by police who surrounded the pub. A group of Asian and black youths gathered opposite and began chanting loudly. The EDL responded and missiles were soon exchanged between the two groups, with police struggling to keep them apart. The EDL moved on, but there was another stand-off in St George's Square with police forced to deploy mounted officers and dog-handlers. Police eventually escorted the EDL to the train station where they were dispersed.

Two days later, Stephen Lennon released a statement. He said supporters should forget the events at Dudley and now concentrate on the forthcoming Bradford demonstration. He also announced that Kevin Carroll was stepping up alongside him and would now be the EDL's joint leader. Lennon said he was taking a short break from the movement, but would return to take his position alongside Carroll, Smith, Kelway and Marsh. The names Price and Titus were noticeable by their absence from this new leadership list. This would lead to some activists claiming it was the leadership and direction of the EDL slowly being secured by one small group. Lennon also announced a demonstration in Holland, which he claimed would take the EDL '**global**'. Geert Wilders was in court on race hate charges. Lennon said the EDL had been in talks with its '**European counterparts**' and they were proposing to stage a rally in support of Wilders in Amsterdam on the 30 October 2010. Lennon said the protest would be a '**landmark**' demonstration for the future of the Defence Leagues.

On 27 July 2009, news broke that Dorset Police had conducted raids in Bournemouth, in connection with an alleged plot to cause an explosion at a mosque. Police marksmen had shot the tyres out on a van belonging to one of the men, a former soldier, as they arrested him as he drove home from work. Six other men were also arrested by police in connection with the alleged plot and were taken to police stations in Poole and Southampton. Five of the six men were members of the EDL Dorset Division. A spokesman for Dorset Police told the *Daily Echo* the arrests were part of an investigation into threats to a Bournemouth mosque and that a total of seven people had been arrested for conspiracy to cause an explosion.

However, police later released them all without charge, with a spokesman telling the paper that there was '**no indication whatsoever that any of the mosques in Dorset are under threat**'. Following his release, the former soldier said that although he was a member of the EDL, there had been no conspiracy to cause explosions. He told the *Echo* that police had carried out surveillance on a meeting where local EDL members had been discussing possible protests and later told *The Guardian* he had lost his job as a result of his arrest.

The day after news of the Bournemouth raids broke; Kevin Carroll announced that Stephen Lennon and his fiancée had been arrested during a police raid on their home. Lennon was released later that evening and issued a statement saying he had been detained on suspicion of money laundering and mortgage fraud. Explaining that police wanted him to produce his accounts for the last six years, Lennon described his arrest as '**a fucking joke**'. He said his three year old daughter was distraught at the sight of her parents being arrested and claimed that '**Bedfordshire Police, in fact British police are taking fucking liberties**'.

It was turning out to be a busy week. On Friday 30 July, two days after Lennon's arrest, news emerged that charges against the Dudley Two were being dropped. Shaw and McCreery had been due in court the following Monday for committal proceedings, but were informed that the Crown Prosecution Service was not pursuing the case. In a statement, District Crown Prosecutor Gill Casey said that after carrying out a review she had decided there was insufficient evidence for a realistic prospect of conviction. Local paper the *Dudley News* confirmed the story later that afternoon. Most EDL were jubilant, but others wondered if the decision had anything to do with the fact that the original plans for the Dudley super-mosque were suddenly back on the table.

31 July 2010: Blackpool

A protest was called by Casuals United, to highlight the case of Blackpool schoolgirl, Charlene Downes, missing since 2003. During a police investigation into Charlene's disappearance it emerged that she and other young girls from the area had been groomed by local paedophile gangs.

In 2005, police informed the Downes family that they believed Charlene had been murdered and that her murder was linked to abuse she had suffered. In the same year, the *Blackpool Gazette* revealed that 240 children in Blackpool had been identified as '**at risk of exploitation**' and 80 had been rescued from the clutches of paedophiles, some from brothels. The paper said police were focusing on takeaways and '**exploitation hotspots**'.

The girls used to congregate in an area which contained several Asian-owned takeaways. Two men connected to one shop were arrested and put on trial for the murder of Charlene. The jury in the trial failed to reach a verdict, so a re-trial was ordered. That trial collapsed over issues regarding a prosecution witness, and the men were cleared of the charges.

An independent review of the handling of the case by the Independent Police Complaints Commission, found that police surveillance techniques were '**handled poorly and unprofessionally**' and recommended that seven officers face disciplinary action. The report concluded that no-one was likely to ever be convicted of the murder. Charlene's mother, Karen, told the *Daily Mail* she felt let down by the police.

The case of Charlene Downes highlights the very essence of why the EDL and Casuals United exist. Before their emergence, white working class people like the Downes' had no-one to support them and don't have the resources to stick up for themselves. Charlene's case received very little coverage in the mainstream media, especially in comparison to other cases involving either middle class or minority groups. Charlene was from a working class family, and there was also a minority group involved, middle class liberals don't view the white working class as a worthy cause anymore.

In 2007, 15 year old local girl Paige Chivers disappeared. In December 2009, a 51year old local man was arrested in connection with her disappearance and premises he was connected to were searched. However, no charges were ever brought. A report by police concluded that Paige, like Charlene, had been a '**victim of sexual exploitation**'. Nonetheless, the official police line is that the disappearance of Paige Chivers is a missing person inquiry and they are keeping an open mind on her whereabouts.

In parts of the country with large Asian communities, there have long been complaints that some men are targeting under-age white girls for sex. Figures released in 2011, showed that out of 56 men sentenced since 1997 for sex gang crimes involving under-age girls, 53 were Asian. Even in the face of such evidence, the authorities are unwilling to acknowledge there is a problem.

Former Detective Superintendent Mick Gradwell told the *Daily Mail* the problem had existed for decades but police hadn't spoken out about it for fear of being labelled racist: '**You have girls being abused and raped and yet the most senior officers are refusing to comment on it. On what other subject would you get that? How many young girls have been abused and raped because of the reluctance of the authorities to say exactly what is happening? The main pressure police have is being called institutionally racist if they highlight a crime trend like this. There's a fantastic reluctance to be absolutely straight because some people may take such offence**'.

In 2004, a Channel 4 documentary exposing the problem was withdrawn following a request by the Chief Constable of West Yorkshire Police, worried that the programme - which included claims by a Bradford woman that her child had been drugged and gang-raped by an Asian paedophile gang - could spark racial unrest.

However, it is not just under-age white girls who are pursued, in 2007, The Hindu Forum of Britain claimed that hundreds of Hindu and Sikh girls were being intimidated and forcibly converted to Islam by Muslim men. The Sikh Media Monitoring Group also claimed that Sikh women were targeted sexually because of their religion and said a minority of young Muslim men boasted about their exploits with '**kuffar women**'.

The issue has been raised repeatedly by former Labour MP for Keighley, Anne Cryer, who has said the Asian community is in a state of denial about the problem. Cryer believes it arises because young Muslim men are caught between two cultures, brought up in Western society but with the cultural values of the sub-continent. These men are often expected to marry a first cousin or other relative from the country their family came from. Young white girls are targeted because it would bring shame on the family honour if they had sex with a Muslim girl before marriage.

In 2011, former Home Secretary Jack Straw finally admitted there was a problem with gangs of men of '**Pakistani heritage**' trawling the streets seeking to groom young white girls they viewed as '**easy meat**'. Straw was speaking after members of a Muslim gang from Rochdale, Lancashire, were jailed for luring girls as young as thirteen into prostitution. The gang were described in court as sexual predators who had subjected their young victims to a reign of terror.

The demo for Charlene was intended to highlight the inaction of Lancashire Police and Blackpool Council with regards to the paedophile gangs operating in the town. Originally planned for the North Pier, following consultation with the police, the protest was moved to the St Chad's Headland on the South Promenade. Around 200 EDL and Casuals United, joined by the Downes family, assembled at the local Yates's Winelodge. The Downes family were obviously grateful for the support, Charlene's grandmother, Jessie Brock, was heard to say "**you're the only ones who care about my granddaughter. No-one else cares what's happened to her**".

The Casuals left the pub at around 2.00pm and quietly filed along the sea-front, carrying banners and placards which read '**Justice for Charlene is all we ask**' and '**Someone must deal with Blackpool's paedophiles**'. The *Blackpool Gazette* claimed that more than 60 armed police officers were in attendance, but where they got that from is anyone's guess. There were a couple of police vans on the prom but no visible presence on foot. Lancashire Police employed a low key approach and it paid dividends, as the behaviour of the Casuals was exemplary.

Following the demonstration they returned to Yates's, but later that afternoon, activists moved to the north end of the town and settled in pubs close to the takeaway which was linked to the disappearance of Charlene. The shop, which had changed name since the trials, was closed for the day and a number of police were stationed outside to prevent any trouble.

In the week following the Blackpool demonstration, a report by the Royal United Services Institute (a defence think-tank) warned that one in ten Muslim inmates were being successfully targeted by extremists whilst inside prison, creating a whole new generation of potential terrorists. The report suggested that radicalisation in British prisons was taking place at a rapid rate, especially in eight high-security establishments where most terrorists were held. Michael Clarke, of RUSI warned that over the next five to ten years, 800 potentially violent radicals would be released and back in circulation.

Only twelve months earlier, officials had warned of a growing problem with Muslim gangs in the prison system. Some former inmates and even staff have claimed that Muslim gangs run some jails. Colin Moses of the Prison Officers Association told the *BBC News* that Muslim gangs were a growing problem in prisons and that some people were being forcibly radicalised by the gangs. A former prison officer who worked at the high security HMP Long Lartin, also told the BBC that non-Muslim prisoners had been seriously assaulted for refusing to abide by rules, imposed by the prison's Muslim gangs, such as not eating pork or not listening to Western music. Muslims constitute over 12% of the prison population, and that figure increases in higher security prisons.

The *Daily Mail* revealed that a soldier who had just arrived home from Afghanistan had been refused service at a Co-op store in New Addington, Croydon because he was in uniform. Sapper Anthony Walls called into the shop for beer after a 34-hour journey home, following a four and a half month tour of Afghanistan. When he went to the till the cashier refused to serve him. When a manager was called, he told Wells he couldn't do anything about it while he was in uniform. The 27 year old soldier, in the Army since he was 17, said he walked out of the shop '**in a daze**'.

When news broke of the incident, members of the EDL bombarded the press and the Co-op with complaints, threatening to hold a demo outside the store (which one Suffolk activist had traced using photos of the soldier standing outside the shop which were published in the press). This led to a hurried statement by the company denying that it was policy not to serve members of the Armed Forces in uniform. A Co-op spokesman told the *Mail* it had been a '**genuine mistake on the part of two members of staff**' and apologised. They added that it had nothing to do with anyone being against the war in Afghanistan, but was 'a **simple case of a misunderstanding of company policy**'.

On 13 August 2010, an article covering the EDL Jewish Division and activist Roberta Moore appeared in Israeli newspaper *Ha'aretz* '**what are Israeli flags and Jewish activists doing at demonstrations sponsored by the English Defence League?**' Moore told *Ha'aretz* that hundreds of

Jews had now joined the EDL. This was simply untrue; there were a handful of active members of the Jewish Division using a number of online pseudonyms.

The Jewish Division wasn't universally popular amongst other EDL supporters, not due to anti-Semitism as they claimed; but more to do with the attitude of the Jewish activists. The Jews seemed impatient to educate EDL supporters that the Israel-Palestinian issue wasn't a land issue, instead it was promoted as part of the struggle of the West against Islam. Obviously the Jewish Division helped to dispel allegations that the EDL was linked to the far-right, but this only applied as long as the shining examples of diversity didn't start behaving like the far-right themselves.

The article was the second in *Ha'aretz* regarding Jewish involvement in the EDL. The first report, by journalist Miriam Shaviv, explained that support of Israel was becoming prevalent amongst far-right groups in Europe (this support didn't come out of nowhere, it had been cultivated. The Jewish press would suggest it was right-wing groups courting Jews, when in fact it was the exact opposite). Shaviv had warned Jews in Europe to keep away from '**bigots**' such as the EDL, no matter how sympathetic to the cause of Israel they appeared.

Following publication, the Jewish Division had apparently contacted *Ha'aretz*, demanding an apology. Shaviv failed to respond; therefore she was denounced her as a '**traitor**' and a '**Jewish Kapo**' by the Jewish Division. The last insult was strong even by what would become Jewish Division standards; a Kapo was a collaborator, a Jewish trustee prisoner in the Nazi concentration camps during World War II.

This time, an article penned by journalist Shaul Adar, covered the Jewish Division more fully with an interview with Moore and Alan Lake, who was again described as '**bankrolling**' the EDL. Moore was described as a petite 39 year old woman who worked for a commercial firm. Born in Rio de Janeiro, the paper claimed she had also lived in Israel but now resided in north London. The paper described Moore as an '**unrestrained Kahanist**', a follower of an extreme right-wing Jewish ideology, developed by Rabbi Meir Kahane. Kahane's Kach movement was barred from taking part in Israeli elections as certain policies, such as preventing Jews from marrying non-Jews, were adjudged racist. Meir Kahane moved to the US, where he founded the Jewish Defence League. Kahane was assassinated in New York in 1991. However, his philosophy lives on in two groups, Kahane Lives and Kach.

Moore told *Ha'aretz* that the Jewish Division targeted anti-Semitic and anti-Zionist organisations, by sending them letters and if no response was forthcoming, took action to expose them. Obviously, now these letters could now threaten the weight of the EDL if their demands were not met. This theory was seemingly substantiated, when, in answer to the suggestion that, as Jews they were being exploited by the EDL, Moore had reportedly replied: '**They think the league is exploiting us, while it is really we who initiated the Jewish division. If anything, we are exploiting them**'.

Moore told Adar that they were not anti-Muslim, but anti-Islam '**as everyone should be. Islam is not a religion, but a cult**' this was obviously not the EDL's founding ethos, which was anti-Muslim extremist. That however, had evolved into condemnation of '**Islam in its barbaric seventh century form**' since people like Lake and Moore had become involved. Moore denied they were fascists and claimed that Muslims '**accuse us of everything - the Israelis, the Jews and the Zionists are to blame for everything**'.

Moore bizarrely claimed there were no Muslims in the land of Israel during the 19th century and that there was archaeological evidence to back that assertion: '**who are the Palestinian refugees? They are people who have a place to return to and they are not our problem**'. Some EDL supporters claimed this statement was complete nonsense and that most readers of the article would see it as proof that the EDL were now in collusion with the Jewish lunatic-right. Moore was keen to tell people to leave Britain and Israel, but the fact of the matter was, she was Brazilian. It left the door wide open for opponents to question how she could talk of expelling people when she was an immigrant herself.

Lake also featured, the article claimed he had recruited football hooligans into the movement. Either he was misquoted or he didn't really understand the EDL rank and file, particularly the mentality of its hooligan members. Implying that someone from his background could enlist working class football lads to a cause was laughable. The hooligans had answered the call of other hooligans, notably Jeff Marsh.

With what would become his familiar style of conspicuous condescension Lake said that he found working with 'street people' from the working class 'very frustrating but also very satisfying', although they didn't know how to organise a meeting or debate persuasively. Lake said that the EDL was chaotic and management of the group wasn't tight enough, therefore it would never be a political movement.

One member of the EDL's Internet forum asked if Lake had told the paper he had recruited football hooligans to the movement, they also questioned his terminology when referring to the EDL rank and file. Lake posted a reply on the *Ha'aretz* website claiming it was a long interview and it was easy to get a few things out of place. He said it was hard for him to accurately describe a position in a limited time, so he often used what he termed 'verbal shorthand'. Explaining the burden of genius, Lake said that at times he would exaggerate a point, in case it was too subtle for the interviewer to pick up on, but denied that he had said he had recruited any 'soccer hooligans' to the EDL. Digging himself a deeper hole, Lake added that when he had said 'street people' he wasn't referring to where people slept, but where they acted, adding it was: 'a refreshing experience to get away from all your books and computers and get out on the street, it's actually reminiscent of childhood. So I too am a street person!'

EDL supporters were now questioning the supremacist nature of the Kahanist movement. They asked why, if the EDL were shunning the British right-wing, they were allowing extremist Jews into the organisation. Some EDL supporters were openly questioning the benefits of the Jewish Division given its far-right links and also the fact it now appeared to have control over the EDL website, after several bizarre pro-Israel statements were released, seemingly penned by Moore.

BNP leader, Nick Griffin claimed that the EDL was now being manipulated by Zionists. He said he had initially thought the EDL was a state-sponsored honey-trap to embarrass his party, but now believed that there were far more sinister forces at work. He claimed the EDL was a neo-con operation, a Zionist false flag operation, designed to create a real clash of civilisations between Islam and the West on British streets. Through his *4freedoms* site, it was obvious that Lake was a fervent supporter of Israel and now with the emergence of the Jewish far-right, Griffin's claims weren't as outrageous, if not wholly accurate, as they had first seemed.

The day after the *Ha'aretz* article was published, around 60 pro-Palestinian protesters gathered outside a shop selling Israeli goods in Covent Garden. They were celebrating a victory in court, which saw four of them acquitted of blockading the store. Pro-Zionist groups counter-protested and there was a peaceful stand-off as both sides played music and sang on opposite sides of the road. The atmosphere changed markedly, when Roberta Moore and the other two members of the Jewish Division appeared.

Moore shouted and gestured aggressively towards the pro-Palestine protesters. She was soon joined by members of the EDL Croydon Division. The EDL mingled amongst the Zionist counter-protestors, handing out leaflets. They then unfurled a large 'Croydon EDL' flag and began chanting. The police made an appearance, as insults began to be traded between the two groups. Although the ante had been raised by the appearance of the EDL, the demo still remained fairly peaceful.

There was public infighting in the wake of the unrest with Snowy Shaw. Two Yorkshire EDL activists fell foul of Jeff Marsh and were threatened with expulsion. An ex-member of the Swansea WDL, Ken Jacks, weighed into the scrap; his group had been banned from EDL demos due to purported right-wing links. Jacks claimed Marsh's attitude would lead to more 'top lads leaving the movement' and said some had already left because of the approach to any dissent. Paul Ray was accused of being behind the unrest; as some people involved had links to him or Greger.

Marsh instructed members not to air their dirty laundry in public and questioned the motives in carrying out disputes so publicly. The Welshman said that becoming involved with Casuals United and the EDL had been like gaining a thousand stalkers and claimed that people jumped on every word he uttered and analysed it for their own agenda. Marsh said that Defence League members criticising other members in public provided their enemies with the ammunition they required and that mixing with associates of '**deluded Paul Ray and banned Nazis out to hurt the EDL**' were grounds for permanent exclusion from the movement. Just because the EDL didn't have a membership as such, Marsh said that didn't mean they could not '**physically remove unwanted losers from a demo**', adding that anyone who intended attacking EDL leaders would receive a big shock if they attempted anything.

A day later, Stephen Lennon addressed the unrest and laid the blame firmly at the feet of Ray and Greger. Lennon claimed that if the Government or any other '**dark forces**' wanted to bring down the EDL they would create an enemy within, one that tirelessly worked to undermine the movement. He said Ray and Greger were that enemy within and claimed they had been actively recruiting from the EDL for their group '**Original English Defence League**'.

Ray couldn't be trusted, said Lennon, he had never attended a demo and although he was jobless, he lived in a large house in Malta. He questioned who was paying Ray's bills. Lennon said anyone who was tempted to join Ray and Greger should do so, because their heart obviously wasn't truly in the '**real EDL**'. Lennon then announced the introduction of a Code of Conduct, which had been agreed upon by the group's Regional Organisers. Lennon claimed it would help manage the movement more efficiently and anyone who didn't like it was free to leave.

EDL Code of Conduct.

1. Personal Responsibilities
a. No member shall act to the detriment of the EDL movement or bring it or it's members into disrepute.

b. In particular, members shall at all time refrain from public or private attacks on the competence, reputation, and honour of any other members of the EDL movement. Any issues with competence should be raised up the relevant channel.

c. Any threats of physical or verbal violence will be met with the removal of said party/s from the movement if found to have substance of truth.

d. In making public statements and in their contacts with the media members must always be vigilant about the fact they are EDL and anything that they convey to the media will be taken as a formal statement and be construed as representation of the entire EDL movement, and shall act accordingly with the utmost integrity, dignity and professionalism

2. Mutual Assistance
a. Members shall assist each other in every practical way, and shall conduct themselves respectfully towards their fellow members and the EDL movement.

b. Members shall maintain complete confidentiality at all times and treat any information, which may come to them in the course of their work/endeavours as privileged information, Not to be communicated to any third party without authority. They shall also require all those assisting them in their work to be similarly bound.

c. Also no member shall disclose at any time privileged, or personal information about any other members.

3. EDL Business
a. No members of the EDL shall make any personal gains from any information that has come to them due to their work /endeavours for or on behalf of the movement of the EDL

b. No EDL member may accept any monies from any outside parties what so ever during the carrying out of their work/endeavours for the EDL.

c. Excluded will be personnel expenses or monies paid out by members personally.

4. Protocol
a. All members must adhere to the correct chain of command and this must be observed at all times.

b. Any and all complaints, queries and problems must be filtered through the correct channels i.e. Divisional Leaders & Regional Organisers.

c. No member should supersede this chain of command without good reason i.e. their issue is with there division leader or RO it must be obeyed and respected at all times.

5. Discipline
a. Any person/s found/proven to a breach of this protocol/conduct will be discussed with the relevant Division Admin, Regional Organiser and leadership.

b. Decision will then be made on the person/s future in the EDL, whether they receive a warning are removed of a status or are asked to leave the EDL altogether and are told to not attend future demonstrations. Leadership reserves the right to hold the final resolution in the said matter.

c. Once the decision is made the relevant person/s will be expected to accept the decision quietly without stirring up any more trouble for the movement.

d. Should there be an issue with any leadership not adhering to this code of conduct then this should be flagged through the same channels. This will then be discussed at a meeting of all Regional Organisers and a decision will be made that ensures the EDL is the most important factor.

6. Allegiance
a. All members agreeing to this document are herby also swearing an oath of allegiance to the English Defence League and its members, leadership, and infrastructure.

b. Any person/s found committing known treachery to this will be disciplined according to the protocol, and if found guilty removed from the EDL with immediate effect and boycotted from any and all contact from EDL members and the EDL movement itself in whole. Any request to reconnect with the EDL should be made to the leadership.

Outside the Saudi Arabian Embassy (11/9/2010)

Nuneaton (28/11/2010)

Leicester (9/10/2010)

Blackburn (2/4/2011)

GARY-GLITTER WOULD LOVE SHARIA-LAWS DO CHILDREN WANT? NO!

Blackburn (2/4/2011)

Halal Chicken Man

Batley, prior to Dewsbury (11/6/2011)

Stephen Lennon, Dewsbury (11/6/2011)

God Help
The English
Coz
The Gov't Dont
Care

English

EDL = SCUM

Dudley (4/4/2010)

Dudley (4/4/2010)

Wolverhampton Flash Demo (28/11/2010)

Dudley (17/7/2010)

Peterborough (11/12/2010)

The Big One

Bradford sits in the foothills of the Pennines, in the manufacturing heartland of West Yorkshire. A former industrial powerhouse, the city was traditionally associated with textiles and once widely accepted as the wool capital of the world. Most of the old mills and chimneys have long gone, but the tower of Manningham Mills, once the largest silk factory in the world, still looms over the city, reminding inhabitants of Bradford's proud industrial past.

Bradford has welcomed large numbers of immigrants since the 1950s, many of them settling in the Bradford Moor, City, Little Horton, Manningham and Toller areas of the city. Close to 20% of Bradford's population is now Muslim and over 80% of them have roots in the Mirpur region of Kashmir. As a result of this, the city has been dubbed Bradistan.

Although promoted as a modern multicultural city, in reality Bradford has a history of racial tensions and disturbances. In 1984, Bradford council introduced a new education strategy for the city's schools, claiming that different cultures could all be accommodated and educated simultaneously. Instead of promoting integration, the city's schools would now follow a policy concentrating on the differences between ethnicities.

Ray Honeyford was the headmaster of Drummond Middle School in Bradford. He penned a series of articles and letters criticising the council's new policy and claimed it was succumbing to intimidation from minority groups. Honeyford contended that like elsewhere in the world, immigrants should accept the education on offer and that it was the responsibility of newcomers to adopt their new culture not vice versa. He believed that promotion of an immigrant pupil's mother culture over the host culture was ill-advised and that the education system was subject to a sweeping revisionism, where British Imperialism was criticised and text books were vetted for any negative references to race or colour. Honeyford said this policy was patronising to immigrant communities, that only the common needs of children should be met and concentrating on one group over another would hinder not promote equality.

Honeyford also addressed the effects on white children in schools dominated by children from families in which English was a second language. He said the interests of these children were disregarded because their parents, many of whom were uneducated, couldn't form the required pressure groups. Honeyford also claimed that many schools turned a blind eye to children who were sent back to Pakistan and Bangladesh for months or years at a time, to discourage them from adopting any British cultural characteristics. He pointed out the negative effect this would have on people who would presumably spend the rest of their lives in Britain.

His last article was picked up by the mainstream media and Honeyford faced widespread criticism from politicians and Muslim leaders. Demonstrations were held outside the school and the headmaster needed police protection to enter and leave the premises. He received death threats and police installed a panic button in his home. It was mob rule and he was hung out to dry when he was investigated but acquitted for '**disloyalty**' by a council education tribunal. Honeyford eventually took early retirement but soon after his departure, after adopting an Urdu name, the school was closed following an arson attack.

Nothing was done to even acknowledge, never mind address, the issues this experienced teaching professional had highlighted. In that time honoured tradition of local government, Bradford Council ignored the opinion of someone with years of hands on experience and continued with its vive la difference policy. As a result the city has become even more divided. The white community has a festering resentment of what they consider the favouritism shown to the city's Asian population. Most schools in the city are either majority white or majority Asian. Half of Bradford's primary schools are totally white, while a quarter are more than 70% Asian. Bradford Council has since attempted to encourage integration by linking schools from the city's opposing communities.

In 1988, Bradford Muslims held the first protests against the *Satanic Verses*, burning copies of the book. Sayed Quddus, secretary of the Bradford Council of Mosques, said Rushdie deserved to hang for '**torturing Islam**' and that he would willingly sacrifice his and his children's lives to carry out the fatwa on the author.

In June 1995, the Manningham area of the city erupted in violence, spurred by alleged mistreatment of local people by police. £9million was pumped into the area by the Government following the riot, fuelling further discontent from Bradford's white residents that the Asian community was again being favoured, this time for bad behaviour. On 5 November 1997, there was more trouble in Manningham. Police attended the area, following complaints from motorists that their cars were being attacked with fireworks by Asian youths. A year later, on 6 November, 1998, the *Bradford Telegraph and Argus* reported that 80 Asian youths, armed with petrol bombs and fireworks, had clashed with riot police in Manningham.

In 2001, following racial disturbances across the north of England, the National Front applied to hold a march in Bradford. The application was refused, but an Anti-Nazi League counter-protest was still allowed to take place. The ANL marchers attacked a pub containing local football fans and Bradford erupted into three days of rioting. The disturbances saw a UK record set for the number of people arrested for riot. An inquiry concluded that the Asian and white residents of the town were living separate lives. Vive la difference!

28 August 2010: Bradford

Searchlight's Hope Not Hate group organised a petition against the EDL protest, supported by the *Bradford Telegraph and Argus*. West Yorkshire Police supported a ban but told the paper that the EDL could only be banned if the force received compelling evidence the demonstration posed a threat to public safety.

On 5 August 2010, around 100 people gathered at the Girlington Community Centre in Bradford for an anti-fascist meeting. Guests included Rev Chris Howson, Bradford East MP David Ward and Weyman Bennett. Two police officers also attended. Several speakers argued that the protest should be banned; some argued that the EDL should be allowed to demonstrate but confronted on the streets; others suggested a counter-protest held well out of sight of the EDL. The meeting decided a counter-demonstration would take place, and be called We Are Bradford, not considering for a second that the EDL would have any local support.

Two days later, *The Guardian* published an article covering local opposition to the EDL. It quoted local MP Marsha Singh, who claimed that it would only take one spark for local people to '**repel the invaders**'. If someone had used the term invaders to describe a minority group, they would rightly be castigated, but time and time again, the rules which apply to minorities in Britain aren't applied to the white community. EDL supporters took exception to the term and claimed it was further proof that some areas of Britain were no-go areas for whites.

The *Telegraph and Argus*, which EDL supporters christened the Taliban and Argus, claimed the group was '**the most significant far-right, street movement since the NF of the 70s**'. The EDL had no links to the NF, but the mention of the NF in the same sentence as the EDL was the current, slander by stealth being practiced by the press. There had been a slow softening in the descriptive words the media coined when describing the EDL, some newspapers had even started to suggest the group had links to UKIP rather than the usual BNP or NF. In the build-up to Bradford however, the gloves were off again and it seemed suggestive terminology was being fully re-employed.

On 10 August, the EDL released a statement to assert the importance of a peaceful event with the world's media watching, claiming it would give the group a '**massive win**'. The EDL said the aim was zero arrests in a city they termed '**the extremists Northern stronghold**'. The statement added, hinting at the riot which was expected to follow, that once the protest was over they would leave the extremists to do as they wished to the city. It would show the world, claimed the EDL, who was the peaceful of the groups in Bradford on the day. The group said they would be fully liaising with West Yorkshire Police as it would show West Midlands Police that the failures of Dudley were down to the force's incompetence. This time, the assembly point would be in the city centre, ensuring EDL supporters did not have to rely on the police to transport them to the demonstration. West Yorkshire Police, who had been in contact with their counterparts in Northumbria, had assured the EDL they wanted the protest to pass of peacefully. The EDL was pleased with the site it had been allocated but added that women and children were being asked not to attend because of concerns about safety. This provoked an angry response from female supporters and the EDL eventually withdrew the request, but asked that people ensured they were fully aware of what they were going into.

On the 14 August, the *Telegraph and Argus* announced that the '**stop the invasion of hatred**' petition had reached 10,000 signatures and said that the Chief Constable of West Yorkshire, Sir Norman Bettison, was considering applying for a ban. A force spokesman told the paper that Bettison was now reviewing all options, one of which was to ask the Home Secretary to ban all marches in the city. Two days later, Bettison released a statement saying that an application to prohibit any public procession on 29 August had been submitted, but added that there was a clear distinction between an application to ban a march and the fundamental right to hold a static protest. If the Home Secretary agreed to a ban on a march, it would not prevent a static and visible demonstration taking place. Nonetheless, Bettison said he believed that a static protest could be better contained.

Of course, it was all propaganda to show Bradford's Muslims that the authorities were at least attempting to stop the protest. The EDL hadn't even applied for a march so the decision by Bettison only affected the anti-fascists if they intended to march. Guramit Singh told *BBC Leeds* that the EDL didn't want any ugly scenes and was aiming for a peaceful demonstration. Weyman Bennett said UAF welcomed the news that a march by the EDL looked unlikely, but the fact remained that the group would still be turning up for a static rally. Bennett correctly claimed that on previous occasions, the police had escorted the EDL to their protest point, thereby creating a de-facto march regardless of any ban.

Stephen Lennon had accused Paul Ray and his followers of hoping for a disaster in Bradford so they could propagate an extreme far-right mentality within the EDL. He now said West Yorkshire Police would help them achieve that by applying to have the protest banned. In applying for a ban said Lennon, the police knew that it would cause a riot and yet another protest was being engineered to go wrong for maximum bad publicity. Kevin Carroll told *Sky News* later that preventing the EDL from marching was damaging to democracy and giving in to mob rule. Carroll said that regardless of any ban, the EDL would still travel to Bradford in their thousands.

A '**multicultural celebration**' planned for the same day as the EDL rally, was moved from the city centre to the Manningham area following concerns that its location could increase the possibility of violence. UAF had attempted to attach itself to the event but organiser and Liberal-Democrat councillor, Jeanette Sunderland, told the *Telegraph and Argus* that people were suspicious of the group's motives. Possibly because UAF numbers had been falling since Bolton, Hope Not Hate had spotted an opportunity to become the main opposition to the EDL. Obviously aware of the difficulties UAF had encountered, the group did not intend to directly oppose the EDL, but instead planned to hold a peace vigil the day before. A spokesman told the *Telegraph and Argus* that a counter-protest on the same day as the EDL's visit would play into the group's hands as they wanted to provoke trouble.

With a week to go, on Thursday 19 August, Snowy Shaw announced that Tommy Robinson a.k.a. Stephen Lennon was set to reveal his true identity on *Channel 4 News* the following day. Shaw said Lennon's real name was Paul Harris. This contradicted information previously released on the *Searchlight* website which had exposed Robinson as Stephen Yaxley-Lennon. Shaw said they thought it only fair the truth should come out now as anti-fascists had been targeting an innocent man and had put his family in danger. He asked the people responsible to stop hiding behind their anonymity and put their names to the websites which were naming Yaxley-Lennon, just as he claimed Paul Harris was now doing. Shaw included a picture of a passport for a Paul Harris, which showed a picture which resembled the ones *Searchlight* and Ray had put out regarding Lennon.

When the programme was aired, Lennon was named as Stephen Yaxley-Lennon, not Paul Harris as Shaw had predicted. It was retracted later by Ch4 correcting the 'mistake' and saying that Robinson's real name was Paul Harris. It was all very bizarre. In a brief interview, Lennon said he was neither racist nor fascist and claimed he had many Muslim friends in Luton. He said that the EDL had given their community a voice again; all they wanted to do was go to Bradford to have a peaceful demonstration and then leave the city. He said a lot of people were more fearful of how the Muslim youth would react, rather than of the EDL.

The day after Lennon's television appearance, news emerged that police had raided the home of Jeff Marsh. He was only held overnight, but police seized his mobile phone, allegedly telling Marsh they considered him a '**Pied Piper of hooligans**'.

With two days to go, the EDL released its plans for what it predicted would be its most successful demonstration yet, despite the obstacles that had been put in the way by West Yorkshire Police. The statement pleaded for a peaceful protest and said anyone intent on causing violence was not welcome. The statement reminded activists: '**Most of all remember why we are here and this is to demonstrate against Islamic extremism not to fight with UAF, police or anyone else. Stay safe and be sensible**'.

The *Telegraph and Argus* said traders in the city were making their own minds up whether to open and pubs in the area would be asked to close at certain times. British Transport Police announced a blanket ban on alcohol on the day of the protest, for trains travelling to Halifax and Bradford. However, two pubs on the outskirts of Bradford would be used as assembly points for those travelling by coach. The demonstration site was in the Urban Garden area of the city centre, a green space which was ringed with steel fencing. The location received criticism from some EDL supporters. They claimed it was surrounded by high fences and the protest would only be seen from tall buildings overlooking the site.

On the eve of the protest, Stephen Lennon released a video entitled '**A quick chat before Bradford**'. On the video, Lennon was asked, considering Bradford's history of race riots, if it was fair that the media compared the EDL to the National Front. Lennon replied that the EDL were nothing like the NF and said the group was going to Bradford to voice the concerns of the average Bradfordian. He claimed the white working class of Bradford had no voice and they were contacting the EDL to let them know what was going on in the town. He said some people from Bradford had claimed their daughters had been taken away, pimped, beaten, raped and abused and no-one was doing anything: "**Every time a Muslim is interviewed on television, they will say they feel it every time a Muslim in Afghanistan or Iraq is killed, well it's the same for me. Every time I open a national newspaper and read that a thirteen year old girl had been purposely targeted by Islamic gangs, and taken away from her family and raped, beaten and pimped out and no-one is doing anything about it**".

There were twelve towns and cities in the north of England, where the practice of targeting under-age white girls was an epidemic claimed Lennon. He said that if you drew a graph of the crimes by the Islamic community against non-Muslims, people would see that a jihad had already been launched in the UK. People were being beaten, raped and murdered daily he claimed, and the common denominator was that the perpetrators were Muslim and the victims were non-Muslim.

Lennon said people only had to look at the prison figures, 4% of the population was Muslim, but Muslims constituted 12% of the prison population – he claimed this meant that a Muslim was three times more likely to break the law than a non-Muslim. Lennon said the reason for this was that Muslims did not respect British law and were brought up being anti-British and pro-Sharia. The UK was not encouraging Muslims to integrate by allowing Islamic banks, schools and Muslim-only sessions at local swimming baths said Lennon, it was a time-bomb and the clash of cultures was inevitable unless the problems were tackled. He said that "**politicians should grow some balls**" and stand up for their electorate rather than bowing to the Islamists.

Lennon was then asked about the racist image of the EDL and if the group was against all Muslims. He replied that the first time he realised the extent of media bias was following one of the Birmingham demos when the *Daily Mail* published a picture of a young man who was pictured lying on the floor being attacked by a gang of Asian youths. Lennon said the paper printed a caption underneath which said '**a fascist is attacked by anti-fascists**' when in fact, an innocent young man had been viciously beaten up by "**religious nutcases**". When he saw that, Lennon said he realised what the EDL was up against, as the only way government or media could deal with them was to label them racist, fascist or Nazi. He said they had caught anti-fascists infiltrating EDL protests to give Nazi salutes, just so the EDL could be painted as racist.

People just had to attend a demonstration and they would find normal hard working people from different backgrounds said Lennon, uniting together for a common cause, normal people who had grown up in these towns and lived it. He said the next generation would never forgive his generation if they stood by and did nothing; it was now time to make a stand and put pressure on Britain's spineless government. Lennon said there was a reason the EDL was sweeping the country and some people had been waiting for years in the hope someone would one day do something. People were now finally doing something, it was happening now he said, and it was the English Defence League.

On the morning of the protest, as expected there was the expected heavy police presence in Bradford. A line of police vans blocked the entrance to the Urban Garden, with six metal-detecting arches situated in the middle. Wooden hoardings, painted green, skirted the sides of the demo site.

Just before midday, already surrounded by the press, small groups of EDL started to congregate across the road from the entrance. Police announced that demonstrators from both sides were entering the city with no reported problems. Casuals United reported that Bradford Interchange station was surrounded by groups of anti-fascists and Muslim males, the group also claimed that three white youths had been attacked near the city's university. At around 1.00pm more EDL started to arrive, one supporter, carrying a flag bearing the legend '**EDL Kent Division**' was stopped and searched by police before being allowed in. More police marched into the site, while officers on horseback trotted up the road.

Fifteen minutes later, the EDL reported that all coaches were en route to the demo site. Two coaches arrived outside the Midland Hotel and activists waved flags as they got off. They were greeted by chants of "**fascist scum off our streets**" from a crowd of Asian youths who the police had allowed to gather nearby. There were scores of journalists with cameras on the balconies of The Midland Hotel immediately opposite the site, one of them was quickly picked out by EDL supporters and identified as Nick Lowles of Hope Not Hate. The NUJ was actively supporting the counter-protest, a fact which many members of the public watching the news reports or read the newspapers would be unaware of.

Around 200 EDL gathered just behind the entrance to the site, they stood and exchanged pleasantries with anti-fascists and Asian youths who the police had allowed to come perilously close. The anti-fascists outnumbered them by this point but more coaches full of EDL were arriving all the time. The EDL congregated next to police vans which, along with a line of mounted officers, separated them from the Asian youths and anti-fascists. Police drafted in reinforcements as the exchanges between the two groups became more and more vociferous. Nine more coaches containing EDL activists arrived; one of them had been attacked on the way to the demo and some of its windows were smashed. The EDL getting off carried placards which said '**we will never submit to Islam**' and '**Britain does not welcome the religion of hatred**'. They waved flags and chanted as they joined their comrades.

Abdul the lapsed Muslim activist from Scotland was giving interviews to the press, some of whom were active anti-fascists. They repeatedly questioned Abdul about racism within the EDL. He continually replied that he had never experienced any racism at EDL protests. He said he had experience of real racists with the BNP in Scotland but the EDL were nothing like them. Wayne Baldwin, an alleged right-winger from Birmingham with connections to the Swansea Nazis banned by the EDL, was also speaking to journalists. He was called over by a journalist interviewing Abdul.

After brief exchange and at the behest of the press, the two men shook hands. Abdul, seemingly unaware of Baldwin's background, now faced a barrage of questions from the press and abuse from anti-fascists. Baldwin put a protective arm around the Scot, telling him to walk away and not react to the provocation.

The police now estimated there were around 700 EDL at the site, 250-300 anti-fascists at the Crown Court Plaza, and 150 at Infirmary Fields, where a '**Bradford Together**' carnival was being held. More police arrived where the EDL and anti-fascists were confronting each other. Although separated by lines of police vans, mounted police and officers on foot, the two groups were ridiculously close to each other, leading to claims by the EDL that police had engineered the situation to justify their response and its subsequent cost.

More EDL flooded down the road towards the demo site as smoke bombs were hurled towards the Urban Gardens by anti-fascists. Both *The Guardian* and *Sky News* blamed the smoke on the EDL, totally omitting the anti-fascist and Asian input into the disturbances. Police, with mounted officers assisting, moved the anti-fascists back. Officers in riot gear also went into the EDL side of the police vans to get them further into the protest site. As police pushed the EDL back, one activist unfurled a flag which said '**We are the famous EDL**'.

Hundreds of fluorescent-jacketed police now stood in front of the EDL but still struggled to push them away from the anti-fascists. It was a disappointing turnout for the group after the pre-protest claims about it being the '**Big One**'. However, EDL supporters were still arriving in the city and a small group were attacked as they left the train station. The crowd inside the Urban Gardens surged towards the opposite side of the site with EDL stewards racing to control them.

The speeches started with activists either side of the speakers holding up placards which read: '**76 thousand Islamists in Bradford, why?**' and '**England will never become an Islamic state**'. Snowy Shaw was introduced as "**someone who had gone to prison for the movement**" and took the microphone to rapturous applause:

> "**Yorkshire is one of the most important counties in the country. Yorkshire is one of only two counties on the Royal Standard. The make up of England and our English royalty can be traced back to the history of our county. Why do we have a situation where we are under attack from Islamic extremists? Yorkshire has a proud tradition of fighting for England, it also has a proud history as the backbone of this country, and now we are at the centre an Islamic fundamentalist invasion. For years Yorkshire has accepted all nationalities and made welcome the immigrants of the old Commonwealth countries. We didn't distinguish between Indians, Chinese, nor did we object to the West Indians and the first Pakistani's. Yorkshire understands the idea of hardship and struggle, its people have spent their lives fighting oppression. We fought in the Industrial Revolution, we fought the oppression of working conditions in the pits and in the steel mills, we fought to oppression of successive governments failing to protect the ordinary working man and woman of Yorkshire. The Yorkshire tradition of struggling and fighting for our communities has never changed; we have never been defeated or destroyed!**
>
> **We have fought battles that have gone down in history, from Bosworth to the Orgreave coking plant, and still we have never given up. They have tried to destroy our spirits, they tried to destroy Yorkshire by shutting the mines and closing the steel plants, but still we have fought back.**
>
> **We now face an enemy who cares little for our people or way of life, who given the chance would wipe us of the face of the earth if we do not conform to their ideology, what I am talking about is radical Islam. These extremists have invaded our communities and begun to radicalise them, they have started to demand that we bend to the will of radical Islam and that we change our traditions to suit them. They have started to gain control of our local councils and make changes to suit their radical Islamic ideology. They want to take**

over. Radical Islam has declared war on the West and a holy war against all non-Islamic religions. They will not stop until no other religion is practiced in the known world. How does this affect you in Yorkshire you may ask? Well let me tell you this, links to the 9/11 Islamic terrorists and the 7/7 bombers were traced back to our region. This showed without a doubt that Islamic terrorism is alive and well in Yorkshire, and we're not fucking having it!

We all have to wake up and realise what is going on around us. Our Government is doing nothing but strangling us with our own political correctness. Yorkshire is now paying the price, we have whole areas that are no-go areas for non-Muslims and the police, they don't want us there, well, we don't want them there either. In Parts of Yorkshire the first language is no longer English as these communities don't want to become part of our society. They don't want to be part of our traditions, they don't want to understand our history or our heritage, all they want is Islamic enclaves where they can continue to do what they like without submitting to British rule and British law. One rule for one, fuck Sharia! How much longer are we going to put up with this?

They abused and spat at the Yorkshire Regiment when they returned home, they threatened to demonstrate by marching through our county, well no more. No longer are we going stand by and watch them abuse our Yorkshire hospitality. No longer are we going to allow extremists to ride roughshod over our traditions and our values, enough is enough! Yorkshire's had enough, fuck me, England's had enough! It's up to us to carry on these Yorkshire traditions, it's our duty to force the British Government into protecting our heritage and force them into fighting for the people of Yorkshire and England. They must remove all Islamic extremists, all fundamentalist groups from our shores, we don't want them, they're not welcome. There is no place in our country or on our island for them, England is our country and at last, we want it back!"

When Shaw finished his speech, the crowd repeatedly chanted "**We want our country back, we'll take our country back!**" Next to take to the podium was Kevin Carroll, who started off by saying he hadn't thought he'd make it because he had been told by local Muslims that he wouldn't be allowed to enter Bradford. He said Muslims now considered the city to be the UK version of Mecca and as a non-believer in their eyes he had no right to enter:

"How can that be when we live in a democracy? Millions died achieving this democracy and our grandparents, fathers, our mothers, our daughters and our sons have all paid with their blood and still are. I entered this city as a free man, and free men and women we will remain, free from the tyranny of Sharia law which has been allowed to shackle us while we were asleep. Well my brothers and sisters the lion has awoken and it is roaring and it is roaring so loudly it can be heard throughout the world.

I stand before you today with a clear head, and I say the light of democracy is slowly being smothered by this 7th century dogma that they call Sharia. If not challenged, and we allow that light to go out, then our children and our grandchildren will suffer terribly at the hands of these Jihadists. Jihadists who would enforce the burqa, the stoning of women, the chopping off of limbs, and the lowering of the age of consent for sexual intercourse. Our belief system is worth fighting for, tell your children about Islam because we need to give them protection from the evils of this ideology, so we can clear the way for them and they can vote untouched by Sharia, and we call that vote democracy".

Sky News claimed there were 300 people at the anti-fascist event - *Socialist Worker* was claiming 1500 were present. The EDL announced that members of right-wing Combat 18 had been ejected from the event by EDL stewards and police (Casuals United later claimed one of them was Wayne Baldwin).

Fighting broke out between EDL members in their compound after one supporter was wrongly identified as UAF after being spotted with a camera. It was resolved following a brief scuffle but highlighted extensively by the press.

A group of around 80 EDL scaled the fences at the side of the site and got into an adjacent building site, where they hurled missiles at police. Some of this breakaway group got into surrounding streets and eventually clashed with a gang of Muslims, said to be members of the newly formed Muslim Defence League (an Islamic version of the EDL set up to oppose the EDL). The two groups were involved in running battles until police arrived. One Muslim male was filmed hitting an EDL supporter during the clashes, the video was widely publicised on social networking sites to the chagrin of EDL members and joy of their opponents. The breakaway EDL group was eventually contained on the street outside the Urban Garden by riot police.

Following the speeches, the EDL requested that they be allowed to disperse. Police refused to bring in any buses, they said they required the area to be calm first. Large numbers of Muslims had gathered in the vicinity and were trying to break through the police cordon. When finally allowed to leave, police refused to escort the EDL heading back to Forster Square train station and small groups of EDL making their way there were involved in clashes with roaming Asian gangs.

As the last of the EDL coaches left the city, one coach from Birmingham passed a small group of EDL being chased by an Asian gang. A number of Brummie EDL jumped from the moving coach to help their comrades. After a brief scuffle, the Asian gang backed off and police intervened, beating the EDL back.

The coaches ferrying EDL supporters back to the Halifax assembly point were attacked by carloads of Muslim males who threw bottles at them. A window on one of the coaches was smashed and other bottles were hitting them and bouncing off the road. Police escorting the convoy made no attempt to stop the cars, even though officers on board said they would report the incident by radioing ahead. When the coaches arrived in Halifax, police detained the EDL on board, demanding their names and addresses. As they did this, gangs of Asian youths toured the area looking for EDL returning to their cars.

West Yorkshire Police said they had arrested fourteen people in total, thirteen on Saturday and one more the following day. The arrests were mainly for possessing an offensive weapon, assault and public order.

Following the demo, Casuals United issued what it called a '**non-violent fatwa**' aimed at left-wing journalists who the group claimed were infiltrating protests. Casuals said that in Bradford anti-fascists had wandered around the EDL protest, pretending to be journalists. These '**plants**' the group claimed, were photographing EDL supporters to identify and harass them away from demonstrations. Casuals United announced that at all future liaison meetings, police would be informed that left-wing journalists inside protests would be considered a threat to public order and would be removed by stewards.

The EDL announced its next demonstration would be outside the Saudi Arabian embassy in London, on 11 September 2010, the anniversary of the 9/11 terror attacks on New York. The group also planned to counter-protest outside the American Embassy on the same day, in response to an announcement by Muslims Against Crusades that they intended to hold a rally there and burn a US flag. The EDL cancelled a proposed demonstration in Luton on 9 October and announced instead they would now be demonstrating in Leicester.

Some supporters questioned why the group was targeting Leicester as it had more Hindu and Sikh residents than Muslim. A statement from the EDL said the city was being targeted because it was due (according to the BBC by 2012) to be the first city in the UK with a minority white population: '**Leicester is an important demo, by 2012 according to official figures it will be the first English city to be lost and will no longer be a majority indigenous English people who inhabit it. We need a massive turnout to hopefully wake the rest of the nation up**'.

On Saturday 4 September, a meeting of the northern divisions was called by Snowy Shaw, primarily to discuss activism, in particular a surprise flash demo planned for Oldham a week later. The rooftop hero wasn't happy, he wanted to take the EDL down a similar route to the campaign group Fathers for Justice and stage high-profile smaller flash demonstrations. Lennon and Carroll had apparently disagreed and dismissed the idea. There were rumours circulating regarding the proceeds from the EDL merchandise website, some people were claiming that ten members of the leadership were flying to America to meet with US anti-jihad groups a.k.a. the US organisers of the ICLA, funded by merchandise sales.

At the meeting Shaw claimed he had received information that Lennon was pocketing the proceeds from the merchandise site and that the girl Carroll had produced on the BBC documentary wasn't actually his daughter. Some people present at the meeting took exception to the allegations and walked out.

During the following week, some high profile supporters announced they were leaving the EDL. After making enquiries why, Lennon found out about the allegations, but not of Shaw's involvement. On Tuesday 7 September, he released a statement dismissing them and comparing the events to a television soap opera. Lennon also announced he was shutting down the merchandising website. He said that people had tried time and again to ruin the movement, different police forces, special branch, anti terrorist branch, UAF, private investigators, Nazis and the government led media machine. Some of the problems they had faced were an example of a concerted effort from all those parties, and still, said Lennon; people who put their heart and soul into the EDL faced a constant barrage of abuse by some supporters.

Lennon said whatever money had been generated by the sale of merchandise had been put back into the movement, used to purchase flags, placards and to pay for the legal fees of Shaw and McCreery. Lennon said he wasn't in the EDL for fame or money; he was in it to defend his country. He said the so called EDL supporters spreading the rumours needed to realise the harm they were causing. All the leadership had been attacked at some point said Lennon; it was his turn now, with his integrity being called into question.

A day after his statement, people who had walked out of the meeting contacted Lennon and put him in the picture about Shaw's allegations. This news angered Lennon and Carroll, as Shaw had made no attempt to contact either of them to discuss the claims. It was obviously something which could split the movement. Shaw was a popular member of the EDL, lately the leadership had been widely criticised for being aloof from rank and file members, whereas Snowy was still seen as one of the lads.

Both Lennon and Carroll told Shaw of their suspicions and he issued a statement, claiming the meeting had been called so people could air any concerns they had and to make arrangements for a demo. Shaw said he had raised the allegations in good faith, but now knew they were '**100% untrue**' and offered an apology to both men. Shaw said some people had used his passion and commitment to the cause to manipulate him for their own agenda and admitted it had been a '**grave error**' on his part. Shaw added he would never reveal the source of the allegations, but by saying that, he left the whole thing wide open and could never truly prove they weren't his own suspicions.

11 September 2010: New York

America planned to mark the ninth anniversary of the 9/11 attacks with a series of services across the US, the biggest of which was to be at Ground Zero where relatives of those who perished planned to assemble and hold a memorial service.

The EDL announced that a number of activists would travel to New York to attend the service and a protest against plans to open an Islamic cultural centre and mosque a couple of blocks away from the Ground Zero site. The group said they planned to meet with other '**counter-jihad groups**' heralding '**a new phase of international outreach and networking**'. In actual fact they were meeting representatives of the Freedom Defense Initiative (FDI) now remodelled as the International Civil Liberties Alliance and the Stop the Islamisation groups.

Founder of FDI and counter-jihad polemicist Robert Spencer runs the website *Jihad Watch*. Spencer claims to have become interested in Islam whilst researching his Greek family's origins in Turkey (Spencer has described himself as a Melkite Catholic - mainly Greek speaking branch of the Catholic Church originating in the Middle East). He has published countless articles and ten books on Islam and counter-jihad, including two best-sellers.

Spencer had recently commented on the EDL, in March 2010, on *Jihad Watch* when he said: '**The EDL is standing up to violent thugs from both the Left and the increasingly assertive Islamic communities in Britain, and they deserve the support of all free people**'. Spencer runs Stop the Islamization of America (SIOA), modelled on Anders Gravers Stop the Islamisation of Europe, with Pamela Geller, who first rose to prominence after her website, *Atlas Shrugs*, published the Danish cartoons.

Geller is a fervent supporter of Geert Wilders, calling him '**the bravest man in Europe**' and has also voiced support for the EDL: '**I share the EDL's goals. We need to encourage rational, reasonable groups that oppose the Islamisation of the West.**' Geller is also involved in the Tea Party, but has been accused by her critics of bringing Islamophobia into the movement. Like Moore with the EDL, Geller has been accused of shifting the Tea Party away from its roots in trying to turn it into a pro-Zionist lobby group. Ibrahim Hooper, of the Council on American-Islamic Relations said of Geller: '**People say don't give her too much credit, she's a fringe character, but she is a fringe character who every day is on CNN, Fox, The Washington Post, and The New York Times**'.

Geller and SIOA were leading the protest against the location of the proposed mosque and cultural centre, originally termed Cordoba House but renamed Park51. Opponents questioned the size of the project and the source of its funding. A number of opinion polls showed most Americans also opposed the plans.

A pastor from Florida, Terry Jones, announced that he would burn a copy of the Qur'an to mark the anniversary of 9/11. Jones faced widespread criticism in the US and abroad. The US commander in Afghanistan, General David Petraeus, warned that the lives of troops would be endangered if Jones carried out his plan. Afghan President Hamid Karzai said he hoped Jones would not proceed with the plan, saying that the Qur'an was in the hearts and minds of all Muslims and an affront against the holy book was a humiliation of the people. Ex-presidential candidate Sarah Palin said that people had a constitutional right to burn a Qur'an if they wanted to, but doing so was insensitive and an unnecessary provocation - much like building a mosque at Ground Zero.

Jones called off the event on 9 September, saying he had brokered a deal with the imam of Park51 and was travelling to New York to discuss moving the Islamic centre.

Two days later, in New York on 11 September, the EDL, minus Stephen Lennon, gathered in Lower Manhattan with other anti-jihad activists - including Geert Wilders - to protest against the plans for an Islamic cultural centre close to Ground Zero. Lennon had been met by two policemen as soon as he stepped off the plane at J.F. Kennedy Airport. They took him into custody, refused him entry to the US and put him on a plane back to London. The official explanation was that Lennon had incorrectly filled out his entry form, but it was widely suspected that the British authorities had informed the US Department of Homeland Security that he was on his way.

At the protest, the remaining EDL, wearing matching tee-shirts specially made for the trip, unfurled banners and flags with the slogans '**No mosque at Ground Zero**', '**the more Islam, the less freedom**' and '**No Sharia**'. Pamela Geller told the audience that the site was a war memorial and burial ground and it was unconscionable to build a shrine there to the very ideology that inspired the attacks: "**Only you can stop this triumpheral mosque on the cherished site of conquered land**". Also addressing the crowd, Geert Wilders said: '**As we all know, America, New York and Sharia are incompatible. A tolerant society, like your city New York, must defend itself against the powers of darkness, against the forces of hatred, the blight of ignorance. We must never give a free hand to those who want to subjugate us**'

11 September 2010: London

In Britain, the EDL had a day of action planned like never before. Activists from the midlands and south travelled to London to commemorate the 9/11 anniversary, but also to oppose Muslims Against Crusades who planned to burn American flags outside the US embassy. On the morning of the protest, around 150 EDL gathered in the Hog in the Pound pub on Bond Street in London's West End. There was a police and press presence outside the pub and the EDL, holding their flags aloft, happily posed for photographs.

They intended to march to the American Embassy and then onto the Saudi Embassy. At midday the group set off headed for the US Embassy, singing and chanting, a mass of flags. After a short walk they arrived at the embassy, laid a wreath and observed two minutes silence for the victims of 9/11. Then, accompanied by press and police, the EDL carried on to the Saudi Arabian Embassy. When they arrived, they found barriers had been set up and they took their places opposite the building. They chanted as a throng of press stood in front photographing them. Some EDL were masked; others hid their faces behind flags. Some had photocopies of the Shahadah, which they held aloft and set light to. After a short protest, they then made their way back to the Hog in the Pound.

Shortly afterwards, large numbers of police surrounded the pub and refused to let any EDL leave. News soon reached them that MAC had arrived at the American Embassy. A number of EDL stormed down the road, but police halted their advance and there were scuffles as they were contained. Eventually, police allowed them to march back to the embassy, accompanied by countless officers and riot vans. As they neared their destination, they saw a group of Muslim radicals clutching black flags walking across a small park. The EDL ran to confront them but police managed to halt them. Some EDL who had missed the mass exodus were still making their way down to the site and a confrontation between them and radicals took place in the surrounding streets.

The EDL were herded into a small section around 200 yards from MAC, where police had set up crowd control barriers in readiness. Following chants from MAC, there was a series of scuffles between the EDL and police. Someone let off a firework and the EDL again surged against police lines. On the other side of the barriers, MAC supporters burned American and British flags. A few EDL came up behind them, but were held back by police as they traded insults with the Islamists.

Eventually both groups were escorted away from the area by police. As the EDL were finally dispersed, one young male was immediately arrested for allegedly letting off the firework. Other EDL tried to intervene and there was a brief struggle with police before more officers arrived.

Most of the EDL headed up Park Lane towards Marble Arch as MAC were thought to be heading for Baker Street. The EDL set off in pursuit but when they arrived at Baker Street they were told the radicals had gone to Regent's Park Mosque. It was decided that a protest outside the mosque would reflect badly on the EDL, so the pursuit was abandoned. Others headed towards Whitechapel on the tube, but found police had closed the station in anticipation of them doing so.

11 September 2010: Oldham

In Leeds, the Socialist Workers Party planned to protest outside the Army Careers Office on the city centre. EDL activists from the north secretly travelled there to counter-protest. The rendezvous point was a bar in Millennium Square, where the EDL intended to wait for the SWP to turn up.

Around half an hour later, three SWP activists turned up outside the careers office. Finding it closed, they were quickly surrounded by 40 chanting EDL, led by Snowy Shaw, who, speaking later on Facebook, said that every protest aimed at British troops would now be opposed by the EDL. Police were quickly in attendance and the SWP activists were escorted from the area for their own safety. Snowy and the boys then made their way to Oldham for their second demo of the day.

Oldham is a large mill town in Greater Manchester which sits amid the Pennines, surrounded by rolling moors. Oldham, like Bradford, is a gritty northern town synonymous with textile production and at one point was the most productive cotton town in the world. Since the demise of the textile industry, manufacturing in Oldham has all but disappeared. The town's other main employers, such as Seton's, Ferranti's, British Aerospace and the more traditional companies, such as Stott's and Platt Brothers have long left Oldham. Since 2008, unemployment in the town has rocketed, and isn't predicted to recover to pre-08 levels until 2023.

Oldham is home to one of the largest Muslim communities in the UK. More than one in four people are of South Asian heritage and the town has the largest Bangladeshi community outside London - on its own amounting to around 5% of the population. Along with other shining urban examples of diversity in modern Britain, Oldham is a town divided, split into distinct white and Asian areas and with a history of ethnic tensions.

In the summer of 2001, along with Burnley and Bradford, weeks of ethnic tension between the town's white and Asian communities, Oldham erupted into racial violence. When police intervened they became the focus of aggression of a large mob of up to 500 Asians. The riot which followed lasted for three days and was said to have cost the taxpayer £2million.

Ten years on from the riots and the divisions in the town persist. In 2011, a study by Bristol University revealed that schools in Oldham were the most segregated in England. Pakistani or Bangladeshi children are effectively educated separately from white pupils, especially at primary level.

The town was linked to extremism in August 2011, when a couple from Foster Street in Oldham appeared in court charged with offences under the Terrorism Act. The couple were accused of engaging in conduct in preparation for acts of terrorism in alleged offences said to have been committed between August 2010 and July 2011.

There had been rumours amongst anti-fascists that the EDL was staging a flash demo somewhere in the north. Following the counter-protest in Leeds, Jeff Marsh of Casuals United hinted that it was Bradford they were heading for. In response, local Muslim youths turned out in Bradford to oppose the EDL but only ended up attacking a group of anti-fascists who had headed into the town on the same pretext.

As the EDL made their way to Oldham, they clashed with police in the Chadderton area of the town, close to Westwood. A group of around 50 EDL reportedly hurled bottles at a police car which stopped, leading to four arrests. Their presence close to Westwood wasn't as sinister as it seemed. The only rail-line available into Oldham dropped them at Mills Hill station nearby. They were merely following directions they had been given by local EDL supporters.

The rendezvous point in Oldham was the Greaves Arms pub, but there were groups of EDL standing outside various other pubs in the town. They eventually all met up and headed towards the town's war memorial, where Shaw gave a brief speech and laid a wreath which said simply 'WHY?' Two minutes silence was then observed, followed by two minutes of applause. They then marched around the main shopping area, through the market and back to the war memorial.

Police were slow in responding and it took them over an hour to get organised. Feeling they had made their point, the EDL walked towards the train station shadowed by police riot vans. However, a police attempt to kettle them resulted in them splitting up and heading back to the town centre. Police headed them off and there were scuffles as officers tried to contain them. There was a pub containing more EDL on the street, they were quickly extracted by police and joined the group being held. After an hour of standing around, they were issued with Section 27 Dispersal Orders and told to make their way to the bus station.

Following the demo, the *Oldham Evening Chronicle* claimed **'Hate mob's terror reign'** even though the paper admitted there were no reports of any injuries or damage to property. Nick Lowles of Hope Not Hate called the day's activities a **'worrying development'** and claimed that EDL members were **'actively hunting down their opponents, including myself'**. Lowles told *The Guardian* that the EDL operated on two levels, street activists, such as those that demonstrated in Oldham and London, and a group of Christian fundamentalist leaders pursuing a political agenda, which included an international aspect where the uniting issue was opposition to Islam.

Lowles was half-right, the EDL leadership, largely due to the influence of Alan Lake, did have a dual strategy and was now following an international agenda, but the unifying issue wasn't as much anti-Islam, as it was pro-Israel. There had been a gradual but deliberate shift by the movement, away from the basic principles of opposing militant Islam and defending the British way of life. This change was obvious as the statements from the leadership became more and more vociferous in their support of Israel and the '**global anti-jihad struggle**'.

12 September 2010: Nuneaton

The next day there was more activism, as activists answered appeals to support a parade by The Royal Regiment of Fusiliers, which was being granted the Freedom of the Borough of Nuneaton and Bedworth.

On Facebook, some local people had claimed that on the last occasion soldiers had paraded through the town they had faced abuse from sections of Nuneaton's Asian community. Appeals went out on EDL websites asking activists to travel to Nuneaton to support the parade.

Nuneaton is a small town to the south east of Birmingham. It was, like Oldham and Bradford, associated with the textile industry, but also known for the production of bricks, beer and munitions. For its size, the town has a substantial Muslim community and has two mosques. In 2007, Nuneaton became home to the first sharia tribunal in the UK, established at the Hijaz Islamic College.

On the morning of the parade, a large number of locals were joined by around 80 EDL. The Dudley and Rowley Regis divisions were the first to turn up, identifiable by their EDL '**colours**' (the hooded tops and EDL shirts with the divisions the wearer hailed from emblazoned on them were now frequently referred to as colours by activists – it is an interesting term for them to promote, football hooligan culture deliberately shies away from colours. However, non-football EDL activists embraced the wearing of EDL colours – possibly a further statement of identity, more immediate and not evolved) and carrying flags. As the parade neared, other small groups of EDL emerged, seemingly from all directions. As the troops marched, the crowd cheered and clapped in support and appreciation.

Following the parade as most people headed home, the majority of EDL headed for a local Wetherspoons pub. Around 1.45pm, around 60 EDL headed into the, mainly Asian, Edwards Street area of Nuneaton. As they walked up the road, police blocked their path, so the group chose a pub on Queen's Road, called The Crew. At first, the landlord refused them entry, but following the intervention of a police commander, it was decided they could stay. They ordered drinks and stood outside drinking with police officers supervising proceedings. They hung flags outside the pub and this soon attracted the attention of the local Asian community.

A group of around 100 Asian men gathered a few yards away and before long bottles and missiles were exchanged between the two groups. As their numbers grew, a local imam tried in vain to calm the Muslims and police ordered the EDL inside. A passing car which signalled support for the EDL was attacked by the Asian mob. Officers from neighbouring West Midlands Police were drafted in, but police were unable to disperse the Muslim gang. Police informed the EDL they would have to be taken out on a bus, but following a discussion, it was decided it would be easier if they walked out with a police escort. At 5.00pm police escorted the EDL to the train station and they left the town. Speaking on the force's website, Chief Inspector Chris Lewis of Warwickshire Police said: '**The day began with a peaceful parade to celebrate the granting of the Freedom of Entry to the Borough to the Royal Regiment of Fusiliers. The day has been sadly marred by the situation which broke out this afternoon in Queens Road. It has been a very tense afternoon but I believe that the situation is now under control. Throughout the afternoon we have worked closely with local community leaders and I would like to thank them for their very active support. I am also grateful to the landlord of The Crew public house who was also very proactive in helping us get the situation under control and achieve good dialogue with the EDL.**'

Speaking the next day, Chief Inspector Lewis admitted that although many of the EDL had travelled from other parts of the country, there were local supporters amongst their number. Yaseen Ahmedabadi of the Nuneaton Muslim Society told the *Coventry Telegraph* he was pleased with the way the police had handled the situation and claimed that the local community had staged a peaceful protest against the '**unexpected and unwarranted presence of visitors from the EDL, who have no place in our society**'.

Following news that the Ghurkha Regiment would be parading through Nuneaton on the 26 September, Stephen Lennon announced that the EDL would again visit the town to support the troops.

Three days later, the EDL Gateshead Division announced that following a raid the Bugle pub in Felling, Tyne and Wear, two of its members had been arrested for allegedly inciting religious hatred. The arrests were in connection with a video, posted on the Internet, showing several masked men, some wearing tea-towels around their heads, setting fire to what appeared to be a copy of the Qur'an. As the book burned, the men danced and laughed, one of them shouted: "**This is for the boys in Afghanistan. September 11, international burn a Qur'an day, for all the people of 9/11! This is how we do it in Gateshead, right!**"

The EDL issued a request for members to attend a flash demo outside Gateshead police station where the men were being held. Over thirty activists from the north-east made their way to the station and held a demo outside. Police admitted they were forced to lock the doors because feelings were running high. Two hours after the EDL issued the request for support, the men were released on bail.

The video was apparently filmed in the backyard of The Bugle, a barman from the pub told the *Daily Mail* the pub had been targeted by police because some of the regulars had links to the EDL: '**I had nothing to do with the fire. I smelt the smoke so I went outside to put it out. The police came to the pub and searched it. We were closed for hours. They took my mobile phones, some empty boxes the phones had been in, some CDs and DVDs, and all the tea towels. They arrested me and another man and took us to the station. They were asking questions about who had been burning the book**'.

A week later, four more men from Gateshead were arrested in connection with the incident. A joint statement by Northumbria Police and Gateshead Council said that the kind of behaviour displayed in the video was not representative of the community as a whole and they would work together with community leaders, residents and people of all faiths to maintain good relations. One of the accused, referring to the flags MAC had burned outside the US Embassy told the *Daily Mail*: '**Muslims are allowed to burn British flags. It wasn't so much planned as more we were driven to do it. Now there seems to be one law for them and one law for us. They can burn a Union Flag and the Stars and Stripes, but we get arrested for burning a few sheets of paper**'

The CPS looked at a number of areas for prosecution but eventually decided there was insufficient evidence. Northumbria Chief Prosecutor, Wendy Williams, said it was a serious incident which the vast majority of people would find repugnant. However, they could only prosecute if there was sufficient evidence for a realistic prospect of conviction and they could not identify who had recorded or posted the video online, there was no evidence of threatening behaviour and there was no evidence anyone present was upset. Therefore, she said they had decided that no-one should be prosecuted. Williams stressed that CPS policy was to prosecute racist and religious crime fairly and robustly, but that could only be done in cases where there was sufficient evidence.

On the evening of Friday 24 September 2010, a reporter visited the Bugle Pub, taking photographs outside and entering to make enquiries. Inside, he was asked to leave by drinkers and delete the pictures from his camera. He was followed outside and barracked as he drove off. It wasn't the response the reporter was expecting, but of course ordinary people supporting the group's actions was the last thing the press expected.

Also in the north-east, Hope Not Hate reported that an SWP meeting in Newcastle had been '**attacked**' by the EDL. The anti-fascist group claimed that up to 20 EDL had attacked two doormen as they tried to storm the meeting, but added there were no arrests. Local EDL divisions denied any knowledge of any attack or any meeting for that matter.

Later that week, Muslims Against Crusaders protested against the visit to London of Pope Benedict XVI. Over a hundred radicals, accompanied by Anjem Choudary, assembled on Duke of Wellington Place as the Pope was due to make his way through Wellington Arch to a prayer vigil in Hyde Park.

Surrounded by police, the protesters, some of whom carried placards proclaiming '**Jesus hates the Pope**', '**Jesus is not God**' and '**Jesus loves Islam**', chanted "**Pope Benedict, you will pay, justice is on its way!**" MAC organiser, Abu Rayah, spoke to the protestors, referring to Pope Benedict as a "**leader of the crusades**"; he said that the "**war against Islam and Muslims**" was ideological as well as military. Rayah said Islam would eventually dominate all other religions, and expressed hope that the Pope would face the '**lions of Islam**' for criticisms he had made about the religion. Rayah, cheered by the crowd, also said that anyone who insulted the Prophet deserved capital punishment.

The MAC protestors chanted "**Burn, burn, burn in hell**" as the Pope passed them in his Pope mobile.

26 September 2010: Nuneaton

Two weeks after the Fusiliers parade, the Queen's Gurkha Signals were also given the Freedom of Nuneaton. After the scenes at the Crew, the EDL was determined to attend again, but this time in larger numbers.

The meeting point was the Felix Holt pub on Stratford Street in the town centre and by 11.00am there were around 150 EDL inside. A few police were stationed outside the pub, with hundreds around the town, drafted in from neighbouring forces. A two-man police Evidence Gathering Team entered the pub and started filming. One EDL supporter followed the team round the pub filming them with his camera, provoking laughter. There was a loud cheer from the EDL as the EGT finally left.

As the Gurkha parade approached, the EDL rushed to greet them. They lined both sides of the road and as the soldiers passed they clapped and cheered, chanting '**heroes**" at the troops. One woman carried a sign which simply said '**Thank you Gurkhas**', others waved Union Jacks as the soldiers marched by. As the parade passed they followed it to the Town Hall, where the Freedom of the Borough was bestowed by Lord Mayor Don Navarro. The EDL were respectful, there was no chanting as they mingled with the large crowd of locals who had also gathered to pay tribute. The Gurkhas then marched back through the town, cheered on the crowds.

Following the parade, the majority of EDL returned to the Felix Holt, followed by a large number of police. The officers seemed relaxed and allowed the EDL to tie flags to some railings opposite the pub and to come and go as they pleased. It seemed it would be a trouble-free day.

However, from the direction of Queen's Road, a small number of Asian youths walked through the town centre, past a few EDL making their way back to the Felix Holt. Words were exchanged between the two groups, shouts were heard and the Asian youths were chased down the street by the EDL. Police intervened quickly, detaining some EDL, one of whom was female. The Asian youths were chased towards the Town Hall and police quickly formed a cordon preventing the EDL from following them. The mood changed; police now blocked off Stratford Street, searching anyone entering or leaving. The heavy police presence was maintained for an hour or so, with three vanloads of riot-police on stand-by nearby. Some EDL were picked out and arrested as they stood outside the pub, presumably after video footage had been studied.

Up at Queen's Road, The Crew was closed, but a small number of anti-fascists from Coventry were outside handing out leaflets. Another group of Asian males made their way down towards the town. They were stopped by police just before they came into view of the EDL and persuaded to seek an alternative route to wherever they were headed.

Eventually the mood relaxed a little, people were allowed to come and go more freely and most EDL started making their way home. Some had parked in the vicinity of Queen's Road and walked towards their vehicles. A number of Asian youths had gathered by The Crew, they saw the EDL and started to walk towards them gesticulating angrily. As soon as they were spotted, the EDL charged, forcing the Asian gang back. The EDL found another pub, but as they walked into the car-park there was a confrontation with another gang of Asians. After a brief scuffle, police arrived and dispersed the Asian group, telling the EDL to leave the town. Around 4.00pm there were further clashes between the EDL and missile throwing Asian youths. Police were again in attendance and this time issued Section 27 Dispersal Orders to the EDL.

The following day, Chief Inspector Adrian Knight of Warwickshire Police said the policing operation had worked well and seven people had been arrested, for a range of public order offences. Knight added that the town's CCTV system had proven invaluable and that police had been in touch with, presumably Muslim, community leaders throughout the operation. *BBC News* reported there had been a disturbance and arrests, showing pictures of police cordoning off a road. The *Coventry Telegraph* reported '**No trouble as Gurkhas are cheered in Nuneaton parade**' and said the massive police operation had prevented any trouble.

2 October 2010: Blackburn

A week before the planned visit to Leicester, a KFC restaurant on Haslingden Road, Blackburn, was again targeted by the local EDL division. The demo was a continuation of the EDL's campaign against halal meat and the group planned to protest outside the restaurant for a week.

Around 80 EDL activists attended the protest, the Blackburn Division was obviously well represented, but others had travelled from Bolton, Burnley and Preston to join in. Activists flitted between the demonstration site and the Observatory pub across the road, as they handed out leaflets and displayed signs and banners which read '**No to halal meat at KFC**' and '**Boycott KFC**'. The EDL claimed that a lot of customers left the restaurant after being made aware it was participating in the halal trials.

Around 4.30pm a large number of police appeared, prompting rumours that a gang of Muslims were making their way to the area. The EDL were shepherded into the Observatory and police surrounded it. After a short while, police decided to clear the pub. As they did, a group of Asian youths appeared on nearby Brandy House Brow. They were dispersed by police, obviously keen to stop the two groups clashing. The EDL re-grouped at a pub called The Crescent in Shadsworth. Police appeared again and detained five people. Everyone not from Blackburn was told that they should leave the town, otherwise they would face arrest.

The following day there were further scenes of disorder outside the restaurant. A rubbish skip was set on fire and four men were arrested for public order offences. Two days later, the *Blackburn Citizen* reported that Lancashire Police had obtained a Section 14 Order limiting the number of demonstrators to nine and stating protests must finish by 7.30pm each day. A police spokesman told *The Citizen* that whilst police were keen to respect the right of people to protest, restrictions were necessary to maintain order and reassure the public. KFC told the paper that they were carrying out the trial due to demand from customers and the response had been positive, adding there was a non-halal store nearby, so customers still had a choice. Local MP, Jack Straw, called the police action sensible, saying he ate halal meat and had not received any complaints about it being served in local stores.

Chairman of the Lancashire Council of Mosques (LCM), Salim Mulla, backed the police but added that the LCM did not accept that the meat served at the store was '**truly halal**' as KFC stunned the animals and used a mechanical slaughter device. Therefore, Mulla said LCM could not endorse the trials: '**We don't want any confrontation. We have asked the youth to keep away from the area. That is the message we are sending out and to let the police do their job. The EDL are totally unrepresentative of British society. We don't want to give them any prominence. Most people are willing to work together for better understanding of each other.**' The next day, it appeared the EDL were sticking to the conditions as only eight activists turned up to picket the store.

Know your Enemy

Prior to the Leicester protest, pictures of journalists and anti-fascists were posted on the EDL's Internet forum under the heading: 'Leicester 9 October - Know your enemy'.

Along with anti-fascists, numerous pictures of members of the press who the group claimed were anti-EDL were posted. Articles by some of the journalists, riddled with suggestive terminology, were also posted as evidence that the people in question were deliberately painting the EDL in a negative light. There was a definite sense of frustration among EDL activists, who felt they were being unfairly represented by a supposedly unbiased media.

Activists upped the ante even further on Sunday 3 October 2010, when an EDL team from the Internet forum attended an SWP *Right to Work* march in Birmingham, planned to coincide with the Conservative Party conference in the city. The EDL had virtually declared war on the trade union movement; they saw it as being infiltrated, corrupt and run by communists.

Your average union leader in Britain is now as remote from their membership as premiership footballers are from the fans who pay their astronomical wages. Thirty-eight union leaders in the UK now earn over £100,000 a year. There is no attempt by any senior trade union official to engage with disgruntled working class people, possibly because they simply can't relate to their concerns anymore. These people are supposedly the representatives of the working class, some of them at the 2010 TUC conference even called for a class war. They still haven't got it; the seven million drop in union membership isn't just down to governmental measures against the movement, ordinary people simply no longer feel represented by out of touch, Sunday socialists with their snouts firmly in the trough.

A week before, a prominent member of the TUC had complained to police that EDL supporters had made threats against him. Alec McFadden, a vocal anti-fascist campaigner, alerted Merseyside Police after discovering a doctored image of himself on the website of the EDL Merseyside Division. Local EDL activists had used a picture of McFadden taken in Liverpool city centre, holding a placard opposing cuts in public spending. However, apparently unbeknown to the EDL, the image had been doctored so the placard read '**protest against our homecoming troops**' rather than '**protest against Lib-Dem betrayal**'.

Comments were allegedly posted on the Internet alongside the picture, calling McFadden a '**scumbag**' and a '**marked man**'. McFadden told the *Liverpool Echo* that he had contacted police as soon as he had seen the picture. He said they had visited his house and were driving past it every hour. McFadden was obviously extremely traumatised by the incident, so much so, he was later listed as a supporter on the website of the hackers who broke into EDL websites and released details of EDL supporters.

In Birmingham, the EDL met at the Shakespeare pub on Summer Row early on the morning of the SWP demo. They waited till it was underway then entered the car park which the pre-march rally was taking place. They walked around the demo freely, taking photographs of the left wing celebrities present. Martin Smith and Weyman Bennett happily posed for pictures, but little did they know the class warriors taking the snaps weren't actually the left-wing variety, they were hardened EDL activists. The mission was a psychological victory, it was the '**taking ends**' hooligan mentality. They acted with impunity, walking into their opponent's gathering because they chose to. As a result, more photographs were published of people who opposed the EDL, putting further pressure on the far-left. It was a trick the left had been fond of playing for decades, but they found themselves uncomfortable targets now the tables were turned.

9 October 2010: Leicester

Leicester is a large city in the East Midlands, built on trade and particularly associated with textiles and footwear. The city also had a plethora of other industries, with factories and works manufacturing anything from hosiery to machine tools. Famous household names such as Co-op, Gillette, Walkers and even the makers of the famous Glacier Mint, Fox's, all had bases in the city.

Following the Second World War, Leicester welcomed large numbers of immigrants from the Commonwealth. Many of the newcomers were from the sub-continent, in particular Gujarat and Punjab, but were followed by Asians from East Africa who were expelled from Uganda by Idi Amin. Leicester's Indian community settled around the Belgrave and Melton Road part of the city, now known as the Golden Mile and latterly Oadby. The majority of Muslim migrants settled in the Highfields area close to the train station. Most of Leicester's inner city areas are now multicultural (the city's white community are predicted to be a minority group by 2012), although the city's outlying council estates remain largely white.

During the 1990s, a large number of Dutch-Somali immigrants also settled in the area, according to the press they were attracted by the large number of mosques. Ethnic minorities now make up over 40% of the population, speaking over 70 different languages; they make Leicester one of the most ethnically diverse cities in Britain.

In the run up to the visit by the EDL, Leicester's MP's released a joint statement, which said the protest would not affect Leicester's long and proud history of community cohesion. Leader of the Leicester Council of Faiths, Manjula Sood, said the city had built a reputation of community harmony and they didn't want it damaged. A spokesman for the EDL told the *Leicester Mercury* they expected a good turnout, but didn't think the protest would see similar violent scenes to those witnessed in Bradford.

Senior Leicestershire police officers met on 7 September to discuss the protest. Chief Superintendent Jason Masters told the paper that senior officers were working with '**key partner agencies**' and '**stakeholders in the community**' to consider the options for policing the event. Masters added that police were assessing the various legal powers available to them to restrict or prohibit certain aspects of the protest. The police always seemed to be in consultation with community leaders or community stakeholders or whatever, but none of them ever seemingly English and working class. This is one of the main the reasons the EDL had attracted such support. When was the last time you saw the police or local authorities consulting white, working class people?

Searchlight told the *Leicester Mercury* the EDL was travelling to Leicester for '**one reason only**' and brought disharmony and disruption wherever it went. A meeting called to organise a UAF counter-protest was disrupted by a small group of EDL, who walked in and distributed EDL literature to astonished anti-fascists. The EDL were asked to leave and a scuffle took place. Police were called and made two arrests.

The EDL had applied to march in Leicester, just as it had in Bradford. Two weeks before the protest, Leicester City Council announced it intended to apply to the Home Office to ban any march. Leicestershire Police had told the council they believed the EDL planned to attack a mosque before marching into Highfields, the heart of the city's Muslim community. Chief Constable Simon Cole said that an intelligence and threat assessment indicated a march by the EDL represented a major threat to public order. Council leader, Veejay Patel, said the council was determined to obtain a ban preventing any march, as evidence showed that it would cause disruption and possibly violence.

Where the mosque attack intelligence came from is anyone's guess. There were no plans to attack any mosque; it simply wasn't in the interests of the EDL to do so. Logic was abandoned however, in favour of sensationalism to fulfil an agenda. It was believed, simply because the police and press had convinced the public that is what the EDL do, they attack mosques! Somewhat justifiably, Muslim groups told the *Leicester Mercury* they were concerned by the police reports. Suleman Nagdi, Chairman of the Federation of Muslim Organisations, said an attack on a place of worship was an attack on everyone, but added that he didn't think the protest would break the unity of Leicester's faith communities. Ibrahim Mogra of Evington Muslim Centre said the news was very worrying and everything possible should to be done to prevent any attack. Guramit Singh rejected the claims and said the EDL was merely going to Leicester to protest peacefully. Singh said the EDL denounced any attacks on mosques, adding that the group was formed to fight militant, not moderate, Islam.

A week before the protest, EDL activists from Leicester met in the city centre to distribute leaflets advertising the event. They came across a handful of Hope Not Hate activists who were also in the city. Standing around a paste table, the anti-fascists were encouraging people to sign a petition against the EDL. They were quickly surrounded by the EDL. Police were quickly on the scene, but didn't intervene and just kept an eye on proceedings.

Hope Not Hate followed a different tack to that of UAF, mainly because they had even fewer activists than UAF to call on. The group would face criticism from local UAF supporters when, with the police, they attended local schools and colleges, advising students not to attend the UAF counter-protest. The anti-fascist group had also organised activities on the Friday and Sunday either side of the EDL demonstration. Singer Billy Bragg was booked to appear at an event on the Sunday, which caused anger among EDL activists who condemned Bragg as a class traitor, the archetypal champagne socialist. Pictures of Bragg's luxury mansion in Dorset, the like of which the working class people he claims to speak for could only dream about, were subsequently widely posted on EDL websites.

On Monday 4 October, five days before the protest, bowing to the wishes of police and councillors, Home Secretary, Theresa May, issued a '**blanket-ban**' on any marches taking place in Leicester on the 9 October. The Home Office said that anyone organising a march on that day could be jailed for six months or face a £2500 fine and anyone found guilty of taking part could be fined up to £1000. Guramit Singh said the ban was '**bang out of order**' and '**a breach of freedom of speech**'. The EDL believed that although the Home Secretary had banned the march, they should be still allowed to walk to the demo point, which had been agreed on as Humberstone Gate East, a remote and largely derelict square in the city centre. The EDL claimed this was so supporters got the chance to stretch their legs and didn't feel contained like they had on previous protests when, after enduring long coach journeys, they had then spent an hour or so being led to the demo site by police. When eventually allowed off their coaches, they were then usually immediately kettled. This, claimed the EDL, led to frustration, and they believed it was a deliberate tactic to gain a reaction.

The EDL claimed that recently in Birmingham, the Islamist organisation Hizb ut-Tahrir had been allowed to assemble unannounced and unhindered to oppose ex-Pakistani President, General Musharraf. The EDL claimed that Hizb ut-Tahrir supported proscribed extremist Islamist groups, yet it did not have to co-operate with local police weeks or even months beforehand as the EDL had to do. The EDL said it highlighted a two-tier system in the country and they were now of the opinion that liaison with local police was not the best approach to take. As stated previously, the group had learned that the threat of non-cooperation was a powerful bargaining tool. The EDL said they felt they could not guarantee the safety of supporters if they agreed to be policed in a similar fashion to how they had been at Dudley or Bradford. As they believed that Leicestershire Police did not want a peaceful and successful demonstration, the group said they were now planning to hold a flash-demo and would not be releasing any details.

A spokesperson for Leicestershire Police told *BBC News* they were keen to keep talking to everyone involved in order to facilitate peaceful demonstrations, but they would be putting methods in place to gather evidence and prosecute unlawful behaviour should it occur.

The EDL published more photos of journalists who they considered were biased against the movement. Freelance journalists' website *Demotix* warned reporters they should take precautions to avoid their faces ending up on an EDL database. Again the Internet was proving to be a great leveller, the press, with all the resources available to them, were running scared from a few EDL activists with cheap digital cameras. The campaign against the press certainly started to bear fruit, as Leicestershire Police announced they would be issuing their own press passes for journalists working at the demonstration. A police spokesman said the measure was being put in place to ensure the safety of journalists, after photographs and threats had appeared on EDL and Casuals United websites. The passes would be issued at a press briefing on the morning of the protest and journalists would be required to prove they were there for legitimate reasons.

There is a UK Press Card already in operation, but that is a voluntary scheme which not all journalists subscribe to. Jeremy Dear, of the NUJ, said they were not advising members to wear the passes. He said the UK Press Card was the only recognised form of identification for journalists and was accepted by the Association of Chief Police Officers. In response to Dear's comments, one journalist claimed that a lot of local newspaper reporters didn't have press cards as they didn't need them, some didn't even belong to the NUJ. He said the NUJ was attempting to speak on behalf of other unions who may not hold the same view and statements by the union which openly attacked the EDL were hardly encouraging independent reporting and also endangered journalists. This highlighted the discontent amongst some journalists regarding freedom of reporting, and the powerful left wing NUJ, which tries to exert control over what appears in the press and also pushes its own politically motivated agenda.

With a day to go, the *Leicester Mercury* reported that the police and council had received reports of text messages spreading unfounded rumours linked to the demonstration. One was said to incorrectly claim a young Asian woman had been attacked. Sheila Lock, Chief Executive of Leicester City Council said that people should not take the texts at face value and the council didn't want groups mobilising on the basis of unfounded rumours. The Leicestershire Federation of Muslims said a rumour that the EDL were planning to start their protest from outside Leicester Central Mosque in Highfields was also false. A spokesman said they were deeply upset by the false information and urged Muslims not to travel into the city centre on the day of the protest.

Chief Inspector Martin Halse of Leicestershire Police asked people not to be manipulated by the texts and said it was a known tactic of certain people to try to manipulate others into reacting. He said the police were encouraging people to speak to their local councillor or community leader if they received one of the messages. Since the Leeds protest, the left-wing and anti-fascist movement had been trying to inflame and mobilise Muslim youth with a series of misleading rumours on social networking websites. Now it seemed police had finally realised that certain groups were attempting to agitate the Muslim community.

Later that day, the EDL announced that Stephen Lennon had again been arrested by police. Kevin Carroll had apparently visited the police station where he was being held and given police an ultimatum, if Lennon wasn't released or charged, the EDL protest in Leicester would be redirected to Luton. Lennon was eventually released, nine hours after being arrested, although it was unclear what the arrest was in connection with.

On the morning of the protest, people travelling into Leicester along the main Narborough Road were greeted with a large banner hanging from a railway bridge which simply said 'EDL 9 OCT'. It was the biggest operation by Leicestershire Police in twenty-five years, with over two thousand officers on duty. Police warned residents that they may see convoys of police vehicles with their lights flashing and using sirens travelling across the city, but stressed it wouldn't automatically indicate an incident; officers could just be deploying where they were needed. Calling the day's proceedings *Operation Stay Safe*, police had advised shops to board up their windows and told the public they should keep out of the city centre. Police revealed they were utilising Section 14 legislation to impose a time limit on the EDL protest, from 2.00pm to 3.30pm.

Apart from police officers, who were on the streets in force by 9.30am, it appeared the general public had taken police advice and stayed away on the day of the protest. The city centre streets were deserted, many shops had chosen not to open, and a lot had boarded up their windows. By 10.30am, EDL supporters started to flood into the city. Those arriving by train were stopped, questioned and filmed by police, then transported by bus to four local pubs on Hotel Street, The Square, Molly O'Grady's, Market Tavern and The Goose. Some small groups of EDL clashed with anti-fascists and Muslims who had begun to roam the city centre.

Unbeknown to police, one group of EDL from London had headed for nearby Loughborough, where they staged a flash demo before heading to Leicester. Other EDL had ignored police muster points and met in neighbouring Market Harborough, over 400 had gathered by the time police were dispatched to monitor them. After a peaceful assembly, the EDL were applauded by locals as they left the town on their coaches. It was becoming clear that the EDL was beginning to garner increasing support in some areas of the country.

By midday, the numbers in Hotel Street were increasing. All four pubs were ringed by police, as EDL, inside and out, sang songs and chanted. There were a handful of anti-fascists on the other side of police lines, some of them photographing the EDL, who were returning the compliment. At the end of the street, a large number of people had gathered to sightsee. Police reported that the atmosphere at all pubs was good natured. They were carrying out Section 60 searches on protestors and had detained one man for a drugs offence. EDL supporters were still pouring into Leicester, one group chanted as they marched past Leicester's Central Library.

As the pubs steadily filled, a man arrived outside The Square and started to make an impromptu speech. Pointing to anti-fascists across the road, he started to rant about UAF. He was quickly identified as ex-BNP councillor Richard Barnbrook., who was quickly told by the EDL that they were not the BNP and were perfectly aware of how to deal with anti-fascists. Accompanied by another man and a female, Barnbrook then went into the pub and circulated amongst EDL supporters.

At 2.10pm, coaches arrived to ferry the EDL to the demonstration site. Police roughly handled EDL supporters onto the coaches and this resulted in a number of scuffles. As officers entered the pubs to clear them, there were further clashes which resulted in two arrests. Again the police were unnecessarily heavy-handed, and it caused resentment among EDL supporters, which would manifest itself later on. As the coaches passed, many of the spectators standing at the end of the street cheered and waved. Many EDL saw this as vindication of their visit to the city; like Market Harborough, members of the public were turning out and showing their support. At Leicester train station, groups of Muslims and anti-fascists were ambushing EDL as they arrived and scuffles between the two groups were broken up by police. Coaches full of EDL headed towards Humberstone Gate and a number were attacked by Muslim youths gathered along the route.

The site was in the middle of a dilapidated part of the city centre, a square formed into a dead end by police barriers. The obvious decay of the area no doubt mirrored similarly neglected areas of the country many EDL hailed from. The press photographed the EDL as they arrived; they were lambs to the slaughter with the media allowed so close. This resulted in confrontations and the press being ordered further back by police.

A number of Muslim males and anti-fascists had gathered at the other side of police lines. This factor, along with the presence of the press, caused the EDL to repeatedly surge against the fences, again, like in Bradford, police allowed opposing groups too close to each other. It seemed bizarre that lessons never seemed to be learned from previous protests by what is considered one of the best police forces in the world. Obviously this leads to constant speculation it is a tactic by police to encourage trouble and either give the authorities an excuse to ban the EDL or make arrests which would result in restrictions being imposed. Police battled to contain the situation, resulting in several EDL supporters being struck with batons. A couple with their heads cut open needed medical attention. One of the injured was asked about a head wound he had received. He said he had been pushed into the area where the confrontation was taking place and had been struck by a riot shield. Asked by a *Central News* reporter if he blamed police for his injury, he said he didn't as the police had just been doing their job by trying to keep people in the compound.

One man did manage to break through police lines and run towards the anti-fascists, but he was quickly wrestled to the floor by three officers. Another man was also arrested as he also attempted to break through the cordon. More EDL supporters were arriving all the time and each new coach was greeted with rapturous applause by those already on site. Not everyone getting off the coaches were young men. One elderly lady pushed a walking frame in front of her, other people were on crutches.

There were further clashes with police as the number of EDL at the site grew. Mounted officers were introduced, but two fireworks thrown from the crowd panicked the horses, forcing them to withdraw. The EDL repeatedly surged at police lines and at one point seemed to have broken through. Police just about managed to regain control and beat the EDL back into the compound. Police and press found themselves under a hail of missiles. A smoke bomb was then thrown, adding to the general sense of mayhem and confusion which was unfolding. At this point the police ordered the press further away, some protested but officers insisted. More police reinforcements arrived and the mounted officers were reintroduced.

At 3.10pm, *Sky News* reported that it was the largest EDL protest to date. *BBC News* reported there were over 2000 EDL present. Leicestershire Police estimated there were 700 at the UAF counter-protest, but they would later blamed by anti-fascists of preventing people from attending. Guramit Singh was organising the PA system. There was a problem with it and activists in the square became restless. A camera was spotted at a window overlooking the site and missiles were hurled at the building as rumours circulated it was either UAF or the press. Clashes were still taking place between EDL and the police at the bottom of the square, some young EDL supporters climbed buildings or lampposts to unfurl flags or banners. The EDL sang **"You're not English anymore!"** at the police penning them into the compound.

Coaches were still arriving all the time. Outside the demonstration site, *BBC News* interviewed onlookers. Mark James, 40, told the BBC that being black gave him his own perspective on the event: **'The EDL invited me in to hear what they had to say. I was ready to go in, but the police said I couldn't, it was too dangerous, it could provoke trouble. You hear and see terrible things about Islamic extremism, so you can see why people would not want that. The neighbourhood I live in, here in Leicester, is mostly Muslim and every community has its own racism, you don't always hear about that'.**

Cindy McCammon, 19, a student from Burton-on-Trent said that she and her friends had come to see what was happening and added that she had some respect for the EDL: **'You have to stand up for what you believe in. They have a point but they go about it the wrong way. If I see someone walking down the street with a St George's Flag on their shoulders, I feel proud. We shouldn't be afraid to stand up to things which are wrong, even if they are done by people from an ethnic group'.**

The speeches started and a local activist, Chris Lough, took to the stage, claiming that whatever the media said, the EDL was welcome in Leicester. Lough said the city had a reputation for being multicultural and integrated, but that was only true up to a point. He said there were areas where the Islamic population constituted 75-90% and those areas had their own Islamic schools and banks, but he claimed it was a side of Leicester that the authorities didn't want people to know about. Lough said people claimed there was no problem with radical Islam, but radicals wanted to implement Sharia in the city.

As the speeches were being made, Richard Barnbrook was encouraging a large group of EDL down towards the fences and police lines. The majority of the crowd had no idea who he was, but it wasn't the last the EDL would see of Barnbrook. He would resurface a month later at an EDL meeting in London, claiming he wanted to get involved, but most present demanded to know why he was there and Barnbrook was asked to leave.

Back at the main stage in Leicester, arriving late after being released after nine hours in police custody, Stephen Lennon took the microphone to rapturous applause:

> **"I haven't prepared any speech; he's put me straight in it. The truth is, police persecution is what I will talk about. You see all the police around here, it is not the police officers on the street, on the frontline, it is the hierarchy. Since we started this, my Mother and Father, they have had their house raided, they are 63 years old, they had their computers taken. My house was raided, with British police and machine guns, my children, my fiancée who is pregnant, has been arrested and charged/bailed on money laundering. The truth is they would not dare to arrest a pregnant Muslim woman. You wouldn't fucking dare do it! When the police went to my parents' house, I haven't lived there for six years, I don't how they gained warrants to search their house, but they searched and ransacked their house. Now, when they ransacked their house, they threw the Bible on the floor like it was any other book. I, myself, am not incredibly religious, but my parents are. They disregarded the Bible on the floor, they would not do that to the Qur'an. They would not do that to the Qur'an. These are exactly the reasons why we formed, to combat a two-tier system. One rule for them and another rule for us.**

It is true, it is oppression, that is exactly what it is, it is apartheid. It is kid gloves for their community and an iron fist for our community, and people won't put up with it for much longer. My missus has been arrested, she has been told she's looking at seven years for money laundering, for all these fabricated charges. I have been arrested three times, three times they have ransacked my house, the British police. Where my little girl goes to nursery, the lady who runs my nursery, lives in the same road as me, now when they ransacked my house, they lifted up the drains of the next door neighbours' houses. It is as if the neighbours are living next to Fred West, or someone like that. It is as if I am some sort of wrong-un, some sort of murderer, yet the truth is I am nothing more than a patriot who isn't going to say No! The police weigh up the situation and rather than deal with the Islamic militant Muslim gangs peddling heroin, taking liberties in our towns and cities, taking liberties with our fucking youth, taking liberties with non-Muslim youth, non-Muslim girls, raping, pimping, beating, abusing our whole system, rather than deal with these gangs, they would rather persecute us, the people who are highlighting the issue. The fact is the police, the councils, the Government, everyone needs to wake up. We aren't going anywhere, we are growing in strength, we are growing in numbers, we will be here next year, we will be here for the next 10 years. People will say where is the English Defence League going? My children are free, and I have a newborn on the way, they will be members of the English Defence League. The English Defence League is going nowhere. It is here now, it is not going anywhere. We will combat militant Islam. Wherever it raises its ugly paedophilic, disturbed, mediaeval, fucking head, we will be there. And, even standing here today is historic, every demonstration is historic, people are united from one corner of England to the other corner, not just England, Wales, Scotland, everywhere, coming together for a united front. The united front is that we will not tolerate what has gone on for the last 15 years. Liberties have taken across our whole nation and the days of militant Islam walking across our country, unchallenged, are gone.

The English Defence League's here. People mention how much we cost the taxpayers, they say we cost the taxpayers £500,000, yet for the first time ever you have got people who pay taxes, protesting. We are the British public, we pay our taxes, we have the right to democratically assemble in city centres to oppose militant Islam.

People want to say we are racists, that we are fascist, that is the weakest argument to our cause. What is the easiest way to get away from the argument, it is to say "they are racists", "they are fascists", "they are Nazis" - the truth is we are not Nazis, we will smash Nazis the same way we will smash militant Islam. We are exactly about, black and white unite, every single community in this country can come and join our ranks, fill our ranks, we don't care if you arrived here yesterday, you are welcome to protect our Christian culture and our way of life and we will not tolerate this any more!"

EDL supporters responded well to Lennon's ad hoc speech. The chant of "**Tommy Robinson's, barmy army!**" echoed around the protest site.

At 3.45pm, the police started to prepare for the end of the protest. The surrounding streets were swept and some blocked by rows of police vans. At around 3.45pm, they relaxed their cordon at the bottom of the site and EDL supporters flooded out. Police tried to force the EDL onto buses but large groups simply ignored them. A large number of EDL burst through police lines to confront a large gang of Asian men. The EDL scattered the Asian gang and both groups engaged in a running battle towards the city centre.

Sky News claimed that one of their vans had been attacked by the EDL, damaging some of their equipment. Reporter Robin Powell said that fearing for their safety, he and his colleagues had been forced to lock themselves inside the vehicle. Powell said that following the attack, the EDL had headed for Highfields. This was later proven not to have been the case and in fact the van had been attacked by anti-fascists. *Sky News* later removed the report from its website, but spurred by the Powell report, rumours now circulated that the EDL was headed for Highfields. A large group of Muslims gathered outside the area's main mosque to defend it, as police attempted to dispel the rumours, asserting the EDL was nowhere near the area.

At 4.07pm, Leicestershire Police announced they had made five arrests, adding that none of the detained men were from Leicester. Minutes later, a convoy of police cars and ambulances were seen heading down Maidstone Road in the St Peter's area of the city. EDL flooded towards the city centre, scattering any opposition in their wake. Police commandeered buses to block off roads. Two men were bitten by police dogs, one so severely that he required surgery. The chant of "**E, E, EDL!**" could be heard reverberating around the city streets.

Another large breakaway group of EDL clashed with Muslim youths on the junction of Queen's Street and St George's Way. With police in attendance but totally ignored, the two groups met in the middle of the road and hurled missiles at each other. Asian males, who were touring the city looking for EDL supporters, jumped out of passing cars to join the confrontation. The EDL gave a sudden roar and ran towards the Asian men, forcing them to flee. They were pursued by the EDL, with some seeking sanctuary in a fast-food restaurant and others in a supermarket. The EDL followed and swarmed round the restaurant, smashing windows. Manager of the restaurant, Usman Ali, told the *Leicester Mercury* that EDL supporters had smashed four windows and entered the shop. Ali said it had been a very frightening experience for both staff and customers.

At 4.30pm, police announced they had closed the inner ring road. Large tailbacks of vehicles could be seen, as sporadic clashes between opposing groups took place. Back at the demo site, the remaining EDL were boarding coaches, some bound for the train station and others to ferry them home. As some of the coaches made their way through Leicester they were attacked by Asian gangs. Some EDL jumped off to confront their attackers and nearby police were forced to intervene.

Leicestershire Police announced they had made seventeen arrests, mainly for public order offences. They claimed that rumours which resulted in locals taking to the streets of Highfields were unfounded and that there had been no reported incidents in the area. However, days later, local group St Peter's Neighbourhood Monitoring released three photographs which showed baton wielding riot-police confronting masked Asian youths on Conduit Street. The trouble was quickly brought under control, but a neutral observer can only speculate why Leicestershire Police maintained there were no reported disturbances in the area, when there obviously had been.

24 October 2010: Israeli Embassy, London

The EDL re-launched its website, which was now overtly pro-Israel and contained new links to the websites which formed the pro-Zionist blogger alliance, including Robert Spencer's *Jihad Watch* and Pamela Geller's *Atlas Shrugs*.

Devin Burghart, of the Institute for Research & Education on Human Rights said he believed Geller was now acting as the bridge between the EDL and the Tea Party and that her stature within both movements had increased substantially following the Ground Zero mosque controversy. He was right, Geller's profile had certainly increased within the EDL, and she now seemed to be taking more of a role than that of a passing observer. It seemed the discussions in the US had resulted in a few substantial changes within the movement, especially regarding agenda.

The EDL also announced what it considered to be a coup. Apparently invited to the UK by Alan Lake, American Rabbi Nachum Shifren would address an EDL protest outside the Israeli Embassy in London. The rabbi would later tell Norwegian television news show *TV 2 Nyhetene* that Lake had a very decisive role in working with him and other people in the United States. *The Observer* agreed, claiming that Lake was believed to have been in touch with a number of anti-Islamic Christian evangelical groups in the US. *Searchlight* suggested that Lake had been using images of the EDL taking on militant Islam on the streets of the UK to garner credibility and support in the US.

This was also a view now shared by some of the EDL rank and file, who were worried about Lake and Moore's input especially with the sudden lurch towards Zionism. As the Tea Party was discovering, the most willing backers in the fight against the perceived '**global jihad**' were wealthy Jewish Americans. With their support came conditions, the main one being support of Israel. The EDL was considered too chaotic an organisation, therefore control would have to be asserted directly from the US and a lengthy power struggle for the EDL would begin.

Shifren, nicknamed the Surfing Rabbi, was a Republican candidate for the upcoming election for the US Senate and also involved with the Tea Party. He had also previously worked as a fitness trainer for Israeli paratroopers and as a driver for Rabbi Meir Kahane. The demonstration was held on a Sunday, apparently because Moore insisted it be staged before the US elections, believing it would enhance the rabbi's chances of being elected. Saturday demonstrations were too problematic to organise with the Metropolitan Police, so Sunday it was.

Rabbi Shifren said he was attending the protest to express his solidarity with patriots in England who were on the front line in the jihad. He said that multiculturalists had brought the West to the brink, insisting on degrading host cultures while pandering to '**forces of darkness**' that threatened to completely transform Western society. Shifren said the multiculturalists sought to destroy religious foundations, loosen patriotic bonds and were responsible for a '**wave of Middle Age darkness in the Muslim religion**'. He added that the American people were facing the most insidious threat to their way of life, but like the British, they were asleep.

Following the announcement, a spokesman for the Israeli Embassy said they wanted to disassociate themselves from the event and also from any attempts to link Israel to the EDL. Speaking for the Jewish Board of Deputies, Jon Benjamin said that Shifren was displaying breathtaking naivety and ignorance in associating with the EDL, especially as (presumably as a rabbi) he characterised the Jewish community. Benjamin said that whatever the dangers of radicalisation, they applied just as much to the right-wing as to the left or Islamism. Calling the EDL violent and intimidating, Mark Gardner of the Jewish Community Security Trust said that any Jews involved in the EDL were deluded. He said the Jewish Division was a tiny part of a far larger movement, dominated by white males who would previously have made up the numbers in National Front marches and football hooligan gangs.

Moore countered the opposition by saying that it was Rabbi Shifren who had contacted the EDL, who had then invited him over to speak. She said that they were going to the embassy to show support for Israel and added that not enough Jews were taking to the streets to protest. Moore claimed the Jewish Division was causing ripples amongst the Jewish community because they were achieving things that other groups couldn't. She said the CST and the Board of Deputies spoke out but what people really wanted to see was action on the streets.

On the morning of the protest, the EDL assembled at the Hereford Arms on Gloucester Street in central London. Prior to the demo, many divisions had reported little interest and it soon became apparent the turnout was low. Around 200 people eventually turned up, it should've been a clear message to the leadership that the majority of the EDL rank and file didn't believe that Israel was as important an issue as they obviously did, or were being persuaded that it was. It wasn't anything to do with anti-Semitism; it was more about relevance, or the lack of it to the lives of ordinary members.

At around 1.30pm, the EDL left the Hereford Arms and made the short walk to the Israeli Embassy. UAF had announced a 1.00pm counter-demo but only 30 anti-fascists had turned up. The EDL were providing the rabbi with security and a handful of activists shadowed him closely. As the EDL arrived at the demo site, one anti-fascist rushed forward and threw water over the PA system. Rabbi Shifren was therefore forced to make his speech with a loud hailer, but it only added to the siege mentality he was promoting.

The rabbi said he welcomed the abuse he had faced from the UK Jewish community. He said some had called him a Nazi and asked why he was poking his nose into England's business. He was here he said, because British Jews didn't have the guts to stand up themselves and '**take care of business**'. Shifren said there was only one group in England with the moral courage to do that and he wished that just one politician had the backbone to stand up and agree with the EDL, but added that they wouldn't because of Arab petrodollars. He would not stand by and watch the destruction of the USA and UK, said Shifren, and he wanted to ask the liberals who preached multiculturalism, "**why don't you go to Saudi Arabia and start there?**" Shifren concluded by claiming that history would record that one group lit the spark to liberate the West from the oppression of government and the leftist, fifth columnist, quisling press. That group, said the rabbi, was the EDL.

Following the demonstration the EDL made their way back towards the Hereford Arms. Once there, the rabbi suddenly told his minders that he wanted to go to Speakers' Corner in Hyde Park. The area has long been synonymous with free speech and protest, but more recently with radical Islam, due to the number of Muslim fundamentalists who flock there.

Shifren strode off purposely with his security team in hot pursuit. They soon realised that only a handful of them had left with the rabbi, it was a fair distance to Speakers' Corner so phone calls for reinforcements were made. As they approached the park, they could see it was full of Muslims listening to various speakers. The rabbi didn't break his step; he strode into the middle of the Muslims, immediately engaging several of them in debate. The atmosphere changed and became intimidating, some radicals started shouting abuse.

Just as things appeared to be getting out of hand, a roar of "**E, E, EDL!**" was heard and over the perimeter of the park, a mass of flags appeared. The cavalry had arrived. EDL swarmed through the park, some tables with Islamic literature were overturned and scuffles broke out between the two groups. The EDL surrounded the rabbi and completely took over Speakers' Corner. Most of the Muslims disappeared, but some stayed and continued to debate with the rabbi. A small number shouted abuse, although they were confronted by the EDL and shepherded away by police. Three EDL were arrested for affray and public order offences.

The next day, writing in *The Times* Labour MP for Dagenham and Rainham, John Cruddas, called the EDL a '**small, violent street militia**' which spoke the language of a disenfranchised class. Cruddas warned that although the EDL might burn out as its predecessors (presumably and predictably comparing the EDL to the NF or BNP) had, it may not, because the group tapped into '**a politics born out of dispossession, but anchored in English male working class culture - of dress, drink and sport.**' He said the EDL operated outside the political centre ground, but it represented a large portion of the electorate. Many of its supporters, said Cruddas, were traditional Labour voters, who believed they had been robbed of their birthright and were in search of community and belonging.

Cruddas was merely echoing what Labour's Frank Field had been saying for years. In 2006, Field said the only way that traditional Labour voters could oppose the aggressive social values being imposed on them by a '**hostile metropolitan elite**' was to vote for extremist parties and he warned of a working class revolt. In March 2008, Field again warned that if government policy wasn't aligned with public opinion and large numbers of the electorate who felt disenfranchised, then trouble would erupt '**in all sorts of ways**'.

The discontent which Field warned of had appeared. Cruddas suggested the promotion of a '**modern England**', but this totally missed the point, probably purposely, because people were taking to the streets in opposition to a new, manufactured identity which was being forced upon them. They wanted a return to their traditional English way of life; they didn't want to embrace any new identity created by middle class socialists. The political establishment were still only considering skirting the issues to placate the masses, not confronting them and attempting to solve the concerns of the white working class.

30 October 2010: Amsterdam

The Amsterdam protest was arranged under the umbrella of The European Freedom Initiative, basically yet another front for the ICLA. It had initially been called to support Wilders, who was on trial in

Holland for inciting religious hatred. It appeared however, that the Dutchman was distancing himself from the protest and in particular the EDL.

Wilders told Dutch newspaper *De Telegraaf*, that he had no involvement with the demonstration and that he had never been in touch with the EDL. Up to this point, Wilders and his small army of Internet bloggers (many of them the same people who were the foot-soldiers of the ICLA) had relentlessly courted the support of EDL members on social networking sites, regularly providing them with news or updates. However, that suddenly changed following the Amsterdam announcement. It was obviously too obvious a link to the EDL for Wilders liking.

Following the disassociation by Wilders, the EDL changed the purpose of the demonstration from supporting the Dutchman, to opposing restrictions on free speech. It was also seen as a chance for the various European Defence Leagues to meet up. There had long been interest in the EDL from individuals in Europe. Denmark, France, Germany, Hungary, Sweden and Holland all now had Defence Leagues modelled on the English template, as there were similar concerns in many parts of Europe as there were in the UK. But there was no getting away from the fact, the Europeans were few in number, the same spirit of resistance that was being shown in Britain was lacking on the Continent.

In 2004, the European Union predicted that by 2050, its population would decline by 16million. New estimates project that it will have increased by 10million by 2060. This is mainly due to the number of Muslims who have settled in the EU and their higher birth rate. Europe's Muslim population has more than doubled in the past 30 years and will have doubled again by 2015. Muslims now make up a quarter of the population in cities such as Marseilles and Rotterdam, 20% in Malmo, 15% in Brussels and 10% in Paris and Copenhagen. Libyan leader Colonel Gaddafi famously once said: '**There are signs that Allah will grant Islam victory in Europe - without swords, without guns, without conquests. The 50 million Muslims of Europe will turn it into a Muslim continent within a few decades**'.

It was hoped, certainly by the ICLA, that a European gathering would create a pan-European movement along Tea Party lines. EDL activists hoped it would cement the EDL at the centre of any European counter-jihad organisation. Professor Matthew Goodwin, a Home Office advisor on far-right groups, told *BBC News* it would become much more difficult to control groups such as the EDL when they started linking up with other like-minded organisations abroad. Goodwin said the EDL and other groups across Europe were trying to form a broad coalition against Muslims, especially in light of the proposed entry of Turkey, and 90million Turks, into the European Union.

Goodwin wasn't the only one worried about the EDL reaching out to Europe; the Metropolitan Police '**Communities Together Engagement Team**' was also frantically trying to get in touch with EDL supporters once news of the European event became public. Activists they spoke to, allegedly countenanced by the leadership, said the police told them they hoped Lennon knew what he was doing, as the right-wing on the Continent was traditionally far more extreme than their British counterparts.

Holland has just under a million Muslims, constituting 5% of the population, many of them originating from Morocco and Turkey. The country has also witnessed two high profile murders involving Muslim extremists.

As Wilders was now doing, Dutch politician Pim Fortuyn campaigned to repeal the first article of the Dutch constitution, which forbids discrimination. Fortuyn believed that Islam was a major threat to world peace and declared what he termed a '**cold war**' on the religion. On the eve of the Dutch National Elections of 2002, with his party on the verge of government, Fortuyn was gunned down in the street. His assassin was white Muslim convert, Volkert van der Graaf, who claimed he had killed the politician to stop him targeting Muslims.

In 2004, film-maker Theo van Gogh was assassinated following his involvement with writer Ayaan Hirsi Ali in the film *Submission*. Two months after the first screening of the film, which explored the role of women in Islam, van Gogh was murdered whilst cycling to work. His killer was Dutch-Moroccan Mohammed Bouyeri who, after he had shot his victim eight times, pinned a warning letter addressed to Hirsi Ali to van Gogh's body with a knife. Bouyeri also attempted to decapitate van Gogh.

Following the murder, hundreds of violet retaliatory attacks took place across Holland, including several arson attacks on mosques. Ayaan Hirsi Ali relocated to the United States. A letter like the one left on van Gogh's body, describing Wilders as a **'disgusting faggot'** and calling for his death was posted on the Internet. From that day, the Dutch authorities gave Wilders 24-hour protection at a cost of €2million a year.

Amsterdam City Council announced it was considering banning both the demonstration and a counter-protest planned by various anti-fascist groups such as ANTIFA. Eventually the council decided on a compromise and the EDL protest was moved three miles out of the city centre, to an industrial site in the Generatorstraat area.

There were also rumours that thugs attached to FC Ajax were not happy that English football hooligans were apparently travelling to their city to demonstrate. British anti-fascists flooded Ajax fan websites, claiming the EDL was going to smash up Amsterdam. Some Ajax hooligans posted messages on the Internet saying they would attend the counter-protest to oppose the EDL. It seemed that Dutch hooligans were keen to use it as an excuse to try and get one over on anything remotely looking like an English football firm. In fact, many of the younger hooligans who follow the Dutch club are of Moroccan or Tunisian descent, pumped up by left-wing propaganda, they believed they were turning out to defend Islam from British Nazis.

On the day of the demonstration, Dutch police in riot gear cordoned off all roads leading to the protest site. Small groups of mainly EDL ran the gauntlet of anti-fascists as they made their way there. One minibus, containing a number of EDL, including Lennon, Carroll and Singh, arrived close to the demo site. They were told by Dutch police that they would have to leave the van where it was and walk the rest of the way to the site.

Lennon got out wrapped in a St George Cross and spoke to a Dutch journalist. He said they had received death threats for coming to Europe. He said it was a sad day when they had to wear bullet-proof vests because of concerns for safety. He said the protest was the first of many across Europe. A number of anti-fascists approached the EDL, as the two groups faced each other Lennon's flag was snatched from his hands. More anti-fascists arrived one the scene and the EDL were forced to retreat back to their van. Fighting broke out in the road and anti-fascists also pelted the minibus with stones and bricks, smashing the windows. Dutch police were forced to intervene, making a number of arrests.

Early arrivals to the protest site were mobbed by a horde of media, but it was apparent from early on that the numbers were disappointingly small. Hundreds had turned out for the counter-demonstration, where Chairman of the Dutch National Moroccan Council, Mohammed Rabbae, wound up the crowd by telling them: **"the struggle against fascism begins today!"** Martin Smith of UAF addressed the crowd. He warned that fascist groups across Europe were growing and said anti-fascist groups needed to join together. Smith ended his speech by, rather inappropriately, encouraging the crowd to chant **'Fuck the EDL!'**

Hooligans from Ajax started arriving in the surrounding area, clashing with EDL supporters. Dutch police decided to halt any further entry into the counter-protest site, holding a large number of Ajax thugs at the local train station. As this was going on, Dutch radio reported clashes between the two sides across the city.

The speeches began at the EDL protest site, Bert Jansen of the Dutch Defence League spoke about life under Sharia. Jansen was barracked by one spectator who started shouting about the Crusades. The heckler was led away by police, but it became apparent there were more anti-fascist infiltrators. Next up was Michael Mannheimer from Germany, who warned of the Muslim demographics in Europe. Near the end of his speech he was assaulted and the lead of his microphone snatched away by two anti-fascists. They too were led away, shouting obscenities. Mannheimer was handed another microphone and continued. He asked for a police officer to be placed in front of the podium, but the request was ignored by Dutch police, who clearly didn't want any of them there.

At this point, Lennon was told by British police who were present that they would have to leave the protest, as it wasn't safe to stay. Due to this advice, Lennon addressed the crowd earlier than planned.

Showing the audience a bullet-proof vest he claimed he had been advised to wear, he criticised the Dutch authorities for their inability to protect a peaceful protest. Lennon said it was a disgrace how the Mayor had moved the demo to the **"middle of nowhere"**, but told the small crowd they were lucky to have Geert Wilders in Holland as in the UK the people had no-one to stand up for their freedoms. Then he delivered a message to the Islamists: **"From your caves in Afghanistan, to your houses in Malmo, in Berlin, in Rome, in London and across Europe, get the hell out of Europe now. Europe will never surrender to Islamism, we will never surrender to Islam, we are free men today, tomorrow and forever in Europe and will unite Europe against Islamism"**.

The small crowd applauded his speech, but it was somewhat subdued as it was obvious it had been a poor turnout and that fact was compounded by the level of opposition they had faced. Guramit Singh admitted to *BBC News* that it hadn't been the best of days, but said they were there to support the Dutch Defence League and would stand with anyone who was sympathetic to their cause. Not too long after Lennon's departure, the audience started drifting away. As activists stood at the train station they could see Dutch police clashing with anti-fascists near the counter-protest site.

Police spokesman, Rob van der Veen, said that 34 people had been arrested and five of those were Britons, detained en route to the protest for not being able to produce identification. ANTIFA released a statement calling the day a success, claiming that hundreds of people had shown their disapproval and anger that the EDL were allowed to protest. The anger of EDL activists at home was palpable. Many blamed the Ajax hooligans and pledged to get revenge next time the Dutch side played in England.

Two days later, Lennon was featured in *The Times*. Making sure readers knew the sort of person they were dealing with, the article opened by describing Lennon as '**a stocky figure with the swagger of a man used to standing his ground amid the push and shove of the football terrace with the more volatile fans**'. It got worse, with apparently '**every taut sinew and muscle**' of his body '**exuding rage**', Lennon told the paper: '**People are at fucking boiling point. There's an undercurrent of anger from people living in towns like this. It's ready to explode. And the Government needs to listen. Before we started, the working class across this country were ignored by the Government. We are bringing these issues to the forefront. They would have ignored us for another ten years if we didn't do nothing**'.

Lennon insisted that neither he nor the EDL were racist. He argued that Islam is not a race, it is an ideology and countered that some elements of the Qur'an were prejudicial towards non-believers. Lennon admitted that some division in the EDL had been caused by the far-right but claimed an organisation only seventeen months old and without a membership scheme, could not control individuals who claimed to support it. He said the fact that one of the most prominent EDL activists was Sikh, and the fact that the EDL also supported Israel, should show it was not a racist organisation.

When asked if the EDL would enter politics, Lennon replied that it wouldn't and said the group's intention had always been to make the two main parties accept and act on what the EDL was saying: "**If the politicians aren't going to stick up for us we will make them, because we will cause so much fuss and so much noise they are going to have to listen. We will not back down or be beaten into submission. We don't care if you call us racists. We are going to continue doing it until someone listens**".

Following the 7/7 attacks on London, Lennon said that politicians had met with Muslim leaders. He said that the Government could now do similar deals with the EDL instead. Lennon said that now, before decisions in towns and cities were made, the people concerned had better start thinking '**what is the EDL going to say?**' Asked what being leader of the group was like, Lennon replied: '**To be honest, mate, I didn't want this on my shoulders. I didn't want to be the leader of the EDL. I want to be home with my missus and kids. I don't want fatwa's on my head and death threats. I don't want to be the next fucking Nick Griffin. But I am not backing down**'.

The next day, on 3 November 2010, Bedfordshire Police carried out a raid on a tanning salon in Luton owned by Lennon, seizing tills and computers. In a statement, Lennon said the police were now '**pulling out all the stops to shut us down**' and announced a protest in Luton. Lennon said that by arresting his pregnant girlfriend and raiding him on five occasions, Bedfordshire Police had '**taken the piss for the last 18 months**'. Confirming the protest on its website, the EDL said it was '**bringing it back to where it all began**' and the demo was not only against the Islamification of the UK, but also against the police, who continued to treat EDL members with total disrespect with the aim of preventing free speech.

Later that same day, Roshonara Choudhry, a Muslim woman described as a promising university student, was jailed for at least fifteen years for the attempted murder of British MP Stephen Timms. She had become radicalised online by extremist preacher, Anwar al-Awlaki (US born al-Awlaki is also suspected of masterminding a plot to blow up a plane, which would be discovered in the US and UK weeks later).

Choudhry told detectives that she had wanted to die as '**a martyr, because that is the best way to die**' and that the crime had been worth ruining the rest of her life, because millions of Iraqis were suffering and she had to do what she could to help them. She said she had targeted Timms because he had voted in favour of the declaration of the war in Iraq. She had allegedly seen a list of MPs who had voted for the war on a website called *revolutionarymuslim.com*, which had called on Muslims to '**raise the knife of Jihad**' against the MPs.

A man from Wolverhampton was later charged with soliciting murder in connection with the website. He was also charged with three counts of possessing information likely to be useful for terrorists and one count of inciting religious hatred. Bilal Zaheer Ahmad, 23, an IT graduate from Dunstall Hill in Wolverhampton, pleaded guilty at Bristol Crown Court to using the website to encourage the murder of MPs who had supported the 2003 invasion of Iraq. The prosecution alleged that Ahmad had used the website, now closed down, to encourage others to attack MPs. On the website's forum, Ahmad had instructed people how to find out details of constituency surgeries and also posted a link website which sold knives.

The court heard that the day before Choudhry was sentenced Ahmad posted on Facebook, '**This sister has put us men to shame. We should be doing this**'. When he was arrested, e-books entitled *39 ways to serve and participate in jihad* and *Zaad-e-Mujahid: Essential provisions of a mujahadid* were found in his possession. Defending Ahmad, Imran Khan said that aged 16, the defendant had fallen in with al-Muhajiroun: '**This is not the case of a man indoctrinating but of a man who has been indoctrinated by others, it was wrong, it was perverted and he now absolves himself from it completely. He was a follower and not a leader**'.

Describing Ahmad as a '**viper in our midst**' who was '**willing to go as far as possible to strike at the heart of our system**', the judge, Mr Justice Royce, said: '**whatever our views on the Iraq War, we are a democracy. You purport to be a British citizen, but what you stand for is totally alien to what we stand for in our country**'.

Ahmad was jailed for 12 years and ordered to serve an additional five year period on licence. Following the case, head of West Midlands Counter Terrorism Unit, Detective Chief Superintendent Kenny Bell told *BBC News*: '**Online extremism is an area of counter terrorism policing that we are increasingly focussed on. We need to protect vulnerable individuals from being urged to commit serious crimes by extremists and radicalisers who are exploiting the internet. We can and will track offenders down**'.

Adding Insult to Injury

Presumably attempting to cause as much offence as possible in the shortest amount of time, Muslims Against Crusades announced it would demonstrate at the annual Remembrance Service for British war dead, held on 11 November at the Cenotaph in Whitehall, London. The EDL obviously announced they would counter-protest and asked all activists who could make it to attend.

11 November 2010: London

Hundreds of police were drafted into the area around the Cenotaph, the risk of disorder seemingly magnified as the previous day students protesting against tuition fees had rioted in the capital, causing widespread damage to buildings and national monuments.

The EDL assembled at the Willow Walk pub in Victoria. Just before the service was about to start, around 50 left the pub and made their way to Whitehall. Around 30 MAC turned up ten minutes before the customary two minutes silence at 11.00am. Some were masked and some carried placards proclaiming '**Islam will dominate!**' and '**British soldiers burn in hell!**' They were quickly ringed by police on Exhibition Road, opposite Hyde Park and close to the Royal Albert Hall. The radicals scuffled with police and one was wrestled to the floor by officers and handcuffed before being led away.

Speaking for the group, Asad Ullah, said violence was not their intention but if it did occur, they were the kind of people who would defend their honour. He said the group was demonstrating because the day was a day of remembrance, to remember soldiers, including those killed in Afghanistan and Iraq. Ullah said it was disgusting that innocent people, including children, had been killed in what he called '**illegal and unjust wars**'. Adding that MAC wanted the Britain to pull its troops out of Muslim countries and to stop interfering in their affairs, Ullah said they would have liked to have protested closer to the Cenotaph, but they still intended to break the silence and ask "**what about the silence for others that have died?**"

MAC organiser, Abu Rayah, from east London, told the *Daily Star*: "**This is Remembrance Day and we will never forget the thousands of Muslims dead in Iraq and Afghanistan. British soldiers are mass murderers and your politicians are oppressors. By wearing poppies, you condone mass murderers**".

The EDL counter-protest was nearby. Two of the group's activists had already been arrested, after reportedly rushing forward and throwing pork at MAC. As the clock struck 11.00am and the silence for Britain's glorious dead began, protected by British police officers, members of MAC burned a model of a poppy, the symbol of sacrifice of millions and chanted "**British soldiers burn in hell**", "**British troops are murderers**" and "**La ilaha IlAllah!**" (There is no god but Allah). One of the group, Abu Asadullah, told the *Daily Star*: "**we wanted to upset people and we wanted them to hurt. If you hurt for two minutes you'll understand the hurt we feel every day**".

The burning of the poppy outraged the EDL and there were scuffles with police as they tried to break through to confront MAC. After their short protest, the MAC group were escorted away by police. Suddenly, Stephen Lennon broke through police lines holding the EDL. He sprinted across the road and vaulted a steel fence to confront MAC. As he landed, Lennon grabbed the pole of one of the black flags MAC were carrying. Police officers immediately pounced on him and after a brief scuffle Lennon was arrested. He joined five other EDL who were also arrested, on suspicion of affray.

MAC were then marched out of the area by police, along Exhibition Road and past the Victoria and Albert and Natural History museums. Police said two MAC protesters had been arrested for public order offences and one police officer had been taken to hospital with a head injury.

Lennon was released on bail and would appear at West London Magistrates' Court on 22 November where he pleaded not guilty to a charge of assaulting a police officer. The *Daily Star* had warned, '**Riot fear over EDL court case**' and said '**heated clashes**' between the EDL, Muslim extremists and anti-fascists were set to take place. When Lennon appeared, supported by around 30 EDL outside the court, he was granted unconditional bail and a trial date was set for 12 January 2011. The day before he was due to reappear, police announced they were dropping the charges. Lennon said the attempt to '**fit me up**' had failed miserably.

Of course the press cranked up public anger over the protest. The *Daily Mail* labelled MAC as '**fanatics burning with hate**' and said they had brought shame to the memory of the dead. *The Daily Express* said horrified onlookers had been appalled by '**the ultimate insult to the war dead and soldiers still risking their lives in Afghanistan**'. Christine Bonner, whose son Darren was killed in Helmand province in 2007, told the paper: '**I'm disgusted. There are people like myself that at 11.00am today were remembering the lives of our children, and then there are some people doing something so hurtful as that. I think it's atrocious. We're talking about individuals who have died for their country.**'

Under the headline of '**Flames of hatred at mob demo**' *The Sun* called the MAC group '**jeering Muslim extremists**'. Christine Gennell, of the Army Widows' Association, told the paper that: '**every poppy we wear symbolises a serviceman who gave his life. They were burning the memory of someone.**' Mohammed Shafique, of the Muslim Ramadhan Foundation, told the paper that the MAC protestors were a '**vile, evil minority who do not respect life and certainly not Muslim life**'. '**Thugs burn poppies**' said the *Daily Star* and called the MAC '**vile Muslim protestors**' who had '**labelled heroic troops mass murderers**'. For some reason, the paper claimed MAC had lashed out against anyone wearing a poppy, which presumably was meant verbally.

The Daily Express followed up the next day with a warning that the group was planning further outrages: '**Muslim fanatics: We'd burn more poppies**'. Asad Ullah explained to the paper he had become radicalised aged thirteen. He claimed his parents, who were from a "**colonised Islamic state**", had been reduced '**to pieces of dirt**' when they came to Britain: "**We are revolutionaries, but do not practice violence, we believe there are ways to bring about our goals other than violence**". *The Sun* named three of the '**poppy thugs**' as, Abu Assadullah, Abu Ubaidah and Abu Rahin Aziz. Following the exposure, Aziz was given police protection. A police source told the paper that senior officers feared for his safety and were therefore taking the necessary precautions.

Two days later, on 13 November 2010, the *Daily Star* announced '**Poppy burning scum: Two arrested**'. White Muslim convert and MAC supporter, Ali Hussein, said it was clear who the police sided with by the arrest of '**two innocent Muslims**'. He said their actions made it clear that the police hated Islam and Muslims, adding that the radicals reward for burning the poppy would come from Allah.

The fallout amongst the general public was as huge as it had been following the Luton outrage. 300,000 people joined a Facebook page with the subtle title '**Let's Show These Poppy Burning Bastards How Many People Want Them Deported**'. The EDL saw numbers rocket on both its Facebook page and website forum, with the Facebook page reaching 70,000 members. The act spurned a spate of protest across the country.

The following Saturday, twelve men stormed a RESPECT Party meeting at a Pakistani Community Centre in Glodwick, Oldham. Up to 40 people were at the meeting and a large disturbance broke out as the men entered. Police blamed the trouble on the EDL and said that four men had been arrested on suspicion of affray.

In Portsmouth, a poppy was painted on the front of the Jami Mosque, on Victoria Road North, Southsea. The following day, two protests were held outside the mosque. More than 100 people gathered there at lunchtime and again later in the evening. A spokesman for Hampshire Police said one man had been arrested on suspicion of a public order offence. Imam, Muhammad Muhi Uddin, told *BBC News* that he was saddened and mystified why his mosque has been targeted twice in two days but added that he condemned the poppy burning.

Two weeks later, on 28 November 2010, West Midlands EDL staged a flash demo in Wolverhampton. West Midlands Police were tipped off about the protest on Facebook, so officers, and a small number of anti-fascists, were waiting for the EDL when they appeared and attempted to gain access to Dudley Street in the city centre. Police refused them entry, so the EDL walked back along Garrick Street and returned through the Wulfrun Shopping Centre. Police stood at the doors of the centre to try and stop them, but were powerless as the EDL flooded past them and onto Dudley Street.

As shoppers looked on, the EDL marched up the street chanting **"Poppy burners off our streets!"** The advance of the EDL was eventually checked by police outside Marks and Spencer. Following a discussion, they were allowed to proceed up Dudley Street to Queen Square. A small band of anti-fascists held up '**Hope Not Hate**' signs as the EDL marched, but seemed inconsequential compared to the numbers of EDL. After a speech on the two-tier legal system in the UK by local organiser Pat Whitehouse, the EDL dispersed peacefully, with some leaving on buses provided by police. Local newspaper, the *Express and Star* dramatically claimed the demo had brought '**chaotic scenes**' to Wolverhampton and incorrectly added that '**alarmed passers-by**' had sought refuge in shops.

On the same day, north-east EDL supporters staged a demonstration outside the former Bishop's Palace in Benwell, Newcastle. They were protesting against a proposed Islamic school and cultural centre for the site.

The Grade II listed building, used as the location for BBC TV children's drama *Byker Grove*, was purchased for £300,000 by the Newcastle-based BAHR Academy. After the plans were revealed, someone placed a pig's head on the railings outside the building. Benwell councillor, Dipou Ahad, told the *Daily Mail* that '**This is going to be a project for the whole community, the Asian community in the west end of Newcastle are short of facilities and this is much needed**'.

More than 100 people, including one dressed as Osama bin Laden, marched from the Fox and Hounds pub on West Road to the site in Benwell Lane, where they held a protest. Organiser Alan Spence claimed that locals did not want the Islamic centre. Labour councillor, Nick Forbes, told the *Sunday Sun*: '**They should have better things to do with their time on a Saturday morning than marching around wearing stupid costumes and chanting. Newcastle is a very diverse city and communities have to live alongside each other. My colleagues and I are working hard to make sure barriers are broken down and this kind of action does not help, but inflames the situation**'.

Protests were springing up across the country. The next day, protesters chanting slogans against Muslim extremists marched through Kingston upon Thames in south-west London. Around 60 people, carrying flags and a large wooden poppy chanted **"Muslim bombers off our streets!"** as they walked from Hampton Wick station to the front of the Bentall Shopping Centre in the centre of Kingston. After a thirty minute protest, they all dispersed peacefully. Organiser Ben Baty told the *Kingston Guardian* that it was a protest against the burning of poppies, but denied it was linked to any group. However, the paper claimed that one man had carried a St George's Cross bearing the letters '**EDL**'.

Later that afternoon, a gang of masked youths threw bottles of beer and left bacon on cars near a local mosque. Police officers who attended the disturbance recovered two pieces of wood and arrested three white males. Rizwan Khaliq, spokesman for the Kingston Muslim Association, said that under the pretence of protesting against extreme Islam, a group of masked men had congregated outside the mosque shouting obscenities. He claimed they had urinated against the mosque walls, thrown bottles and used baseball bats to smash windows. Khaliq said it was a miracle nobody was injured and that only superficial damage to the mosque was caused. Detective Chief Superintendent Martin Greenslade said police were investigating any link between the attack on the mosque and the earlier march.

Ben Baty told the *Kingston Guardian* that he was saddened and shocked by the attack and hoped the people responsible would be brought to justice. He said he had wanted people from other communities to feel welcome and when people were shouting **"Muslim bombers off our streets"** although he was not happy, he realised that it was simply because they did not know how to express themselves.

27 November 2010: Preston and Nuneaton

The EDL announced it would stage two simultaneous protests on the 27 November 2010, showing the movement was growing, not only in numbers but also in confidence. There would be a protest in Preston against a large mosque planned for the site of an existing one in Watling Street Road. The Nuneaton demo was against the introduction of Sharia, the town chosen because the first UK Sharia tribunal was established there.

In the week preceding the protests, anti-fascists were stunned when the new National Coordinator for Domestic Extremism, Detective Chief Superintendent Adrian Tudway, denied the EDL was an extremist group. Tudway said the police walked a tightrope when targeting small groups which they believed were intent on violence, but said they did not consider the Defence Leagues as extreme right-wing groups: '**The present particular challenge to us, constitutionally, is they are not extreme right-wing organisations. On the one hand, they are seen by many as the single biggest threat to community cohesion in the UK, but they are most certainly not extreme right-wing organisations**'.

In Preston, some shops had decided not to open and taxi drivers had vowed to stay off the roads for the visit of the EDL. Police said that traders should operate as normal, even though they were describing the operation as '**the biggest thing Lancashire Police has probably ever done**'. Chief Superintendent, Tim Jacques, told the *Lancashire Evening Post* that all leave for officers had been cancelled and that assistance was being drafted in from across the county. Jacques said he was confident they had the resources to handle any flashpoints, in spite of a proposed UAF counter-protest. He said police were aware of the history of when the two groups met but even so, they would not be flooding the city centre with riot-police.

Following a meeting between police and local councillors prior to the protest, councillor Michael Lavalette complained to *Socialist Worker* that police had told him that the EDL website stated that it was a non-racist, peaceful organisation and that they would have to take that assertion at face value. They had also allegedly told Lavalette that the EDL had a right to protest and they would stay neutral, adding it was UAF counter protests that caused trouble and the anti-fascist group was just a front for the Socialist Worker Party. Lavalette said he believed that the police wanted to clamp down on any anti-fascist counter-protest and criticised the fact that the EDL was being allowed to assemble on the High Street, within a minute's walk of Preston's Asian community and a five minute walk from Preston's main mosque.

On the day of the protest, Preston Council announced it was '**business as usual**' as around 1000 EDL protesters descended on the town, gathering in the vicinity of the Jazz and Reflex bars. The rear of both pubs backed onto each other and the short walk along back streets to the Flag Market demo site was completely obscured from public view by buildings. As around a thousand EDL left the pubs and walked to the site, police insisted that everyone removed any face coverings.

The UAF rally was being staged in the Fish Market area of the town centre. They had applied for the Flag Market but to their consternation the application was denied by police, who preferred it as the venue for the EDL. Local anti-fascists claimed that UAF had been too overeager to appease the police and that the Fish Market site was agreed upon without any consultation with them. To compound the feeling of victimisation, police informed UAF that they were setting a time limit on their demonstration and it was to be over by 2.00pm. If that condition was breached, they were told that organiser Michael Lavalette would be arrested.

It was a poor turnout for UAF, with no more than 80 anti-fascists present. It compounded the general feeling of demoralisation in the anti-fascist movement. However, true to form, presumably by sticking its fingers in its ears and singing loudly, UAF later claimed that over 250 anti-fascists had been present.

The walk to the demo site on was a peaceful one for the EDL, apart from the usual chanting and a firework which was thrown at them by anti-fascists. As they assembled on Flag Market, it soon became apparent that the police and council had under-estimated the numbers. People began to get crushed as police pleaded with the crowd to move back. There were some exchanges between the EDL and anti-fascists who had gathered on the other side of police lines. Anti-fascists were discovered infiltrating the EDL compound and scuffles broke out as they were ejected. Smoke bombs were hurled into the neutral area, which resulted in the police pushing the public and press away from the square assisted by mounted officers.

The EDL staged their rally, although the PA system couldn't be heard by large sections of the crowd. During the speeches, a fight broke out in the crowd, caused again by the discovery of anti-fascists. Police didn't intervene and left it to the EDL stewards to quell the trouble and eject the interlopers. Following the protest the EDL were allowed to disperse. One large group were escorted back to the coaches and others were allowed to make their way to local pubs. During the walk back to the coaches, a group of around 100 EDL breached police lines on Church Street, but after charging into nearby Deepdale for no apparent reason, they were rounded up by mounted police.

The event was largely ignored by the media. Tim Jacques of Lancashire Police told the *Lancashire Telegraph* the event had passed off peacefully but they had arrested fourteen people for being drunk and disorderly.

27 November 2010: Nuneaton

Days before the Nuneaton protest, a number of local councils, including Bedworth and Nuneaton, complained to the press that they were being blackmailed over the removal of the word 'Christmas' from council literature. The EDL had written to a number of local authorities warning them not to lose the meaning of Christmas by referring to the Christmas Holidays as Winter Festival - threatening to visit their towns and cities if they did. In the letters, Lennon, using the pseudonym Tommy Robinson, said:

> **'As I'm sure you are aware Christmas is a long-established tradition in British history and indeed other cultures and religions and dates back as far as 400AD. Please keep Christmas as Christmas and not let our culture and traditions be eroded and preserve English values. Any council that does not keep the word Christmas in the annual celebrations and opts for Winter Festival, out of the politically correct appeasement of others to the detriment of our traditions, will have their town/city visited by the English Defence League throughout the following year. The average cost to the council is £500,000 when the English Defence League demonstrates at any given location and it is hoped this will be avoided by your council keeping the word Christmas alive. Do not lose the meaning of Christmas by changing it to Winter Festival'**

Nuneaton and Bedworth Council leader, Dennis Harvey told the BBC that it was 'a **bit of a blackmail letter really**'. He said they had always celebrated Christmas traditionally in Nuneaton, but to receive a letter threatening them that if they didn't they would be targeted was appalling. Harvey added that he did not think blackmail played any part in a traditional English way of life. Telford & Wrekin Council confirmed it had also received a letter and had passed it onto West Mercia Police. Another recipient, Shropshire County Council, told the *Shropshire Star* that the Christmas celebrations would proceed in the borough as normal and it would not be advising organisers to alter any titles.

Nuneaton was by now used to seeing the EDL (it was the third visit in as many months) and Warwickshire Police were using the code-name *Operation Cavendish* for the day's proceedings. The police and council assured the press they had contingency plans in place, some roads would be temporarily closed as the EDL were being allowed to march around the town. Assistant Chief Constable, Bill Holland, said the policing operation would be effective, but proportionate and fair. Council Chief Executive, Christine Kerr, told the *Nuneaton News* that they had been working to keep the town fully open for business during the protests. Apologising to anyone affected, Kerr added:

'We live in a democratic society in which individuals and groups have the right to air their views, even if their views are not shared by everyone.'

On the day of the protest, EDL supporters started gathering in the town from 10.00am. There was a huge police presence and the EDL gathered at three pubs a short walk away car park the rally was being held in. Just before 1.00pm the EDL started making their way to the site. There were well over a thousand, many of them with banners and flags. Once there, they were addressed by West Midlands local organiser, Pat Whitehouse, who to cheers and applause, confirmed that they would be allowed to march.

A huge snaking mass of flags and banners, totally surrounded by police, made its way around the town. There was one minor flashpoint as the EDL passed a small group of anti-fascists and Asian youths. Abuse was hurled by both sides and the march stalled temporarily. Smoke bombs and bangers were hurled by the EDL and they made repeated attempts to breach police lines. Police in riot gear were deployed at the back of the march to hurry things along and it eventually continued.

The marchers passed the Nuneaton Justice Centre on their route around the town. It was a good turn out, especially considering there was also a demo in Preston. The public were kept too far away and behind rows of fluorescent jacketed police officers, to gauge the strength of casual local support, but the local regions of the West Midlands were well represented. They finally returned to the demo site, where Guramit Singh made a speech. He was followed by singer Citizen Steve, but as he broke into song, the crowd seemingly having had their say, started to disperse.

There were sporadic clashes between small groups of EDL and Asian youths but police intervened, quickly extinguishing any trouble. Inspector Adrian Magee told the *Coventry Evening Telegraph* they had put a lot of planning into the operation and they were pleased with how it had gone. One EDL organiser told the *Evening Telegraph*: **'It's not often we are given the privilege of getting permission to have a march and we have to thank Warwickshire Police for their co-operation. Our aim was to have a peaceful demonstration, without causing any aggravation. It was a good venue for us and we had a good day.'**

Following the march, the leaders of Nuneaton and Bedworth Council sent a letter to Home Secretary, Theresa May, asking her to ban any further EDL demonstrations in the town. Dennis Harvey said that the demonstration had badly affected Nuneaton and even though the council had declared it was business as normal, many shoppers had stayed away.

The councillors obviously missed the point. The EDL had protested successfully in Nuneaton against Sharia, the prior two visits had been to support parades by returning soldiers. There was no reason for the EDL to return to the town. The day was seen as a success, the EDL had staged two demonstrations, with over a thousand people at each. Also, the police appeared to be waking up to the fact that serious trouble at demonstrations only occurred when the left-wing were permitted to counter-protest.

11 December 2010: Peterborough

Peterborough is a large city in Cambridgeshire, in the east of England. The city was traditionally an industrial centre, famous for brick making and engineering, but the majority of the areas main employers are now service industries. Even so, Peterborough has relatively low unemployment levels in comparison to the rest of the UK; this has led to it being one of the most popular UK destinations for migrants.

Since WWII, large number of immigrants from Italy, Pakistan, India and more latterly Eastern Europe have settled in the city. The majority of Peterborough's Muslims live in the Millfield and New England areas of Peterborough.

In 2001, 17 year old Ross Parker was beaten and stabbed to death by a Muslim gang as he walked home with his girlfriend in Millfield. The attack on was ten days after the 9/11 attacks on the US. The Muslim gang had simply gone out to find a white male to attack and found 5'5 tall Ross. His attackers, some of them masked, told his girlfriend to run, sprayed Ross in the face with CS gas and stabbed him three times in the neck and chest. As he fell to the ground he was struck with a hammer and kicked. Ross Parker bled to death.

One of men arrested for the attack was recorded chanting '**Osama bin Laden**' and '**Taliban**' while in a prison van being transported to court. Four men eventually stood trial for the murder, three of them, Shaied Nazir, 22, Ahmed Ali Awan, 22, Sarfraz Ali, 25, were found guilty and handed life sentences. Safraz Ali was given a character reference at the trial by the Deputy Mayor of Peterborough, Raja Akhtar and Labour Party councillor Mohammad Choudhary. Akhtar, a Conservative who went on to become Mayor in 2004, and Choudhary, would later be jailed in 2004 following a police investigation into vote rigging.

In May 2004, gangs of Pakistani men clashed with Afghan and Iraqi asylum seekers who had moved into Millfield. Houses and cars were torched, windows were smashed and people were injured during running battles between the two groups. Two months later, a festival to celebrate the city's diversity exploded into violence as Pakistanis and Iraqis repeatedly clashed over a period of two days.

In the run up to the EDL protest, local paper the *Peterborough Evening Telegraph* reported that hundreds of pantomime fans were to be left disappointed after the local Key Theatre revealed it would close on the day of the EDL demonstration. The *Telegraph* said the cancellation of *Jack and the Beanstalk* was due to the EDL protest passing near the theatre. It was at least a novel approach, the EDL were now accused of ruining Christmas and disappointed children could now be added to the growing list of people who they had upset. As almost an aside, the paper added that the TUC counter-demonstration would end in the theatre's car park. Superintendent Paul Fullwood told the paper that police hadn't asked the theatre to close.

Guramit Singh predicted an EDL turnout of around 3-4000, telling the *Evening Telegraph* that the route, a short walk from the football stadium to a small square on the outskirts of the city centre, had been thoroughly planned. The pubs nominated as assembly points were along the route and EDL supporters would join the column as it made its way down London Road to the protest site.

Around 1,000 officers from eighteen forces were being drafted in to assist Cambridgeshire Police, costing an estimated £750,000. Peterborough United announced it was rearranging its match against Rochdale to avoid clashing with the protest. Irene Walsh, of Peterborough City Council said it was in the city's best interests to pay as little attention to the EDL as possible. Local MP, Stewart Jackson, said the EDL had a right to march, the community was strong enough to cope with the demonstration and the best advice was for people to '**keep calm and carry on**'. Local Muslim, Asif Ali, said the biggest concern for his community was the policing of the areas near the mosque, but he believed the EDL had the right to express their beliefs.

Speaking in Peterborough Cathedral, Reverend Jonathan Baker criticised the EDL and said he hoped the city greeted them with the apathy and indifference they deserved. Baker said the group should be renamed the Amnesiacs Anxiety Division, amnesiac because their understanding of English identity was fundamentally opposed to history, anxiety because their desire is to define what is English by feeding on insecurities and division because they have been brought together to sow discord and disharmony. Baker was one in a line of Christian clerics to criticise the EDL.

The Bishop of St Albans, Right Rev Dr Alan Smith, would use his Christmas sermon to speak about the '**destructive powers of groups such as the EDL, led by individuals who wanted to stir up unrest**'. Smith said such groups were trying to commandeer Christianity in an attempt to 'divide **communities, races and religions**'. The Bishop said that the proposed Luton demonstration could seriously undermine community relations. These comments wouldn't, and probably weren't designed to, reach the ears of most EDL activists. The Church of England had long abandoned the white working class and was as irrelevant to the life of the average EDL supporter as the political parties or trade unions now were. None of these institutions represented working class people anymore, and in actual fact some now lined up in opposition to them.

On the day of the protest, even so close to Christmas, it was obvious it was a good turnout for the EDL. With over a thousand in attendance, the protest made its way down London Road, a mass of flags and placards. Some EDL carried sheets of paper with '**A question of time**' printed on them. As it made its way past the pubs nominated as assembly points, more EDL joined. Coming down a slight hill, the marchers could see members of the public thronging either side of the protest site, eager to see the demonstration. Many of these local people waved, applauded and cheered the marchers into the site.

The protest began with a two minutes silence for the British service personnel killed in conflicts at home and abroad. The silence was keenly observed by EDL and members of the public alike, until one anti-fascist shattered the silence by shouting "**shame on you!**" In unison, the crowd roared its disapproval and some near the front surged forward to confront the person responsible. As police battled to control an angry EDL mob, Stephen Lennon took the microphone and pleaded with the crowd not to attack the police. As he spoke, there were numerous police officers standing on the steps to the Magistrates' Court opposite, some filming proceedings and others making notes.

Calming the situation, Lennon said he didn't want police officers going home saying they had been attacked by the EDL. He said the EDL supported the British police and were their allies. Lennon said the people demonstrating against the EDL, such as the students (referring to the violence seen at protests in London only a few days before, where a statue of Sir Winston Churchill had been vandalised) aimed to destroy the nation. The police of Peterborough had upheld democracy and allowed the EDL to march said Lennon, which, he rightly claimed, wouldn't have been possible eighteen months earlier. There was a two-tier system in the country, Lennon said he and his family had been victim to it, but he still supported every British police officer who was doing their duty. He said every EDL supporter should shake the hand of a police officer for allowing their right to free speech. Lennon said the police saw the true face of militant Islam and true EDL members would never attack them.

He said he believed the police were now finally accepting the EDL as a community in its own right. It was only in the UK where ordinary people didn't have politicians speaking for them, said Lennon. As members of the EDL, he said they were on the forefront of the war to defend Britain. They were writing their names in history to protect the future for future generations: "**It is our duty, as members of the British public, as patriots of this great nation, as fathers to children; it is our duty to defend this nation.**"

Lennon said that in the 1930s, if people had held the attitude they had today, everyone would be speaking German. Britain had stood up to tyranny then and they would do so again today. He said the EDL would lead England in the worldwide fight and militant Islam's days in the UK were numbered. Lennon then went on to mention five EDL members, who he said showed exactly what the EDL was about. They had travelled to London the day after student protests to clean the statue of Sir Winston Churchill, which Lennon said had been '**desecrated**' by communists who had hijacked the student protests: "**Winston Churchill was one of the most famous and best men to grace this country. Winston Churchill is every single thing England is about, he is every thing Britain is about. We will stand and admire this man as a true patriot, not even as a patriot, the man is a fucking prophet of this country. You had students, living off their dads fucking bankcard, who have never ever lived a normal day in their life, they do not understand what it is to be a working class member of this community. They do not know what it is fucking about**".

Lennon called three EDL members to the stage, he said one of the lads had travelled from Watford to London on a bicycle to meet the others and clean the graffiti from the statue of Sir Winston Churchill. Lennon said the statue of Churchill stood for everything the nation stood for, that the people who attacked it had defaced the history of the nation. The EDL were demonised by the national media as scum, said Lennon, but people were now seeing through it and realising that they in fact were the true people of the country, the patriots. He warned that the next time the students protested in London, the EDL would be there to defend their country's national monuments against attack. To this the crowd roared its approval.

Then referring to an attack by "**communist scum**" on Prince Charles and the Duchess of Cornwall during the student protests, Lennon declared (and it is a view common with working class English people) that they were not the Government's people, the EDL were people of the Queen. Lennon said the EDL was now making a direct appeal to the Queen, to intervene and stop what was happening to the country.

It was an effective speech, he had hit all the right notes with his audience, especially regarding Churchill and the monarchy and also set a tone of police cooperation, even withstanding his own turbulent relationship with the forces of law and order. Lennon was followed by Guramit Singh, who thanked him and the people of Luton for "**starting the revolution**". Gesturing to the Magistrates' Courts, Singh said the judges inside did not realise what a threat militant Islam was, then went on to list the reasons why. During a speech littered with profanity and bizarre claims, Singh said "**I may get arrested for this shit, but fuck them, I'm not having it**". He was correct, eleven days after his speech, Singh was arrested on suspicion of causing religiously aggravated harassment. He was questioned by police in Nottingham and bailed until February.

Singh was followed by a local woman who spoke about the subjugation of women in Islam. At this point the crowd began to drift away. To their left they could see the small counter-demonstration, but lines of police barred them from getting any closer if they had wanted to.

Superintendent Fullwood said there had been some issues of disorder but they were promptly dealt with by officers. There were eleven arrests in total, for possession of an offensive weapon, assault and public order offences. There was some unrest following the march in the mostly Asian part of the city and vanloads of police were diverted to deal with a large mob of Asian men who had gathered. In the city centre, a masked mob of Asians chased three men they believed to be EDL supporters, forcing one to hide in a building until police arrived.

Peterborough was seen as a success by the EDL, but the mood changed a day later, when news emerged that the group's merchandise website had been hacked. Names and addresses of people who had donated or recently purchased merchandise were posted on various Internet sites. The leak caused panic amongst some EDL members, who immediately received threats from anti-fascists. However, the leak was met with a wall of silence from the leadership. This caused anger, simply because some members had broached the issue of Internet security when EDL sites had previously been hacked. With no real leadership, ordinary supporters, especially those connected to the Internet forum, looked after their own. Using existing networks they ensured that everyone on the list was informed and had support that was only a phone call away.

The EDL did eventually release a short statement informing members they had reported the matter to the police who were now investigating. The statement said they believed that the hacking was designed to cause annoyance rather than anything more sinister. They instructed any supporters who were worried to contact their local police and explain the situation. Amazingly, they also advised that anyone who hadn't seen the list should email them with their details so they could check if they were on it. The irony of a group which had just had its website hacked asking people to send them more details was obviously lost on the EDL leadership. Many other EDL websites were hacked, including the personal Facebook accounts of some activists.

Later the same week, EDL members Richard Price and Collum Keyes pleaded guilty to public order offences at Aylesbury Crown Court. The pair were arrested following the EDL protest in the Buckinghamshire town. After denying charges of violent disorder, a deal was struck with the CPS and the two defendants agreed to plead guilty to reduced charges. Price pleaded guilty to a charge of Section 4 of the Public Order Act (he was told the prosecution would recommend a non-custodial sentence), while Keyes pleaded guilty to breaching Section 5.

As the case opened, the judge, Lord Parmoor, enquired why the plea bargain had taken place, questioning why, if the police had enough evidence for the original charges, they had entered into a plea bargain. The prosecutor responded by informing the judge that the decision to offer the deal had come from "**as high up in the police as is possible**".

Prosecutors were applying for a CRASBO (Criminal Anti-Social Behaviour Order) to be placed on the men, designed to prevent them attending future EDL events. That would prove to be the objective of a lot of EDL prosecutions, under the direction of the Domestic Extremism Unit, the police were seemingly playing the long game.

The court heard that police were forced to spend around £350,000 on a huge operation for the Aylesbury protest. Even though the defendants had pleaded guilty, their barristers were contesting various points in the CRASBO restrictions. Prosecutor Gavin Holme said that EDL protests regularly involved '**racism and abuse**'. The intention of the CRASBO was not only to prevent Price and Keyes from continuing in that manner, Holme said it was to send out a message to other EDL supporters that it was unacceptable behaviour.

Defending Price, David Miller claimed his client had been punched and kicked by police and he had played a minimal role in the violence that broke out at the demonstration. William Harrington, defending Keyes, said that his client's behaviour was no worse than what he had admitted to. After the court was shown video footage, strangely filmed by an anti-fascist rather than police, Harrington said his client had not been seen acting in a violent way and there could have been 30 or 40 other arrests.

Lord Parmoor questioned the validity of the CRASBO in the interests of free speech and also a sentence which said '**and groups with similar aims**'. When asked to clarify this, the prosecution said that the National Front was a group of similar aims, as it was racist like the EDL, but was forced to admit that the EDL had broader objectives and minority divisions. Voicing concern over free speech, the judge decided to retire and consider the case overnight.

The next day any concern regarding free speech seemed to have evaporated, as Lord Parmoor said he could find no valid reason for the EDL protest in Aylesbury. He said the only reason for the demonstration was to provoke some reaction from the local community and to have a fight with the police.

Price was jailed for three months and ordered to pay £85 costs. Keyes was fined £150 and £85 in costs. Issuing a ten year CRASBO to both men, the judge said: "**You each have a right to freedom of speech and freedom of assembly. Your behaviour in joining these open air events is simply and solely to join a crowd and provoke violence. Residents and visitors to towns such as Aylesbury have rights too. I take the view that it would be unfair and disproportionate to prefer your rights over the rights of those others who wait in fear of the arrival of you and like-minded hooligans and are expected to pay the price of these anti-social events.**"

The CRASBO forbade them to organise, promote, travel to, participate in or control, any march, demonstration or similar event in the open air more than ten miles from the centre of their hometown of Birmingham. PC Mike Ellis, Anti-Social Behaviour Coordinator for Thames Valley Police, said it was a clear signal to those who used violence to further their extreme and racist views to create fear within minority communities. Detective Constable Andy Haworth of the National Domestic Extremism Unit said he was pleased with the result which prevented '**two violent criminals**' from using demonstrations to commit violence and cause distress to others: '**While the Defence Leagues are legitimate protest organisations, violence has been a persistent feature of their demonstrations, and we hope the success of today's application will prevent that violence. We will work to support all police forces with CRASBO applications against any who persistently commits criminal acts at Defence League demonstrations, regardless of whether they profess to support the Defence League or oppose it, in order to ensure future demonstrations are peaceful and lawful**'.

It was the first time a Criminal Anti-Social Behaviour Order had been issued to an EDL supporter and fellow activists reacted angrily to the length and terms of the restrictions, arguing the CRASBO wouldn't be out of place in communist China. The main concern was the length, ten years. There were also concerns over the effects on the individual's freedoms of association and speech. One activist claimed the conditions of the CRASBO contravened Article 11 of the European Human Rights Act, and predicted it would be rescinded at any appeal.

A campaign to '**Free Richard Price – EDL Political Prisoner**' was immediately launched and Price immediately gained hero status within the movement. Six days later on Christmas Eve, he was released from prison, pending appeal. His comrades saw his release as an indication that the sentence had been harsh and hoped it indicated that the CRASBOs on both Price and Keyes might be quashed.

Then on Tuesday 4 January 2011, EDL supporters were hit by a bombshell. *The Times* ran a story claiming that Price had been convicted of making four indecent images of children in June 2010 and as a result had been placed on the sex offenders register. The conviction had apparently followed his arrest in 2009, on the morning of the Manchester demonstration, when police had conducted a dawn raid on his Birmingham home. His computer was seized and analysed leading to the discovery of images of children which he had allegedly downloaded. Also, during the search of his home, police had also discovered cocaine.

At Birmingham Crown Court, Price claimed he had inadvertently downloaded the images from an Internet file-sharing site, believing them to contain music, which the judge said he accepted. He admitted four counts of downloading indecent images of children and two charges of possessing cocaine. Price was given a three-year community supervision order, placed on the sex offenders register for five years and banned from owning a computer for a year.

It was a body blow for the EDL, especially those who had supported Price so fervently. Price claimed he was told that if he pleaded guilty to the charge then the matter would be "**hushed up and brushed under the carpet**". That aspect of the story did have some truth in it, as his conviction for possession of the images and cocaine wasn't reported at the time (which was strange as Birmingham had experienced three eventful visits by the EDL and Price had been a prominent member from the start, so at least locally it surely would have been newsworthy), neither was it mentioned along with his other previous convictions during sentencing at the Aylesbury trial. Some people claimed it was an obvious stitch up and suggested police had been lining Price up as an informant, when he hadn't played ball and became a hero after Aylesbury, the press were given the story. However, many others claimed '**there's no smoke without fire**' and questioned why an innocent man would plead guilty to such a charge.

Lennon initially issued a statement supporting '**Pricey**' saying that it had been a second-hand computer and that the pictures were considered '**low level**' images. At the same time, he denied Price had ever been a leader or organiser of the EDL, which contradicted a statement issued following trouble with Paul Ray the previous June, when Price was named alongside Lennon, Marsh, Kelway and Titus as an EDL leader.

Two days later, Lennon issued another statement claiming his previous statement was issued before *The Times* story had appeared and was a mistake. Lennon said he had been acting on what he had been told by Price and a journalist. After seeing the full story, Lennon said the EDL now completely condemned Price and he was being expelled from the movement (Price had already left by this point). He added that although Price's name had been linked to the leadership in June, a subsequent statement issued in July clearly showed he had no leadership involvement. Lennon concluded by saying that all paedophiles should be hung. Price's later appeal was unsuccessful and he was returned to prison to finish the rest of his sentence.

22 January 2011: Shotton and Leicester

A protest was called at short notice to oppose plans to build an Islamic cultural centre at the site of a former social club in Shotton, near Chester. Flintshire Muslim Society was aiming to develop the site of the former Shotton Lane club, which had been empty for six months. Mohammed Monchab Ali, chair of the (Bangladeshi) Greater Sylhet Development and Welfare Council told the *Flintshire Chronicle* they wanted more cooperation and cohesion and the centre would help to build understanding as it would be open to the wider community.

The BNP was campaigning against the centre, but was keen to distance itself from any EDL protest. BNP councillor John Walker said he was against an EDL protest and believed the issue should be solved politically. A spokesman for the EDL Chester Division told the *Chronicle* they had fully liaised with North Wales Police and the aim was for a peaceful protest. Sergeant Antony Heaword of North Wales Police said he was aware that comments opposing the centre had been posted on social networking sites and that some of the comments were being investigated. He said police were working with the whole community to address concerns and provide reassurance and they would respond to any threat.

The Reverend Steven Green of local St Ethelwold's Church criticised the protest. He told the *Flintshire Chronicle* that he found it difficult to believe such a demonstration had anything to do with the people of Deeside. In response, one EDL member said: **'People are angry that this is being pushed on them with no choice. Who do they have to turn to? No-one, the local authority is already branding them as hateful for daring to disagree!'**

EDL supporters gathered in Chester at noon, before heading by train to Shotton. At the Central Hotel they were met by locals and marched to the club. In all, around 200 people turned up, which the EDL claimed was a good turnout at such short notice. When they arrived at the site, speeches were made opposing the mosque. The week after the demo, the site was hit by a blaze which destroyed the building and led to 100 local residents being evacuated. Police they were treating it as suspicious and offered the local Muslim community CCTV cameras for their protection.

On the same day as the Shotton protest, East Midlands EDL staged a flash-demonstration in Leicester. Around 50 EDL, some bearing flags, assembled at the Clock Tower in the city centre around midday and as bemused shoppers looked on, chanted **"Muslim bombers off our streets"**.

Police arrived and quickly surrounded them. A handful of anti-fascists gathered on the other side of police lines, one of them had a megaphone and led the chant of **"EDL off our streets!"** with the EDL replying in kind with a chants of **"we pay your benefits!"** and **"where's your EMA gone?"** (A reference to cuts in the Education Maintenance Allowance which students had recently been protesting against) Anti-fascists later claimed police asked them to stop chanting at the EDL as it was antagonising them.

Police eventually led the EDL away at around 1.30pm and they were taken to the Queen of Bradgate pub. They stayed there for a few hours and were joined by more EDL as the day wore on. Eventually a large group left the pub and walked into Highfields where they became involved in a confrontation with Muslim youths. Police arrived and arrested ten EDL, but they were all released without charge the following morning.

The following week, the British Government announced it intended to reform Control Orders (issued to people suspected of involvement in terrorism) by introducing the Protection of Freedoms Bill. The orders had proven controversial since their implementation in 2005; critics claimed that the judicial process and justice had been set aside in favour of suspicion and secret security service assessments. A worldwide coalition of human rights groups had condemned the orders as **'punishment without charge'** and an **'affront to democratic values'**.

The new provisions, renamed Terrorist, Prevention and Investigation Measures (TPIM), changed the requirements for people believed to pose a threat, instead of **'reasonable grounds to suspect'**, the Secretary of State was now required to have **'reasonable grounds to believe'** that someone posed a terrorist threat.

Other aspects of the orders, such as forced relocation, a ban on Internet and telephone use and restrictions on association with others, were to be dropped. However, electronic tagging, travel bans, limited house arrest, curfews and monitoring would remain. There was to be a two-year limitation on a TPIM but that could be extended at the discretion of the Home Secretary, making them potentially limitless.

The new bill did however have some positive implications for civil liberties, reducing the limit on detention without charge from 28 to 14 days. It also regulated police **'stop and search'** powers under Section 44 of the Terrorism Act. However, it didn't, as some people had suggested, broaden the reasons to ban controversial organisations such as the EDL, erring on the side of freedom of expression.

5 February 2011: Luton

The Luton demonstration was initially a reaction to the arrest of Stephen Lennon by Bedfordshire Police. However, it was quickly repackaged as the group: '**returning to where it all started, where United People of Luton first gave us our voice**'.

The *Daily Star Sunday* sensationally announced that the EDL was planning to bring '**chaos to the streets not seen since the summer of 2001**'. The paper said the group was also planning a series of protests against Muslim gangs targeting young white girls across the north-west and Yorkshire. Lennon explained:

> "**This has been going on for two decades, yet it has been ignored by the Government and the police for too long. There is an undercurrent of anger in Britain and I don't think the Government are aware of it. And as more of these gangs are highlighted in the media, the more people will get angrier. We are not being represented by government or any political parties, so this is why the EDL is getting so much support. And if it doesn't stop there will be civil unrest across the country - riots like we haven't seen in a long time. We as a group are trying to avoid that. We want to channel that anger and frustration into mass, peaceful protests. But the longer it's ignored and brushed under the carpet, it will happen. It will just need one incident in one town and it could trigger a reaction across the whole country. We are not racists. But we live in towns and cities where we see the influence of Islam on our country. Do you know people who are addicted to heroin sold to them by Muslim gangs? I do. Do you know any 11 or 12-year-old family members being pimped out by Muslim gangs? I do**".

Luton was already linked to extremism and those links were further strengthened when, a month earlier on 11 December 2010, a man from Luton, Taimur Abdulwahab al-Abdaly, blew himself up in Stockholm, Sweden. Prior to the attack, which inured two people, a Swedish news agency received a threatening email regarding Sweden's participation in the war in Afghanistan. The email had warned '**now your children, daughters and sisters shall die like our brothers, sisters and children are dying**'.

Of course, the attack prompted renewed claims that Luton was a '**hotbed of extremism**'. Chairman of Luton Islamic Centre, Qadeer Baksh, told the *Luton & Dunstable Herald and Post* it saddened him to hear the town described in those terms. There were more than 20,000 Muslims in Luton said Baksh, and probably only a handful of those had extremist links. He said that the vast majority of Britons were tolerant of all religions but he was concerned that incidents like this could cause people, particularly in Luton, to turn against Islam.

A week later, *The Observer* revealed that the website of the Luton Islamic Centre which Baksh represented contained a link to a lecture by Dr Bilal Philips, a Muslim preacher who was barred from entering Britain because of his extreme views. In response, Baksh told the paper that Philips had made some errors and promised to remove the link. However, *The Observer* claimed there was even more '**contentious material**' on the website, including one publication which called for homosexuals to be executed.

Muslims in Luton told *The Telegraph* that the authorities were to blame for ignoring the activities of radicals who were still openly operating in Luton, close to the former home of al-Abdaly. The paper said former members of al-Muhajiroun now called themselves The Reflect Project and intimidated anyone who spoke out against them. A spokesman for The Reflex Project said that al-Abdaly was a '**lone wolf**' and denied that he had anything to do with the group. Local radical and veteran of the Anglian parade, Sayful Islam, told *The Sun* that it was the EDL and '**Britain's hatred of Islam**' that had inspired al-Abdaly: '**Luton has become a battleground between Islam and those who oppose Islam. The English Defence League started in Luton. And because of this conflict this has made Muslims more aware of situations around the world like Iraq and Afghanistan and made people do something about it**'.

In a speech at Leicester University, Baroness Sayeeda Warsi, herself a victim of Luton's radicals, warned against dividing Muslims into moderates and extremists as such labels fuelled misunderstanding. The Baroness accused the media of reporting on Islam in a patronising, superficial way and said that many Britons now saw anti-Muslim prejudice as normal and uncontroversial. Warsi said Britain was a less tolerant place for Muslims and she would use her position in government to fight an **'ongoing battle against bigotry'**. The terror offences committed by a small number of Muslims should not be used to condemn all, said the Baroness, but she also urged Muslim communities to alienate those among them who resorted to violent acts.

The news that the Stockholm bomber was from Luton gave the EDL a clear mandate to protest in the town. Councillors in Luton wrote to the Home Secretary requesting a ban, claiming the group's visit could result in serious disorder. Councillors believed that a **'provocative'** protest would compound the negative media coverage regarding the Stockholm attack and cause **'deep dismay and anxiety among the wider community in Luton – of whatever background, faith or outlook'**.

The EDL accused the council of **'trying to silence free speech and democracy'** and said that stopping the march would only cause more problems. Guramit Singh told *BBC News* that **"when you ban marches you take away a key element of the demonstration and the logistics of the demonstration crumble and you get a lot of trouble"**.

Dr Fiaz Hussain from the Luton Council of Mosques said ordinary Muslims were living in fear at the prospect of the protest. He said people just wanted to get on with their lives and didn't want groups coming to Luton throwing abuse and hate around. Hussein said his message to the EDL would be to sit down and talk about their grievances to see how they could be addressed. One youth worker told *The Guardian* that he had detected the influence of the EDL in the town and believed the group was specifically targeting young people: **'No one comes out and says "I'm an EDL member" but the tell-tale signs are there. It comes out in the arguments that they make - the idea that minorities get priority in social housing, that the police are scared to stop and search Asians. For some of the young people I work with, the EDL are very appealing – people like street cred. When you're young you want people to respect you and this is one way of gaining respect. There are some kids who are being manipulated – they think they're the big guns'**.

UAF informed the *Luton News* it would counter-protest, but as in Preston, anti-fascists were annoyed the EDL had been given the prominent St George's Square location. UAF was supporting a **'mobilisation to defend Bury Park'**; even though the EDL had repeatedly stated it had no intention of entering the area. Sian Timoney, a councillor for Luton's Farley Ward, said the vast majority of Lutonians were not racist and agreed with the UAF that anti-fascists, not the EDL, should occupy St George's Square. Timoney opposed the EDL demonstration but believed UAF and the people in Bury Park had every right to protest. She told *Socialist Worker* that the EDL was a violent, racist group which wanted to create the impression that it owned Luton.

Bedfordshire Police were calling the day's proceedings *Operation Missouri* and said the money to police the events was coming from the Bedfordshire Police budget. They estimated it would cost over £500,000, at a time they stressed, when many public agencies were dealing with a highly challenging financial situation. The police said they and the council were working to ensure the demo passed off peacefully and would work within the guidelines of the law to protect communities whilst balancing the rights of those who wished to protest. Police said their priority was public safety and they would do everything in their power to bring to justice anyone who broke the law. The lengthy statement went on to say that several events and visits out of the county had been arranged to prevent local youngsters from attending either protest.

Police said that the banning order preventing the EDL from marching in Luton in 2009 had been based on the small number of events that the EDL had organised by that point which had resulted in serious disorder. However, since that time there had been many EDL events where there had not been any serious disorder and where serious disorder had occurred, it was caused by opposing groups. On that evidence, police said there were no grounds to apply to the Home Secretary for a ban and any such order would only prevent the EDL from marching, not from holding a static assembly. Police added that in Leicester a marching ban had been in place, but protestors from a variety of groups still arrived to exercise their right of static assembly, resulting in more police resources being needed than if a march had been allowed.

Luton South MP, Gavin Shuker, said he was disappointed that police were unwilling to '**take a punt and put it in the Home Secretary's in-tray**' and criticised the Home Office for not having done more to combat the EDL, which he said he considered an extremist right-wing group.

Nine days before the protest, at 10.30pm on Thursday 27 January, the EDL claimed that shots had been fired outside the Luton home of Kevin Carroll and that armed police had cordoned off the area. Stephen Lennon issued a statement claiming armed police were also at his home but he was determined the demonstration would still go ahead, even if one of them was killed.

EDL supporters reacted angrily, especially on Facebook where some said it was tantamount to a declaration of war. The group requested members tone down their language as it might '**play into the hands of the Home Secretary**' and see the march banned.

It later emerged that Carroll hadn't claimed shots were fired. He told *BBC News* he was at home when had heard a loud bang. He had looked out of the window and saw a man standing across the road. He went out and challenged the man, who said he was out jogging. As he returned to his front door, his wife screamed out of a window that the man was following him, but now brandishing a shotgun. Carroll said he had run across adjacent gardens to get away, landing poorly at one point, fearing for his life. Police were called and carried out a search of the area, but no-one was found. Bedfordshire Police said they wanted to talk to any witnesses. Carroll described his attacker as a tall Asian male aged around 26-27.

The EDL claimed that violence and intimidation was not new to Islam and compared the attack on Carroll to the fatwa issued on Salman Rushdie and the murder of Dutch film maker Theo van Gogh. *BBC London Tonight* reported that Lennon had been advised to leave Luton by police, after threats were made against him. Two days later, the EDL staged two flash demos in Dewsbury and Derby. Around 80 supporters from across Yorkshire travelled to Dewsbury and in the East Midlands, around 50 EDL marched through Derby city centre.

Days before the Luton protest, Lennon appeared on the BBC *Newsnight* programme. Host Jeremy Paxman stressed that thousands of police were set to be deployed at considerable public expense for the demonstration (accusing the EDL of racism and fascism hadn't worked, this was the new line by the establishment, emphasising the cost of the group's protests in a time of economic depression and widespread public spending cuts. It's strange how it was never mentioned in connection to the student demonstrations). Paxman said police were unsure how to classify the EDL as they were vehemently anti-Islam but also had non-white and gay members (anti-Islamist might have been a start).

In a feature before the interview, Lennon was pictured donning a bullet-proof vest. When asked by the reporter if wearing the vest was a little extreme, he replied "**we aren't up against Mickey Mouse, we are facing militant Islam**" and claimed his home and business had been attacked.

Paxman, somewhat patronisingly asked Lennon what the EDL was defending people from. Lennon replied the group was combating the introduction of Sharia, Islamism and the spread of militant Islam. Paxman tried to ridicule Lennon's claims regarding the introduction of Sharia, but Lennon replied that there were now over 100 Sharia courts in Britain, even though in 2003 the European Human Rights Court had ruled it was incompatible with Western democracy. Paxman was incredulous and asked him if he really believed that, Lennon replied that yes, he believed that 100 Sharia courts were now operating in the UK.

Moving on, Paxman then asked if Lennon was against all Muslims and if a Muslim could join the EDL. Lennon said the EDL was against militant Islam and Islam in its '**seventh century barbaric form**', not Muslims per se, and yes, a Muslim would be able to join the movement. Lennon went on the offensive, asking Paxman if he knew anyone who was hooked on heroin sold to them by Muslim gangs or knew any beautiful girls from school who now wore the burqa and didn't see their families anymore, or if Paxman knew anyone murdered by a Muslim gang. Paxman replied that they were all personal issues of Lennon's, but Lennon replied they were issues facing lots of people in many towns and cities across the country. Paxman countered that there were white drug dealers or Sikh gangs and other types of gang. Lennon asked Paxman if they were seriously going to sit there and pretend there weren't Muslim gangs out there **'trying to pimp British youth'**. It was a cultural issue said Lennon, and for years councillors and the police had conspired to deny there was a problem and had therefore allowed **'the systematic rape of our youth''**.

Paxman said Lennon was tarring the whole of the Muslim community with the same brush. He then alleged that Lennon had called the Qur'an an evil book, Lennon replied that he hadn't, but he'd agree with Paxman on that point. Lennon was getting more confident, his typical working class offensive had unsettled Paxman who was obviously far more used to harassing nervous middle class intellectuals. Lennon said the Government was going to waste a lot of money looking into Muslim paedophile gangs, but they should save the money and simply look into the Qur'an. One of problems, he said, was that 97% of imams in the UK were from abroad, they brought a barbaric form of Islam to the UK, from countries such as Afghanistan and Pakistan.

It wasn't going well, Paxman introduced the EDL Facebook page; reading out some racist comments from it and asked Lennon if he could understand people being frightened by that sort of thing. Lennon replied they were frightened by militant Islam and Sharia and said the EDL had genuine grievances and a righteous cause, at which point Paxman drew the interview to a close.

On the eve of the demonstration, Guramit Singh alleged that three carloads of Asian men had allegedly turned up at his house the night before and threatened him. Police had apparently moved Singh to a place of safety, but he left of his own accord and was reportedly staying with friends.

Stephen Lennon appeared on *Sky News* claiming that Bedfordshire Police had issued him with an Osman Warning informing him there was credible intelligence to suggest an attempt may be made on his life (A legal ruling by the European Court of Human Rights in 1997 declared that police have a duty of care to warn individuals if they have intelligence to believe their life may be in danger. The ruling came about following the failure of police to protect several people from Paul Paget-Lewis, a teacher suffering from psychotic tendencies. In 1988 Paget-Lewis shot and wounded a former pupil, Ahmet Osman, killed his father Ali and two others). Lennon said police had advised him he shouldn't attend the demonstration and claimed his family were now under 24-hour police protection. Anjem Choudary told the *Daily Star* that Lennon could find his life in danger if he and his supporters continued to insult the Prophet Mohammed during demonstrations, **'I don't think a bullet-proof vest is going to be enough to protect him if he continues to go down that line'**.

Lennon was also interviewed by Adam Boulton on *Sky News*, who asked him why he was masked on a poster advertising the demonstration. Lennon replied that it was a picture from the original UPL demonstration, the picture was chosen because the group was returning to Luton where it had all began and he had originally worn a balaclava at the time to hide his identity and protect his family. Pursuing a line of condescension, Boulton asked Lennon if he knew the difference between Islamism and terrorism. Lennon replied that Islamism was the political wing of Islam and that the Palestinian group HAMAS were an Islamist terrorist group. A smirking Boulton replied that HAMAS were also an elected government, but Lennon stopped him and said they were an elected government whose first charter concerned obliterating Israel off the map. Again going on the offensive (they don't like it up 'em Mr Mainwaring); Lennon asked Boulton if he agreed with that aspect of the elected government in question. Boulton floundered and quickly changing the subject implied that Lennon wanted to draw attention to his personal dislike of Islam by having confrontation on the streets. Lennon replied he would attend the demo, he wouldn't bow down to intimidation and the British public wasn't going to bow down to it anymore either. He said the EDL had liaised with police and suggested that he and Boulton should start discussing the Muslim Defence League, as that group had given the police no details whatsoever of what their plans were.

At this point Boulton decided to halt the interview. It was yet another assured display by Lennon; he refused to be intimidated and in true working class fashion had taken the argument to yet another sardonic middle class inquisitor. It was a depth of coverage which the group was previously unused to, but would prove to be a poison chalice, as it attracted people seeking to use the movement to further their own agenda, some of whom were already positioned in the background, waiting for the right moment.

It was proving to be a busy day, as news broke that at an international security conference in Munich the following day, Prime Minister David Cameron planned to make a speech claiming multiculturalism had failed the UK. He would say that instead, Britain needed a strong identity to halt radicalisation. The speech was previewed to the press, in it Cameron said that the country needed to wake up to what was happening in UK communities under the doctrine of state multiculturalism. He said certain groups had been encouraged to live separate lives from the rest of mainstream society and called for an end to the "**passive tolerance**" of divided communities. Cameron said that members of all faiths needed to integrate into wider society and announced that groups which failed to promote British values would no longer receive public money or be able to engage with government.

Britain had sleepwalked into the current situation. The public assassination of people like Enoch Powell or Ray Honeyford had ensured that people were fearful of broaching the subject. If they did break ranks they were immediately pounced upon by various anti-fascist groups and their comrades in the media, who publicly humiliated anyone who didn't toe the multicultural line. The subject was widely discussed in the straight-talking, working class pubs and clubs of England, but even so, until the foundation of the EDL no-one had actually tried to do anything about it.

It was obviously a coincidence that the security conference clashed with the Luton protest, but was the content of Cameron's speech influenced by the growth of the EDL or even apprehension of the events about to be played out? Reacting to the speech, Dr Faisal Hanjra, of the Muslim Council of Britain said Cameron's comments were disappointing. Mohammed Shafiq, of the Muslim youth group Ramadhan Foundation, told *Sky News* that Cameron was trying to score cheap political points in a way that would '**rip communities apart**'. Stephen Lennon said Cameron was "**saying what we're saying. He knows his base**".

A joint response was issued by Luton Borough Council and Bedfordshire Police (who had previously denied there was a problem in Luton), admitting the town had problems. The statement said they believed the issues raised in the speech affected the whole country, not just Luton, adding that there were a '**tiny handful**' of people from a variety of backgrounds, who '**have a message of extremism and hate**'. Local people lived in harmony said the statement, and they were very proud of Luton and its '**exciting and diverse culture**'.

Anjem Choudary told the *Daily Star* that he believed Cameron was a spokesman for people who hated Islam and Muslims:

> '**They find themselves in many guises such as the English Defence League, who are useful idiots on the streets, and their pseudo-intellectual backers and the people who are blatantly anti-Islam and anti-Muslim like Geert Wilders in Holland. These are all in one camp. Their objective is to silence Islam and Muslims and to have a Christian civilisation based upon secularism where Islam has no say and no prominence whatsoever. They know that Islam is coming – that there is a tsunami in the prevalence of Islam across Europe. We are on the brink of something as far as the Islamic uprising is concerned and the Government is aware of that. The EDL only have numbers because there are football supporters on the streets anyway**'.

In an interview with ITN, Lennon said the EDL was using the Luton protest to highlight local issues, such as Islamic centres no-one wanted (such centres were planned for the Arndale Centre and an old drill hall in Hightown, which had initially been reserved as land for social housing by the council but sold to a Muslim group for the development of a mosque). Lennon said local politicians might be in bed with local Muslim groups but they weren't, and as people who had grown up in the area, they wanted these issues debated.

He said nationally the EDL was stating that they had had enough of Sharia and Islamic extremists, they wanted politicians to grow a backbone and speak out for them, if not they'd speak up for themselves. For the first time in 20 years, people who actually paid taxes were protesting, said Lennon, not students or the local Islamic community who weren't working, but taxpayers. Apologising to the people of Luton for the disruption, Lennon said he understood the effect the protest would have on local businesses but it was the price they had to pay to stop the spread of militant Islam.

Council leader, Hazel Simmons, said it would be a challenging day and she was sure many people like herself, would rather the event was not coming to Luton. Simmons said the council wanted to get back to normal as soon as possible and look forward to positive things instead. The cost of the police operation was now being estimated at £800,000. Chief Supt Mike Colbourne told *BBC News* that officers from forces across the country were being drafted in and would be there to look after the town. Colbourne revealed that pubs and off licences in Luton would be ordered not to serve alcohol until the protests had finished.

On the day of the protest, there was trouble in the town as early as 10.00am. UAF were staging their static protest at the other end of town from St George's Square in Park Square, but anti-fascists were blockading the train station and clashed with arriving EDL. Police rushed to contain the trouble, as anti-fascists chanted "**who protect the Nazis? Police protect the Nazis**".

The assembly point for the EDL was in Hightown, around half a mile from St George's Square. EDL supporters had travelled the length and breadth of the UK for this symbolic protest. They were also joined by activists from across Europe, including Holland, France and Germany.

They set off at 12.15pm, around 2,500 strong, accompanied by officers on foot and mounted police. The column was a mass of colour, the flags and white placards of the EDL, contrasting with the grey, damp morning. One banner amongst the crowd stated '**More Islam = Less Freedom**' another said '**Sharia law oppresses women**'.

As the huge snaking mass made its way to the town centre, a few spectators and press lined the sides of the road, some children even ran alongside the EDL as if it were a parading Boys Brigade band. At the front, riot-police walked backwards, attempting to stem the speed of the advance. As they were halted temporarily, the crowd burst into a rendition of "**I'm English till I die!**" Nearing the square, the police funnelled the crowd into single-file to enter the site. As they stood waiting to enter the square, the sound of "**E, E, EDL!**" reverberated off the surrounding buildings.

It was a return, a homecoming, even for those not from Luton. It was the realisation of 18 months of determined endeavour for those present, not the people on the stage, but in the crowd. Selfless, loyal, determined, they had gone about their business quietly but steadfastly, attending anything they could, simply to fight for their community and preserve their way of life. It had been a long winding road for many. Some, especially those involved from the early days, had risked reputations, livelihoods, even the personal safety of them and their families. They didn't seek to push themselves forward into the spotlight, they were just happy to be part of it all, and now here they stood, in this small square in south-east England, triumphant.

This English horde might not be everyone's cup of tea, brutal, crude and forthright, but they exuded honesty, the sort of honesty which is only bestowed on those who know what it is to struggle. These weren't the sort of people who were taking to the streets in pursuit of some romanticised political ideal; they were on the streets because they believed their very existence depended on it. As far as they were concerned, they were patriots, following a very long line of patriots who hadn't gone missing when their country, and more importantly what it stood for, had needed them. These were the proud descendants, not just of the men who had fought in the trenches of Flanders or the deserts of North Africa, but of the common folk of Peterloo or Jarrow who had also stood up for what they believed. The spirit of those ancestors, lied to time and time again by the establishment about wars to end wars, land fit for heroes or simply food on the table, burned brightly in the hearts of every single one of them.

Lennon arrived with a police escort and told *Sky News* he didn't want the day marred by violence: '**We want it to be peaceful. We want to get our point across. We want our local and national**

issues at the forefront, not anything else'. As he made his way through the crowd he was caught in a crush as people rushed forward to shake his hand. After struggling through the well-wishers, with the EDL spanning out in front of him in their thousands, Lennon got up to speak:

"Look around you, Feel your strength. You are part of a tidal wave of patriotism which is sweeping this country at an uncontrollable rate. We will not be held down, we are reintroducing patriotism, Britishness, Englishness, a non-racist Britishness. No matter what colour your skin is, we would rather stand with one proud Black patriot than a hundred scumbag racists, that is where we stand. I see before me, many Lutonians. I am born and bred in Luton, Lutonians, where are you let's hear you. So all the Lutonians are at the EDL demonstration, not the UAF, where we are led to believe, from that town hall, from Hazel Simmons the leader of our council. We don't need weak leadership, we need strong leadership, we need leaders, we don't need appeasers we need leaders to lead our community, to lead our youth, to lead our families, to stand in the face of extremism instead of pretending Luton is in harmony. You can say Luton is in harmony, you can write Luton is in harmony, you can keep on telling everyone Luton is in harmony, it is not in harmony!

West Indian youth, Sikh youth, Jewish youth, Christian youth, all religions apart from Islam are in harmony. There are no racial tensions in this town, there is no such thing as racial tensions, there is nothing of the sort. There are religious tensions, not racial tensions, religious tensions.

Icknield High School, Lutonians know what I'm talking about, Icknield High School last year banned the emblem of St George. Banned it! They sent letters home to the parents of our children, that if they brought in, even the emblem on a pin badge, they would be suspended. Last week in Icknield High School, a Muslim maths teacher said to his pupils "Us Muslims are ready for the English Defence League". And who do the parents of them children contact? They contact the English defence League, that's who they contact.

This sign says 'Say no to the mosque at High Town drill hall'. High Town drill hall was owned by Luton Borough Council okay? It was earmarked as affordable housing, for us, for us, affordable housing for Lutonians, for our community, so they could afford to buy houses. The land was valued at £2.5million, Luton Borough Council sold it to the Muslim community for £1.7million. And guess who sits at the head of the planning authority for Luton Borough Council, Mahmood Hussein. You got it. We do not want a mosque in High Town. We want affordable housing for our community, that's what we want. That is our land, Luton Borough Council's land is our land. You are not selling it to the Muslim community to build a super-mosque, you are building affordable housing. We stand here today, proud, look at this turnout, look around you, we stand here to tell Hazel Simmons, you sell out! We are here to tell Luton Borough Council, you sell outs!

The other that many Lutonians are probably not aware of, I'm sorry to keep talk about Luton but this is where we are and this is where it feels in my heart and this is my Arndale Centre. This is my shopping centre; this is where my family shop. They are opening, in this shopping centre, a mosque! In the shopping centre! But it's not called a mosque; it's called a multi-faith prayer room. Although we have St Mary's Church, which is a Christian church, we have Our Lady's church, which is a Catholic church. And when we heard about this multi-faith prayer room I went into the Arndale and I went to businesses that are next to it, family run restaurants that have been established for thirty years, in this town, where our community meet, in this town, in our shopping centre. And I asked them what do you think about this multi-faith mosque that's gonna be opening next door to you? Do you want this? They were petrified, they did not want it. None of them wanted it. All the businesses I went to didn't want it. So I rang up the Mall and spoke to the manager and said who wants this mosque then? If no-one in our town wants it, from our community, why are you building it? Have you done any consultation periods in this town with our community before you go and build a mosque? Shopping centre's are for shopping, okay? That is what it's about. This shopping centre has been here for forty years, without a mosque, we don't need somewhere to pray five times a day, we go here to shop. While we stand here, we're telling the council now, we apologise to the residents of Luton for the cost of this demonstration okay, you have seen no shops need to board themselves up from the English Defence League. Nowhere needs to, these are scaremongering tactics by our council, no-one needs to board themselves up, no-one has anything to fear from the English defence League.

But we are telling Hazel Simmons and Luton Borough Council, you are not building a mosque in High Town, you are not opening a prayer centre in Luton Arndale Centre. Do you know why you're not? Because the people of Luton don't want you to. And that's who we are, that's what it's about. We are a democracy, you do what the people want, you appease the majority, not the minorities. And the majority of people are standing here today, and that's what we're doing, we're telling you enough is enough. Stop buying us out of our community, stop steam-powering through our community, stop building mosques in our community, we've had enough of it, we're standing here to make a stand. God bless our troops and God bless every single one of you. Every single one of you is on the forefront of the fight against militant Islam. We are writing our names in history. We are the only country who is doing this, but we have representatives here today from France, where are you? We have the French here, we have the Dutch here, we have the Germans here, we have the Swedish here, we have the Norwegians here, we have the Australians here, we have the Americans here, we have the Jewish here, and we've got fucking Guramit here. We did not chose to be in the European Union, if you want to put us in the European Union, we will unite Europe like you have never seen, and that is what we're doing. God bless everyone, and remember, stay peaceful."

The crowd roared its approval and Lennon was mobbed as he stood down. The demonstration was well organised, it was peaceful. There was an unusual feeling surrounding this protest, as one *Guardian* journalist surprisingly put it, there was an '**air of legitimisation**' about the whole event. There was a pervasive feeling of victory, whether it was simply relief at getting this far, or the fact they now felt vindicated by the build-up and outcome. Whatever the reason, it was palpable. This would prove to be a landmark for the EDL, sadly possibly not in the way most supporters expected as some people would now make their move to hijack the movement for their own ends.

Speaking at the anti-fascist rally, Labour MEP Richard Howitt claimed the EDL had bussed in a '**ragtag coalition of racist thugs from France, Germany, Holland, Belgium and all over the UK**'. Howitt said Luton could never be a home for neo-fascists as they were not welcome in the town. There were reports of trouble in Bury Park. A large gang of Asian men had gathered and were clashing with police, who deployed '**community mediators**' to reason with the group and try and pacify the situation.

As EDL supporters made their way home, *Luton News* reported a large police presence at the train station and Hightown. Chief Supt Mike Colbourne said the day had gone well, with the minimum of arrests and injuries. He said the operation was weeks in the planning and he was pleased with the professionalism of officers. Colbourne added that seven arrests had been made, for possession of offensive weapons and assault.

The *Luton and Dunstable Express* revealed that two houses in Argyll Avenue, Luton, had been targeted with EDL graffiti daubed on walls. Two days later, two houses in nearby Alexandra Avenue would also be vandalised in a similar fashion. Over the next week the local Labour Party offices were also attacked, windows were smashed and the initials EDL were sprayed on the walls of the building. Stephen Lennon told the *Luton and Dunstable Express* that he did not believe EDL supporters were responsible for the vandalism and added that if the EDL wanted to damage anything they would have smashed up Luton when they protested in the town.

The paper revealed that the day before the attack on the Labour Party offices, local Labour MP, Gavin Shuker and Lennon had discussed a possible meeting. However, the MP told the paper that the attacks had derailed the chances of any meeting with the EDL 'any time soon'. Shuker said the EDL could be their own worst enemy at times, adding that Lennon needed to get his house in order.

The day after Luton and obviously exuding confidence, the EDL announced it would now return to Birmingham on 19 March. The protest was in response to the actions of two local councillors, Salma Yaqoob and Mohammed Ishtiaq, who had recently sparked controversy by refusing to take part in a standing ovation given to honour a Royal Marine. Both councillors remained seated during a ceremony in the council's chambers for Lance Corporal Matthew Croucher, who had been awarded the George Cross after throwing himself onto a grenade to save his comrades during an ambush in Afghanistan in 2008. Stephen Lennon told the *Daily Star* that the EDL would go where they were needed and that the Birmingham protest would be the group's biggest to date: **'What those councillors did was disgusting. It just shows that they don't care about offending us. But we're not allowed to say anything that might upset them'.**

However, the announcement upset some in the EDL as it was a week before the Casuals United demo in Blackpool in support of the family of Charlene Downes. Some feared that in the face of the success of Luton, the movement was suddenly trying to distance itself from its football hooligan roots. There was little doubt the announcement was intended to disrupt the Casuals protest, following legitimisation of Luton, people in the shadows now stepped forward, believing the EDL now offered a respectable platform for their agenda. These people believed such football hooligan associations would prevent the more socially acceptable middle classes from joining the movement.

In response to the announcement, the *Birmingham Mail* claimed police and council officials, already 'making huge budget cuts' would face a £1 million bill for the protest. The paper added that police resources would be stretched on the day because a game between Aston Villa and Wolverhampton Wanderers, two clubs it claimed had a 'history of trouble with hooligans,' was arranged for the same day.

Selly Oak Labour MP Steve McCabe told the *Mail* that he believed that the Home Secretary should ban the protest. In September 2009, before the last Birmingham protest, McCabe had opposed any ban, claiming 'our system is built on defending the freedom to express all sorts of opinions'. This time however, he supported one, claiming the EDL was a group with a track record of violence. Khalid Mahmood said that if the Home Secretary did not ban the march, then the Government should provide West Midlands Police with extra officers or cash. The MP for Perry Barr said the issue was community safety and claimed that every time the EDL visited a town there was violence (obviously unaware of the trouble-free Luton and Peterborough protests, which is understandable as both had been peaceful thereby attracting little interest from the mainstream media).

Days later, the EDL cancelled the protest, claiming it had been informed by media contacts that Birmingham City Council and West Midlands Police had applied to the Home Secretary for a ban, mainly due to football fixtures that weekend. The EDL claimed that 'as usual' WMP had refused the offer of a dialogue and instead had applied for a ban. The EDL said they knew their legal rights and they could not be stopped from holding a static demonstration, but not wishing to upset or disrupt the public and due to the football match, they would postpone the protest. The EDL said it would not forget what had been happening of late in Birmingham and vowed to return.

Adding weight to the speculation that the date of the demo was no error, the EDL announced a replacement demonstration in Reading, Wiltshire, on 19 March, and also Blackburn, Lancashire, on 2 April. Both dates sat either side of the Casuals demo. This confirmed in the mind of many supporters that the announcement was intended to squeeze out the Casuals and also Marsh from the leadership. Marsh is a well liked character amongst rank and file EDL members, down to earth and approachable, qualities which many members accused the current leadership of lacking. There seemed to be a determination to make the movement more acceptable, and in the eyes of those now in control of the

EDL that meant shedding the football hooligan founding fathers. Unfortunately, even in the wake of Luton, replacements from the more socially acceptable middle class weren't rushing to take their place.

However, cementing the leadership into as little a group as possible left the movement open to infiltration, the smaller the group, the easier it was for outside forces to influence particular individuals and assert control. The recognised original leadership had shrunk in size for various reasons, Price had left because of his conviction for the images, Tutus was awaiting trial for a football related matter so had dropped out of the spotlight, and Trevor Kelway had also virtually disappeared. With fewer recognised leaders, surrounded by a small clique of sub-leadership 'yes men', the EDL was seemingly becoming a dictatorship, in all but name.

Operation Hummingbird

The *Daily Star* had announced the proposed Birmingham protest on Tuesday 8 February 2010, ironically the day it was cancelled: '**English Defence League: We'll stand up and fight for Britain's heros.**' [sic]

The *Star* ran another story the next day, accompanied by the results of a readers' phone-poll, which showed 98% support for the EDL. With a front-page headline '**English Defence League to become a political party**', the *Star* claimed the EDL was considering a move into politics. Lennon had always been adamant the group wouldn't enter the political arena and when asked by the paper if he would consider it, he replied although they were not ruling it out, it was hoped that one of the main parties would address the issues the EDL was concerned about:

> '**I think this country needs a party that's not afraid to say things some would consider unpopular. My hope is still that the Tories will take a tougher stance. We are a single issue group and at the moment we would rather have a dialogue with the other political parties – but that could change. I think we would get millions of votes. The main political parties are so out of touch with working class people. They keep saying Islam is a religion of peace, but it's not. All we see is raging wars. Our last four demos have been peaceful. We are a legitimate organisation. We are not driven by hate, it's the Left who have got us into this mess. Labour have destroyed this country and we want our rights back for British people. We have done all this in just two years without any funding or marketing. We have really struck a chord with the working classes that the three main parties have failed to do.**'

Lennon did however tell the *Star* that he wanted to appear on BBC discussion show *Question Time*. Unlike Nick Griffin of the BNP, who sparked a UAF protest when he appeared on the show, Lennon said he would have ten thousand people outside the studio supporting him. An EDL demonstration had never attracted such numbers, it appeared that it was either a misprint, sensationalism or people close to Lennon were convincing him that following the Luton protest, the EDL was suddenly more socially acceptable and would be attracting considerably more support.

To the surprise of EDL activists used to negative media coverage, the *Daily Star* ran a further story the next day, '**EDL Boss Tommy Robinson says he has 24-hour armed guard**', which recounted claims made by Lennon before the Luton protest; that Bedfordshire Police had issued him with an Osman Warning following threats from Muslim extremists. With the success of the Luton protest, and now the attention of the press, many EDL activists started thinking the movement had turned the corner and the group might be about to go mainstream. It proved to be a false dawn, as they weren't the only people who had noticed the *Daily Star's* sudden obsession with the EDL.

On Thursday 10 February 2010, *The Independent* ran an article speculating that *Daily Star* owner, Richard Desmond (whose media empire includes the Express Newspapers Group and Channel 5), had decided to back the EDL, '**Has Richard Desmond decided to back the English Defence League?**' A *Daily Star* spokesman told the paper that Desmond was away and knew nothing of the articles, so *The Independent* changed its headline to '**Has the Daily Star decided to back the English Defence League?**' *The Independent's* Ian Burrell said it was rare for the *Star* to report on politics and although the report had referred to the EDL as a '**far-right group**' it had been largely uncritical. It was the left-wing journalistic closed-shop springing into action, simply because someone wasn't playing ball and attacking the working class.

Burrell explained that the *Star's* editor, Dawn Neesom, was someone he said almost accusingly, who supported West Ham United and was proudly in touch with the *Star's* working class readership (the crux of the issue). Making sure everyone knew exactly who he was putting in the firing line; Burrell explained that the EDL drew much of its support from football fans and that sources had revealed it had been Neesom's decision to give the group such a high profile and not owner Richard Desmond. It was transparent, the nouveau machine in action.

Following *The Independent's* article, the *Daily Star Sunday*, under the same owner but with a different staff and editor, Gareth Morgan, chose a different tack, '**EDL – Not in my name says hero**'. Describing the EDL as '**far-right extremists**' the paper said a '**hero soldier**' had '**slammed**' the group. The soldier in question was the one which the two councillors had refused to stand for in Birmingham, spurring the cancelled Birmingham protest. Referring to Lennon as a '**tanning salon boss, who has a conviction for assault**', the paper said he had been '**bleating**' about concerns for his safety, adding that Lennon had '**joined the British National Party in 2004 and attended at least one BNP meeting in Luton in 2007**'. Describing the EDL as football hooligans and '**hoodlums**', the *Daily Star Sunday* then took the opportunity to remind readers that they had already revealed how '**prominent EDL member**' Allan Hetherington-Cleverley had spent four years in prison for smuggling Chinese immigrants across the English Channel in an inflatable speedboat.

Obviously eager to make amends for its earlier transgressions, the *Daily Star Sunday* ran another story in the same edition, '**Paedo rap for EDL leader**', recanting January's news that Richard Price had been convicted of possessing indecent pictures of children. The paper claimed Lennon had been '**blasted**' for defending Price.

Although there was a different editorial staff involved, the *Jewish Chronicle* reported that the '**Star no longer shines on the EDL**' and claimed that Dawn Neesom had '**refused to say whether the stories were a deliberate shift in editorial stance**'. Neesom obviously wasn't responsible for the editorial content of the negative stories, but nonetheless, the *Chronicle* claimed a spokesman for the *Daily Star* had said that the paper would in future '**clearly not be endorsing EDL**'. Danny Stone, director of the All Party Parliamentary Group Against Anti-Semitism told the *Chronicle* that the EDL created tension and anger wherever they went, their tactics were violent, and therefore they deserved no sympathy and should be shunned by the media. A spokesman for the Board of Deputies said that whether the EDL had political aspirations or not, the press should be exposing the group's '**insidious agenda of intolerance and intimidation**'. The were implying the EDL was merely the BNP reinventing itself following failure at the ballot box and said the media shouldn't '**become an unwitting, and still less a willing accomplice**'.

It had been a breakaway by the *Daily Star*, but one which was rapidly contained. Here was a newspaper, aimed at working class people, running stories on working class issues. They had found the EDL sold newspapers, to the extent where they had produced the '**political aspirations**' story out of a denial by Lennon. Working class people wanted to read about the EDL, because the group addressed some of their concerns. However, the left-wing middle class mafia which controls the British press wanted to be certain all stories about the group were loaded with the obligatory negative prefixes i.e. '**right wing**', '**extremist**', '**racist**' and so on, it certainly didn't want the EDL described as standing up for heroes.

Weeks later, *The Guardian* revealed that a disgruntled *Daily Star* reporter, Richard Peppiatt, had admitted to producing a number of fictional stories about celebrities and said the story suggesting the EDL was planning to enter the political arena was known to have been an exaggeration. Peppiatt said he was resigning because of the *Daily Star's* sympathetic coverage of the EDL and accused paper of inciting racial tensions and Islamophobia. The paper rejected the claims and said that Peppiatt had never voiced any disquiet over the tone of the articles and had been spoken to in the past regarding the proposed content of some stories.

On Saturday 19 of February 2011, the English Nationalist Alliance (a small right-wing group, which had supported EDL demonstrations and tried to garner support from doing so) held a demo in Dagenham at the site of a proposed new mosque.

The Becontree Heath Islamic Society had acquired four shops on one corner of Burnside Road and Green Lane, intending to turn them into a mosque and cultural centre. Barking & Dagenham Council had approved the plans, despite a local petition opposing it which had raised 1,300 signatures. A number of residents were surprised the council had approved the application because the area already experienced severe parking problems. A lot of shops in the area had closed and the majority of local people seemingly wanted these replaced with more shops, not Islamic centres.

Although not an official EDL protest the group said its supporters were free to attend. About 60 people attended the protest and it passed off noisily but without incident. However, the *Barking and Dagenham Post* did claim that some locals said they were intimidated by the protest. Following the demonstration, one young EDL supporter was sadly struck and killed by an oncoming train at Chadwell Heath Station.

The following day, the BBC broadcast a *This World* documentary '**Geert Wilders: Europe's most dangerous man**?' which followed Wilders on the campaign trail during recent Dutch elections and featured members of the international anti-Islamic network who support him.

The programme featured Chaim Ben Pesach a.k.a. Victor Vancier of the American based Jewish Task Force (JTF). Vancier is currently the head of the JTF, a Kahanist organisation which he founded in 1991. The JTF raises money to fund Jewish settlers in Judea and Samaria; it also broadcasts on public-access cable TV and runs a website.

Vancier is banned from entering Israel because of his support of Rabbi Meir Kahane's Kach Party, which as stated earlier is banned in Israel. He was formerly National Chairman of Rabbi Kahane's Jewish Defense League, formed to oppose anti-Semitism in the US by '**whatever means necessary**'. In 1978, Vancier was jailed for bombing Egyptian targets in an attempt to halt the Israeli withdrawal from Sinai. In 1987, he was convicted on charges connected to a series of eighteen bombings on Soviet targets in New York and Washington and served five years in federal prison for his involvement.

Seemingly believing it would boost her credibility and that the programme had been a positive portrayal, Roberta Moore announced that she had been in discussions with Vancier. The announcement was quickly picked up by EDL and anti-fascists alike. Most EDL were furious, not only had the Jewish Division seemingly been given preferential treatment by the leadership since its formation, they now claimed it was forging links with convicted terrorists. Moore defended Vancier, claiming that although he had carried out eighteen bombings, they had all been on empty diplomatic cars and '**no-one had been killed**'.

Some EDL called for Moore to be shown the door. The Jewish Division was closely linked to the LGBT Division and lately a lot of ordinary activists felt that both groups, although tiny in comparison to other divisions, wielded far too much influence. In an effort to show it wasn't Nazi or homophobic, both groups had been given unnatural prominence. It seemed that both groups believed that due to that prominence they could now steer the EDL towards their individual agendas. Some LGBT members had even recently tried to claim that the EDL was now a gay rights pressure group.

Both groups had recently raised eyebrows within the EDL when one member of the LGBT Division admitted that he and Moore had been meeting regularly with representatives of the Metropolitan Police Communities Together Strategic Engagement Team. In fact, at one point the LGBT activist referred to his police contacts as his '**handlers**' which set alarm bells ringing amongst some EDL. When challenged on the wisdom of these meetings, the LGBT activist replied that they were meeting the police with the blessing of the leadership and would continue to do so. He added that oyther members of the leadership had also had similar meetings with the same team. These revelations did little to ease the unpopularity of Moore and the Jewish Division with the EDL rank and file.

A small but influential group steadfastly defended Moore and the links with the JTF. They reasoned that the Jewish Division represented Israel; a country on the forefront of the fight against Islamism. A larger majority however, were aghast at the thought of the EDL being linked to extremists such as the JTF. The EDL they said, was formed to fight extremism, forging links with extremist groups would just bring unwanted bad publicity. Vancier issued a statement explaining he had been contacted by the

EDL and they had agreed to work together on joint projects. Vancier said he had '**wanted to be sure they were not the BNP, we would never work Holocaust deniers or Nazis**'. The EDL waved Israeli flags, they supported the Jewish people and wanted Jewish members said Vancier, so he was happy to work with the group to '**save England from the millions of Muslim invaders**'.

Anti-fascist websites pounced on the announcement and published pictures of one JTF activist on EDL demonstrations in Amsterdam and Luton. It became obvious that the JTF was already active within the EDL. The next day the EDL issued a statement, denying any link:

> '**With reference to recent statements posted online by JTF leader Victor Vancier and his purported links to and support from the EDL, the EDL would like to renounce those affiliations and reiterate their own position. The EDL is a non political pressure group, dedicated to raising awareness of the incompatibility of radical Islam in the West and the creeping Islamification in England and Great Britain as a whole. It seems our success has been hijacked by those who have a different and more sinister agenda and we do not want to be associated with radicals of any persuasion. The EDL has a Jewish Division, who have their own opinions and goals and while in some instances these may dovetail with ours, their relationship with JTF is not sanctioned or supported by the leaders of the EDL and we will not be used for others as a platform for their own publicity.**'

The Jewish Division responded by calling the statement '**poisonous**' and claimed it had been released by a rogue website administrator. The Jewish Division claimed it had done more than any other division to persuade people that the EDL was a credible group and added that the *Daily Star* wouldn't have covered the EDL if it wasn't for them as the paper's owner was Jewish: '**You are all the same: Blame the Jews. It was ok to have the Jews supporting you when you had zero credibility and only 10k members. But now you have 78k you don't need us any more. You are scum!! We don't need you! And remember this: Rabbi Schifren [sic], who all EDL think is great, was the driver for Rabbi Kahane, who all EDL think is a terrorist. You cannot get anything straight because you are so fucked up!!**'

It was a hysterical statement, and the only reason it needs further examination is because of the bizarre claims it contained. Was the Jewish Division really suggesting that the *Daily Star* only covers organisations that support the Zionist claim to Israel and that appearing in the paper was really a stamp of credibility? The statement also claimed that since the involvement of the Jewish Division the EDL had gained 68,000 members, again this was nonsense. In fact, Islam4UK or MAC had done more for EDL recruitment than the handful of Jewish right-wingers, who in all honesty even the Jewish quality press ridicule, could ever hope to do. With the comment '**you are all the same**', the Jewish Division was doing exactly what the EDL condemned the Muslim community for doing, using minority status to assert its will and claiming victimisation when it didn't get its own way.

On the JTF website, Vancier said that there were elements in the EDL with no principles or courage who desperately wanted to be accepted by the left-wing establishment and media. In contrast, he said Roberta Moore and the Jewish Division represented the courageous and noble elements within the movement. Vancier said if the EDL was not willing to work with JTF, it was rejecting all right-wing Jews, evangelical Christians and others who supported the right of the Jewish people to the land of Israel (presumably there will be some evangelical Christians in the Bible belt of the American Mid-West somewhat surprised to suddenly find they have become far-right Zionists).

The *Jewish Chronicle* revealed the links to the JTF and the opposition the move had faced within the EDL. Moore told the paper she was determined to continue the affiliation and the EDL leadership who had released the statement were '**complete idiots**'. Moore said she had been forced to '**put my foot down; I am the one in contact with the JTF. If some people don't like it, then screw them**'. Moore also claimed there were lots of Jewish people (presumably more than the handful who seemed to be the sole Jewish members of the Jewish Division) who were very upset at the EDL statement. She said she hadn't received any messages telling her to cut contact with Vancier. Another statement from the Jewish Division claimed there was a '**witch hunt**' against Moore because she was a '**strong Jewish woman**'.

An EDL spokesperson told the *Chronicle* that the group would never have any affiliation with the Jewish Task Force and that Moore had caused a great deal of unrest within the EDL because of her '**gung-ho attitude**'. The Jewish Division responded by saying that Lennon should '**sack the Nazis from the admin and apologise to Roberta**' warning that Moore had '**powerful allies in the US and in politics**'. The next day, the EDL released a further, blunter statement:

'**A member of the Jewish Division this week decided to link herself with terrorist organisation JTF. This was the decision and wishes of one single individual within the EDL, and does not in any way shape or form mean that the EDL is linked with this movement. We would like to make it clear that the decision to release a statement of this fact was done so without any consultation or agreement with anyone in the EDL leadership team.**

The EDL will never be associated with something that it was formed and exists to eradicate 'TERRORISM', and hopes its members understand and realise this.

As we have stated before hysteria and realisation in this country has seen the EDL has grown at an unprecedented rate over the 20 months of existence. Unfortunately this means it is impossible for the EDL to be held responsible for the actions of every individual; unless a decision and statement is released on the EDL official fan page or the EDL website then it does not represent the decision of the movement.

The English Defence League has worked closely with the Jewish Defence League since its formation as it has with a number of other faiths and religions. The EDL is open for all to join but its purpose still stands to defend England from Islamism and Islamists, while forging links with similar groups around the globe.

Any one person can create a story and put it on Facebook for all to see and the rumour hungry left swallow it up and spew it out with headlines such as 'EDL forges link with terrorist'. Well we have not and never will forge links with this group.

There are also a number of pictures that have been 'exposed' by the left of people wearing JTF jackets at the Luton demonstration. With over 5000 people in attendance again this is something impossible to police, and again doe not mean the EDL support this group.

The EDL will now hold further discussions with the JEDL and if the JEDL continue with their plans to forge links with the terrorist JTF, the EDL will have no option but to sever its links with the JEDL as we can not support terrorist sympathisers.

This however does not in anyway mean that we will sever ties with any Jewish people who wish to support the EDL and hope that the Jewish division of the EDL can grow stronger and assist us in our fight against the Islamisation of this great nation. The critical issue for the EDL is English sovereignty and opposition to Islamic Jihad.

The EDL Facebook Admin team have also become involved in a number of statements from the JEDL. The Leadership would like to point out that the admin team are made up of the core team that sit under the leadership in the EDL structure, they are involved in all decisions regarding the EDL movement and will continue to do so. The work these guys dedicate to the cause is unprecedented and any member of the movement should not disrespect them'.

19 February 2011: Barnsley & Blackburn

UAF and local trade unions organised a rally in Barnsley, South Yorkshire, against what they termed '**the policies of the far right**'. UAF had been struggling for numbers of late, especially in opposing the EDL. It was hoped that an operation against the BNP, who didn't oppose them as vociferously, would rally morale and help UAF regain some momentum.

Around 20 anti-fascists gathered in Churchfields in Barnsley, intending to march into the town centre. As they were about to set off and to their horror, dozens of EDL suddenly appeared and marched towards them chanting. A small number of police officers present intervened but it was obvious the EDL weren't intent on violence; just there to peacefully oppose the UAF. Police reinforcements arrived and the EDL were soon surrounded by officers, including dog handlers.

From behind police lines the EDL chanted and mocked the anti-fascists, who appeared dumbfounded by their sudden appearance. The EDL were held by police for over an hour, before being marched to the town centre. They soon found a pub, the Courthouse, where they hung flags and stood outside drinking and chanting.

The news was greeted with jubilation by most in the EDL, but commenting on Facebook, Snowy Shaw, quiet since his public fallout with Lennon, said the counter-protest was a mistake. Shaw, who had recently set up his own group United British Infidels said the UAF demo had been against the right wing and the BNP, he was neither, so hadn't attended. He claimed that opposing a UAF rally against the BNP implied that the EDL was protecting the BNP. One EDL supporter who was present replied: '**The UAF were marching against the BNP, however no BNP members were present in the area, the EDL decided to hijack the UAF march to show them that they will be challenged on the streets. We were not there to support the BNP, none of us have any interest in the BNP or their politics. Since the formation of the EDL, the UAF have decided to try to make our lives a misery, so on this occasion we decided to ruin the UAF march**'.

It was a tactic which EDL supporters enjoyed employing, it was also, for the first time, making anti-fascists in Britain look over their shoulders. They had put themselves up in opposition to the EDL and in true working class fashion EDL activists savoured the prospect of directly opposing them wherever possible. Psychologically they started to expect the EDL to turn up, rather than wonder if they would make an appearance. It definitely started to have an effect on their numbers.

On the same day as the action in Barnsley, the EDL Blackburn Division was again protesting again at the KFC restaurant in Haslingdon Road, Blackburn, involved in the halal trial. The EDL said KFC hadn't listened to them regarding the matter, therefore they would return to the Blackburn store every day for a month-long demonstration. Its main concern, said the EDL, was the serving of halal produce to a public who hadn't been properly informed.

In 2010, the *Mail on Sunday* revealed that halal food was widespread in schools, hospitals, pubs and sporting venues and the public were generally ignorant of the fact. Alison Ruoff, a member of the General Synod, told the *Mail*: '**The Church is only just waking up to this. We have been pathetic and mealy-mouthed but we should be really concerned about this. There is a lot of fear about upsetting Muslims but as a Christian you have to stand up for Christian values. Because we are unwittingly eating halal meat, we are spreading the practice of sharia law**'.

The Church of England had recently finally acted on the spread of halal food and told schools under its control to ensure the food they were serving was non-halal. The instructions followed concerns that a number of schools were actively sourcing halal meat (why would they do that other than for political correctness? One presumes they hadn't actively sourced kosher products?), in effect spreading Sharia across Britain.

Around 80 EDL supporters attended on the first day of the protest. The group claimed that a number of potential customers changed their minds after being made aware of the halal trial. Some passing cars sounded their horns in support. Inspector Gary Crow of Lancashire Police told the *Lancashire Telegraph* the demonstration had passed off peacefully: '**We've got a couple of officers up there now and it's all been reasonably well behaved. It's something we've been routinely dealing with over the last few weeks and months. We've been in constant contact with the KFC staff, who are aware about what is going on and are comfortable with it, and we've talked with EDL organisers who have been compliant and helpful. They are within the boundaries of their right to have a** peaceful protest, but we know what those boundaries are, and if they step beyond them we will take action'.

The next day, the protest wasn't so peaceful. Even with a police presence, cars containing Muslim youths drove past and hurled rocks at the EDL Later that evening, EDL supporters claimed that one of the cars had mounted the pavement narrowly missing a protestor and that police had stood nearby and ignored the incident.

Days later, the *Daily Mail* claimed that Anjem Choudary was planning to hold a rally outside the White House in Washington. The *Mail* said that Choudary was set to lead a protest which would call for Sharia to be established in the US. There was obviously no chance of the protest happening, it was a non-starter very much in the same way his threat to protest in Wootton Bassett had been. However, as a student of Omar Bakri Mohammed, Choudary knew how to give the tabloids the headlines they wanted and at the same time, gain easy publicity. He told the *Mail* that he expected thousands to turn up and support the march. The article descended into farce when it suggested that Abu Izzadeen and Sayful Islam were being invited to speak at the event (you can imagine US Homeland Security hitting DefCon5 when informed of the plan).

23 February 2011: Belmarsh Magistrates' Court, London

On 23 February 2011, Mohammed Haque from Bethnal Green and Emdadur Choudhury from Spitalfields appeared at Belmarsh Magistrates' Court in south London, accused under Section 5 of the Public Order Act of causing '**harassment, harm or distress**' during the Remembrance Day protest.

Supporters of both the EDL and MAC attended the hearing and were kept apart by police outside the court. Around 30 MAC chanted "**democracy, hypocrisy**" and "**British troops, burn in hell**" (anti-fascist group Hope Not Hate claimed they had also chanted for the formation of a Waffen SS Muslim Division). Opposite MAC, around 80 EDL from across the country chanted and sang songs, holding placards with pictures of poppies on.

In court, prosecutor Simon Ray said both defendants had been part of the Remembrance Day demonstration by MAC. Ray said the protesters, who were carrying placards which were '**critical of Britain's role in Afghanistan**' and had chanted that British troops were rapists and murderers throughout the two-minute silence. Shortly after the end of the silence, the prosecutor said the accused had lit large pieces of red and black plastic which were designed to resemble poppies. Ray said that the right of freedom of speech was very important and the decision to prosecute had not been taken lightly, but in this case the actions of the defendants had gone beyond reasonable protest and freedom of speech. The prosecution was brought, he said, in order to protect the right of the British people to exercise their right to the two-minute silence.

Grandson of a First World War veteran, Tony Kibble, told the court that he and his friend Paula Allen had found themselves close to the demonstrators as the two minutes silence started. He said that members of MAC shouted throughout the silence: '**Halfway through, I looked up to see what was going on around and I saw a ball of fire fall to the ground. Literally, my stomach turned over. I felt sick inside. It is something that means so much to me and to see what I believed to be a wreath of poppies fall to the ground - it is just despicable.**' In a statement read to the court, Ms Allen said she had felt '**insulted, sickened** and **offended**' by what she had heard. She said her father, grandfather, great-grandfather had all served in the Armed Forces and her nephew was currently serving.

The verdict was delayed until 7 March. Supporters of Haque and Choudhury joined EDL activists in the public gallery. As the court adjourned and was told to rise, the MAC activists refused to stand. The EDL reacted, calling them "**scumbags**" and "**traitors**" telling them to stand and respect British law. Court officials informed the judge and police were called to eject the radicals.

When the court resumed for sentencing, Haque was found not guilty, but co-defendant Choudhury was found guilty and fined £50 (the maximum fine for the offence was £1000). These were the sort of decisions which angered ordinary people. In the eyes of the British public burning a poppy and disrespecting Remembrance Day was one of the gravest offences imaginable, sadly it appeared the establishment didn't share that view.

Birmingham MP Khalid Mahmood told *Sky News* the sentence was not adequate to make up for the hurt it had caused: **'we don't take it seriously enough, he hurt a lot of people - people who are simply going out and doing their jobs'**. Shaun Rusling, vice-chairman of the National Gulf War Veterans and Families Association, told *Sky News* that every serviceman would see the sentence as **'disgusting'** and it would just encourage the radicals to make more offensive protests:

> **"If we set fire to a Qur'an there would be uproar and they would go after us but because this is Britain people just get upset. It is a futile sentence. For them to insult those who have given their lives for freedom is an affront. It is one law for them and one law for others. Remembrance Day is a very special day for those in the armed forces. It is a day when we remember those who have lost their lives for freedom and fighting for their country. The contradiction in their behaviour is that it is the armed forces who have given them the right to protest and free speech. I do not object to their right to protest, but what I do object to is for them to insult the people who have fought for their country to give them that right"**

In the same week that Emdadur Choudhury received his £50 fine and further illuminating the two-tier legal system, an EDL supporter from Lincoln received a ten year CRASBO for a public order offence at Doncaster railway station. Three EDL supporters were travelling back from the protest in Newcastle, when they became involved in a disagreement with three Muslim men, who were accompanied by a woman and child. Words were exchanged, the police were called and the three EDL supporters were arrested.

The three attended Doncaster Crown Court on the 9th march 2011, where charges against one of them were dropped. The remaining two, charged with Section 4 of the Public Order Act, saw that dropped to a lesser Section 5 (racially aggravated) public order offence. Both men were found guilty and received a £500 fine and a ten year CRASBO.

It was the same charge, bar the racial aggravation, that Choudhury had faced. Even though he had insulted a nation, it wasn't considered a racial offence, in the same way the vandalism of the war memorial in Burton wasn't. You have to question the motives of an establishment which interprets the law in such a blatantly unbalanced and unfair way. Mind you, when you look at the background of members of the current establishment, former militant communist students, it maybe isn't so surprising. The difference was £450 and a ten year restriction on the activities of an individual for members of the majority and a slap on the wrist for any member of a minority group. If it wasn't a two-tier system it was certainly doing a good impression of one.

As in the case of Keyes and Price, officers from the Metropolitan Police Domestic Extremism Unit travelled from London for the case. DC Andy Haworth said: **'It is only the second time a CRASBO of this nature has been granted to individuals participating in Defence League demonstrations, and it is widely anticipated other police forces will follow suit and apply for CRASBOs to stop violent individuals from subverting otherwise legitimate, lawful, protests. We are working to support all police forces with CRASBO applications against any individual who persistently commits criminal acts at (or travelling to and from) Defence League demonstrations, regardless of whether they profess to support the Defence League or oppose it, in order to ensure future demonstrations are peaceful and lawful'**

The unrest in the movement, sparked by Moore's links to Victor Vancier, still persisted. She remained in the EDL and was as vocal as ever, much to the consternation of a growing number of activists. For whatever reason, it appeared the leadership hoped it would all eventually blow over. Kevin Carroll denied there were any problems, describing it as **'internet talk'** fabricated by **'Bolsheviks and hard-line Socialists'**.

On the 26 February 2011, the EDL issued a statement which many supporters hoped would deal with Moore. Instead, it announced the breaking of all ties with the English Nationalist Alliance and the expulsion of its leader, Bill Baker. There had been growing antagonism between the EDL leadership and Baker, who had attempted to gain exposure for the ENA through the EDL. However, the recent ENA demonstration in Dagenham was effectively hijacked by the EDL and was subsequently referred to by the press as an EDL rally. This had seemingly angered Baker, who had also been highly critical of the way Roberta Moore had been censored by the EDL (Moore was allegedly a founding member of the ENA).

The statement called Baker a '**parasite of a man**' and '**an opportunist**' who had attempted to exploit the EDL. The EDL gave two reasons for his expulsion; firstly that he had links with '**Nazi groups such as Combat 18 and Redwatch**' (a far-right website that publishes photographs and personal information of far-left and anti-fascists). Secondly, that Baker had participated in a televised debate with a Muslim convert which was publicised on the Internet. The statement said although Baker made some valid points, he had '**made a complete fool of himself**' during his appearance.

The statement then addressed Roberta Moore, saying that the EDL didn't approved of her discussions with the JTF and hoped it was '**just an error in judgement**'. The statement said the EDL felt forced to publicise Moore's actions as she had failed to admit to an error and instead had criticised those who had issued statements denying the link with the JTF. Because of what it called '**this farcical JTF story**' the EDL said it was sending a clear message to those who wished to drag the group down: '**Take your agenda elsewhere, it is not wanted, and it is not needed. We will continue on a righteous path, one of clarity, and one of morality rather than hypocrisy. This battlefield is littered with mines and you have laid more than your fair share. We will not allow you to lay anymore!**'

The irony of the statement seemed lost on many supporters, the EDL had expelled English activists for alleged links to right-wing extremist groups, yet Moore, a Jew who followed a supremacist Kahanist ideology and had links to a group led by someone who had been imprisoned for terrorism, was allowed to stay. It was a two-tier system very much like the one the EDL allegedly opposed. Baker retaliated by claiming many people were leaving the EDL because of attacks on individuals and accused the leadership of '**lining their pockets**' and '**engaging nose candy**' through the profits from EDL merchandising, '**if they put some of the profit back into the cause instead of up their noses they would achieve something**'.

With the triumph of Luton rapidly fading from memory, anti-fascists also highlighted photos allegedly showing EDL supporters in hoods and masks posing in front of flags bearing the name of Northern Ireland paramilitary group, the Ulster Volunteer Force (UVF). In another picture a man was seen making a Nazi salute. The *Daily Star Sunday* obviously jumped on the story '**EDL blasted for sick gun taunt**', calling the photo's '**chilling**'. They were obviously keen to further disassociate the *Daily Star* brand with support of the EDL. Seemingly eager to promote the alleged Irish paramilitary link, the paper claimed that both '**former BNP member**' Lennon and Kevin Carroll were second generation Irish and had both spoken in the past of their pride in their roots. The *Daily Star Sunday* omitted the fact that both Lennon and Carroll were of Irish Catholic heritage, not Protestant, which might've been a sticking point for any association with the UVF. Hope Not Hate claimed the UVF link had sparked fears factions of the EDL could now launch terror attacks against British Muslims.

The same day, the *Sunday Mirror* revealed: '**Leader of right-wing English Defence League investigated for money laundering**'. The *Mirror* said Lennon's bank accounts had been frozen and claimed he had told supporters it was inevitable that he would go to jail, despite being innocent. Calling Lennon's video response to the charges a '**hate-filled rant**' the paper said he was being investigated over the source of several sums deposited into bank accounts. Lennon would later explain that the investigation concerned a period between 2007 and 2009, when he had deposited £160,000 in deposits on five properties. Lennon said the police were saying he hadn't paid enough tax during that period to be able to afford to do that, but he would fight the case if it was brought to court.

On Tuesday 1 March 2011, the EDL revealed that Lennon had been rearrested for the disturbance at the MAC protest on Remembrance Day. He was now charged with Section Five of the Public Order Act, and pleaded not guilty a week later at West London Magistrates' Court. A trial date was set for 11 May 2011. Lennon claimed there was to be a legal argument before the case started, due to what he called: **'abuse of power by CPS and the police'**. He was also awaiting trial over an incident at Luton football ground (he would later plead not guilty to using threatening, abusive or insulting behaviour on 24 August 2010 at Luton Town's Kenilworth Road ground. Following a trial, Lennon was found guilty and handed a 12-month community rehabilitation order, 150 hours of unpaid work, £650 in costs and a three-year ban from football. Ironically the case was heard by Carolyn Mellanby, the judge who had handed sentences of two-year conditional discharges and £500 costs to the Luton radicals who had abused the Anglian Regiment).

As if to temper the news of Lennon's arrest, days later Cambridgeshire Police announced that Guramit Singh would face no further action following his arrest on suspicion of causing religiously aggravated harassment at Peterborough. A spokesman for Cambridgeshire Police told the *Peterborough Evening Telegraph* that following an investigation and advice from the CPS, they had decided to take no further action. Stephen Lennon told the paper that he was pleased the charge had been dropped as it was baseless.

Also, a report published by Her Majesty's Inspectorate of Constabulary said that senior police officers were struggling to cope with the rise of protest groups in the UK. The report said the police needed to adapt to the changing face of public protest and naming the EDL specifically, said the group was by far the biggest drain on police resources. The report said the EDL had staged more than 50% of all significant demonstrations in the UK in the preceding 18 months and, barring one student demonstration, EDL protests had required the largest amount of police resources.

5 March 2011: Rochdale, Greater Manchester

The northern divisions of the EDL announced a demo in Rochdale, a market town recently linked to a Muslim paedophile gang which was to be the focus of the protest. Rochdale is a former mill town and like many the EDL had visited in the north, traditionally associated with textile production. Following WWII, large numbers of immigrants, mainly from the sub-continent, settled in the town. Now, close to a quarter of the town's population is Asian.

Roger Ellis of Rochdale Council said shops would trade as normal on the day of the protest, but police and council staff would be present to provide a reassuring presence. Ellis said the council respected the democratic right of the EDL to peacefully protest but they would also support the police in dealing with any criminal offences. MP Simon Danczuk said that people angry at spending cuts were looking for scapegoats. He said Rochdale should not be bullied by the EDL which was coming to the town to sow division, fear and hatred.

Mushtaq Ahmed, chairman of Rochdale Council of Mosques, told the *Rochdale Observer* that he had asked local Muslims not to counter-protest. Ahmed said that although they did not welcome the EDL, they had a democratic right to protest and the Muslim community would respect that right as long as there were no problems. Speaking for the EDL, Leon McCreery told the paper the protest was to highlight the paedophile grooming problem in Rochdale and would be peaceful: **'We are not out to cause tension and do not go out intent on causing trouble. If you look at our previous demonstrations in Bolton and Manchester where there has been fighting it has only been because of the police force being against us and from radical Islamists attacking us'**. Chief Superintendent John O' Hare, of Greater Manchester Police, told the *Rochdale Observer* that the event would be policed in a professional, sensitive manner and anyone who was coming with the intention of inciting violence could expect a swift and robust response from police.

Local support had been evident on previous protests such as Dudley and Leicester, but on the morning of the demo a substantial number of local people gathered around the impressive Rochdale

Town Hall to sightsee and some to even support the EDL. UAF were supposedly holding a counter-protest in the Deeplish area of town, but at the EDL demo site there were areas for both sides, 30m apart, either side of the town's war memorial.

By 1.00pm the EDL side was filling up. All the pubs in the town centre were closed, so the main body of EDL assembled at the Hopwood pub in nearby Middleton. There were around 100 counter-demonstrators opposite the EDL; consisting of a small number of white anti-fascists and around 80 local Muslims. Some of them carried placards sporting the Socialist Worker Party logo 'Smash the English Defence League' and 'EDL + BNP = Nazi-racist thugs'. They mocked the EDL numbers and at one point threw an orange smoke bomb toward them, who in response surged against police lines.

EDL coaches from Middleton started arriving, their arrival cheered by their comrades already at the site. The coaches were also clapped in by around 300 locals who had now gathered opposite the site. It was a Bolton scenario; the counter-demonstrators believed only 100 EDL had turned up, but when the coaches started arriving they were stunned, the silence only broken by an EDL rendition of "you're not singing anymore!"

In all, around 600 EDL turned up, some carried flags, others carried banners proclaiming 'Patriotism is not a crime' and 'Protect all children from Islamists'. GMP had seriously under-estimated EDL numbers, the demo site was too small and as the crowd spilled out of the side, police suddenly started to baton charge activists further into the compound. Officers in riot gear were deployed along with dog handlers. A number of EDL were bitten by the dogs as they struggled to avoid the oncoming police. It was a display of abject brutality by GMP; officers were using their batons indiscriminately.

The EDL sang "We're taking it back, it's our country, we're taking it back" as missiles were thrown and each side clashed with the police. Although missiles were coming from the counter-demo, it was treated with a more softly-softly approach by GMP, although officers did wade in at one point to apprehend someone who had attracted their attention.

On the EDL side, there was a short speech by former Blackburn councillor, Michael Johnson, who, through a megaphone which most people struggled to hear, talked about allegations of the sexual exploitation of children in Rochdale. Johnson had represented the far-right England First Party (EFP), but after a dispute left and founded the For Darwen party. In April 2009, he became involved with the English Democrats, a Euro-sceptic party which campaigns for England to be recognised and treated as a nation in its own right. Johnson told *The Citizen*, he had joined the English Democrats to prevent the BNP from gaining a foothold in Darwen.

Following the Rochdale protest Johnson would reveal he had met with Stephen Lennon, Kevin Carroll and Alan Lake at the Luton Hilton to discuss the EDL moving into politics. This upset some EDL supporters, who questioned Johnson's links to the EFP and whether he was the right man to be representing the EDL. Lake had initially hoped to link up with UKIP, but following the party's distancing of itself from the EDL had now turned his attention to the English Democrats. According to *Searchlight*, Lake claimed to have been offered a senior role in the party, but had declined, preferring, as with the EDL, to influence events from the shadows.

The protest in Rochdale was noisy and rowdy, with the EDL crowd swaying from side to side inside the packed compound. GMP again deployed dog handlers who launched themselves into the crowd, the dog's indiscriminately biting people. Officers battled periodically with certain sections of the crowd as they encroached onto what police considered no-mans land. Some Asian youths left the counter-protest early and although they bounced menacingly towards the members of the public gathered across the road, they were gently shepherded away by police.

After the protest the police insisted on filtering the EDL out of the site one at a time and tried to force them onto buses going to the train station. Lots of EDL supporters were local and some had parked in the town, this again caused problems between them and police. The handling of the police operation was inept and amateurish. You'd think by now, someone in authority would have some sort of grasp of human nature, but whether by design or instruction they treat EDL supporters like animals and in some cases they get animals, not people, in return. The EDL dispersed, with most bussed out of the town centre to the applause and cheers of locals.

Following the protest police said they had arrested 34 people for a range of offences, including possession of an offensive weapon, public order offences and refusing to remove face-masks. Leader of Rochdale Council, Colin Lambert, said that the police operation was a complete success and minimal disruption had taken place. He said that '**Rochdale's diverse communities**' were to be commended for their '**co-operation, tolerance and restraint through what has been a challenging time**'.

On the same day as Rochdale, EDL activists from the East Midlands staged a flash demo in Hinckley, Leicestershire. UAF and MDL supporters had caught wind of the protest, but had mistakenly gathered several miles away in Leicester.

The EDL assembled outside Hinckley train station, where the local division handed out banners and placards for activists to carry. They then made their way to a local pub where they chatted to bemused locals, explaining why they were in the town. Accompanied by police, the EDL then marched through the town, flags and banners aloft, singing and chanting.

Speeches were made in the town centre by a member of the Leicester Division and East Midlands Regional Organiser, Tony Curtis. The EDL then marched back to the pub. It was a trouble free demonstration; police were complimented on their approach, a stark contrast to the scenes in Rochdale.

12 March 2011: Becontree, Dagenham

The London divisions of the EDL announced another protest in Dagenham, at the site of the proposed mosque and cultural centre. Its supporters had attended a previous protest organised by the ENA but following Bill Baker's expulsion, the EDL decided it would now stage its own protests at the site.

Dagenham is a majority white working class suburb of east London, traditionally associated with vehicle production, mainly Ford, but Jaguar also had presence in the area. Other famous names such as Ever Ready (batteries), Sterling (arms) and Bergers Paint also had their bases in Dagenham, but have since either closed down or moved elsewhere.

Before marching to the site, EDL supporters assembled at Chadwell Heath station to lay flowers and hold a minute's silence for the young man who had tragically lost his life at the previous ENA demonstration. The EDL said that out of respect for his family they were keeping it low key and refused to name him, simply saying he was '**someone's son and someone's brother, he was a patriot and a good lad**'.

Around 160 EDL marchers were supervised by stewards and police. The EDL handed out leaflets as they walked to the protest site. Passing drivers sounded their horns, local people stood and clapped and some came out of their houses waving flags of St George. Regardless of what the media implied, here were local people supporting a group which some of them now believed represented them. Even so, there wasn't uniform support for the EDL; one activist, the author of blogsite *The New English Review*, claimed that some people had ripped up the leaflets she had given them.

Arriving at the site, the EDL stood behind small metal barriers. The police operation was low key, officers sat in vans parked outside two churches on nearby Burnside Road, relaxed and sipping tea with the radio on. One EDL activist carried a sign which read, '**1300 locals said no! Don't they matter?**' It was yet another small local demo, but now the EDL was attracting more numbers on these demos than it had on early national protests.

A UAF counter-protest attracted only seven anti-fascists and police were eventually forced to load them onto a passing bus for their own safety. EDL supporters bundled the placards left by the anti-fascists into rubbish bins. The anti-fascist movement simply couldn't cope and many simply weren't bothering anymore. The common people of England were revolting, and the policies of the left-wing were the last thing on their mind.

The EDL were confronted by lines of photographers. One young woman, referring to the proposed mosque, shouted: "**don't be bringing this to England. This is London, if you don't like it bugger**

off!" Local people gathered on the opposite side of the road and cheered along with the EDL. One woman opened up her house nearby so the EDL could use her toilet. These were *the people* and regardless of what the mainstream media said about the group, they were welcoming the EDL into their community. Someone burned a photocopied sheet of the Shahadah, cheered on by the EDL and surrounded by eager photographers. Another activist, clutching a megaphone said he was a local man and could speak for the people of both Dagenham and east London. He said they weren't protesting about the traffic which the centre would attract like the local press had claimed, they were protesting against '**creeping Sharia**'. Following the protest, police escorted the EDL back to Chadwell Heath Station where they dispersed peacefully.

Speaking about the proposed centre, MP for Barking, Margaret Hodge, said the people behind the application wanted the centre to be a part of the community and also wanted the area's police to have a base there. Hodge denied that the shops on the site were closing because of the plans and said they had been given the opportunity to relocate to the other side of the road. The MP said she knew the decision was controversial but said the community needed to unite now the decision had been made and not be '**exploited by extremists**'.

MP for nearby Dagenham and Rainham, Jon Cruddas, told the *Barking and Dagenham Post* that local people were appalled at the threatening nature of the EDL. Although the site was not in his constituency (strange he would therefore comment, try writing to an MP who doesn't represent your constituency and see how unwilling to comment, let alone intervene, they are), Cruddas said he understood any applications for religious premises were dealt with by the Faiths Forum who worked with local councils to select the best locations for such buildings.

On 15 March 2011, the spectre of Roberta Moore reappeared. She had been quiet since her public dressing down from the leadership. However, Alan Lake, who Moore was now rumoured to be close to, was far more influential than many in the EDL realised. Moore announced that there had never been any problems between her and Stephen Lennon, claiming that '**horrible stories and rumours**' had been spread by '**very jealous people who have no idea of what's truly going on**'.

There was obviously no dispute that Moore had announced she had been in contact with Victor Vancier, therefore it seemed more a statement of fact that she and Lake had more influence on Lennon and Carroll than anyone realised. Why they continually tolerated Moore's outbursts and extremist links, and followed a pro-Zionist line which the rank and file, although sympathetic to Israel, didn't follow, was obviously open to question. On one Jewish Division Internet blogsite, Moore would later claim Lennon and Carroll were both Zionists.

One veteran EDL activist released pictures of a meeting in London that Moore, Lake, Lennon and Carroll had attended, which was filmed by an Australian film crew. Following the disclosure of the meeting, Moore boasted about how they had discussed their '**goals, tactics and the future of our country**'. She said she was very excited about it all, because the things that were agreed on were '**nothing like we have done before**'.

Posts appeared on the EDL's Internet forum, openly criticising the fact Moore was back, not only in prominence but apparently attending key meetings to discuss the group's future. They questioned why that if white working class Englishman Bill Baker had been expelled from the group for alleged links with extremists, why Moore was being allowed to remain. Not only was she still in the movement, she was seemingly completely without remorse for the damage she had caused and the gift she had handed the group's opponents.

The discussions on the forum evolved into a debate over the whole Israel issue, including the murder of British soldiers and civilians by Jewish terrorists during British Mandate Palestine, something which is still celebrated in Israel. At this point, Trevor Kelway, who had overall control of the forum, suddenly shut it down.

Kelway claimed he had received a complaint from Pamela Geller in New York about anti-Semitic comments on threads about Moore and Israel. Those who staffed the forum pointed out that none of the comments had been anti-Semitic and that this was unwarranted and unfair censorship in favour of Moore and the Jewish Division. Kelway followed the closure by alleging that one of the forum admin had made anti-Semitic remarks and also used the **'Fourteen Words'** (a phrase used by white nationalists which refers to the fourteen word slogan, **'We must secure the existence of our people and a future for white children'**) in a conversation with a member of the leadership.

The EDL had already opened a new forum, claiming they would have more control over a forum which wasn't supplied by an outside company. When it was closed, many of the existing forum members didn't cross over and the EDL lost some supporters, this raised many questions:

How can a single complaint from an American close down an English forum of many dedicated members of an English street movement because of imagined **'anti-Semitic'** comments? Did this amount to, the line the pro-Zionist blogger alliance was always pushing, **'if you are not pro- Zionist you cannot be anti-Islamification'**?

How had Brazilian Moore with her open and unremorseful connections to an extremist group remained in a position of influence when Englishman Bill Baker had been expelled for alleged links with extremists? Who is Alan Lake, (he freely admits to using pseudonyms for 'anti-jihad activities' so presumably Lake is a nom de plume) and how, with virtually no visible support, does he seemingly assert such control over Lennon and Carroll?

Some people obviously suspected that, assisted by Lake, this was a takeover of the movement by American Zionists. Bearing in mind the drastic action taken on the prompting of Geller, they suggested that the EDL was now being financed by Israel or at least American Jews sympathetic to Israel. They believed the EDL was being funded (which Geller's alleged intervention certainly pointed to) for propaganda purposes, the intention to use the group, and its European counterparts, to show grass roots public support in the West for Israel.

The pro-Zionist lobby believed that in closing the forum, they had isolated and censored all resistance to the pro-Israel agenda. However, although many people from the old forum crossed over, others resigned in disgust. All objections to the agenda the leadership now intended to openly pursue were suppressed and anyone who opposed it smeared as a **'Nazi'**. The use of that word was apt in the minds of many EDL activists, as they believed they had just witnessed the EDL's very own, Night of the Long Knives.

The Loyal Rebels

The closure of the forum was followed by an EDL statement concerning the meeting filmed by the Australian TV crew. It had apparently been held close to the Royal Courts of Justice in the City of London and the statement said the location was '**appropriate as the EDL has attracted members of the legal profession and other professions to its base of supporters**'. The EDL claimed it had recently been reaching out to '**Middle England**' and had brought people from a range of social and ethnic backgrounds into the movement. The statement claimed that the EDL had been maligned as a group of thugs and hooligans by the media, but the meeting in the hotel had shown the '**true nature of the EDL**'.

The statement was immediately mocked by some EDL supporters who believed they could see exactly what was going on. Following the perceived legitimisation of the movement following the Luton protest and the national coverage it had received, Lake and his pro-Israel allies, now made their move to commandeer the movement for their own agenda. Football hooligans and ordinary activists, who had done the hard work by standing up in the first place, when no-one else had the courage to do so, were suddenly surplus to requirements now the movement was apparently attracting the middle classes in their droves. Of course there was no evidence of this, no middle class groups had declared their support for the EDL and there was no visible middle class presence on demonstrations. It was a confidence trick. The proof of one member of the legal profession joining the movement would manifest itself later, when a website to oppose new planning applications for mosques would be opened. However, it was hardly proof of professionals flocking to join the movement in their droves.

The content of the official EDL website markedly changed, becoming dominated by Israeli propaganda. Roberta Moore was now calling herself Head of EDL Media. It was a kick in the teeth for ordinary activists who had travelled the length and breadth of the country, risking their reputations, livelihoods and spending their hard-earned cash to stand up for what they believed in. Any criticism by long serving members was brutally censored on the new forum which accompanied the website. Hardly any of the new moderators or admin on the forum were known to the rank and file, which caused concern from some members who questioned who now had access to some private details of members, especially in the wake of repeated leaks from EDL websites. Any problematic members, who weren't complying quietly, were slandered by whispering campaigns emanating from the leadership.

The group had already lost large numbers of football supporters, mainly due to the diversity route it had been intent on pursuing. People had initially stood up for Britain and their traditional way of life. The Pakistani Christian Division is a good example of how minorities were pushed ahead of the white working class majority within the EDL. It is actually one woman, but promoted as a division because it illustrates the diversity mantra. As soon as the sole member of the Pakistani Division joined the EDL, she was promoted straight away to the stage to speak to the Nuneaton rally. EDL supporters wanted to hear from their peers, people who faced the same struggle as they did, not from minority groups who were promoted simply due to their minority status and the perception it would promote, not for their contributions or achievements.

As in society at large, ordinary members now felt they had no representation, they certainly had no representatives at the key meeting which had apparently shaped the movement's future, Jeff Marsh wasn't even aware that the meeting had happened, even though he probably commanded a large proportion of the movement, merely by consensus and respect for the personal sacrifices he had made. The rank and file felt Marsh represented them simply because he was one of them. He hadn't become remote like the rest of the leadership, when the membership leaks had occurred, Marsh, along with other unsung heroes from Humberside and Scotland had coordinated protection for members who were threatened. The fact that Marsh was unaware of proceedings made many ordinary members very uncomfortable with the route the EDL was now apparently taking.

Unfortunately for Lake and his legion of Zionist bloggers, the people who they were seeking to dislodge now shared a common unbreakable bond. They were people who had stood up against the might of the British establishment. They were the British working class, they were *the people*, and they would not submit to anyone.

19 March 2011: Reading

The date of the protest in Reading had initially been allocated to the Birmingham demonstration. There wasn't the same level of support in the south of England as there had been in the midlands and north, this, along with the fallout following the Moore affair resulted in only a moderate turnout.

On the day of the protest, around 200 EDL, chanting and waving flags, marched from the Three Guineas pub to the Town Hall in Market Place. The EDL told the *Reading Chronicle* they were protesting against a proposed mosque on Oxford Road and another in east Reading. Others said they were protesting for wider reasons, such as the number of mosques being built across the country and for more to be done to tackle militant Islam. Around 50 anti-fascists had turned up to counter-protest, referring to the EDL, one of them told the paper: **'We don't tolerate or want them in our town, they are Nazis and fascists.'**

Following the protest, Superintendent, Stuart Greenfield of Thames Valley Police said that no arrests had been made and he was pleased with how the police operation was conducted. Leader of Reading Borough Council, Andrew Cumpsty, said he condemned the **'racist demonstration'** and that the varied and vibrant communities of Reading had excellent relations, the town stronger and richer due to its diversity. Hatred and division have no place in civilised political debate said Cumpsty and condemned the activities of **'this small minority'**. This was further proof of course that all pretence of multiculturalism had been dropped by the establishment, the neo-liberals all now seemed to be bizarrely claiming diversity was making communities stronger. Of course it was, that is why the EDL existed, because everything in the garden was so rosy!

On the same day as Reading, at the other end of the country in Newcastle, local SWP activists were campaigning against spending cuts at Grey's Monument, in the city centre. Everything seemed to be going well, with one wag dressed as a 'banker in need' thanking people for the billions in bonuses he had received. Suddenly, the carnival atmosphere evaporated as around 60 EDL appeared. There was a small confrontation, one of the socialists said they were fighting cuts in spending and opposing massive bonuses given to the bankers, an EDL supporter replied that he didn't mind bankers getting bonuses, as long as they were English bankers.

Socialists complained that for the next couple of hours they were continually abused and that one police officer had posed for photographs with the EDL. One claimed they had been covered in EDL stickers and that a socialist who appeared carrying a Libyan flag was greeted with chants of "**scum, scum, scum**". The SWP complained the EDL were anti-trade union and anti-student (all the clues were there).

The next day, 40 football lads connected to Casuals United met at the Hamilton Hall pub in Liverpool Street, London, intending to protest outside East London Mosque. The mosque was hosting a conference by the Tayyibun organisation, which Casuals United described as a **'hate-fest'** involving **'a motley collection of hard-line Islamic extremists, some being allowed to speak via video link as they had been banned from this country by the Home Office'**.

The Casuals marched down Whitechapel Road towards the mosque, but were intercepted by police. They explained their intentions but the police informed them that they were under orders to prevent anyone from interfering with the conference. The police added that the presence of the Casuals was likely to upset the locals, therefore, if they continued they would be detained. It became obvious that if they pushed the point they would be arrested, many of the Casuals felt that they had made their point and left the area.

26 March 2011: Blackpool

Activists were instructed to assemble on the South Shore from 10.00am for the Casuals United demonstration in support of justice for Charlene Downes. The meeting place was again Yates's Winelodge, which by the allotted time was full of Casuals activists, the outside of the pub festooned with flags and banners.

Lancashire Police had informed the group that shop linked to the disappearance of Charlene would be under 24-hour surveillance so Casuals asked activists not to approach the place as doing so would result in arrest. Casuals said they understood people were angry, but the demonstration had to be staged properly, as it was about justice, not revenge.

At around midday, the demonstrators filed across the road and onto the sea front where the protest was due to be held. It was a quiet, solemn affair with very little chanting or singing. Charlene's mother and sister gave short speeches and a memorial CD of Charlene's favourite music was played. After the protest activists retired back to Yates's and eventually dispersed with no problems.

Casuals United said they intended to carry out a month-long leaflet handout near the shop, to warn tourists not to use the establishment. The group said the demonstrations would continue until they obtained justice for the Downes family: '**The constant pressure we are applying will eventually force the police and CPS to act and re-arrest them, so the family can get justice. This is our aim. We have told the police we will stop our demos once the family get justice**'.

02 April 2011: Blackburn

Blackburn is a former mill town which has produced textiles since the thirteenth century. The Spinning Jenny, a machine which revolutionised the efficiency of yarn production, was invented near Blackburn and contributed to the town becoming one of the first industrialised centres in the world.

What was left of the textile industry collapsed after WWII, the local council and NHS hospital trust are now the town's largest employers. Also following the war, the town welcomed large numbers of migrants from the sub-continent, in particular Pakistan and Kashmir. A quarter of the population of Blackburn is now Muslim, and in some parts of the town, such as Whalley Range, they form the majority group. Although Blackburn didn't suffer race riots at the turn of the twenty-first century like other northern mill towns, the far-right, in the form of the BNP and For England Party, has managed to hold at least a token presence on the local council ever since.

In the week before the demo, the EDL released a statement claiming that several homes in Luton connected to the group had been attacked. There had been eight separate attacks in the first week following the Luton demonstration. Then Labour Party offices had been attacked. Now the group claimed, in the last week, seven cars had been firebombed and a house Stephen Lennon used to live in had been attacked. The EDL said the intention of the attacks was not only to intimidate people, but also to associate the group with criminal behaviour. The group published pictures of two vandalised properties with the letters '**EDL**' daubed on a walls, a car outside one house had been torched.

Stephen Lennon said it was fortunate the car hadn't exploded. It was a diesel model, Lennon said if it had been petrol it might've caused more damage or set fire to the house where a family, totally unconnected to the EDL, now lived. Lennon also revealed he had been approached by local Muslims, who told him that their cars and the homes of local black people had been targeted in a similar fashion. Lennon said he had informed Bedfordshire Police because he believed someone was trying to start a war. Lennon said that police had now arrested someone in connection to the attacks and had confirmed they had no connection to the EDL.

Also in the run up to the Blackburn demonstration, an interview by Press TV with a young member of the EDL was being widely circulated by anti-fascists. A young supporter in a black Adidas tracksuit gave an interview in which, obviously worse for wear, he made several mistakes, confusing Iraq with Iran and Muslim and Islamic, which he fused and termed '**Muslamic**'. A strong northern accent, slurred by alcohol, also made his concerns about '**rape gangs**' sounds like '**ray guns**'.

Many EDL thought the clip was hilarious, others worried that it gave out the wrong impression. The video was however jumped on by anti-fascists. Music was added to the video and the young mans words mixed and repeated. A whole new cottage industry was created by the left-wing, where all manner of '**Muslamic Ray-Gun**' merchandise could be purchased. But as Patrick Hayes, on the website *Spiked* pointed out, the clip may have been funny, but not quite as funny as the left-wing seemed to be making out. There are all sorts of interviews with protestors on the Internet, from the G20 protests to climate change rallies, which contain many people just as confused as Muslamic Ray-Gun Man. It was just another stick to beat the white working class with, and as Hayes suggested, it confirmed every prejudice the middle class left-wing have about the ignorant, drunken, white working class.

Using the video to reinforce the view that Muslamic Ray-Gun Man represented the views and the intelligence of the majority of the EDL and ridiculing him, the left-wing are able to dismiss the concerns of ordinary people more readily. As Hayes commented, it was like '**porn for liberals**' bolstering their smug sense of superiority, allowing them to dismiss the EDL as a joke, a group of confused and ignorant people who simply aren't worth engaging with.

Anti-fascist groups were said to be planning to turn up to oppose the EDL in Blackburn carrying toy Muslamic Ray Guns to embarrass them. Unfortunately it was just another example of how the middle class communists didn't *get* the working class as, in true working class fashion, the first to laugh at themselves the working class EDL beat them to it by taking toy ray-guns and pictures of them on placards to the Blackburn demonstration.

Local paper the *Lancashire Evening Telegraph* said the EDL's visit to Blackburn and was '**deliberately provocative**' because of the town's high Asian population. The *Telegraph* said the EDL was an '**unsavoury organisation**' which attempted to '**build on foundations of fear and breed prejudice and hatred**'. The paper admitted that much more needed to be done with regards to community relations in the town but said its message to the EDL was still '**you are not welcome**'.

They were right, much more did need to be done, Blackburn was divided. In 2009, a report by government advisor Ted Cantle, who led the government's review following the Milltown Riots, said that Blackburn was one of the most ethnically divided towns in the country. Cantle concluded that people from different backgrounds were separated in every area of their lives and concluded that segregation in the town was increasing.

Speaking on *BBC Radio Lancashire*, Guramit Singh said there was no particular reason for visiting Blackburn, other than they wanted to visit every town and city in the country, to raise awareness of radical Islam. Singh had recently been given an ultimatum by some members of the Sikh community who had signed a declaration condemning the EDL. A Hindu and Sikh inter-faith group demanded that he publicly renounce the EDL by the end of the major Sikh festival of Vaisakhi on 13 April 2011. Failure to do so they warned, would result in the matter being referred to Sikh authorities at the Golden Temple in Amritsar, India. Excommunication would permanently expel Singh from the worldwide Sikh faith, which would result in him stripped of his right to be called a Sikh and being banned from every Sikh temple in the world.

Singh responded to the ultimatum by calling it an attempt at blackmail. He said his forefathers had battled against '**Islam-inspired intolerance**' and he was proud of his Sikh faith and its glorious history. Singh said he had been attacked and insulted by a variety of people, including national socialists and '**the usual far-Left Islam-apologists**', but attacks by fellow Sikhs could potentially affect his family life, so he felt he had to make his position clear, he wouldn't be blackmailed into denouncing the EDL.

On the eve of the protest, Lancashire Police announced that in a bid to prevent disorder and disruption to Blackburn town centre, it was imposing restrictions on the demonstration under sections

12 and 14 of the Public Order Act. The EDL demo would be limited to 3000 participants and would be held between 12-45pm and 1.45pm. Assistant Chief Constable Andy Cooke said their priority was the safety of the community and people visiting Blackburn. He believed the restrictions were necessary to minimise the risk of disorder, but added that everyone had the right to peacefully protest and police had a duty to allow that to happen.

As well as the announcement, several activists in the north claimed police had visited them and issued them with orders barring them from the demonstration. Several of these activists, including Blackburn activist 'Diddy' Calvert (who had coordinated the KFC protest), and Snowy Shaw, claimed that police delivering the letters had told them they were on a list of people the EDL leadership didn't want at the protest. The letters informed them that if they attended the demonstration in Blackburn they would be immediately arrested.

On Facebook, blaming the leadership for the letters, activists from the north branded Lennon a '**grass**' and Singh a police informer. They were adamant they would still attend whether the leadership or police liked it or not. Lennon later claimed police had compiled the list themselves, using posts from social networking sites. The relationship between the leadership and the northern divisions had been terse since Shaw's public fallout with Lennon, now the popular Diddy was seemingly being excluded it became even more precarious.

Adding fuel to the fire, Guramit Singh told *BBC News*: '**We don't expect trouble at all. I understand that our organisation attracts some unsavoury characters from the community and some of them left a racist stigma, but we're getting away from that**'. Rooftop heroes Snowy Shaw and Leon McCreery had a public falling out over the letters. Diddy Calvert was discussing the issue on Facebook. Following an accusation that 'Kermit' a.k.a. Singh had given police the list of names, McCreery interjected and dismissed the claim, saying that the police had amassed the evidence themselves based on comments on Facebook.

Telling McCreery to open his eyes, Shaw weighed in and said he had received a letter even though he had made no attempt to join any recent EDL demos, but EDL supporters who had recently publicly called for a mosque to be blown up on Facebook hadn't received a letter. McCreery suggested it may be anti-fascists or even an informer in the north who was providing the police with their information. Shaw dismissed this claim and said that one of the accusations against him was regarding the rooftop protest. He asked why it had taken six months for police to bring that up and also questioned why McCreery hadn't received a letter if the rooftop protest was a reason for being excluded. McCreery said nothing would surprise him, he even suggested there could be a whole division of undercover police in the movement or even Army agents. He claimed the protestations were '**sour grapes**' after the northerners had drawn attention to themselves. Shaw countered by claiming that a prominent member of the leadership had admitted at a recent meeting that they had used the police to prevent certain people from attending the Peterborough demonstration and had allegedly said they would be doing the same again for Blackburn. Shaw said the EDL leadership were now not just liaising with police but collaborating.

Nearly 2000 police officers from across the north-west were drafted in for the protest, in an operation said to be costing around £1million. Lancashire Police would later apply to the Home Office for reimbursement of the cost. Chief Constable Steve Finnigan would tell *The Citizen* that the protest cost a lot of money to police and the Home Office was looking at the impact on forces around the country. Lancashire Police Authority member Tony Jones would suggest that the EDL be treated like professional football clubs who were forced to pay for a police presence at matches.

Roads in the town were closed and many shops and pubs shut. A large central area was completely enclosed by mobile barriers. The EDL assembled at four public houses in Blackburn town centre, Zy Bar, Bar Ibiza, The Sun and the Arena. Coaches were parked nearby and those arriving by train were bussed there by police.

The EDL march to the protest site started just before 12.30pm, a mass of flags and banners such as, '**Garry Glitter would love Sharia law. Do children want it? No!**' and '**Warning! Political**

correctness can badly damage your nation!' Chants of "**EDL!**" and "**Muslim bombers, off our streets!**" reverberated off buildings, as the EDL made its way through the town centre. The route was deserted and totally shielded from public view by the barriers erected at strategic points.

At the demo point outside the Town Hall, Stephen Lennon, surrounded by banners, asked activists to remember why they were there. He referred to a case recently in the news, where Iraqi Kurd Aso Mohammed Ibrahim was jailed for only four months after knocking down and killing local girl Amy Houston. Following the paltry sentence, Ibrahim was told he could remain in the UK as he had fathered children here. Lennon said it angered him but he was proud that the resentment people felt over the case hadn't turned to violence.

Moving on, Lennon said that two years previously the beacon of resistance had been lit and could now be seen shining all over the country. At this point there was some heckling from the crowd and seemingly agitated, Lennon suddenly started to name EDL supporters he considered "**no longer loyal to the cause**". He said before every demonstration they experienced division, caused purposely by some people. He asked if one individual from the north-east was present. When the man made himself known, Lennon beckoned him to the stage. As the man made his way forward, Lennon suddenly embarked on a tirade against him. The crowd, now aware who the man was, started to point at the man and chant "**who are ya, who are ya**?" Scuffles broke out and EDL stewards intervened to remove the man from the demonstration.

Lennon, seemingly suddenly realising he had gone too far, pleaded with them to look at him and not the man, who with blood streaming from a facial wound was being led away by police. Further scuffles broke out and without a hint of irony; Guramit Singh, for some reason wearing a bowler hat for the day, grabbed the microphone and asked the crowd why they were fighting each other.

At this point many tried to leave the site, but found their path blocked by police. As it became apparent that the demonstration had descended into confusion, police relented and let them walk down the street, but barred their path once more further down with mounted officers. Scuffles broke out between the EDL, who simply wanted to go home, and police who were intent of herding them like animals. One man was dragged to the floor and arrested. They were then allowed to move, but only as far as the assembly point, where they were held yet again. Police told the waiting EDL they were being held because Asian youths were causing problems in the town centre. The coaches were parked within the perimeter so those who had come by coach started to board them, while others who had travelled by car and train were forced to wait.

At the coaches, words were exchange between a member of the Luton Division and a member from the north-east. During a heated discussion which followed, punches were exchanged and supporters of both men waded into each other outside the SDL coach. During the fracas, a bottle was thrown, hitting a young female. At this point the boys from the SDL intervened, rushing to the aid of the young woman and calming the situation. It would not help the infighting however and in the following weeks accusations were exchanged between the two sides. Following the protest, EDL spokesman Tony Curtis claimed that the clashes had broken out between the main body of marchers and a more extreme splinter group, telling *BBC News*: '**Once we got rid of the troublemakers it got better. It was a good demonstration.**'

The *Daily Mail* reported: '**Shaming the St George's Cross: Vile EDL thugs in 2,000-strong hate protest wear flag-coloured burkas to confront Muslims**'. The '**EDL thugs**' in '**flag-coloured burkas**' was actually one man with two St George Cross tea-towels on his head. Although the paper reported the violence within the EDL protest, it didn't, as its headline had suggested, report any confrontations between the EDL and local Muslims, in fact Chief Superintendent Bob Eastwood told the *Mail* that there had been no significant disorder.

Police estimated there were 2,000 EDL present, with 500 anti-fascists at the counter-demo (UAF claimed over a thousand). Chief Superintendent, Bob Eastwood, told *BBC News* they had made twelve arrests. One 48-year-old man from Blackburn was detained on suspicion of assaulting a police officer with others arrested for a range of offences including breach of the peace, affray, being drunk and disorderly and using threatening words and behaviour.

Later that afternoon, around 70 Yorkshire EDL staged a flash protest in Halifax. Assembling at The Courtyard public house, they draped their flags on railings outside, which soon attracted the interest of the local police. Also seeing the flags, a carload of local Muslim men pulled up and shouted abuse before driving off.

Around 20 minutes later, police told the group to take down their flags as they were causing offence. The group complied, but only so the flags could be carried through the town centre as they began an unofficial protest. They marched through the town, stopping outside the Town Hall to hold a rally, while police looked on. As they chanted, a group of Muslim youths approached them. The EDL chased them off, forcing police to intervene and make one arrest.

As more police arrived on the scene, the EDL decided to return to the pub. As they stood outside, yet another group of Muslim males approached them. They were chased off with the EDL running through the town centre in pursuit. The Asian youths sought refuge in a local takeaway shop and the road was cordoned off by police.

Following this incident, the EDL gradually dispersed, feeling they had made their point. A worker at a nearby takeaway told the *Halifax Courier* that staff at some shops had been so worried they had closed for the day. Another shopkeeper told the paper a fight started in the street, eight men had tried to get into their shop but police had marched them away.

In the wake of the scenes in Blackburn, local politician Michael Johnson, who had spoken at the EDL protest in Rochdale, claimed he had been asked to speak at the demo by local EDL organisers, but complained that they had been overruled by: '**a few lads from Luton with their own agenda**'. An angry Johnson said he had walked away in disgust and that the days of the north being dictated to by a few lads from Luton were now over. He said the Luton Division had attended the demo with the intention of being '**the big men**' but all they had managed was to do was split the EDL and show themselves to be incapable of running anything in the north.

Johnson claimed that 5000 people had turned our in Preston to hear him speak (there were nowhere near those numbers present) and the leadership had tried to stop the demo (in actual fact it had been rearranged a couple of times due to clashes with other demos). Johnson also accused the leadership of failing to support the Rochdale demo, where he claimed 2000 '**northern lads**' had turned out to hear him speak (again the numbers weren't even half of that and the majority of people present had no idea who Johnson was).

Presumably talking of the disturbance at the coaches, Johnson said that head-butting someone in front of the national media '**while off your face**' wasn't how people should be conducting themselves. Johnson's outburst possibly indicated he had been rebuffed by the EDL after the meeting at the Luton Hilton about representing the group politically and him now making a move for the support of the northern EDL.

There was a lot of discontent in the movement. Lennon's actions at Blackburn had contravened his own Code of Conduct, which had been used to discipline and expel ordinary members in the past. A statement by Manchester EDL summed up how a lot of activists were feeling: '**EDL is achieving nothing, loads of lads are packing it in because fuck all's happening. Snowy's got the right idea with the flash demos. The EDL's not led by Tommy anymore it's told what to do by the police. EDL have become a joke. Taking back our streets? Haha don't make me laugh you have to bend over and beg for permission to walk on them first! I am not getting the same kicks I joined up for in the past because the days of Stoke and Dudley are long gone, there's no buzz there anymore**'.

The EDL promised that Lennon would make a statement. The Scottish Defence League, respected and rapidly becoming the stuff of legend amongst the EDL rank and file because of their dedication to the cause and the hundreds of miles they clocked up supporting demonstrations, replied: '**Here we go again! Watch the body language lads n lassies! Be aware Mr Robinson, Your statement must be the truth, 100% the truth because if not then video evidence** [of the incidents at Blackburn] **is** obtainable. **No one wants a split with any divisions or regions, but we don't want anymore LIES. Ponder that thought before you speak!'**

Some of the northern divisions issued their own statement, claiming that Lennon had broken his own Code of Conduct in front of thousands and must answer for that. He had disgraced himself said one statement and brought a premature end to what should have been a peaceful demonstration. It accused Lennon of causing a rift between divisions and of cowardice because he needed his '**rent-a-mob**' when accusing people. The statement said the scenes at the coaches were disgraceful and accused the leadership of attempting to cover it all up.

In a video statement issued on Tuesday 5 April 2011, Lennon said Blackburn activist Diddy had been prevented from speaking at Blackburn because he was pictured in photos making a Nazi salute in Blackpool at the recent Casuals United demonstration. However, Lennon said the list of people not wanted at the demo was compiled by police and not the EDL.

He then ran through the risks he and his family faced on a daily basis and said that the people making the accusations about him were living anonymously at home without fear of intimidation. He said the accusations against him always came from the same person and there was no evidence that he was a '**grass**'. He said although he felt partly justified for his actions at the demo, he admitted he could've handled it better and said he wanted to apologise to everyone present. Lennon said there was fault on both sides for the trouble at the coaches and he apologised for his division's involvement. He then claimed the EDL had no real leadership, he just decided where demos would be held. This, in the wake of the forum closure, the tolerance of Moore and the expulsion of other activists was obviously questionable.

The SDL responded by calling Lennon a disgrace who had become obsessed with his own agenda for fame and gain. The group said any '**true leader**' would step down and Lennon's body language during the video had implied he was not at ease with the story he was '**spouting**'. Just over a week later, Diddy Calvert from Blackburn would claim that two men had visited his home, claiming that he owed them money. Diddy said he refused to answer the door and claimed one of the men, who had a southern accent, told him: '**Listen Diddy, we've driven 300 miles to come and see you. You better stop putting your shit all over the Internet. What would you do if I put this brick through your window now? Carry on and we will be back**'. Calvert also claimed that prior to the visit; threats had been made on Facebook by someone using the name English Merchandise, who had allegedly said, '**Shit St George Flag in your window Diddy**'.

Alan Lake, who many were now convinced had an unnatural influence over the EDL leadership and was in effect keeping Moore in situ, was again interviewed by Norwegian television news show *TV 2 Nyhetene*. Rabbi Nachum Shifren was also featured in the programme. Speaking about Lake, Shifren said '**Alan has had a very decisive role in working with me and people in the United States**'. In the interview, for the first time Lake admitted to at least financing the EDL in part: '**I mean, I have given some money to help some EDL things happen**.' Critics would claim the there was no evidence of any major funds being ploughed into the movement, so what those things were, was debatable. There were no visible signs on any financial input, repeated claims by the leadership over the proceeds to merchandise that the money had been spent on a PA system and other costs ruled that out. So what Lake was actually helping to make happen was anyone's guess.

9 April 2011: Dagenham & Blackpool

A week after Blackburn, EDL activists from the south-east staged a flash demo in Dagenham, with over 200 people turning up to protest against the proposed mosque.

In the north-west on the same day, 60 Casuals United staged a flash demo outside the Mr Beanz takeaway on Dickson Road, Blackpool, linked to the disappearance of Charlene Downes. The protest started with a minute's silence and then lasted for an hour. A police spokeswoman told the *Blackpool Gazette* that the protest had passed without incident.

A small number of Casuals United stayed in the area following the demo and police said they had increased their presence in the town centre accordingly. Casuals United released a statement: '**Sixty Casuals and locals held a flash demo outside Mr Beanz takeaway in Blackpool today demanding justice for the family of Charlene Downes. The paedophiles inside the shop laughed and even disrupted the minute's silence that was held in Charlene's memory. They are so sure they have gotten away with it, and all the other children they regularly groom and abuse without fear of arrest. Scum. Justice is gonna catch up with you one way or another, that is guaranteed'**.

The demo came a day after Lancashire Police denied covering up the amount of grooming of children for sex which had taken place in Blackpool. An article in *The Times* had accused police of hiding the extent of sexual grooming in the town and also of inhibiting further research into the problem because of political correctness. The paper claimed an unpublished police report showed that more than 60 Blackpool children aged 13 to 15 had been groomed by men connected to local several takeaways. Lancashire Police told the *Blackpool Gazette* that the report in question had been submitted to the Home Office in 2007 and was freely available to view online. Blackpool Council told the paper that child protection had since improved and they had always been completely open and honest that there was a problem.

This news followed the revelation that the men involved in the Charlene Downes investigation and two trials were to receive £250,000 in compensation for police handling of the case. In response to this news, the EDL announced a demonstration in Blackpool on 14 May 2011, demanding that the CPS immediately re-open the investigation into the disappearance of Charlene Downes and also that the government take action against Muslim grooming gangs. The EDL said it realised the demo would be stretching the budget of Lancashire Police so soon after Blackburn, but if they had a quarter of a million pounds to give out to the men implicated in Charlene's disappearance, then they could afford to police the EDL's right to protest against a '**gross miscarriage of justice**'.

Four days later, Casuals United held another surprise flash demo outside the shop. Around 40 activists demonstrated for three hours and in the time they were there, the shop had no customers. A number of passing cars signalled support for the group by sounding their horns. Casuals announced a further demo for the following Tuesday.

11 April 2011: London

On Monday, 11 April 2011, France introduced a public ban on the face veil. The new legislation meant that anyone refusing to lift their veil for an identity check could be detained by police who could then threaten fines if it wasn't removed. Anyone who repeatedly wore a veil in public could now be fined €150 and ordered to attend re-education classes. In an attempt to protect women who were forced to wear the veil, anyone found guilty of forcing someone else to hide their face could be punished with a fine of €30,000 and a year in jail.

A demonstration opposing the ban was held outside Notre Dame Cathedral where two women were arrested for defying the ban. In London, around 30 Muslim and left-wing demonstrators held a protest opposing the ban outside the French Embassy. The protestors carried placards which read: '**Face veil – a woman's right to choose**' and '**Defend religious and cultural freedom**', which was ironic really, as the left-wingers present would most likely have spent the last two years screaming "**fascist**" at anyone English who was '**defending**' their culture. Of course, this contradiction is easily explained by the unique brand of pick-and-mix socialism the British middle class far-left favour.

Suddenly, a large number of EDL turned up, chanting and carrying placards which read, '**Vive la France!**' There were clashes as the two groups confronted each other, one Muslim male struck out repeatedly with a large stick. Police intervened but completely ignored the Muslim man's violence. More EDL came from another direction; this group completely surprised both protestors and police. The pro-veil protest was thrown into chaos. The Muslim male with the stick and another EDL supporter clashed, but after wrestling the stick from the Muslim man, it was the EDL activist who was arrested (apparently released after accepting a caution). Officers rushed to separate the two groups, who then exchanged insults across the street.

Later the same week, Muslims Against Crusades protested outside the US Embassy against an event in the US involving controversial pastor, Terry Jones. The radicals marched, carrying placards which read '**Islam will dominate the world**', '**Allah elevates some nations with this book & He humiliates others with it**' and '**Terry Jones burn in hellfire**'. One young boy carried a placard which said '**Allah showed me the east and west and the authority (sharia) of my ummah was over it all**'.

Anjem Choudary had allegedly threatened to burn a Bible outside the embassy building, but unfortunately for the radicals the site they had wanted to hold their protest had already been commandeered by the EDL. As they couldn't access the planned site, the Islamist group ended up in a side street, surrounded by police. Around 40 EDL counter-protested, chanting "**Poppy burners, burn in hell!**" and "**No surrender to the Taliban!**" from behind police lines. Metropolitan Police officers assured the EDL that if Choudary burned a Bible he would be immediately arrested.

16 April 2011: Grays & Halifax

On Saturday 16 April 2011, Hope Not Hate announced it was staging a national day of action '**delivering a message of hope against hate**' to the country. In Grays, Essex, visiting anti-fascists were met at the train station by a group of EDL, who attempted to stop them leaving. One anti-fascist, who was filming events, asked one of the EDL why they were stopping them, the EDL activist replied that they had done the same to the EDL in Luton, it was a response to that and they were simply "**not having it anymore**".

Later that afternoon, the EDL clashed with police on Grays High Street, after a Muslim stall was allegedly upturned. One Muslim told the *Your Thurrock*: '**They scattered all our books and turned the stall over. One of them then got a lighter out and held the Qur'an and demanded that we burn it. It was very frightening but we remained calm. We are here to preach peace and love and will be back next week**'.

In Halifax, the Muslim Defence League planned to protest against the recent EDL activity in the town. The EDL planned to counter-demonstrate and over 150 people assembled in the Bull Green area of Halifax. There was a large police presence and at 3.00pm officers asked landlords in the area to close their pubs and started clearing them of EDL.

The MDL held their demonstration in the Park Ward area of the town, with around 50 people in attendance. A total of four people were arrested and police said that a man who was part of the EDL counter-protest was taken to hospital after becoming ill. Around an hour later there was an altercation at Halifax train station and police made a further seven arrests.

Two-Tier Britain

Wrexham Borough Council announced it was debating a proposal to ban certain protests in the town. The criteria for a ban would depend if it was deemed '**offensive to public morals**'. However, it was no secret the ban was intended to prevent the English and Welsh Defence Leagues from protesting in the area.

It was feared that if passed, the ban would set a precedent for the government to prohibit any inconvenient demonstrations whenever and wherever they wished. The EDL claimed that demonstrations by Muslim extremist groups wouldn't be banned and said it was yet another example of the two-tier system in operation. To further cement this theory, two high-profile cases hit the headlines.

On Sunday, 17 April 2011, the *Mail on Sunday* reported that an electrician from Wakefield, former soldier Colin Atkinson, faced the sack from his job with publicly funded Wakefield District Housing (WDH). Atkinson was facing disciplinary hearing for gross misconduct after refusing to remove a small palm cross he had placed on the dashboard of his company van. WDH said that the cross could be seen by members of the public and might suggest that the organisation was Christian. Under threat of dismissal, Atkinson, who had worked for the company for fifteen years, told the paper: '**The treatment of Christians in this country is becoming diabolical; I have never been so full of resolve. I am determined to stand up for my rights. If they sack me, so be it, but I will stand up for my faith.**'

According to the *Sunday Mail*, at one pre-disciplinary investigation Atkinson was required to attend, Equality and Diversity Manager, Jayne O'Connell, said employees could demonstrate their personal beliefs discreetly, adding that for instance, WDH would provide extra material for '**employees who wish to wear a different style of uniform**'. When asked whether a Muslim woman who wore a burqa at work would be considered discreet, she said if they did their job effectively then it would be considered discreet (but presumably wouldn't suggest the organisation was Muslim). It seemed that a small palm Christian cross on a dashboard was considered a provocative religious statement, yet in comparison a garment which covered someone from head to foot was not. It was utter madness.

The EDL Yorkshire Division immediately announced a protest in support of Atkinson for 7 May 2011. However, seven days later, WDH announced that he had agreed to move the cross to a vertical position on his dashboard and the company was no longer pursuing disciplinary action against Atkinson. The *Daily Mail* revealed the association had received over a thousand letters and emails in support of the electrician.

A day later, on Monday 18 April 2011, former soldier, Andrew Ryan, 32, appeared in Carlisle Magistrates' Court for sentencing, after earlier pleading guilty to religiously aggravated harassment and theft. Incensed at the burning of the poppies by Muslims Against Crusaders the previous November, Ryan had stolen a Qur'an from the local library and set fire to it in Carlisle city centre whilst shouting anti-Muslim slogans.

The court heard that shoppers and schoolchildren had witnessed the event outside the Town Hall. Ryan had failed in his first attempt with matches but had eventually succeeded with a lighter. After he had burned the book, he threw it to the floor and walked away. He then returned home and admitted what he had done on Facebook. Defending Ryan, Margaret Payne told the court that he admitted the incident was silly and it was not something he would do again. She said he also wanted to make it clear that the act was directed towards radical Islam, such as the burning of poppies and flags, and not all Muslims. Payne claimed Ryan had '**lost it**' after viewing a website showing radical Muslims burning poppies and abusing returning British troops

Jailing the former soldier for 70 days and calling the act **"theatrical bigotry"**, Judge Philip Chalk said it was a pre-planned act and Ryan had wanted **'maximum publicity and to cause distress'**. As they attempted to handcuff him, Ryan struggled with security guards and shouted, **"What about my country? What about the burning of the poppies?"** His supporters in the gallery shouted **"what a joke"** and **"do you call this justice?"**

Speaking to *BBC News*, Inspector Paul Marshall of Cumbria Police said the incident was highly unusual for the county as it experienced low levels of hate crime. Also, it emerged that Carlisle United Football Club was investigating claims that club stewards were among EDL supporters outside the court. Local paper the *News and Star* claimed that Ryan had been flanked by men **'waving the St George's Cross and shouting nationalist chants'** and said it had received reports that some of them worked as stewards for the Cumbrian football club. Carlisle United spokesman Andy Hall assured the paper that the club would carry out a full witch-hunt. One steward later resigned.

The Atkinson and Ryan cases highlighted the two-tier system which is now applied in modern Britain. It is a country where Christians are openly persecuted; registrars are forced from their posts because their Christian faith prevents them from officiating at same-sex civil partnerships. Tried and tested foster parents, barred from caring for children because the equality contract they were required to sign contradicted their Christian beliefs. Other faiths would not be publicly ostracised in the same fashion, again they were all examples of equality being applied unequally.

In the Ryan case, a Muslim radical burns poppies, an act which offends millions of people and they are fined £50. Andrew Ryan burns a Qur'an, the incident ironically publicised by the prosecution of the ex-solder itself, not only is he is jailed for 70 days, his supporters are persecuted. It's important to point out that the people carrying out the persecution of people like Atkinson or Ryan aren't Muslim; they are white and middle class. They are products of the British university system, and the communist ethos which infests it.

Look at the facts, a small palm cross suggests a company is Christian, but a full burqa doesn't suggest it is Muslim? Even if it did it seems that not being seen to be Christian is the over-riding, all important factor. Burning a poppy close to the Cenotaph, a symbol of national sacrifice, which insults millions doesn't warrant prison, but burning a copy of the Qur'an in Carlisle, where there are virtually no Muslims, merits a jail term. You would have to be brainwashed to even begin to justify that sort of reasoning, but they still get away with it because of the apathy in society they have purposely engineered.

In the same week, the *Sunday Times* reported that Muslim extremists were believed to be behind a spate of attacks being investigated by police in Tower Hamlets. Both Muslim and non-Muslim women who didn't wear headscarves were being threatened by radicals. One woman who worked in a pharmacy was told to dress more modestly and wear a veil. After she informed the press of the threats, a man entered the shop and told her if she persisted, she would be killed.

Ghaffar Hussain, of the Quilliam Foundation, told the paper the intimidation was the work of **'Talibanesque thugs'** who thought they had the right to impose their fringe interpretation of Islam on others. Other incidents of intolerance were also reported in the borough, including stickers stating **'Tower Hamlets it is a gay-free zone'** (An 18-year-old man from Leamouth, Tower Hamlets, Mohammed Hasnath, was arrested in connection to the posters and charged under Section 5 of the Public Order Act. He later pleaded guilty and was fined £100) and the painting over of advertisements featuring women in bikinis.

East London Mosque (controlled by the Islamic Forum of Europe (IFE), an Islamic group which has faced accusations of being an extremist Islamist organisation) issued a statement condemning the homophobic stickers. However, in the same week, the mosque hosted a **'gala dinner'** with Uthman Lateef, who Andrew Gilligan of the *Sunday Telegraph* referred to as **'a homophobic hate preacher'**. The East London Mosque was also said to have hosted a **'Spot the Fag'** event. *The Sunday Telegraph* also revealed that a Muslim woman who ran a dating agency in Tower Hamlets had been threatened by a local IFE activist, Abu Talha, who had warned her that if she didn't stop her **'activities'** he had **'a huge network of brothers and sisters who would be willing to help me take this further'**.

Paul Rickets of the Metropolitan Police said there was no evidence to suggest any of the incidents were linked (apart from the fact they were all initiated by radicals from the same area. Can you imagine a spate of race hate crimes aimed at a minority group in the same area not being linked?). Rickets said police were working closely with faith leaders in the community to ensure that people felt safe. Anjem Choudary told the *Times* that he was aware of individuals who would '**give advice about their views on Islam**' if they saw a Muslim woman without a headscarf, but insisted no threats would be made and described the allegations of death threats as '**completely ridiculous**'.

19 April 2011: Blackpool & Brighton

Casuals United activists staged another demo in Blackpool. Around 40 activists turned up and demonstrated outside Mr Beanz takeaway for three hours – in which time they claimed the shop had no customers. It was a strategy to at least deprive the shop of business, although to the chagrin of EDL supporters local police officers had recently been pictured leaving the shop carrying food.

Following the protest, the *Charlene Downes Action Group* now organising things on a local level, said: '**Once again the Great British public have spoken, last nights demo was a great success and would like to say well done to all that attended and thanks for the sent messages of good luck, the demo prevented any custom in the shop and the owners know without any doubt what's thought of them, we had a lot of support from passers by and motorists alike with many beeping horns in support. Next event Tuesday 19th April!**'

On the Casuals United website, the group took things one step further, pointing to recent revelations that in 2009, a 51 year old man from Blackpool was arrested in connection with the disappearance of Paige Chivers, who went missing in 2007. Casuals United said the one suspect in the Downes case was now 53 and claimed he was the man arrested in connection with the disappearance of Paige. Both EDL and Casuals refused to let the case go, further demos would be held outside the shop on 27 April and 4 May 2011.

On the same evening as the Blackpool demo, UAF claimed a confrontation had taken place after a group of up to 40 people turned up at an event it was holding in central Brighton. The event was billed '**public meeting to oppose David Cameron's attack on multiculturalism and Britain's Muslims**'. UAF said some people carrying EDL and Union Flags tried to burst into the Friends Meeting House in Ship Street. No-one was arrested and police denied there was EDL insignia on show. UAF claimed that at least one anti-fascist had suffered cuts, but police denied that anyone had been injured.

News also broke that EDL founding member, Joel Titus, had been jailed for nine months and handed a Football Banning Order. A court heard that the nineteen year-old had taken part in a pre-arranged '**pitched battle**' between supporters of Brentford and Leyton Orient outside London's Liverpool Street station in May 2010. Titus and five other men admitted affray.

Titus was also handed a post-conviction Criminal Anti-Social Behaviour Order by Uxbridge Magistrates Court on Friday 6 May 2011. The CRASBO stated that he must not enter a defined area of Whitechapel, nor enter or loiter outside a mosque. He was also barred from being part of a group of ten or more people whose actions could cause alarm or distress and from attending any EDL demonstrations. Detective Constable Andy Haworth, from the National Domestic Extremism Unit, who had been present at all the CRASBO cases involving EDL supporters, said: '**We hope this Anti-Social Behaviour Order will show people that we will not tolerate violence being used at legitimate lawful protests**'.

23 April 2011: Newcastle

Around 11.00am on St George's Day, 20 EDL met in Newcastle for a parade by the Royal Regiment of Fusiliers. When the march was over they decided to head down to the Grey's Monument area of the city to meet other EDL. Some far-left groups had also gathered by the Monument, including the SWP and the Revolutionary Communist Group.

When the EDL arrived they saw the left-wingers. The SWP chanted "**Scum!**" at the EDL, one with a megaphone was claiming that nationalism was evil and that St George's Day shouldn't be celebrated, others carried banners which said things such as '**Stop the racist EDL**'. Police separated the EDL and SWP. One EDL supporter was immediately arrested for trying to launch himself into the communists, but police prevented the EDL from getting anywhere near them. The two groups settled for exchanging chants from either side of police lines.

EDL activists said the attitude of the police was friendly. Police tried to move the EDL back and they staged a sit-in protest, refusing to budge. One EDL supporter told the police that if they released the detained man, then they would withdraw from the area. Police agreed to this request and the EDL left.

The next day news broke that the EDL website and forum had been hacked yet again. This time the hackers published the home and businesses addresses of Lennon, Singh, Carroll and Moore. The hackers were the same pro-Palestinian group which had hacked the EDL previously and made much of the fact that a company accredited to Moore which sold honey and other bee-related products, advocated the Qur'an as a reference to the effectiveness of its produce. One businessman who ran a business accredited to Singh later claimed that the company had no association to either Singh or the EDL. He claimed he had been forced to move his family away following a series of threatening calls.

The EDL Facebook page was also hijacked, but this time it was rebels from within the movement who were responsible. The EDL had always organised through Facebook first and foremost, therefore, practically and symbolically the page was very important to the movement. The rebels said they wanted to return the page to '**the people**' and not the select few who usually ran it. They published several messages attacking Stephen Lennon, then, on 28 April, issued a statement addressing grievances and questions they required answers to. They said the people deserved some answers to questions that had been asked time and time again but not answered.

The first issue was money, something which had been a reoccurring theme amongst critics of the leadership. They demanded that proper accounts be published showing all EDL income and outgoings from April 2010 so the people could see how much EDL was making and where the money was going. If the EDL did this, the rebels said they believed a lot of the accusations against the leadership would disappear. However, they added that they knew that wouldn't happen because they knew what the leadership had been doing with the money.

The statement also requested an explanation as to what had happened to over £800 that was raised to pay for some of the damage caused at the Stoke demo, as they claimed it hadn't ended up where it was intended for. They also wanted to know what had happened to 50% of the legal fees from the solicitors in the Dudley Two case, because, they claimed, as the charges were dropped the EDL was entitled to half of the money to be returned. The rebels claimed there was between £2000 and £3000 of EDL money that couldn't be accounted for.

They also wanted to know why the group was still collecting for the charity *Soldiers off our Streets*, when they had been informed the charity didn't want to be associated with the EDL. They alleged that although money had been collected, the charity hadn't seen any of it. Finally on the issue of money, they demanded to know who paid when the leadership and others stayed in '**the best hotels**' in towns and cities where the EDL staged demonstrations.

The lengthy statement then addressed the infighting which had recently plagued the movement, claiming people had been publicly slandered after questioning leadership decisions. It was time, said the statement, for the leadership to start acting like leaders and not children in a playground. The rebels demanded that the EDL stop holding spoiler demos (as they had done to Casuals United in Blackpool) or hijacking other protests (ENA in Dagenham) by groups with the same aim.

The rebels also asked if it was true that the EDL Internet forum had been shut down at the behest of Pamela Geller due to criticism of the Jewish Division. If that was the case, said that statement, why was an American telling an English street movement what it could and couldn't do or say. They also questioned why Roberta Moore was still being endorsed as part of the Jewish Division. Ordinary supporters now felt the EDL was too pro-Israeli said the statement; the movement was supposedly formed to defend England and Britain, not to constantly bang on about Israel, which in its formation had involved the deaths of British soldiers.

The statement also criticised some in the Support Group, accusing them of '**taking the piss out of us**'. It quoted one member, Hel Gower, who, to the chagrin of some members, referred to herself as '**PA to Tommy Robinson and Kevin Carroll**'. The title had been widely ridiculed by many people, but regardless, Gower had recently worn a hoody at a demo with '**PA to the Stars**' emblazoned on the back. The statement asked if that was how the Support Group saw the leadership, as stars who were detached from the rank and file.

Concluding, the statement said that as long as *the people* received some answers then that would be the end of the matter. If no reply was issued, or if the leadership were dishonest, then they would publish '**all the evidence we have, which includes recorded conversations. You know this evidence exists because you know what you've said and written**'.

.   An initial reply by the leadership said that the hacking was taking the focus away from the group's main aim, fighting militant Islam. The EDL claimed that the account of a Facebook page admin had fallen into '**the wrong hands**', although they admitted they were not sure who had control of the site. The EDL claimed that the new list put out by the hackers of the group's website, which had included the business addresses of some members of the leadership, was old information that was already in the public domain, implying the site hadn't actually been hacked. It was nonsense of course; certain information on the leaked list was definitely not already in the public domain, certainly not the alleged business addresses of Singh and Moore anyway. The statement carried on with the three monkey approach the leadership had been employing of late and failed to address any of the concerns raised by the rebels.

29 April 2011: London

The wedding of HRH Prince William and Catherine Middleton was taking place in London. It was worldwide headline news and of course the opportunistic students of Omar Bakri Mohammed were keen to capitalise. Muslims Against Crusades threatened to turn the event into a '**nightmare**' unless Prince William and Prince Harry resigned from the Armed Forces. On the MAC website, along with a picture of Prince Harry with a swastika and a burning Union Jack, the group announced: '**We strongly advise Prince William and his Nazi sympathiser to withdraw from the crusader British military and give up all affiliation to the tyrannical British Empire. We promise that should they refuse, then the day which the nation has been dreaming of for so long will become a nightmare**'.

Moderate Muslim group Quilliam, called the threat '**deeply disappointing, but entirely predictable**', but of course, just as the people at source had hoped, the press ensured the threat received full coverage. '**Muslim fanatics plot to hijack Royal Wedding by burning effigies of Kate and William along route of the procession**' cried the *Daily Mail*. Abu Abujandal of MAC told the paper they were expecting thousands of people to protest and said as well as models of the couple the group might also burn a flag and a crown. *The Sun* followed suit with an almost identical headline, '**Muslim fanatics plan to hijack the royal wedding by burning effigies of Prince William and Kate Middleton**'. The paper claimed MAC were vowing to turn the wedding celebrations into a nightmare and planned a '**forceful demonstration with thousands of protesters set to burn the Union Flag, images of the Crown, and the bridal couple**'. The paper said this even though there was no evidence (as there hadn't been in the case of the proposed Islam4UK march through Wootton Bassett) MAC could pull such numbers. *The Mirror* reported that there was a banner on the MAC website which told Princes William and Harry to '**watch their backs**'. *Sky News* and *The Independent* revealed that a second group, with '**Middle East links**' had also asked police for permission to protest on the day of the wedding and was in talks with senior officers.

The EDL responded and said it would position people at all underground stations in central London. The group said that if radicals appeared, they would be sent straight back in the direction they came from. The papers reported that MAC was unlikely to be granted permission to protest, unless they agreed to postpone the demonstration until later in the day. MAC apparently refused to comply and failed to turn up at a planning meeting with police. As a result, MAC was denied permission to demonstrate outside Westminster Abbey during the service. Spokesman, Abu Abbas, told *The Telegraph* that MAC now urged all Muslims to stay away from the royal wedding, '**not only because of the drinking, drug taking and sexual promiscuity but because of the likelihood of an attack by the Mujahideen**'. Police told *Sky News* they had no intelligence of a specific terror threat to the wedding.

The wedding passed off without incident, with even the most republican of commentators conceding, due to the number of people who travelled to witness it in person and interest in the coverage, that patriotism was still alive and well in the UK. It was reported that some radicals did appear at Stratford tube, but were refused access to the station by police. They were spotted by locals and an angry mob of patriotic Londoners quickly gathered and started barracking the extremists, who were reportedly escorted out of the area by police for their own safety.

In the north-east, the *Hartlepool Mail* claimed that three alleged EDL members had been charged over race related vandalism at a local mosque. Durham Police charged two men aged 24 and 31, and a woman aged 19, of being behind three spray paint attacks the previous November, including one on the Nasir Mosque, in Brougham Terrace, Hartlepool. A police spokesman said that at the time of the alleged offences all three people claimed membership of the EDL.

30 April 2011: Weymouth, Berwick and Stretton Burton

A demonstration was called for Weymouth, Dorset, billed as a protest against '**the entrapment of youth by Islamic extremists**'. It was in fact a response to a BBC documentary *My Brother the Islamist*, by film-maker Rob Leech. The programmed had featured Leech's step-brother, Richard Dart, who had converted to Islam. Viewers saw Dart refer to British soldiers returning from Afghanistan as "**murderers**".

The tabloids went into overdrive. '**Muslim fanatic in £1k rent benefit**' said *The Sun* explaining that Dart claimed £64 a week jobseeker's allowance and £1,015 a month in housing benefit while insulting British soldiers. The paper said he had stopped working as a security guard 18 months earlier and he had said that his rent was so expensive that it was difficult for him to get a job that was financially viable. The *Evening Standard* revealed that Dart, who now calls himself Salahuddin, lived in a state funded £420,000 two-bedroom apartment in Mile End. Under the headline '**Revealed: How TV Islamic extremist who hates Britain enjoys £1,250-a-month benefits and rent-free luxury flat**' the *Daily Mail* said Dart had been branded a '**hypocrite**' for taking benefits from the state he claimed to despise. The paper also claimed Dart had recently said '**When the Taliban defeat the allies we will establish Sharia and take the fight to the enemy**'. The radical had also featured in a *Daily Mail* article back in July 2009, when he told the paper he would be happy to fight and die overseas, that Islam must defeat Western aggression and that the soldiers taking part in these wars were the enemies of Islam. Dart said he would love to see Sharia in the UK, there were a lot of people who needed to have fear in their lives and Islamic law would bring back standards (presumably not double standards which were already alive and well in modern Britain).

On the morning of the protest, EDL supporters assembled at Moby Dicks pub on Weymouth seafront. There were large numbers of riot-police present, to keep the EDL away from a UAF counter-protest at the Pavilion.

UAF had bizarrely claimed the EDL demonstration was linked to the anniversary of Hitler's death. Many, in fact probably 99% of the EDL hadn't got a clue when Hitler had died. A large number could probably tell you what date Britain declared war on Germany, or the date of the D-Day landings, even the date of the Queen's Coronation, but Hitler? Highly unlikely. It was desperation by the far-left; anti-fascists losing the battle on the streets were seizing any chance to link the EDL, however tenuously, to Nazism.

Police escorted around 300 EDL along the Esplanade towards the demo site at the Pier Bandstand. It was a poor turnout, numbers had been falling lately, no doubt affected by the infighting, but also because of the new middle class friendly, globalised, minority driven agenda the EDL was seemingly taking. However, the infighting also undoubtedly played a major part, the EDL had lost some committed activists, also many northern and midlands activists had stopped attending demonstrations in the south. But the main reason for falling numbers was the EDL seemed to have deviated from its founding ethos, standing up for England, the English people and their English way of life.

One EDL organiser told the *Dorset Echo* they didn't want extremism in Weymouth. He said the protest was a great chance to show that they were not racist or Nazi and they were just people who wanted to protect their way of life. At the bandstand, a retired forces veteran from Dorchester, Ted Caine, gave a speech in which he said he agreed with the protest and that there were people in the UK who did not deserve to be in the country. Caine said he had served in the forces for 25 years, he didn't advocate violence but the British people needed to take their country back. The proud old soldier said it was time that people stood up for what they believe in.

Following the demo, *BBC News* reported that '**EDL Dorset protest passes off peacefully**' and said there had been no arrests. Dorset Police said that around 300 EDL and 50 UAF counter-protesters had descended on the town. UAF, somewhat predictably, claimed 250 anti-fascists had attended the counter-protest.

On the same day as Weymouth, the SDL held a peaceful demo in Berwick which attracted over 100 people. A number of EDL and WDL attended the protest, along with a number of the northern rebels including Snowy Shaw. There was a slight air of tension between the rebel groups and the groups still loyal to the Defence Leagues, but the event remained peaceful. Also, in Stretton Burton, Staffordshire, activists from the East Midlands attended the war memorial which had been vandalised prior to the Aylesbury protest, where a small number of EDL held a protest.

The infighting persisted, and to some observers, the EDL seemed to be slowly imploding. Carroll and Lennon were both missing, purportedly abroad on holiday. The website and official forum now appeared to be under the control of Moore and the international Zionist lobby, as a plethora of pro-Israel propaganda started appearing on the site. All was not well in the camp either though, as Moore set up an anonymous blog attacking other pro-Zionists in the EDL Support Group.

EDL activists from the north of England and Scotland were now openly criticising the Luton leadership. Snowy Shaw claimed that he had been roughed up at his home by some heavies sent by Lennon and Carroll. This led to hostilities being resumed between the northern rebels, taking Shaw's lead and now calling themselves the '**Infidels**', and the southern leadership, with threats against members of each faction openly posted on Facebook.

The activists who had refused to cooperate with the shut down of the old Internet forum opened a new one, *UK Freedom and Democracy Forum*, based on the ethos that free speech within the movement must be maintained. A lot of veteran activists, missing since the forum's closure and the movement's sudden change of direction, reappeared. Most were time-served and trusted supporters, many concerned at the current pro-Israel course the EDL had embarked upon. Some were openly claiming that the EDL had been infiltrated and taken over in a pro-Zionist coup d'etat.

UKFD now formed a credible and resolute opposition to the Zionists and over the coming weeks more patriots would flock to its banner. Unlike the now pro-Zionist '**official forum**', which was now frequented by a number of pro-Israel activists from across the world, *UKFD* became the credible Internet home of a number of hardcore EDL activists. No-one wanted to damage the movement as all were active within it and believed in the cause, but they now believed the group now appeared to be in the wrong hands, and that well meaning British patriots were being used. Therefore, they precariously balanced their inherent loyalty with a constant stream of constructive criticism which the infiltrators shied away from or censored from the official forum, referred to as the '**occupied forum**' by some *UKFD* members.

Days later, Lennon released a video statement to address some of the issues. Firstly regarding the legal fund set up for McCreery and Shaw following their rooftop protest, Lennon said the cost of defending the two men was £5750. When the prosecution dropped the case the EDL was informed that £3000 of the £5750 would be returned. The video then showed letters from the solicitor and County Court explaining that the money wasn't being returned because the Legal Aid originally granted to Shaw and McCreery wasn't terminated by either of them.

Addressing the allegations concerning the charity money, Lennon said the leadership didn't arrange charity collections, they were organised by the EDL Angels. He said that 10% of EDL merchandise profits had always gone to *Help for Heroes* charity, but the charity had eventually declined donations. He then produced proof of donations to *Help for Heroes*, *Afghan Heroes* and *Soldiers Off our Streets*. Lennon said the EDL had donated £100 to *Soldiers Off our Streets*, but the money was returned, as the charity had said the donation **"wasn't enough"** (apparently more because the charity didn't want to be associated with the EDL). Following allegations of impropriety, his PA, Hel Gower, had claimed that the money refused by *Soldiers off our Streets* had been **'returned to funds'**. Lennon said the money was then given to help with the funeral expenses of two EDL members.

Lennon said an allegation that they had sold over 100,000 items of merchandise was ludicrous, he said the figure was nearer 4000 items which equated to roughly £63,000. He said all transactions would be included in the video, which some were, and said the EDL had made £21,000 in total, but £19,000 had been paid out for expenses such as leaflets, placards and sound systems. Lennon said the allegation that he had recently been on holiday financed by the EDL was nonsense. He said he had merely been away on a friend's pre-planned stag-trip and added it had been nice to be away without having to look over his shoulder. He said that before the EDL, he had been a wealthy young businessman with a property portfolio and a normal life; he challenged anyone who wanted to step into his shoes to apply for the job. He said he gave the group a platform and there was no-one else who wanted to do it.

The rebels who had hijacked the Facebook page, said Lennon, were **"in league with the reds"** following recent posts by some former EDL members on an anti-fascist website. Lennon said that while he lived in Luton, surrounded by 45,000 Muslims, the people lining up against him were anonymously living in the countryside **"breeding bloody llamas"** (Snowy Shaw apparently bred llamas on his farm). Lennon said he believed the rebels were paid instigators, the type who had destroyed every single movement like the EDL, paid to destroy it by discrediting the leadership.

He then announced a national campaign called **'Say no to halal'** aimed at the ASDA supermarket chain. Lennon said the EDL would hit 300 ASDA stores in one day, they would **"hit them where it hurts, in the pocket"** reasoning that if the public knew the EDL were at a particular store they wouldn't shop there, which would force the supermarkets to take notice. He also announced a **'no more mosques'** campaign, aimed at halting the building of new mosques in the UK. Lennon said their construction was counter-productive as Islam was unable to sort out its problems. He said so many mosques were **'springing up'** across the country, they couldn't cope with the number of planning applications and oppose them all. Lennon said a national campaign was needed to address the whole issue and the EDL would set up stalls in many major towns and cities encouraging people to sign a petition to demand a referendum on the two issues.

This was the shift in agenda agreed upon at the, now infamous, meeting in London which had caused so much controversy by Moore's attendance. These were the **'goals, tactics and the future of our country'** Moore had claimed were **'nothing like we have done before'**. These were the tactics which presumably Lake and co believed would take the movement mainstream.

Snowy Shaw released a statement in response to Lennon's video release. In the statement Shaw accused Lennon of slandering him in the video by insinuating he was an informer or a communist and said he had considered releasing a video himself, and would do **'if pushed'**. Shaw updated the statement a day later, claiming as he had before Blackburn, that police had visited the houses of certain people connected to the North West Infidels and North East Infidels, with letters warning them to stay away from the forthcoming Blackpool demo. Shaw said he might as well not have bothered issuing the earlier statement as it had obviously fallen on deaf ears.

6 May 2011: US Embassy, London

On 2 May 2011, the US announced that Osama bin Laden had been killed by Special Forces in Abbottabad, Pakistan. The body of the al-Qaeda leader, who was apparently shot through the head, was taken back to a US aircraft carrier before being buried at sea. The Americans claimed they had buried him at sea because no country would accept the body; however, it was all noticeably rushed when you consider they'd waited ten years to catch him.

It is possible bin Laden was executed, if he wasn't dead already as some evidence suggests, because as previously stated the US had no hard evidence linking him to 9/11, a trial was the last thing the US administration wanted, as if acquitted, other perpetrators would have to be sought.

There was no noticeable response in the Muslim world, possibly due to the Spring Revolution which had taken place in many Middle Eastern countries, where people had taken to the streets demanding democracy. Speaking from Beirut, Omar Bakri Mohammed said the '**cold-blooded murder of a helpless man**' and his burial at sea was an '**offence to Muslims and a declaration of war against God, his Prophet and Muslims**'. Bakri added that he expected al-Qaeda to retaliate. Councillor Salim Mulla, chairman of the Lancashire Council of Mosques urged British Muslims to remain peaceful: '**I am appealing publicly to all Muslim communities wherever they may be that there is no backlash. We should now move on. I really hope and pray that there will not be a backlash. I hope it won't happen and I can't see it happening. I have been very critical of American foreign policy in Afghanistan and Iraq, but it is time to move on**'.

Prime Minister David Cameron said bin Laden's death was a great relief, but also urged the people of Britain to be vigilant. Former Prime Minister, Tony Blair, said the fact that 9/11 was the worst ever terrorist attack involving UK civilians should not be forgotten and said his thoughts were with all the victims who had lost their lives in those attacks.

The next day, as Britain placed its embassies and military bases around the world on high alert, five Asian men from London were arrested close to Sellafield nuclear power station in Cumbria. Police said the men were taking pictures of the plant and had been detained under Section 41 of the Terrorism Act (2000) which allows police to arrest anyone they 'reasonably suspect' of being a terrorist. Following the arrests, four houses in east London were raided. Police said there was no evidence to directly link the men to the events in Pakistan and they were later released without charge.

The *Daily Mail* reported that '**hate-preacher**' Anjem Choudary planned to lead a '**funeral prayer**' outside the US Embassy in London, to call on U.S. authorities to return bin Laden's body to relatives. Choudary said that bin Laden's British supporters loved him '**the way they care about their own parents**'. He said that '**more intense fighting**' would occur in Afghanistan and Iraq as a result of the assassination of the '**figurehead leader, someone who sacrificed a lot for the Muslim community**'.

Most of the EDL and Casuals United had managed to stay out of the in-fighting which was plaguing the movement. Marsh had stayed aloof from the mud-slinging most of the leadership were engaging in, and likewise the rest of the rank and file, who were determined to carry on regardless and confront the real enemy, militant Islam.

Around 40 Casuals and EDL met in London on 6 May, to counter-demonstrate against Choudary's rally. Their numbers were dwarfed by a crowd of over 250 radicals who marched on the embassy. They carried placards which read '**Islam will dominate the world**' and '**Western Injustice in Iraq, Afghanistan and Palestine**' and chanted "**Allahu Akbar!**" as their advance was checked by police. There were small groups of EDL popping up periodically along the route, attempting to confront the extremists. Two EDL approached the protest with an effigy of bin Laden on a pole. The men were detained by police, as the Muslim protesters started chanting '**Obama burn in hell**, **USA burn in hell**'. When questioned by a journalist, one of the men detained by police replied: "**Why are we being** arrested? **For holding up an effigy of bin Laden, while these people** [pointing] **celebrate the death and destruction he has brought, not just here but in every country across the world. Why are they being allowed to celebrate it? Why are they allowed to celebrate a terrorist?**"

As some radicals arrived at the embassy independently of the main march, they were confronted by more small groups of EDL. Insults were traded between the two sides; one woman rushed forward, spitting at the Muslim men and shouting "**you scum!**" The hatred was palpable.

When the marchers arrived outside the embassy, they staged a mock funeral ceremony for bin Laden. They warned the press that revenge attacks would be launched. One of them, Abu Muaz, 28 from East London, told the *Daily Mail* that '**It is only a matter of time before another atrocity - the West is the enemy**'. EDL supporters tried several times to get close to the rally, but were continually shepherded away by police.

Following the protest, police kettled around 40 EDL and confiscated several flags. A statement by Casuals United said that '**it seems the police are there to defend Choudary's right to threaten us with another 7/7 and attack our people**'.

The rank and file were also still keen to confront the left-wing whenever possible. In Liverpool on 7 May 2011, fifteen EDL targeted a left-wing bookshop. Several EDL occupied the *News from Nowhere* shop in the city, unfurling a flag which said '**EDL Huyton**'. The protest followed a similar operation where local EDL had protested outside a conference held by the Unite union near Liverpool's Lime Street Station the previous April.

EDL supporters applauded the activists, as by occupying the shop they believed they had kept '**left-wing lies off the streets and out of the hands of our children**'." One activist who was present said that several pieces of literature in the shop were '**anti-royal**' and that as an Englishman, he found that unacceptable. Speaking for the bookshop, Sara Newton said: '**We are still wondering how EDL members asking us if we stock pornography is challenging terrorism or defending England. We've never quite figured out what they are defending England from and why it takes fifteen men and a flag to do it in our shop**'.

Also in the north-west, the *Lancashire Evening Post* claimed the EDL had threatened to demonstrate outside the Little Theatre in Chorley, Lancashire, when comedian Russell Howard appeared there. Howard had ridiculed the EDL on his programme *Russell Howard's Good News* and a Facebook group was initiated which promised to demonstrate outside the theatre when he performed there on May 17 2011. One activist had posted '**We're going to be loud and he's going to know we're there. Hopefully next time he'll think twice before opening his middle class mouth about things he knows nothing about.**' Ian Robinson of Chorley Little Theatre told the paper it was a big night for the town and it would be a shame if a comedy show was ruined by a few people taking offence at a joke.

Also that week, to everyone's surprise, the EDL suddenly announced they intended to demonstrate in Tower Hamlets, London. The announcement was seen as a diversionary tactic by many people, engineered to take the heat off the infighting and many accusations which were flying round, as the more extreme elements of the EDL were always calling for a demo in Tower Hamlets or Birmingham (considered hotbeds of radicalism by activists).

11 May 2011: West London Magistrates' Court

On Wednesday 11 May 2011, Stephen Lennon appeared at West London Magistrates' Court, Hammersmith, in connection with his arrest on Remembrance Day. He was accused under Section 5 of the Public Order Act and around a hundred EDL, carrying flags and placards, attended the court to support him. Lennon wore a tee-shirt with a burning poppy and a £50 note printed on it for the trial (a reference to the fine imposed on Emdadur Choudhury).

Lennon was found guilty and fined £350. Interestingly the prosecution didn't apply for a CRASBO. Presumably with him in charge the authorities knew exactly who they were dealing with, take Lennon out of the equation and they perhaps believed the EDL would be considerably more unpredictable.

Just before the verdict, EDL supporters outside the court clashed with a group of Muslim youths who had infiltrated the protest. During the melee, one female EDL supporter was struck in the face with a bottle. There were reports of further disorder in Margavine Cemetery, near Barons Court Tube station. The *Fulham Chronicle*, running with the headline '**Helicopter circling as EDL thugs descend on Hammersmith**', claimed that the EDL had '**flooded**' into the area to support Lennon. *BBC News* reported: '**Arrests at EDL founder Stephen Lennon's court case**' and said that up to 65 people had been involved in the disturbances and the Met's Territorial Support Group had made five arrests.

On the same day as Lennon's trial, three people appeared in court in the north-east charged with racially-motivated vandalism at the Nasir Mosque in Hartlepool. They were also accused of carrying out vandal attacks at the Albert Guest House and Milko store, both in Shotton Colliery. The case was committed to Durham Crown Court and all three were granted unconditional bail.

A Durham Police spokesman told the BBC: '**At the time of the alleged offences, all three people claimed membership of the English Defence League.**' Casuals United claimed the three were informed they faced substantial sentences and compared the prosecution to a case the 12 months previously, where a Muslim man had painted graffiti on a war memorial in Burton upon Trent and received a conditional discharge.

16 May 2011: Darlington, Hull and Middlesbrough

Northern EDL divisions organised a flash-demo in Hull, Yorkshire. Around 80 protestors marched from the Old Zoological pub in Princes Avenue towards Queen Victoria Square in the city centre. Around 50 police, including mounted officers and a helicopter supervised proceedings, making two arrests. Sergeant Julian Hart told the *Hull Daily Mail* they had received information about the protest but the EDL had a right to assemble.

On the same day, two men aged 49 and 40 and a youth aged 17 were arrested in Darlington, following what was described as '**serious disorder**' outside a local mosque. Police were called to the Jamia Mosque in the North Lodge Park area of the town after a group of around 30 EDL had gathered nearby. Calling the protest a '**racist demonstration**' the *Darlington and Stockton Times* reported that the group had chanted '**nationalistic slogans**' and had intimidated local residents.

Superintendent Paul Unsworth of Northumbria Police said the people concerned were acting in a '**rowdy, abusive and offensive manner**' and he believed their actions were racially motivated. Unsworth said officers had attended to ensure the group dispersed without any problems. Local councillor Eleanor Lister claimed it was very frightening for the local community but said the police had handled it well. Lister said she believed people had done the best thing by not reacting and added they didn't want that sort of thing in Darlington. Local MP, Jenny Chapman, also condemned the protest and encouraged the police to take the '**toughest possible line**' in dealing with people who '**come to Darlington to cause trouble**'.

Three days later, Carlisle's *News and Star* revealed that the Ministry of Defence was investigating claims that soldiers from the 1st Battalion of the Duke of Lancaster's Regiment had showed their support for the EDL by posing for photographs with the group's supporters. One picture allegedly showed eight soldiers standing next to an EDL flag bearing the words '**EDL supports Duke of Lancaster Regiment**' at a homecoming parade for the regiment in Blackburn. Another reportedly showed a masked soldier, allegedly in Afghanistan, brandishing a pistol in front of an EDL flag.

A spokeswoman for the MOD assured the paper a thorough witch-hunt was now underway, but said some of the soldiers may have been hoodwinked into posing next to the flag. Former Chair of the Commons Counter Terrorism Sub-Committee, Patrick Mercer, urged members of the Armed Forces to steer clear of the EDL and said the pictures could be used as propaganda by extremists in Afghanistan.

On Thursday 19 May 2010, UAF claimed that a trade union sponsored anti-fascist meeting in Barking, east London had been attacked by the EDL. UAF alleged that windows of the building where the meeting was taking place were smashed. Labour councillor, George Barratt, said it was '**extremely disturbing**' that the meeting had been targeted. RMT organiser, Steve Hedley, said they wouldn't be intimidated by '**street thugs**'.

A week before the Blackpool demo, the EDL organised another demonstration in Shotton, Deeside, over the proposed mosque on the site of a former social club. Over 100 EDL marched through the town to the site of the club, which had mysteriously burned down three months earlier.

Also, in Leeds on the same day as Shotton, around 25 EDL staged a protest against the presence of an Islamist stall in the city centre. They met at the train station and then made their way to where the radicals usually gathered, close to the city's Debenhams store. There was a considerable police presence, indicating they had prior knowledge of the protest.

When they arrived at the site, there was only one radical present but regardless, the EDL held a noisy, but peaceful demonstration opposite. EDL activists chanted and sang songs such as the National Anthem and Rule Britannia. Activists spoke to members of the public as they distributed leaflets, while around 30 police, including mounted officers looked on. Feeling they had made their point the EDL marched back to the train station. When they arrived there, police held them, demanding their names and addresses. However, the EDL pointed out that no offences had been committed, nor arrests made, therefore most refused to comply with the request.

24 May 2011: Downing Street, London

President Obama was visiting the UK and scheduled to meet British Prime Minister David Cameron. MAC had threatened to protest against a meeting between the two in Downing Street, London. The EDL issued an appeal for anyone who could make it to attend a counter-protest.

Around 100 MAC turned up, some carrying placards which read, '**Obama most wanted terrorist for crimes against Muslims**' and '**Muslims will conquer the White House**'. MAC chanted "Obama burn in hell! America burn in hell!" while Anjem Choudary told *The Telegraph* they were there '**to expose him for the crimes he committed against Islam and Muslims and which he continues to commit in Iraq, in Afghanistan, in Libya**'. Talking to the *Daily Mail*, Choudary said that Obama was an even greater killer of Muslims than his predecessor George W Bush: '**Just like Osama Bin Laden is the number one enemy for the West, Obama is for Muslims. He is a war criminal, it goes without saying. He has slain more Muslims than even his predecessor George Bush and has overseen the escalation of the war on Islam. He must be arrested and face a Sharia court for his crimes**'.

Around 30 EDL turned up and were given a site opposite MAC, where they unfurled a Cross of St George and chanted at the radicals. A clash between small groups of both sides took place outside the McDonald's store at Horse Guards, as eight EDL clashed with around 20 MAC. The EDL were apparently outnumbered, but claimed some members of the public reportedly came to their aid, including eight passing removal men.

Police arrived and quelled the trouble, holding and searching both groups. After a search and a warning, the EDL were given directions to their official counter-protest site, but as they made their way there, they encountered more police who immediately arrested them. The EDL claimed that some officers didn't think their arrest was justified but were over-ruled by a sergeant. They were all released without charge two hours later.

26 May 2011: Luton

Around 80 EDL, including Stephen Lennon, demonstrated noisily outside Luton Town Hall, as MEPs, invited by local MEP Richard Howitt, arrived at a meeting to discuss the rise of extremist groups such as the EDL. The protestors carried placards which read '**Patriotism is not extremism**', '**Tackle the REAL extremists Howitt**' and '**The poppy burners were from Luton Richard!**'

Lennon told *The Luton and Dunstable Herald and Post* he was **'disgusted'** that the EDL was being targeted and questioned why Howitt hadn't staged a meeting to combat militant Islam. They hadn't killed anyone said Lennon, and were just using their democratic right to protest. Lennon told the *Herald and Post*: **'I want to get in and talk to him. Are they going to talk about militant Islam? They need to wake up and not be afraid to talk about the real problem. The EDL hasn't got a stall outside Don Miller's (bakers) in the town centre every week. We're not the ones they need to stop. It's just a political stunt by Richard Howitt so he can say that he's stopped racism'.**

As delegates arrived for the meeting they were greeted with boos and shouts of **'scum!'** from the EDL, who had gathered opposite the Town Hall at the Duke of Clarence pub. A council press officer told the paper that the meeting was a private affair arranged by Richard Howitt and not something the council was involved with, despite the fact that the council's Luton in Harmony initiative was one of the subjects being discussed.

Howitt said the demonstration was a typical example of the EDL shouting and screaming from the sidelines and causing upset and fear. He told the *Herald and Post* that the MEPs, from five different countries, all had hands-on experience in tackling extremism and that the aim of the meeting was to show that Luton was a **'centre of excellence for combating racism and extremism'** (of course it is Dick, that is why it became the epicentre for the current ethnic unrest – are these people even on the same planet as the rest of us?).

28 May 2011: Blackpool

Two weeks before the Blackpool protest, the *Blackpool Gazette* revealed that the late-night licence to trade of the Mr Beanz takeaway had been revoked after a judge was told it had become a centre for grooming under-age girls for sex.

Iyad Albattikhi and Mohammed Reveshi were appealing against the revocation of the licence, which allowed them to open the takeaway between 11.00pm and 5.00am. The court heard Albattikhi, who earlier in the hearing had been accused of plying teenage girls with drink and drugs in exchange for sex, had been pictured with a **'provocative and scantily clad'** 14-year-old girl on his knee in his office. However, Albattikhi told the court: **'I have been arrested five times for it but never charged. And each of the five times came after the Charlene Downes case. The police don't like me because I have proved they are corrupt. They have so called intelligence reports on me but they are not right, we are talking about a conspiracy. When the licensing officers go to Club Sanuk there are just two of them when they come to our place there are eight'.**

Mohammed Reveshi told the hearing he and Albattikhi had invested a lot of money in the business, which had suffered when they had been held on remand for over a year awaiting trial for the murder of Charlene Downes. He claimed a teenage girl mentioned in police reports who had been seen in his car was his foster daughter.

Judge Jeff Brailsford said he was **'entirely certain'** the original decision to revoke the licence had been correct and he had no doubt it would reduce crime and disorder in the area, thereby improving the quality of life for those who lived there.

Ahead of the EDL's visit, the *Blackpool Gazette* reported that Peter Billington, secretary of the Lancashire Trades Union Council, had declared the EDL were not welcome in Blackpool. Regarding the disappearance of Charlene Downes, Billington said the group were in **'no position to sit in judgement on anyone"**. Casuals United replied that if left wingers like Billington put as much energy into trying to help the Downes family get justice as they did opposing Casuals United and the EDL, then they would not have to had to get involved. The fact of the matter said the Casuals, if it wasn't for them, the case would be long forgotten.

Casuals staged a small demo outside the shop on the evening of 13 May 2011. Charlene's 72-year old grandmother, Jessie Brock was present as usual, sitting on a nearby bench watching the protest. Along with other activists, Charlene's grandmother was issued with a Section 14 Notice by police forcing them to relocate to a spot over the road. Mrs Brock claimed that an officer informed her that a tee-shirt she was wearing which bore her granddaughter's photograph and the legend '**Justice 4 Charlene**' was offensive and she would have to leave the area outside the takeaway.

The *Blackpool Gazette* reported '**Charlene's Gran in tee-shirt ban**' and said the pensioner was distraught at the way police had treated her. Mrs Brock told the paper: '**My tee-shirt only says Justice 4 Charlene, how can that be offensive? I'm disgusted by what they said; I wouldn't have thought they'd have said something like that. The police are supposed to be for justice**'. Charlene's mother, Karen Downes, told the paper she was so disgusted with the notice that she had ripped it up: '**She's no bother to anyone, my mum is lovely and she was sticking up for her granddaughter. They took her name and address, we were so upset. I had to go into a nearby pub and ask if we could borrow a stool for her to sit on. That was a public bench and mum is not a troublemaker**'.

A spokesman for Lancashire Police told the *Gazette* they had received no information from officers present that any tee-shirt had been deemed offensive and that Mrs Brock and a number of others were politely asked if they would move to an alternative site. The spokesman said they apologised if Mrs Brock felt she was treated inappropriately, but they had a duty to ensure the protests were facilitated peacefully and balance the right of those who wish to protest with the rights of those who live and work in the area. Owner of the takeaway, Mohammed Reveshi, told the Gazette '**I couldn't care less if they want to demonstrate, I just don't want them outside my shop**'.

In the run up to the Blackpool demonstration, Stephen Lennon told the *Blackpool Gazette* the EDL would bring 5-6000 people to the town and planned to release 500 lanterns in memory of Charlene Downes. Lennon said the issue had sickened a lot of people across the country and it needed to be addressed.

Also in the weeks leading up to the protest, Guramit Singh announced that he was leaving the EDL. Citing his grandmother's ill-health and the stress it was causing him as the reason, Singh said he was standing down.

News also broke that one of the men connected to the shop and the Downes investigation had been found guilty of assault. The *Blackpool Gazette* reported that Iyad Albattikhi had '**brainwashed another young girl into a sex and drugs lifestyle**'. The court heard Albattikhi had a seven month relationship with the 18-year old girl, during which he had '**plied her with alcohol and cocaine**' at his late night takeaway.

Albattikhi had head-butted the girl during an all day drink and drugs spree after she had told him that she had miscarried his child. The accused alleged that the girl had assaulted him after telling him she had a new boyfriend. He said the girl had tried to strike him again and he had '**pushed her away with his head**'. However, the court heard he had followed her outside, grabbing and smashing her mobile phone. The girl told the court: '**There was loads of food, alcohol and drugs He brainwashed me and there were others too. It was the biggest mistake of my life**'. When police investigated the matter they found images of the incident had been deleted from the shop's computerised surveillance system.

Adjourning sentencing for four weeks and imposing a Restraining Order preventing him from contacting the victim, magistrate Eileen Oldroyd said there had been '**substantial force used**'. When the court resumed, Iyad Albattikhi was sentenced to 20 weeks in prison (later reduced to twelve weeks on appeal).

On the eve of the Blackpool protest, four Muslim radicals from Tower Hamlets were jailed at Snaresbrook Crown Court for a horrific attack on a local teacher. Akmol Hussain, 26, Sheikh Rashid, 27, Azad Hussein, 26, and Simon Alam, 19, ambushed religious studies teacher Gary Smith as he made his way to work. They attacked Smith because they disapproved of a non-Muslim teaching religion to Hussain's niece. The gang slashed Smith with a Stanley knife and kicked and punched him repeatedly. They also battered him with a concrete block and an iron rod, leaving him with a fractured skull and jaw. The court heard that the four men drove away after the attack, '**praising Allah**'.

The four believed they had got away with the vicious assault, but didn't realise they were being investigated by British security services, who suspected they may have been involved in a terrorist plot. MI5 had planted a recording device in Akmol Hussain's car and heard them discussing the attack on Smith. In a recording played to the court, Azad Hussein could be heard to say: '**He's mocking Islam and he's putting doubts in people's minds. How can somebody take a job to teach Islam when they're not even a Muslim themselves?**'

The defendants claimed they had heard rumours that the teacher had raped a girl at the school, but Prosecutor Sarah Whitehouse said that Smith was '**targeted as the victim of this attack quite simply because of his position as head of religious studies at the school.**' Hussain and Hussein were given an indeterminate sentence, with a recommendation they serve at least five years. Alam was sent to a Young Offenders' Institute for five years and Rashid was told he would serve at least four years, with both men subject to a five year licence on release. Badruzzuha Uddin, a neighbour of Rashid, was jailed for two years after admitting hiding the blood-stained clothing of the four men. Sentencing the men, Judge John Hand QC told them: '**If you think that people around you in society present an insult or threat to God then you will not hesitate in attacking again**'.

In the weeks following the case the *Sunday Telegraph* claimed that people in Tower Hamlets had accused the police of ignoring or downplaying incidents of hate crime. Police were also accused of suppressing evidence implicating Muslims as being responsible, simply because they feared being labelled racist. One Muslim man who was attacked and left partially blind and with a dislocated shoulder, told the paper he was attacked by a mob of radicals in Cannon Street Road for smoking during the Muslim holy festival of Ramadhan. When he reported it to the police, he was told they couldn't track anyone down and there were no witnesses, although the street is busy, covered by CCTV and lined with shops.

It appeared as if the extremists were attempting to turn Tower Hamlets into an Islamic enclave. Teachers in the area told *The Sunday Telegraph* they felt pressurised following campaigns by extremists in the local community to force Muslim girls to wear the veil in schools. One teacher told the paper they had faced hostility over the matter from both pupils and parents. Other instances of intolerance include the spate of homophobic stickers left around the area, as the recent conviction of 18-year-old Mohammed Hasnath showed. Alongside this, homophobic attacks in the area have risen sharply. In 2008, a 20-year old male was left paralysed following an attack outside local gay pub, the George and Dragon. In 2010, a gang of Muslims stormed the pub and assaulted customers. *The Sunday Telegraph* reported that homophobic attacks in the borough have increased by 80 per cent since 2008.

Lancashire Police, aided by officers from forces across the country, set up a ring of steel around Blackpool for the visit of the EDL. Police were on seemingly every bridge along the M55 motorway into the town and were stopping coaches and minibuses full of EDL and escorting them in. Arriving late, the East Midlands Division were taken in with a police escort President Obama would've been proud of, much to the amusement of those on board, and to the amazement of people they passed, possibly wondering who on earth the bus contained.

The assembly point for the protest was at Yates's Winelodge on the South Shore. The area behind the pub was fenced off with portable steel screens. Activists also had the use of the nearby Sun pub. UAF were counter-protesting by the Central Pier. Some from the *UKFD Forum* were unhappy with the assembly point and arranged to meet up at a pub at the north end of the town, with everyone instructed not to wear any colours to identify them as EDL. It was a tactic used for decades by football hooligans, if the police asked who they were; they were told to say they were with a stag-party and not connected to the EDL. In the face of it, with so many stag and hen parties in Blackpool at any given weekend, there was little the police could do when met with this reply.

Around 60 EDL and Casuals United gathered at the pub and it wasn't long before it attracted the attention of the police. One officer went inside and informed everyone they were being bussed to the demo point. Activists replied that they were nothing to do with the EDL and the police were powerless to argue, as there was nothing to link them to the group. A short time later they decided to leave, splitting up and arranging to meet by Blackpool Tower.

There were hundreds of EDL on the streets of Blackpool, it was a working class movement and the town was really somewhere many of them considered home turf. After the group from the pub assembled at the Tower they walked down the seafront, being joined by more EDL all the time. As they passed Central Pier they noticed a small group of around twelve anti-fascists across the road. Four of the EDL and SDL, three men and a woman, went straight over. It was the SWP Central Committee, accompanied by some members of Hope Not Hate.

Weyman Bennett stood motionless, staring at the floor seemingly transfixed, as the patriots bombarded them with questions. Also present was Martin Smith, who tried to joke it off, but it was obvious most of them were paralysed with fear. The anti-fascists were ridiculed but just stood there quietly, behind a small number of police. The EDL and SDL were eventually moved on by officers. It was a terrible turn out for the UAF, only 34 hardcore communists eventually turned up; they were rapidly becoming an irrelevance.

At the assembly points, both pubs were packed with EDL. The police had totally sealed off the area and access to the demo site was only gained by a road at the side of Yates's. The majority of police officers were relaxed and it paid dividends as the EDL were well behaved and some friendly exchanges took place between them and police.

At around 12.30pm they began their march to the demo site. As usual the column was a mass of flags, and activists chanted and sang as they marched along the seafront, cheered on by members of the public who stood and watched on the other side of the road. The EDL carried placards which read: **'If you're not outraged – you're not paying attention'**, **'Charlene's blood on police hands'** and **'Someone must deal with Blackpool's paedophiles – EDL defending our youth'**.

The demo site was close to the South Pier and many members of the public stood on the pier to watch. East Midlands organiser Tony Curtis opened proceedings. Flanked by placards bearing a picture of Charlene Downes, Curtis asked supporters to remember why they were there. Referring to the infighting, he said anyone who was thinking of causing trouble was not welcome and asked everyone to show respect for the family of Charlene. Curtis said they weren't there to argue with the people of Blackpool or disrupt their Bank Holiday, but they felt they had to make a point. A minute's silence was then held for Charlene, fallen troops and in the memory of West Midlands activist Roger English, who had sadly recently passed away.

Curtis said Charlene was **"brutally taken from us, by scumbags"** and criticised the compensation paid to the two men linked to the case. With boos and chants of **"scum!"** from the crowd, Curtis said that the EDL would return to the town until Lancashire Police had closed down all the **'honey-pots'** linked to Blackpool's paedophile problem. Curtis said Blackpool wasn't the only town the problem was happening in, it was also happening in Nottingham, Leeds, Lincoln and Birmingham. If the EDL could just save one life, stop one young girl from sharing Charlene's fate, Curtis said it would be worthwhile. He then introduced Karen Downes, the mother of Charlene She thanked Casuals United and the EDL for their support and for making the day possible:

> **"Charlene was a young, beautiful typical teenage girl taken from us by two brutal takeaway owners. Charlene loved life, her family and friends and her infectious smile lit up a room. She would be so proud of you all today and I know she will be looking down on us all from above with pride. She has missed out on so much, the chance to leave school, take her exams and the chance to one day to become a mother. And very recently Charlene became an auntie, to her beautiful nephews, baby Ashton and more recently to newborn baby Ryan, who I know she would've adored, she loved children. We miss her more than life itself, but how badly Charlene was let down by the police and CPS. We saw her vile court case collapse and then the police brushed it under the carpet. And to add insult to injury those two scumbags have walked away from this £250,000 richer. This was the biggest insult to us and above all Charlene. The police have also covered up the grooming of 60 girls by takeaway owners, still to this day the police choose to protect**

those murderers, paedophiles and rapists, who they still continue to defend. We want this case reopened and Charlene's case looked at again, we demand a new investigation. Bring those two responsible back to justice. Still there is no justice for Charlene, but with the support of EDL and Casuals United, we are confident that justice will be done, the justice which is rightfully hers. We now feel that the EDL and Casuals are the police force for Charlene's justice. We cannot thank them enough and we owe a debt of gratitude to you for the rest of our lives. Charlene, we miss you more than words could ever describe, you will always be loved and never forgotten and we will continue to fight until justice is done for our angel. God bless each and every one of you, we will never surrender, ever".

The group had been given a mandate, the Downes family had been let down by the establishment, and now looked to two working class street movements to provide them with the justice they were morally due. It was permission, it was justification for their existence, the EDL and Casuals United spoke for large unrepresented sections of society. Stephen Lennon then took to the stage. He said the demo wasn't about the EDL, it was about Charlene:

"First off I thank Jeff Marsh and everybody needs to give Jeff Marsh a round of applause it was him and Casuals United who brought this to the forefront. The police's reasons for not highlighting this, was because they didn't want to be called racist. You can call us racist every day of the week, whenever you want if it stops the rape of our children. The lion is not awake yet, because that chicken shop should not be there anymore, and that is what people need to wake up to. And the message we want to give them, so long as we know where your businesses are, so long as we know where you live, you will never live another peaceful week you are murdering scumbags and we will follow you wherever you are. That's it, God bless Charlene, let's hope her family get justice".

Following the protest, the EDL dispersed peacefully, most returning to pubs in the area. Some EDL tried to walk up to Mr Beanz (the shop would seemingly change ownership and its name to Mario's in the weeks following the protest), but were met by a large number of police who were stationed outside the shop and in the surrounding areas. Richard Debicki of Lancashire Police told *BBC News* he was pleased that the protest had passed off peacefully and he was satisfied that they had given both sides the right to demonstrate and also ensure it was business as usual for Blackpool. Police announced that ten people were arrested, for a variety of public order offences. The *Blackpool Gazette* estimated the EDL numbers at around 2000 and 34 at the UAF protest.

11 June 2011: Dewsbury

The in-fighting still persisted but was showing signs of calming down. There were three distinct camps: The Luton leadership, supported by the sub-leadership, which included Jack Smith, Guramit Singh (who would reappear following Blackpool, appearing on BBC Radio WM as the EDL West Midlands Regional Organiser), Steve Simmons and Hel Gower. More importantly they were supported by the pro-Zionists, including Lake and Geller. The second group was the northern rebels, who following Blackburn had been largely quiet, Snowy Shaw had been true to his word and kept away from demonstrations, but the leadership were still bothered by certain vocal members of the North-West Infidels. There was another third faction, people who were still loyal to the movement but who didn't share its current pro-Zionist agenda. A lot of these, still loyal, rebels were of the opinion that autocratic, localised flash-demonstrations were the way to go and also that liaison with police should be abandoned following the recent treatment of EDL activists at demonstrations.

This last group was key, a lot of them were very active and well known throughout the movement, and they also had coherent and valid arguments against the path the EDL had chosen to take. The leadership were slightly hamstrung by this. It was obvious since the handover of the website, and statements by the evermore increasingly vocal Roberta Moore, that the leadership were somehow under the spell of the pro-Zionists. However, with the recent loss of a lot of support in the north, they weren't prepared to gamble on a total collapse by denouncing the current opposition.

In the face of this unrest, the Yorkshire Division called what it termed an '**unofficial demo**' in Dewsbury, West Yorkshire, in response to a number of attacks in the town, which they claimed police refused to classify as racist incidents. In one incident, the EDL said a 14 year-old boy was left unconscious following an attack by 10-15 Muslim youths, but West Yorkshire Police refused to regard the attack as racially motivated. However, the boys father claimed that it was a racist attack, and his son's attackers had called him "**white trash and white this, that and the other. This is why people are angry about what is happening in this country. If it had been an attack by whites on an Asian it would have been a definite race attack**'. In another attack the previous October, a 46 year old local man was surrounded punched to the floor and repeatedly kicked by a gang of Muslim men in another totally unprovoked attack.

Dewsbury is a former mill town, which formed part of the wool-belt, close to Leeds and Bradford. The Chickenley, Dewsbury Moor and Ravensthorpe areas of the town are amongst the most deprived in Britain. Following WWII, Dewsbury welcomed a number of migrants from Pakistan and India, attracted by the opportunity of work in the town's many woollen mills, settling in the Ravensthorpe and Savile Town areas of Dewsbury (the population of Savile Town is now believed to be 98% Muslim). Even though the Muslim population has expanded over the years, the fact that Dewsbury has 25 mosques for a population of 50,000 does seem somewhat disproportionate.

The town also has its own Sharia court. Dewsbury's Muslims are mainly followers of Deobandi Islam, considered one of the more austere branches of the faith. Dewsbury's Markazzi Mosque is run by Tablighi Jamaat, a political offshoot of the Deobandi faith which runs its European operations from the town. Kaheel Ahmed, the Indian doctor who died following the attempted car-bombing of Glasgow Airport, was said to have been involved with Tablighi Jamaat. The town was also the home of 7/7 bomber, Mohammad Sidique Khan. It was also the birthplace of Haroon Rasheed Aswad, who was arrested in Pakistan in 2005 with a suicide bomb belt and explosives in his possession

In 2007, classroom assistant, Aishah Azmi lost an employment tribunal appeal following her dismissal from local Headfield Church of England School. Although she had attended the interview for the job in a hijab, soon after commencing employment Azmi requested that she be allowed to wear a full face veil. It was deemed unacceptable by her employer, Kirklees Council, who suspended her pending the appeal. *The Sunday Times* claimed that Azmi had made her decision to wear the veil following a discussion with a local Tablighi cleric.

The town also experienced racial unrest in 2007. Dewsbury's Muslim community clashed with newly arrived Iraqi Kurds. A year later, they clashed again, this time with newly arrived Gypsies from eastern-Europe.

Local newspaper *The Press* announced the EDL demonstration, referring to the group as '**far-right**' and terming the protest '**provocative**'. An EDL spokesman told the paper that the protest was not a national demo but an unofficial local divisional demo regarding local issues (The EDL actually had another demonstration (this one seemingly sanctioned by the leadership) in Maidenhead planned for the same day). The paper said a number of left-wing and pro-Muslim groups were planning to counter-demonstrate, including Islamic Resistance, the MDL, UAF and members of the Huddersfield Anarchist League. In a letter to the paper entitled '**Why should we protest in Dewsbury?**' John Cross of Yorkshire EDL claimed that there were 36 mosques within one and a half miles of Dewsbury and that open '**warfare**' between white and Asian pupils from certain schools was '**hushed up**'. Cross also alleged that certain '**no-go**' areas for whites existed in the town and that countless racist attacks by Asian youths were being dismissed by police.

A police spokesman said they had received a letter informing them of a possible protest and they were trying to establish its authenticity. Chief Superintendent John Robins said West Yorkshire Police would facilitate peaceful protest and they had vast experience of policing such events and he assured the EDL that police would treat them firmly, but fairly. Dewsbury councillor, Khizar Iqbal, urged people to stay away and said it was not going to help the town. Councillor Paul Kane said that although he didn't agree with the EDL, he believed in democracy and people's right to protest.

During discussions with representatives of Yorkshire EDL, the police initially agreed to a protest outside the Town Hall and allocated the group two pubs in Dewsbury town centre. However, following the announcement of a counter-protest by UAF, police reneged on the agreement and ruled that neither group would be allowed to protest in the town centre. Chief Superintendent Robins told the *Dewsbury Reporter* that after discussions with local businesses, the council, the community and the EDL, West Yorkshire Police had decided that the venue of the planned EDL protest should now be on a car park outside the train station. Robins said the decision was made to ensure that any possible disruption was kept to a minimum and added that the counter-protest would be held further along the ring road on Wellington Road East. Police also announced that the majority of pubs in the town would not be opening on the day of the demonstration.

The EDL claimed that although they had agreed to original terms of the protest with local officers, the decision to change the venue had come from higher up in the force. Following the news, many EDL activists suggested that police liaison should be abandoned altogether. The EDL now announced they would be gathering and drinking in pubs in towns outside Dewsbury and would not cooperate with West Yorkshire Police in future.

Two days before the protest, Stephen Lennon surpirsed Home Secretary Theresa May during a surgery in her constituency of Maidenhead. Lennon posed as the companion of a man claiming the police were treating him unfairly. When the pair sat down, Lennon said to Mrs May: '**Do you know who I am? I'm the head of the English Defence League**'. Lennon then complained about how the EDL was treated in comparison to Muslim groups and asked for an official appointment to see the Home Secretary, which was declined. Mrs May told the *Daily Mail* she had walked away and said: '**My concern now is that he will try to make something of it, which he should not do. He did not have a meeting with me, I was completely door stepped. I did not even recognise him. This is a group whose purpose is to divide and to encourage hatred in our society and I condemn them for that**'.

On the day of the protest in Dewsbury, a large number of EDL from across the country met at The Union pub in nearby Batley. The message to meet in Batley had been spread through the grapevine of text messages and phones calls rather than the Internet, which many now realised couldn't be trusted. They were joined by Stephen Lennon and Kevin Carroll, who had travelled up to support the demonstration. Police had caught wind of the assembly point and around 50 officers surrounded the pub, preventing people leaving. Around an hour before the protest was due to begin they informed the EDL they would be marching them to the train station from where they would be escorted to Dewsbury by officers.

Around midday, around 200 strong, the EDL left The Union. They marched towards the train station, completely surrounded by police. There was a brief flashpoint as a lone anti-fascist emerged to the right of the column and shouted abuse but after a brief pause they continued. There was a further flashpoint as a group of Asian and white males appeared from a side road, with the EDL surging towards them thinking they were MDL or anti-fascists. They were in fact members of the EDL East Midlands Division; two members were of Sikh heritage, EDL in the crowd who recognised them rushed over to quell the trouble as police battled to cope. The East Midlands lads were absorbed into the crowd and they continued towards the train station.

The EDL were held outside Batley station for around half an hour, before police announced that they would now be bussing them to the protest site. Three buses were brought and the activists treated like prisoners as they were completely surrounded and filtered onto the buses one at a time. It was totally out of proportion but West Yorkshire Police were obviously taking no chances. The buses laden with EDL, standing as well as sitting, made there way out of Batley, towards Dewsbury. As they arrived in Dewsbury, some pedestrians and drivers applauded them as they passed. Again like in so many areas of the country, there was a degree of local support. The buses passed the UAF demonstration, where around 20 dejected looking anti-fascists surrounded Weyman Bennett. With the EDL safely on the passing buses and accompanied by police, Bennett was less subdued than he had been in Blackpool and gave the EDL repeated 'v-signs'.

As they neared the protest site, it became obvious that the town centre was virtually deserted. Local councillor, Mehboob Khan announced on *Twitter* that he had walked around Dewsbury town centre and the view of local people was that the '**EDL travelling thugs**' were not welcome. At the demo site, or rather the zoo which had been created by police, there were ridiculous numbers of officers. The area had been halved with steel cages and was completely fenced off. As the buses, and coaches which had travelled independently, unloaded, the EDL were surrounded and forced into the compound by police (it was something akin to animals being shepherded into an abattoir).

The speeches were made quickly, the EDL seemingly aware that the crowd were angry. Wanting to get it over with quickly to ensure less opportunity for flashpoints, Stephen Lennon spoke to the EDL:

> '**Dewsbury, where do we start? An Islamic enclave, in Yorkshire, that's where we are. I hear all the time 'whose streets?' do the streets of Dewsbury belong to heroin peddling Muslim gangs? No they don't. Do the streets of Dewsbury belong to paedophilic Muslim gangs? No they don't. Do the streets of Dewsbury belong to imams? No they don't. The streets of Dewsbury belong to us, they are British streets in England, and we are taking our streets back, city by city, street by street and there ain't no-one that's going to stop it.**
>
> **I thought by now the police would've realised the English Defence League is not going to go away. We're not going anywhere, we are here to stay. We offer the olive branch for every demonstration, we want peaceful protest, we put our hand out but we want equal treatment. We want the same treatment as Islamic organisations, why have we been treated like animals all day, out in cages? We should be outside Dewsbury Town Hall, and we will be outside Dewsbury Town Hall, because what was a regional demonstration, has now turned into a national demonstration. At no point do we blame your average bobby on the street, we know it's not their problem it's the hierarchy, they have surrendered and bowed and appeased to Islam again. In the last six months our demonstrations have been peaceful, we have liaised and cooperated, we have had peaceful marches with low arrests, so why, why can't we go outside Dewsbury Town hall? Because you're [pointing towards police] worried that militant fucking Islam is going to riot. It's got nothing to do with us, you've surrendered our rights to them once again, and it won't be tolerated. So after Tower Hamlets, the EDL bandwagon will be coming to Dewsbury in their thousands.**
>
> **We hear so much how much these demonstrations cost us, you've just cost yourselves another million pounds and it's out of your budget. When we talk about money, our demonstrations cost peanuts in comparison to the PREVENT scheme. Since Muslims rioted in Bradford, their communities and their religion have been given millions of our taxpayers money for rioting, what's all that about? And then we're penalised for having demonstrations, using our democratic right to freedom of assembly when we're aggravated and frustrated at what's happening to our communities, our women our youth and our country, this is the right way of doing it. The authorities and the police are lucky that the English Defence League are following democracy, we're using our democratic right. God help you if the day comes when people turn the other way. We are trying to channel anger, channel frustration, so that we have our voices heard and you wake up to what is happening in our towns and cities.**
>
> **I was reading the local paper, Luton is exactly the same as Dewsbury, until you've grown**

up in a town or community like this you don't know what you're talking about. So when you've got politicians, telling us that Dewsbury is in harmony, no it's not, we live it, you don't live it. These people who are telling us our towns and our communities are in harmony they live in leafy suburbs, and they're telling us how to live our lives. I open up my local paper, you can read this every week, gang attack as a man walks home, a man in his 20s was attacked by a gang as he walked through Luton in the early hours of Sunday morning. The victim was stopped by three men, they surrounded him prevented him from moving, they didn't try and rob him, they punched him, they kicked him and battered him to the ground. He eventually struggled and ran away, and the offenders are described as three men of Asian appearance [crowd chant "Scum, scum!"]. Asian appearance, we all know, I'll bet my bloody life on it, they're Muslim, not Asian, they're Muslim, that's the problem. Now you can open up your local newspaper in Dewsbury and you will read that every week, every week. And we're told we live with community cohesion, in harmony, if we joined the dots in our communities of the attacks by Muslims against non-Muslims we would wake up and realise they launched their jihad on us years ago.

Shahid Malik [ex-MP for Dewsbury], I watched a video on YouTube, anyone can watch it type in 'Shahid Malik's speech'. He's supposed to represent Dewsbury, the Muslims and the non-Muslims of Dewsbury, In this speech his says in 2001 we had one Muslim MP, in 2002 we had two Muslim MP's, in 2004 we had four Muslim MP's, in 2007 we had eight Muslim MP's, [inaccurate but Malik did say something along the same lines] in between all this he says Inshallah, which is Allah willing, he then goes on to say that in ten years every MP will be Muslim. That's what he says; he's supposed to represent the Muslims and non-Muslims. InshaAllah, so what's he's telling us is that Allah is willing them to take over our democracy. He then says within twenty years time we will have a Prime Minister who will share our faith, there was a crowd of a thousand Muslims who stand there cheering, getting excited about what he's saying.

Well we're in Dewsbury Shahid Malik, we're in your back yard and we're here to tell you, England is awake, England will never have a Muslim Prime Minister, you've got away with it for fifteen years, you've taken liberties, you've extorted us, you've destroyed our communities and did you think we'd stand there while you take our country from within? No we won't.

This is a regional demonstration, as I've said after Tower Hamlets we're coming back here. When we come back we're not standing in cages like this, we're going to Dewsbury Town Hall. We'll come peacefully, we'll offer the olive branch, we'll liaise with you, we will give stewards and we will facilitate a peaceful protest, but you give us the same rights you give the Islamic community of Dewsbury. You wouldn't put them on buses, you wouldn't put them in cages, the offers there it's the last chance for West Yorkshire Police. If not then the trouble that happens at the demonstration is down to yourselves.

I've seen loads of flags here today, I've seen shit-loads of Scottish lads, my message to you boys is, God bless you, thanks for coming over the border to support us, we are you, you are us, we are Britain, we will travel to Wales, we will travel to Scotland, we will travel wherever we need to go, we are by your side, you are by our side. God Bless'

It was an effective speech, the fact he had vowed to return to Dewsbury following police treatment of the EDL that morning appealed to many in the crowd. They were starting to realise, especially following back to back demonstrations in Lancashire, that in the face of cuts in spending, budgets were a major consideration for local councils and police forces. Now if a town or police force treated the EDL in an unfair or shoddy way, they would now pay for it where it hurts, in the pocket.

Lennon talked of offering olive branches in his speech; the last part was he himself offering an olive branch to the Scottish Defence League. As stated previously, the dedication to the cause of the SDL has reached legendary status amongst EDL activists. The SDL clock up thousands of miles, mainly supporting their English comrades and it hasn't gone unnoticed south of the border. In working class circles only length of time served ranks alongside such dedication, therefore the blessing of the SDL would be an important factor should a leadership challenge ever occur.

The Luton led leadership were trying to reassert centralised control over the whole movement again, supporting an unofficial demonstration in the north, when there was a protest in the south and the special mention to the SDL was all part of the plan to achieve that. The movement was in danger of moving away independently of the Luton leadership; they were attempting to rein it in again.

Following the protest, most EDL were either taken into the train station by police or put on their coaches at the site. The people bussed in from Batley were informed by police they were being taken back there, where many of them had left their vehicles. However, they were taken directly to Leeds instead. One of the EDL told everyone to catch a train back to Batley and was threatened with arrest by police if they did. In response, they decided to hold a flash-protest in Leeds, marching through the city centre, chanting. Police deployed a number of officers to contain the EDL, but they only ended up chasing the shadows of the younger and fitter EDL around Leeds city centre, much to the amusement of shoppers.

West Yorkshire Police announced there were 500 EDL in Dewsbury and 75 UAF. Six people were arrested in connection with the demonstrations, but none of those were detained at either protest site. Mehboob Khan, leader of Kirklees Council, said the community had '**decided to reject messages that would divide the community in Dewsbury perpetrated by those who have no interest in Dewsbury**'.

11 June 2011: Maidenhead

On the same day as Dewsbury, the EDL was staging an '**official**' demonstration in Maidenhead, Berkshire. The protest was against a proposed new cultural centre next to an existing mosque in Holmanleaze, Maidenhead. The EDL alleged that the £1 million project would be funded by the local council, as the Muslim community were unable to find the cash. However, both the council and the Islamic Trust behind the project denied the allegation.

The protest was called following the announcement of the unofficial Dewsbury demonstration and it undoubtedly affected the turnout in Yorkshire. Some activists suggested it was again a subtle '**spoiler demo**' as the EDL had done to Casuals United in Blackpool, but there was no proof of this, especially with the appearance of Lennon and Carroll in Dewsbury. However, there seemed little sense in staging it on the same day as a demonstration in a considerably more sensitive and potentially explosive area such as Dewsbury.

On the morning of the protest, police had a visible presence in Maidenhead from around 10.30am. The Maidenhead Carnival was also being staged and organisers pleaded with the public to still attend regardless of the protest. Some EDL supporters were escorted into the town centre by police, they joined around 100 EDL gathered outside Noctors pub in Queen Street. The EDL stood outside the pub drinking and chanting with various flags on display. Members of the press stood across the road, photographing and filming events.

At 1.00pm, the EDL marched to King Street where an area had been fenced off for them to hold their protest. Local EDL organiser Chris Jones made a speech and they dispersed soon after with no problems.

Following the protests in Dewsbury and Maidenhead, the EDL claimed its supporters were being sent letters by police, barring them from demonstrations. The group said it would not tolerate '**this shameful violation of the right to peaceful protest**' and if the letters continued it would stop all police liaison and organise flash demos instead. The EDL said it was important that it continued to hold peaceful demonstrations and work with the authorities, but it was just as important that people's voices were heard. The EDL would not allow the freedoms of patriots to be attacked by the very authorities that should be working hard to preserve and protect them.

Four days later, on 15 June 2011, news broke that Stephen Lennon had been arrested by Lancashire Police for an alleged assault. He was bailed to appear at Blackburn Magistrates' Court on the 24th June 2011. Lennon was also arrested by Bedfordshire Police for an alleged offence at the demo opposing MEP Richard Howitt in Luton. He was also bailed on that charge, to appear in front of Luton Magistrates on the 29th June 2011.

This time Lennon's bail conditions restricted him from doing anything EDL related. He was required to attend Luton Police station every Saturday and was prevented from attending any EDL protests. Lennon released a statement in which he said, due to '**ongoing harassment**' by the police, he had decided that there would no longer be any police liaison with any force.

When Lennon appeared at Blackburn Magistrates' Court he pleaded not guilty to a charge of assault, alleged to have occurred at the Blackburn demonstration. He was bailed to stand trial at Preston Magistrates' Court on 29 September. The bail conditions again prevented Lennon from any involvement with the EDL and also prevented him from travelling to any demonstration ten miles outside the centre of his hometown of Luton. He was also ordered to report to Luton Police station every Saturday between midday and 2.00pm.

Following the hearing, Lennon and his supporters noticed Blackburn MP and former Home Secretary Jack Straw going into a local restaurant. Lennon and a couple of others followed Straw into the building and a bemused Straw was photographed with Lennon, before police arrived and moved the EDL on.

At Luton Magistrates' Court, Lennon stood accused of a public order offence which was alleged to have been committed at the protest which opposed Euro MEP Richard Howitt. He was granted conditional bail to reappear on October 31 for trial. As part of his bail conditions this time, he was required to tell Bedfordshire Police if he moved address. As in Blackburn, Lennon was also banned from organising, attending or participating in any EDL related activity, but this time was also prohibited from participating in any protest within ten miles of Luton. Calling his bail conditions '**pathetic**' Lennon said "**we have taken a stance that we will be peaceful, if not we would have been a rioting mob. We are an organised peaceful protest movement. These conditions mean I can't be leader of the EDL. They obviously want to get rid of me. This is about who I am, not what I am accused of doing**".

That same week, the *Evening Standard* reported that police were investigating a number of '**poison packages**' containing white powder which had been sent to five mosques in London, Luton and Birmingham over a period of ten days. Some mosques were evacuated while specialist officers in protective suits investigated the suspect powder. A package sent to Finsbury Park mosque also contained drawings of the Prophet Mohammed similar to the Danish cartoons. Imam of Finsbury Park Mosque, Ahmed Saad, told the paper: '**Our security guard was in the office when I opened the letter and he called the police right away. He told me to wash my hands and face just in case the powder was dangerous. The police arrived with ambulances and evacuated the building. It could have been anything in the envelope, my first thought was that it could be anthrax, or it could be some kind of [other] poison. It was very frightening. Something like this should not happen; we live in a multi-cultural society**'.

Detectives were said to be studying CCTV footage as many of the packages were not stamped and were thought to have been delivered by hand. Scotland Yard was said to be so concerned about the threat to community cohesion, it had sent a warning to more than 200 London mosques. In the warning, the Association of Muslim Police warned people not to touch any suspicious mail, but added that the packages contained a non-hazardous substance. Police said that inquires were ongoing and no arrests had been made. They said they recognised the distress and disruption caused by such incidents and no line of enquiry had been ruled out.

Manager of Finsbury Park Mosque, Mohammed Kozbar, told the *Evening Standard* he believed people with right-wing views had sent the packages. A BNP spokesman told the paper they were in the political business now and did not indulge in any activity of that sort. Ghaffar Hussain of Quilliam said it was a reminder that British Muslims could also be the victims of extremism and intolerance.

While newspaper headlines focused on the threat of Islamist terrorism, Hussain said far-right extremists were posing an increasing threat. He said the packages sent to mosques were not one-off incidents and were part of a campaign to intimidate British Muslims.

18 June 2011: Dagenham

The EDL was demonstrating in Dagenham again. The group claimed there had been no response to the concerns of local people opposed to the proposed mosque. The EDL also alleged that at a recent planning meeting one local councillor had sneered at residents opposed to the plan telling them they couldn't afford to stop it. The group said that as a response, money was now being put aside to oppose the project in the courts.

Pro-EDL blogsite *The New English Review* claimed that the local Islamic Society had already moved into the premises, a former butcher's shop, despite the fact that they were £400,000 short of the £500,000 purchase price. The blog claimed that prayer services had started and the flats on the upper floors were now occupied, but worshippers were using a back door to hide the fact the building was in use.

The New English Review also revealed that the mosque was advertising events where the sexes would be segregated and pointed to the industrial action at the Ford plant in Dagenham led by women machinists in 1968. Those ordinary, working class women had fought long and hard for equality, it seemed their sacrifice was now for nothing, as discrimination in the name of diversity was being openly tolerated in the borough.

The assembly point was the Rendezvous bar in Chadwell Heath, with activists gathering at 9.30am. The event was apparently being filmed by Channel4 for an upcoming documentary and around midday, the EDL set off for the demo site. There were no police, just stewards, the EDL were seemingly being left to police themselves. This infuriated anti-fascists and even surprised many EDL activists.

At the centre of the march was a huge flag of St George with the words 'Dagenham EDL' emblazoned across it. Again, the group was warmly welcomed by some local people, who lined the route and applauded. Some passing cars also signalled their support. The EDL again stopped at Chadwell Heath train station where a young EDL supporter had tragically lost his life and held a minute's silence. At this point a police officer arrived on a pushbike, but kept his distance while observing proceedings. They then proceeded to the demo site.

There were some photographer's present and there was some antagonism between them and some EDL who objected to having their picture taken. On Valence Avenue some of the younger EDL clashed with four Muslim men who they claimed had spat at them. EDL stewards were forced to intervene and shepherded the Muslims away. The EDL later accused the Muslim men of attempting to attack the demonstration and said their stewards had intervened to protect the women and children present.

The sound of police sirens filled the air and a number of officers arrived on the scene. However, they still kept their distance and allowed the EDL to proceed to the demo site. Once there, in heavy rain, Kevin Carroll pledged the EDL's continued support to the people of Dagenham. The power for the PA system was supplied by a local shopkeeper, obviously sympathetic to the EDL's cause. The leader of the EDL Dagenham Division was introduced as Diane. Addressing the crowd, she said: **'Dagenham has always, and will always be a multi cultural town; we don't have a problem with that. But according to Margaret Hodge our MP, because we oppose this temple of hate she calls us racist and accuses us of dividing the community. When have you ever seen one of these mosques help anyone apart from Muslims? It is not us who cause divisions in the community. So Margaret, jog on. We are not racist. You don't live here and you know nothing about us. We have always welcomed immigrant here and we have always shown tolerance to those that choose to live by their own customs. There is nothing racist about wanting to preserve our local identity. Margaret Hodge, you have done nothing. What about our rights Mrs Hodge? Why are you supporting criminals instead of local residents?'**

Following the speeches and due to the heavy rain, the rally was cut short and the EDL marched back to the Rendezvous. *Searchlight* almost wetting themselves, claimed that the EDL had '**shockingly without a police escort**' taken over the area and were '**even directing the traffic**!' The anti-fascist group said they had pictures of the attack on the Asian men and claimed two of its photographers were assaulted by a breakaway mob of EDL. The *Barking and Dagenham Post* reported '**Three hurt during Dagenham protest skirmish**' and claimed that one of the Muslim men involved in the confrontation had required hospital treatment.

Later that day, an UAF concert in Leeds was stormed by Yorkshire EDL activists. The EDL reportedly hurled rocks and bottles before charging into the 150-strong Rage Against Racism crowd at The Well venue, close to Leeds city centre. The *Yorkshire Evening Post* reported that two people were injured during the disturbance and three people had been arrested. The paper said the EDL had posted its plans on Facebook beforehand and afterwards had boasted about what had happened on the Internet. Kevin Berry, assistant manager at The Well, told the *Evening Post*: '**A group of around 15 people, estimated to be aged between 16 and 23 barged into the premises shouting and chanting EDL. They were throwing bottles and rocks. The police attended quickly and arrests were made**'.

A spokesman for West Yorkshire Police told the paper that officers were called to the venue shortly before 2.40pm. One man received a serious facial injury and others received minor injuries, with damage also caused to the premises. Three men were arrested on suspicion of affray and were bailed pending further enquiries.

In the days following Dagenham and Leeds, news broke that a radical Muslim preacher, supposedly banned from Britain, had entered the country and delivered speeches to a packed halls in Leicester and London. According to the *Jewish Chronicle*, Raed Salah had '**strolled through immigration checks at Heathrow Airport**' despite being excluded from the UK by the Home Secretary. A spokesman for Salah, Lubna Masarwa, said it wasn't the first time he had visited the UK. They claimed Salah had arrived on a scheduled flight from Tel Aviv on Saturday June 25. After presenting his passport, the radical preacher was asked about the purpose of his visit, and allowed to continue.

Police were said to be trying to hunt him down (perhaps they should've just checked his itinerary?), but Salah managed to evade them and Border Agency officers for three days to carry on with his speaking tour. Incredibly, Salah was booked to share a platform in Westminster with the Palestine Solidarity Campaign, of which left-wingers such as MEP Richard Burden, Labour MPs, Yasmin Qureshi, John Austin and Jeremy Corbyn and union figures Rodney Bickerstaffe and Bob Crow are members.

Conservative MP Mike Freer, who had accused Salah of '**virulent anti-Semitism**', said the UK Border Agency had made a very serious error in letting him walk through passport control. Yvette Cooper, Shadow Home Secretary said the Government's rhetoric of being tough on border controls had been exposed as an '**incompetent sham**' but made no mention of her Labour Party colleagues plans to meet with Salah.

Salah was finally was finally arrested and held at an immigration removal centre, but refused to fly home on his return ticket. His lawyers claimed that kicking him out would be a breach of his right to freedom of expression, i.e. preventing him from preaching (stopping him from preaching was the whole idea of him being banned in the first place). Salah was bailed after a hearing at the High Court on a surety of £30,000 on condition that he report to the police every day, refrain from preaching, live at a specific address and obey a curfew.

Beware of Greeks Bearing Gifts

On 21 June 2011, Stop Islamization of America and Stop Islamisation of Europe announced they were to hold their first joint conference in Strasbourg, France, on 2 July. The groups said the summit would feature, amongst others, Pamela Geller, Robert Spencer, Anders Gravers, Bulgarian presidential candidate Pavel Chernen and Roberta Moore of the EDL.

EDL activists immediately jumped on the announcement, questioning why Moore was speaking on behalf of them. There was outright anger that someone they believed had caused so much division and had linked the EDL to a terrorist group was now representing the group on an international stage. One activist asked why someone with such minuscule support and who had caused so much trouble was representing the EDL. Another suggested it was because Moore represented a minority within a minority and it was a symptom of the EDL becoming too politically correct. People suggested that Moore was the major reason for the leadership losing a lot of grass roots support and questioned why, in the face of the drop in support, they still seemed to not only support her but pushed her forward. Other activists suggested it was Moore's alleged close relationship with Alan Lake which had resulted in her being chosen.

Moore's supporters, somewhat predictably by now, accused her detractors of being anti-Semitic and Nazi. They also claimed that Lennon couldn't attend the conference because of his bail conditions; neither could Carroll, so Moore was the obvious choice. Since the takeover of the main website and forum, any anti-Zionist discontent had been stamped out, but this latest announcement seemed a step too far and many moderators and admin on the new forum openly criticised the decision. People also now openly attacked Lake and his henchmen within the movement. One of them, flustered whilst trying to defend Moore, revealed that Lake's group was called '**Section 9**'. When pushed by EDL activists on the reason for the name they refused to comment further. However, following research it emerged Lake's shadowy, pro-Zionist entryist group was named after '**Public Safety Section 9**', a fictional Japanese Ministry of Home Affairs intelligence department from Masamune Shirow's *Ghost in the Shell* anime cartoon series. In the cartoon, the group's operatives are trained in various disciplines ranging from investigations to cyber-warfare.

This revelation was met with widespread ridicule amongst EDL activists. Some could see it for what it was, Section 9 was an entryist group, very much in the same manner of the SWP, or even Militant which had infiltrated the Labour Party during the 1980s. One activist complained that it was highly embarrassing being infiltrated by a group of cartoon characters. Lake's allies accused people of embarking on a witch-hunt against Moore and accused the person who had leaked the photographs from the now infamous London meeting (which had included one of Moore and Lake in an embrace) was a traitor who had breached trust. In response, other EDL countered that the person responsible was a true patriot, that the meeting itself was a breach of trust and those photographs had woken a lot of people up to what was really going on.

To further fan the flames it also emerged that two limited companies had been set up in the name of the EDL. The first company, registered on 23 December 2010, had one director, who had resigned immediately after the company was created. This company had Roberta Moore as a contact and gave the same address as her honey business. The second company was seemingly registered by Hel Gower and a collection of EDL Angels.

When quizzed on the matter, one Angel was forced to concede that Moore, not the EDL, now apparently owned the rights to the name English Defence League. The second company was seemingly set up in response to the EDL discovering that Moore had registered the EDL as a company. The second company owned the rights to the names, The English Defence League (EDL), English Defence League Angels, EDL Angels, British Defence League, BDL, British Defence League Angels and BDL Angels. Even so, the people behind the second company still hoped Moore would hand over the rights to the name English Defence League '**with no bother**'.

The criticism of Moore continued and one Jewish Division activist in particular came to her aid. Robert Bartholomeus is from The Hague in Holland. He was the activist who had been pictured at EDL demos wearing a Jewish Task Force jacket. Oddly, Bartholomeus has admitted that he isn't actually Jewish, but had become interested in the Zionist cause due to his admiration of Geert Wilders. He was seen as one of the more fanatical members of the Jewish Division, his posts on the Internet were littered with comments such as **'monkeys'**, **'primates'** and **'sub-human'** when referring to Muslims and especially Palestinians.

Bartholomeus claimed that blowing up an empty car in an isolated area was **'in no way terrorism'** and that someone could not be a **'proper Jew'** unless they were a Zionist (a bizarre statement coming from a non-Jew). When tackled about racist comments he made on the Jewish Division Facebook page, Bartholomeus replied: **'I will call anyone a monkey if they give me a reason to. White trash, Muslim monkey's, wigger-in-the-white house'**. It was an incoherent tirade which many EDL found repugnant. However, Bartholomeus saved his most outrageous comment for one female EDL activist who had criticised Moore: **'You are a filthy liar with an [sic] Nazi agenda, and full of shit. I hope a Muslim rapes you'**.

It was open warfare on the Internet as EDL activists responded to the outburst by Bartholomeus. Showing either how out of touch he was with the whole affair, or deliberately ignoring the severity of the situation in the hope Moore's position could still be salvaged, Alan Lake suggested that the warring factions should just keep away from each other.

The next day there were fresh clashes on Facebook, this time between Moore and Snowy Shaw. It was the reoccurring issue of terrorist atrocities committed against British soldiers in British Mandate Palestine. Moore questioned if the perpetrators of the murders of British troops were terrorists and if the soldiers concerned were innocent. That was it, Moore and Bartholomeus had committed EDL hara-kiri. Saying that you hoped a female EDL activist would be raped by a Muslim and that British soldiers deserved to be murdered in cold blood by terrorists would never win you many friends in the EDL.

As the word spread, division after division came out against the Jewish Division. Barnsley was the first, followed by Grimsby, Yorkshire and Lincolnshire. Soon the Facebook pages of divisions across the country, bar a few in the south-east, all carried the same message, **'I stand shoulder to shoulder with my fellow patriots, but I do not support the EDL Jewish Division or its leadership, not in my name please'**. It was an open loyal rebellion by ordinary rank and file EDL who had been pushed to respond in such a fashion. It was the EDL's Summer Revolution, it was people power.

Moore responded angrily, inflaming the situation she offered to fight all the northern divisions at the Tower Hamlets demonstration. She said she would challenge them with the Jewish and LGBT divisions and said the leadership would back her up if it came to a fight. That was obviously the final straw; the southern leadership were just about hanging on, never mind in a position to challenge the whole of the north of England to a fight. Moore had gone too far this time, she had to go. The following day, Moore released a resignation letter entitled **'The world is your oyster'**:

> **Dear all, I have been made a great offer yesterday and therefore I am stepping down from the Jewish Division in order to take up that offer, which will take most of my time. While we are aware that the EDL is doing a fantastic job, but there are elements within that have hijacked the EDL for their own Nazi purposes.**
>
> **I do not wish to be part of it any longer, but I will however help their genuine cause in whatever they need now that my arena has increased to an international level.**
>
> **I do wish the EDL the best of luck in this fight, as they surely need it. And I sincerely hope that the leaders will get the strength to squash the Nazis within, for they will destroy this movement if allowed to remain, and thus lose the fight against the Islamization of their countries.**
>
> **Meanwhile, I shall carry with me the voices of all those warriors who are genuinely fighting for justice and human rights around the world. My support remains with the EDL leaders and all the genuine patriots out there who struggle to get their voices heard, and I shall make their voices a deafening scream in the International arena.**

In response, one of Moore's supporters claimed 'They must be pleased as punch they have won. The Nazis within us have won. Sad, but that is the way this world is going, it is the 1930's relived. Jewish hatred is prolific. God help the Jews and Israel'. Other EDL weren't so subdued however, 'best news I've heard in a long time, she had to go she was a liability to the movement'…. 'At work now but need a beer to celebrate later. Good riddance!'…'If that's real then I'm buzzing, people power works!' On Moore's allegation of Nazis in the EDL forcing her out, one activist from the West Midlands commented, 'Good news if true, but she's the one who hijacked the EDL for Nazi purposes'.

Some EDL believed that while Moore had apparently gone, the elements which had held her in place for so long, namely Alan Lake's Section 9 group, should also leave. One of Lake's errand boys on the official EDL forum was immediately asked if he was going to do the honourable thing and fall on his sword.

The *Jewish Chronicle* reported Moore's exit 'EDL Jewish Division leader Roberta Moore quits'. The paper said that the 'hardline activist' had announced that she did not wish to be a part of the EDL any longer because of Nazi elements. Mark Gardner, from the Community Security Trust, seemingly ignoring the Kahanist beliefs of Moore and her associates, told the paper that the latest development showed why Jews shouldn't be involved in 'such circles'.

The next day Pamela Geller released a statement on Moore's departure. Geller said she was an early supporter of the EDL 'I liked who they were and what they were doing. I noted their strong support of Israel: Israeli flags at their rallies, and forthright expressions of solidarity with the Jewish State in its resistance to the same relentless jihad that is advancing in Britain'. Geller said that 'the jihad-loving Left' had claimed the EDL was neo-Nazi, neo-fascist and white supremacist, but when she had investigated she found that the group had Sikh, Pakistani, gay and Jewish divisions, the latter she claimed being decisive in her decision to back the EDL. She said the EDL had seemed 'a genuine anti-jihad group, strongly pro-Israel as every legitimate anti-jihad group must be, since Israel is at the front lines of the global jihad'.

Here it was, the crux of the issue, Geller was claiming that support of Israel and the fight against militant Islam were intrinsically linked. This was the line all the shadowy Internet 'counter-jihad' blogger groups, such as the ICLA or SIOE promoted. With recent events in mind, it was obvious Geller and Spencer believed they had a hold over the EDL leadership. Now she was laying it on the line, shape up and support Israel, or ship out of the 'global anti-jihad' movement.

Geller continued, saying that it had become clear that the EDL had 'morphed and diverged from its original course' and had now 'clearly been infiltrated by the worst kind of influences'. She claimed she had stopped covering EDL events some time before, as she was waiting to see if 'the forces of good would recapture the heart and soul of the group. Alas, it was not to be'. She suggested that the 'decentralization of the group or the loose grip Tommy Robinson held on its tether' was responsible for this 'terrible shift' in the EDL's direction (by decentralisation or loose grip, she presumably meant not controlled from New York).

Geller said she was withdrawing her support from the EDL that now Moore had resigned. She said that she also hoped that genuine 'anti-jihadists' in Britain would follow suit and leave the EDL to 'work with Roberta on starting a new group that will resist definitively and firmly all attempts to divert it from its mission of fighting against jihad and for human rights'. The Geller statement was followed with one from Stephen Lennon on *Atlas Shrugs*:

> 'The English Defence League was formed two years ago. One of the fundamental beliefs that this movement was built on was its support for Israel's right to defend itself. In our first demonstrations, we went to Birmingham, and we flew the flag of Israel, the Star of David. In the first public speech I ever gave, I wore the Star of David in Leeds. The reason for this is because Israel is a shining star of democracy. If Israel falls, we all fall. This is what our movement has been built on for two years.
>
> The English Defence League will not be deterred from its support for Israel and the Jewish people. Recently, in the EDL there have been internal arguments, which are nothing more

than that. Every large family has its disagreements, but when push comes to shove, we all stand on the same side.

Meanwhile, some people on the fringes of this movement wish to direct it toward their own agenda. This will never happen. Israel is a beacon of democracy amid repressive Arab states. Recently some people have jumped on the EDL bandwagon and tried to use our platform to express anti-Semitic views. These statements are not in accord with the fundamental beliefs of the English Defence League. These people are not welcome, never have been welcome and never will be welcome within the EDL. We reject all anti-Semitism. The EDL stands where it always has stood, which is side-by-side with Israel.

We repudiate any individual, group or writing that favors anti-Semitism, neo-fascism, and any race-based ideology. Any rogue elements within the EDL who go against our mission statement and our beliefs will be removed from the organization; we are determined to remain true to our mission. Anti-Semitism will not ever be tolerated within the EDL.

The EDL stands for freedom. It always has, it always will. We want the Jewish people and all free people to remain free forever, and we all stand together in this fight against Islamic jihad'.

The majority of EDL supporters were stunned by some of Lennon's comments; for starters he was apparently on bail and not allowed any involvement in the EDL. One presumes that is why it was only published on *Atlas Shrugs*. They also pointed out that it appeared very similar to Geller's statement and contained an Americanised spelling of favours. It could've been the fact that by releasing a statement on an American website, they hoped Lennon wasn't breaking his bail conditions, it could've been that an American wrote it, there were many theories.

Hardcore EDL activists questioned the claim that the EDL had been built on support of Israel. They claimed it was nonsense, that the EDL was formed to defend British troops who were being abused on the streets of the UK. If the original agenda had shifted at all it was only to encompass defending British values, British customs and the British way of life.

After a short subdued period of contemplation following Lennon's declaration, defiant statements again started flooding out from EDL divisions across the country, '**This is England, not Israel**'. The rank and file were refusing to allow patriots, who simply objected to the influence of extremists, to be thrown to the wolves and branded as neo-Nazis, as had happened months earlier. Again it was a total refusal to submit, *the people* were again resisting the pro-Zionist leadership's demands.

This widespread act of defiance didn't go unnoticed and it caused widespread panic amongst the international pro-Zionist blogger alliance. They feared Geller had acted over confidently and too blatantly. An open letter, signed by many people involved in the '**counter-jihad**', called the EDL '**the salvation of England**' and said any attack on the movement was '**an act of treachery**'. The letter said that Geller's accusation that "**neo-fascists**' had infiltrated the group was '**grossly inaccurate and unfair slander against the leaders and membership of the EDL**'. Geller's '**unfortunate statement**' had damaged the international counter-jihad cause, said the letter, adding she should publicly apologise to the EDL.

The letter prompted an immediate response from Robert Spencer on *Jihad Watch*. He had been quiet up to now, but said as Geller had been attacked he felt he should respond. Spencer called the claims in the open letter '**baseless and defamatory**' and accused the signatories of denigrating him and Geller to obtain a bigger '**market share**' (of the international counter-jihad bloggersphere presumably). Spencer said that everyone who signed the letter should be '**deeply concerned about the hijacking of the EDL**' and by ignoring it, they were '**sanctioning this vile racism**'. He claimed the letter had disrespected Lennon by ignoring his statement, which the EDL leader had issued to him and Geller.

Moore's resignation had been followed by that of her ally the head of the LGBT Division. He had been instrumental along with Moore of promoting the importance of Israel, so it was hardly surprising in the eyes of many that he would also go. His replacement as leader of the LGBT Division was Liam Wood from Blackpool. Wood got off to a good start in the eyes of many by immediately issuing a statement which, although he acknowledged they had worked closely in the past, immediately distanced the LGBT Division from the Jewish Division. Contrary to the militant pro-gay-rights line the division had played up until now, Wood said the ethos of the division from now on would be to **'dispel myths and then educate people about the EDL and help integrate people from the LGBT community and then into membership with their local divisions'**.

Many activists praised this new approach, it was how many believed the division should be run, and everyone should just join their local divisions regardless of creed, colour, religion or sexuality. However, the positivity surrounding the change was soon tempered by revelations the following day that Wood had recently admitted to possessing cocaine with intent to supply at Preston Crown Court. The *Blackpool Gazette* reported that Wood was said to have been looking after the drugs for a short period, before returning them to their owner. Sentencing in Wood's case was deferred for six months.

On the same day the revelations about Wood were published, the Muslim Debate Initiative (MDI) sent an official invitation to the EDL, to openly debate their contentions against Islam and Muslims in a live public debate at a neutral venue. MDI had invited controversial groups to speak in the past, including fundamentalist evangelical Christians, atheists, secularists and the BNP, which the group claimed had been peaceful, fair and civilised events. The EDL responded with a curt **'thanks, but no thanks'**, claiming that MDI was merely a front for the Muslim Defence League.

2 July 2011: Chorley, Clitheroe and Simonstone

Regardless of the infighting which was plaguing the EDL, Casuals United was quietly getting on with things. In fact in the face of the unrest, the group came to the fore. On Saturday 2 July, Casuals United activists from Blackburn, Chorley, Burnley, Preston and Wrexham met up, intending to hold a series of flash protests in a number of Lancashire towns.

First on the list was Accrington, 30 Casuals held a short protest in the local ASDA store, accusing the shop of selling unlabeled halal products. Then, with police now in pursuit, they made their way to Clitheroe, where the group claimed the local council had approved plans to convert a church into a mosque, which many local people opposed. They held a small protest in the town centre, before moving on to their next destination, Simonstone in the Ribble Valley, home of Conservative MEP Sajjad Karim.

Casuals United claimed that Karim had voted against a bill which proposed that halal products should be labelled. A number of activists marched up to his door to hand him a letter, but the MEP refused to answer, closing the blinds and calling the police. Karim, who represents the North West in the European Parliament, said the **'huge mob'** had wanted to intimidate him, his wife and young daughter because they were Muslim. Lancashire Police would arrest a number of activists involved in the protest over the next couple of days.

The group then proceeded to nearby Briercliffe to hand out leaflets, where they claimed they received a good response from locals, and then onto Brierfield, a small town near Burnley. As they prepared to hand out leaflets, the Casuals noticed a large group of Muslim youths gathering nearby. There were scuffles as members of both groups confronted each other. Police arrived and separated the two groups, arresting four people. A spokeswoman for Lancashire Police told the *Clitheroe Advertiser and Times* that they would thoroughly investigate the incident and bring to justice those who had committed any offences. Police said that a woman aged 45 and three men 33, 44 and 47 had all been arrested on suspicion of violent disorder.

The *Clitheroe Advertiser and Times* also reported that there was also criminal damage to two vehicles on Glenway in Brierfield the same afternoon. The paper said there were suggestions that the damage was a result of **'the English Defence League suspects holding a protest in Brierfield'** (suspects seemed a strange term to use). A female motorist, her husband and two young children were confronted by a group of people the paper described as **'of Asian heritage appearance'**. One member of this group had caused £500 worth of damage to the vehicle's rear offside passenger door. There was another attack on another vehicle, which an Asian male struck with a golf club.

On the same day as the Lancashire protests, dozens of EDL staged a protest on Market Place in Huddersfield town centre. A spokesman for West Yorkshire Police told the *Huddersfield Daily Examiner* that the EDL had gathered at three town centre pubs and informed the police they wished to march through the town. The request was denied by officers, and around 50 EDL had then held a short demonstration on Market Place. Following the demonstration, the EDL then left the area. Police said six arrests had been made for public order offences.

In spite of the infighting which was plaguing the movement, it appeared that the rank and file were continuing, carrying on regardless, However, Pamela Geller still wasn't finished, releasing a further statement claiming that a **'blogwar'** was being waged against her by **'vultures with an altogether nefarious agenda'**. Even so, Geller said she stood by her concerns about increasing anti-Semitism in the ranks of the EDL, but unsurprisingly added that she and Spencer had no intention of breaking with the group if they **'purge these antisemitic elements'**. Geller said she had been **'immediately reassured that these rogue elements would be routed out'**, if they weren't, Geller claimed **'they will be finished as a force for good in England'**.

It was an amazing threat. Here was an American, again seemingly believing she could shut down an English street movement. Geller was virtually unknown outside of the EDL in Britain. It begged the question what influence she believed she and Spencer wielded over the EDL leadership.

Geller's second statement was followed by another by Roberta Moore, who was now claiming that although the recent controversy had been made out to be about her, that was a diversionary tactic. Moore said that there were **'real issues that need to be addressed; elements that must be purged'** and she was **'relieved that Tommy Robinson said in his statement to SIOA that he would do just that'**.

Moore said the EDL had been struggling with anti-Semitic elements for some time and the leadership needed to act. She said she was still being goaded by anti-Semites, but continuing to **'air this dirty laundry'**, would only serve the enemies of the EDL, which is why she had chosen to resign. She said the whole point in founding the Jewish Division and supporting Israel was that **'Israel is under siege from jihad, and England faces the same jihad'** and claimed her comments over the murder of British troops in British Mandate Palestine had been taken out of context. She said she had not condoned murder of anyone, and she had **'merely stated a historical fact that these Jews were not terrorists; they were freedom fighters who were trying to protect their country'**.

Moore claimed the attacks on her were conducted by **'a small anti-Semitic group, whose sole purpose was to gather as many nationalistic supporters as possible to eventually oust Tommy Robinson and Kevin Carroll from the leadership, while at the same time bringing down our great movement'**. She said this group was coordinating its activities with certain members of other organisations **'which are linked to the EDL but who are not EDL members per se'**. Moore concluded by saying she hoped that the true leaders of the EDL would **'act without any further delay, and act as per their statement to SIOA. We in the Jewish Division confirm that in turn we will cooperate fully, help them with this very much needed "exorcism" and offer every help within our scope in order to ensure they fully accomplish this'**.

Obviously, with this closing statement, Moore was indicating she was still very much a part of the Jewish Division. She had not only refused to withdraw her remarks, she was reiterating her contention that the Jewish terrorists who killed innocent British servicemen and civilians in cold-blood were **'freedom fighters'**. Some EDL supporters, especially those from *UKFD*, replied that on Moore's reasoning, the Muslims that flew planes into the Twin Towers could be considered freedom fighters, or even members of the Taliban or IRA. Others claimed that Moore's smearing of anyone who disagreed with her as Nazi, or saying her comments were out of context, were similar tactics to those of the Islamists they faced. They claimed as well as fighting militant Islam, ordinary patriots were now fighting an **'enemy within'** in the form of the hardcore Zionists who they believed had infiltrated the movement.

Others claimed this was the reason Moore had registered the EDL as a limited company, to control the name and ensure that she could never be stopped from using the EDL brand. The next day, Moore released a further statement on the Jewish Division Facebook page. It prompted one EDL activist to comment **'I am keenly awaiting tomorrow's installment. It must be the longest resignation letter in history'**. Moore claimed she had been attacked, bullied and intimidated by **'envious people'** since she had joined the EDL, but had refused to falter and carried on working for the group. She said she realised that many people thought the Jewish Division had very little support, but they were fools, as they had **'very important people inside who have been doing an incredible amount of work and many of them are intellectuals and** professionals'. She reiterated that she did not consider JTF leader Victor Vancier a terrorist in any way, shape or form, as **'his so-called terrorist acts were simply to blow up EMPTY soviet diplomatic cars in isolated areas and empty establishments'**.

Moore compared the jailing of Vancier to the problems Lennon and Carroll faced with British police. She said that as the EDL was a Zionist organisation, she hadn't thought contacting Vancier would be a problem and the only people who had a problem with it were **'those who have serious issues with Jews owning their home'**. Moore said that **'if they cannot accept that the EDL is a Zionist organisation they should pack up and leave. There is no place for anti-Zionism inside this group. And none will be tolerated'**. It appeared that not only had Moore not gone away; she was now dictating who should stay and who should leave the movement.

9 July 2011: Halifax, Derby, Middlesbrough, Plymouth and Cambridge.

The EDL had announced a day of action on 9 July 2011, planning to protest in Halifax, Derby, Middlesbrough, Plymouth and Cambridge simultaneously. A number of activists were worried that a demonstration in Halifax on the same day as others, was unwise. They claimed Halifax was a hotbed of Islamic extremism and they would face considerable opposition, so argued it should be a national protest. They worried that activists from the East Midlands would obviously support the Derby demo; activists from the North East and North Yorkshire would support the Middlesbrough protest, leaving Halifax potentially undermanned.

There was no real leadership being displayed since Lennon's bail conditions barring him from involvement were imposed. It was claimed that he was on holiday, but other members of the leadership were also conspicuous by their absence. Therefore it was down to the East Midlands Division, who cancelled the Derby protest, so that East Midlands activists could support their comrades in Halifax. The cancellation also enabled activists from the West Midlands to travel to Halifax.

West Yorkshire Police had told the EDL they would be demonstrating on the Eureka! car park, next to the train station. This caused consternation amongst EDL activists and in response Yorkshire EDL withdrew any police liaison, which was limited anyway following the Dewsbury protest. Several alternative locations for the protest were being touted by the organisers, and as a result, West Yorkshire Police issued several leading members of Yorkshire EDL with Section 14 Notices ahead of the demo, confirming the location of the demonstration.

On the morning of the protest, police closed all pubs in Halifax town centre. A large number of EDL met in nearby Sowerby Bridge, but were located by police and handed leaflets confirming the location of the protest. Another group of EDL arrived, they were barred entry to the pub, but found another one nearby.

The EDL started arriving in Halifax an hour before the protest was due to begin. Most were halted by police on the outskirts of the town. There were clashes between EDL and Muslim men in the Kings Cross area of Halifax, where the UAF counter-protest was being held. Some EDL managed to get near to the UAF protest, attended by a small number of anti-fascists. The EDL shouted abuse and were moved on by a small number of stewards and rapidly arriving police officers.

Around 400 EDL were eventually escorted to the protest site by police, they didn't stay in there for long however, breaking down fences and scattering into the town centre. Hundreds roamed the town, clashing with police and small groups of Asian youths. Most were eventually rounded up and escorted back to the protest site, where, after a short speech, they waited to be allowed to leave. After most of the coaches had left, police still held around 200 at the protest site. There were more clashes between EDL and police as the frustrations of activists boiled over.

West Yorkshire Police said that five people had been arrested on suspicion of public order offences and one on suspicion of possessing an offensive weapon. The force also said that a police officer was injured during the protest, suffering a dislocated shoulder. Police said that 450 people had attended the EDL demonstration with 70 at the UAF counter-protest.

The protest in Cambridge was called to oppose the building of what was referred to as a **'super-mosque'** in the Mill Road area of the city. Around 200 people gathered at around 11.00am for a TUC-led counter-demonstration. A helicopter hovered over the city centre, as police patrolled Mill Road. Richard Howitt told the counter-protest in Market Square 'we were here before the EDL as we are going to be here after them too'. As he spoke, five EDL supporters attempted to gain access to the square, shouting at the anti-fascists, before being ushered away by police.

By midday, the EDL started arriving in the city, heading for Queen's Green where they would start their protest. The group was being allowed to march, and the *Cambridge News* reported that anti-EDL graffiti had been sprayed on walls along the route overnight. Coaches containing EDL arrived at Queen's Green, activists carrying flags chanted, "**Burn our poppy and we'll burn your mosques**". Some carried banners which said '**London, Glasgow bombers were from Cambridge**' and '**Stop the Super Mosque**'.

At 1.00pm, the EDL set off on their march around Cambridge. There were scuffles and beer cans thrown at police almost immediately as some EDL, responding to anti-fascist jeers, attempted to break out. There were further scuffles along the route as more anti-fascists, some with megaphones, goaded the EDL. The *Cambridge News* reported that some members of the public joined in with the EDL protest as it passed by. After the march around Cambridge, the EDL arrived back in Queen's Green. Police estimated that around 250 EDL had taken part. A spokesman for Cambridgeshire County Council said the protest had been very rowdy and lively, but added that it had '**gone off quite well**'.

On the same day as Cambridge, up to 400 officers from Dorset, Avon and Somerset and Wiltshire were drafted into Plymouth as around 150 EDL marched through the city centre. Around 200 people attended a UAF counter-protest, billed as a '**multicultural celebration of diversity**'. Devon and Cornwall Police said there had been six arrests, one for a racially aggravated public order offence, one for possession of a weapon, one for assault and three for breach of the peace. Superintendent Craig Downham told *BBC News* that it had been a considerable policing operation, but he hoped the public had felt reassured by the number of officers on duty.

In Middlesbrough, arriving EDL found the police waiting for them at Middlesbrough train station. They were escorted by officers to three pubs which had been allocated as assembly points. The North East Infidels, a group aligned to Snowy Shaw's breakaway British Infidels, were present and there were rumours they planned to disrupt the protest, but in the event there was no trouble.

The start of the protest was delayed. A wedding was taking place on the route and the EDL agreed to delay the march so the wedding could take place unhindered. They eventually set off at 2.00pm, just as it began to rain, heavily. It was a largely peaceful march around Middlesbrough, the only trouble when young EDL supporters tried to break out to confront anti-fascists who were barracking them. After a short speech, and in the face of what was now driving rain, the protest was cut short. The EDL were allowed to disperse by the police. Many of them wandered back to the pubs unescorted. One EDL activist estimated the number of EDL present as around 500.

As the protests across the country were happening, news started to surface amongst anti-fascists that members of the EDL had been seen in London, at Bethnal Green tube station. More EDL were seen in a pub in Stepney, according to some anti-fascists they were on their way to Tower Hamlets. Also in London, eighteen members of the Scottish Defence League, in taxis heading for the East End, were stopped by police. They were held for an hour under Section 60 legislation, then put in police vans, taken to Kings Cross station and put on a train home. *Leeds Casuals Blog* would later claim that over 100 people were arrested for attempting to counter-protest outside what it called a '**hate conference**' being staged by Muslim radical group Hizb-ut-Tahrir, at the Water Lilly Business Centre in Mile End Road.

It emerged that among the arrested was Stephen Lennon. The EDL released a statement claiming that it was yet another chapter in the ongoing police harassment Lennon was facing. The statement claimed that Lennon, who it alleged was getting married soon, was in the East End on his stag party, '**Amongst the large crowd were many of Tommy's friends from the EDL, but none were wearing EDL colours — they were quite simply on a night out**'.

The group claimed that someone had recognised Lennon, and arranged what they believed was intended to be an ambush. The EDL said police had informed them that a large group of Muslim youths had gathered at a venue which was intended to be the next pub on the night out. When Lennon and his friends had tried to leave the pub they were in, they found their way barred by the police, who detained everyone to prevent a breach of the peace.

The EDL said that no explanation was given and the incident gave rise to the belief that the police in Great Britain, were now becoming nothing more than '**Stasi agents**' and the country was on a downward spiral to becoming a state where the innocent were punished and the potential perpetrators allowed to carry on in their '**sharia controlled**' areas.

The group was referring to the news that a number of posters claiming that the area was a '**Sharia-Controlled Zone**' had appeared around Tower Hamlets in London. The posters stated that no gambling, music and concerts, nudity or vice and no drugs and smoking would now be allowed in the area. Anjem Choudary said he supported the implementation of the Sharia Zones as an alternative to the government's attempts to combat violent extremism under the Prevent strategy. Choudary told *Asharq Al-Awsat* that as Islamists, they took a clear stand on gender mixing, taking drugs, gambling, vice, and concerts where everything becomes mixed up and also had a clear stand on democracy which they considered '**unbelief**'. He said that '**Sharia police will include others who do not belong to the fundamentalist trend**'.

Choudary said that the anti-terrorism strategy approved by the Home Secretary, Theresa May, would be confronted during the next two weeks starting with Waltham Forest where the campaign to distribute the posters about the Sharia Zones would begin. He said that this meant that the Muslim community in the zone would not tolerate drugs, alcohol, nudity, gambling, usury, or the free mixing of men and women which were '**the fruits of Western civilization**'.

On its website, MAC backed the plans; saying it was time that areas with large Muslim populations declared an emirate, and use their own courts, community watch, schools and even self sufficient trade. MAC suggested that '**likely areas for these projects might be Dewsbury or Bradford or Tower Hamlets to begin with**'.

Leader of Bradford Council, Ian Greenwood, said people would not allow extremists to provoke them into violence. Greenwood said extremism was less likely to emerge when people get the opportunity to come together and that was one of the best ways to build a tolerant society in which extremism played no part. The *Daily Mail* claimed MAC's plan was a response to the government's Prevent strategy, termed Islamic Prevent. MAC also called for Muslims to remove CCTV cameras from Muslim institutions and accused many mosques of spying on Muslims on behalf of the police and local authorities. The group also called for the release of all Muslim prisoners, a ban on Muslims joining the police or Armed Forces and a rejection of British democracy.

16 July 2011: Portsmouth

The EDL was protesting in Portsmouth. The group was marching through the city, starting and finishing at Victoria Park. The group wanted to lay a wreath at the city's war memorial in Guildhall Square but were denied permission by the council. Leader of the council, Gerald Vernon-Jackson, told local paper *The News*: '**There is no way we would allow this. It's totally inappropriate and we have told the EDL they will not be allowed to lay a wreath there. We wouldn't allow anyone, from the city or outside, to use this memorial, erected in honour of people who died for the country, for purely political purposes**'.

EDL representative, Paul Ness, told the paper that the group still intended to lay a wreath: '**The council doesn't like us, but we just want to be left alone. We want to lay the wreath to remember the people who died for our country. We want a peaceful march and that's what will happen if we're left alone. We'll send in a speaker and six people. They will lay the wreath**'. A spokeswoman for Hampshire constabulary told *The News* that the agreed route didn't include a visit to the memorial. She said the EDL had been co-operative, had agreed not to lay a wreath and wouldn't be allowed to because the council had refused the group permission to do so. UAF announced it would hold a vigil in Guildhall Square.

On the morning of the protest, there was a heavy police presence in Portsmouth city centre. More than 200 officers were on duty with officers drafted in from Thames Valley and British Transport Police. The EDL met at three pubs, the Park Tavern, the Royal Standard and the Painter's Arms. Activists had travelled from places such as Blackburn, Brighton, Colchester, Dudley, London and Plymouth to protest. At around midday, led by countless police officers, the EDL began its march. It wasn't a brilliant turnout, around 300 EDL, but their numbers were boosted by Portsmouth and Chelsea football fans whose teams were playing each other in the city later that day.

One EDL demonstrator carried a placard which said '**Newsflash! Englishman gets job!**' another had the letters EDL shaven into the back of his head. An Israel flag was prominent at the front of the march. There were scuffles between marchers and police as anti-fascists holding placards which said '**Racist EDL not welcome in Portsmouth**' barracked the EDL. The police wouldn't allow the EDL access to Victoria Park so the rally took place on nearby Edinburgh Road. Hampshire Police arrested two people, one on suspicion of assaulting a police officer and the other for a public order offence.

Portsmouth was a disappointing turnout for the group. There were admittedly, a lot more protests being called. There were protests the week before Portsmouth and in the middle of a recession people were struggling to justify the constant expenditure. It was a fact however, that EDL numbers were at best stable, at worst falling, but one thing for sure was they weren't rising anymore.

Some activists argued that a turnout of over 500 people in Portsmouth was positive. However, the demo was a bit of a white elephant. Although it achieved a turnout of between 300-500, Portsmouth is a city which is largely white; there was also a football match in the city between Portsmouth and Chelsea, two clubs traditionally with a patriotic support. It was also the only planned demonstration going on that day.

22 July 2011: Oslo, Norway

At 3.30pm on Friday 22 July 2011, a large bomb exploded in the centre of Oslo, Norway. The explosion killed at least eight people and damaged government buildings, including the office of the country's Prime Minister, Jens Stoltenberg.

Around half an hour later, there were reports of shootings at a Labour Party youth camp being held on Utoya island, around 40 miles from Oslo. A man, dressed as a police officer was roaming the island indiscriminately shooting people, mainly children, some of whom were diving into the sea to escape. Armed police were slow in responding to the incident due to the carnage in Oslo and it took them 90 minutes to arrive at the scene.

The attacks were automatically presumed to be the work of Muslim extremists; al-Qaeda was mentioned as a matter of course. In fact, the man responsible, who gave himself up to police, 32 year old Anders Behring Breivik, wasn't a Muslim, he was an ethnic Norwegian, said to have links with right-wing extremists. Police said that when arrested, Breivik gave himself up even though he still had a lot of ammunition. He had allegedly used dum-dum bullets, designed to cause the maximum damage to his victims.

Only hours before he started his murderous spree, an email was sent to people Breivik had befriended on Facebook, including some EDL supporters. The email, which contained a 1500-page '**manifesto**' entitled *2083*, which Breivik had written, using the pseudonym Andrew Berwick. In the manifesto, Breivik referenced anti-jihad websites *Atlas Shrugs*, *Gates of Vienna* and *Jihad Watch*, he also mentioned both SIOE and the EDL. Breivik allegedly wrote that he '**used to have more than 600 EDL members as Facebook friends and have spoken with tens of EDL members and leaders. In fact; I was one of the individuals who supplied them with processed ideological material (including rhetorical strategies) in the very beginning**'. Two years earlier he had also posted online '**I have on some occasions had discussions with SIOE and EDL and recommended them to use certain strategies. The tactics of the EDL are now to 'lure' an overreaction from the Jihad Youth/Extreme-Marxists, something they have succeeded in doing several times already**'.

A video entitled *Knights Templar 2083*, had also been posted on YouTube by someone called Andrew Berwick two days before the attack. It promoted the fight against Islam and showed pictures of Breivik wearing a wetsuit and pointing an automatic weapon, which were also posted on Breivik's Facebook profile.

The following day the EDL was being directly linked to Breivik. *The Guardian* claimed '**Norway attacks: Utøya gunman boasted of links to UK far right - Anders Brehing Breivik took part in online discussions** with members of the EDL and other anti-Islamic groups'. The paper said that Norwegian officials were working with foreign intelligence agencies to see if there was any international involvement in the attacks.

The *Sunday Express* announced '**Killer was advisor to EDL on Islamic hatred**' and reported that the '**right-wing psychopath behind Norway's bloodbath was involved with the English Defence League**'. The *Daily Express* said that Breivik had '**advised the EDL how to stir up anti-Islamic hatred. He not only admired the far-right group, but also harboured dreams of setting up Norway's version to combat the country's growing Muslim population**'. *Channel 4 News* claimed that online postings by '**Christian fundamentalist**' Breivik had made indicated links between the Norwegian Defence League he claimed to have co-founded and its '**English counterpart**'. *Channel 4 News* also claimed that '**according to unconfirmed reports**' Breivik had attended two EDL rallies in west London and Newcastle in 2010.

The EDL denied any link to Breivik: '**We can categorically state that there has never been any official contact between him and the EDL, our Facebook page had 100,000 supporters and receives tens of thousands of comments each day. And there is no evidence that Breivik was ever one of those 100,000 supporters. Even so, anyone who expresses any extremist beliefs of any kind, be it white supremacist, Christian fundamentalist or Islamic extremists, they all get banned from the site**'.

Scotland Yard was said to be investigating Breivik's claims that he began his '**crusade**' after being recruited into a secret society called the Knights Templar in London by an English '**mentor**' called '**Richard**' who he described as the '**perfect knight**'. Speaking on his blog *Lionheart*, Paul Ray said that although he was a Christian fundamentalist with a deep dislike for Islamic fundamentalism, anyone who knew him would know he would play no part in '**such inhumane savagery that has no place in the civilised world**'. Ray said although it had been implied that he was the mysterious '**Richard**', it wasn't him. Videos of Alan Lake giving a speech and an interview in Norway in October 2009 were posted, Ray said the interview was '**for a documentary there which puts him clearly at the scene of the crime**'. He said that Lake's '**murderous ideals**' were there for all to see when he said that he would execute those who believed in Sharia: '**all arrows point towards Alan Lake, and all circumstantial evidence points towards Alan Lake**'.

Anti-fascists and now Ray were referring to an interview on Norwegian television only months earlier, where Lake, referring to people who promoted Sharia, said: '**I call them seditious. They are seeking the overthrow of the state. They're not respecting that which protects the state. As far as I'm concerned I'd be happy to execute people like that**'. Seemingly oblivious to the gravity of the situation, posting on *4freedoms*, Lake described the Norwegian attacks: '**Apparently, in a long screed Anders Behring Breivik posted on line, he did this attack to protest against the way that Islam is taking over large parts of Europe. By attacking the leftist politicians that are enabling this, the chickens have actually come home to roost – altho [sic] I'm sure it won't be depicted that way**'.

The next day, an article in *The Independent* '**Outcry over the role of English Defence League**', claimed that EDL supporters on the group's website were blaming Norway's immigration policies for the attacks. Nick Lowles of Hope Not Hate told the paper that the decision not to classify the EDL as an extremist right-wing group severely limited the capacity of the police to gather intelligence on it, '**given the mounting evidence of connections between the EDL and alleged violent extremists like Anders Behring Breivik, we don't see how this situation is sustainable**'.

The EDL issued a further statement '**due to some uneducated members of the media, blindly only reporting half a story**'. The EDL said it was '**shameful**' that journalists had been '**all too quick**' to link the group to someone they described as a '**murderous creature**'. The EDL said it could '**categorically state that there has never been any official contact between him [Breivik] and the EDL**'. The statement said there was no evidence that Breivik was ever one of its 100,000 Facebook supporters. Even so, said the group, anyone who expressed any extremist beliefs of any kind, white supremacist, Christian fundamentalist or Islamic extremist was immediately banned from the site.

The group said that if journalists had bothered to give '**due respect to Norway**' they would have read the entire writings of Breivik and found he talked about the EDL in a negative light. The EDL claimed that on page 1438 of his manifesto, the Norwegian claimed his principles and those of the EDL were '**miles apart ideologically**'. The EDL said it condemned any movement, such as the Breivik's Knights Templar, that used terror as a tool. The group also informed the press that Stephen Lennon was unavailable for comment and journalists could attend a press conference with him if they paid a £50 fee.

Anders Behring Breivik appeared in court the following Monday. The hearing was held behind closed doors, to prevent him a platform for his views, but also due to police concerns Breivik might use it to pass a coded message to other suspected cells. Police said they were not searching for anyone, but had also not ruled out more people being involved. Eyewitness reports suggested a possible accomplice and Breivik's was claiming there were two similar cells in Norway and others abroad.

Breivik admitted carrying out the bombing in Oslo, and the massacre on Utoya island, but did not accept criminal responsibility for the acts. His lawyer, Geir Lippestad, told the media: "**He thought it was gruesome having to commit these acts, but in his head, they were necessary. He wished to attack society and the structure of society**".

At a subsequent press conference, Lippestad revealed that Breivik, who he described as a '**very cold person**', saw himself as a warrior who had started a war which was now underway and would continue for sixty years. Lippestad said the whole case indicated that the accused was insane, as he believed the rest of Western world didn't understand his point of view. Breivik was apparently fully cooperating with police, but wouldn't comment on other cells he claimed existed. He claimed his attack had been on Norway's ruling Labour Party for the society they had created. He also said he expected further attacks from the other cells. Breivik planned to read an extract of his manifesto at the trial and had read an excerpt from it to the judge at the hearing the day before.

The *Daily Mail* claimed '**Smirk of the maniac: As mass murderer grins outside court, full scale of his links to British extremists emerges**'. The paper said an EDL source had told them: '**I know people within the English Defence League who claim Anders Breivik was at some of those meetings. Also, people who he knows have been over to the UK many times and are very active within the EDL circles in London. There are definite connections between this man and the UK**'.

Under the headline '**Norway killer Anders Behring Breivik had extensive links to English Defence League**' the *Daily Telegraph* claimed Breivik was understood to have met leaders of the EDL in March 2010, when he had travelled to London for the visit of Geert Wilders. Someone called Daryl Hobson, who the paper claimed organised EDL demonstrations, had allegedly posted on Facebook that Breivik had met EDL members. The paper said another anonymous senior member of the EDL had told them that the Norwegian had been in regular contact with EDL supporters via Facebook: '**I spoke to him a few times on Facebook and he is extremely intelligent and articulate and very affable. He is someone who can project himself very well and I presume there would be those within the EDL who would be quite taken by that. It's like Hitler, people said he was hypnotic. This guy had the same sort of effect**'.

The *Northern Echo* claimed '**Norway killer on North-East march**' and said that it understood, from an anonymous UAF source, that Breivik had taken part in the EDL protest in Newcastle.

On bail preventing him from involvement in the EDL, Stephen Lennon appeared on the BBC *Newsnight* programme, interviewed by Jeremy Paxman. Lennon was asked how Breivik, had been able to attend EDL demonstrations, he replied that he didn't believe he had, and said that people should stop speculating and look at the facts. Paxman asked Lennon if he knew Daryl Hobson, Lennon replied that he didn't and he was probably one of the 100,000 supporters on Facebook. Paxman claimed Lennon had been arrested with Hobson at the poppy burning incident in London in November 2010. Lennon said it might be true they had both been arrested on the same day, but not together and he had no idea who Hobson was.

Referring to Breivik, Lennon said it was more important to '**listen to what this psychopath says in his manifesto**'. Paxman asked him how much of the manifesto he agreed with, Lennon replied by asking Paxman if he would've asked a Muslim leader the same question following 7/7. He said that the EDL believed Islam was a threat, and asked Paxman if they wanted to stop something like what had happened in Oslo or play the blame game.

Lennon then read out a quote from Breivik's manifesto which stated that his group and the EDL were incompatible. Paxman introduced one post Breivik had allegedly made on the EDL website forum, using the pseudonym Sigurd Jorsalfare, claiming it was the last thing the Norwegian had published before he "**disappeared to make his bombs**". Paxman introduced the name of Alan Lake, calling him a founder and a funder of the EDL, both of which Lennon denied. Lennon was asked if he agreed with Lake when he had allegedly referred to the Norwegian massacre as '**logical and inevitable**'. Lennon said he didn't and had been disgusted and sickened by the incident.

Lennon said there were British people across the country gravely concerned about the spread of Islam. He said that in Norway 24% of Norwegians had voted for an anti-Islamic party and that people across Europe were worried about the issue. Lennon said he condemned the incident as a horrific, disgusting, deranged attack, but even so that didn't warrant brushing off millions of people concerned about Islam. He said government think-tanks were not doing their job, simply because there were no representatives of working class community involved in them: "**We are against all extremism and all violence, but you need to listen, because, God forbid, if this happens on British soil. It's a time coming, you're probably five or ten years away**".

Paxman: "**That sounds almost like a threat, hang on a second!**"

Lennon: "**No, it's not a threat**".

Paxman: "**You think something like that could happen in a few years time in this country?**"

Lennon: "**I believe it could, it's not a threat it's a wake up call to say listen, we don't want this to happen. We need to address the problem, the problem's not going to get solved by keep building more mosques and keep flooding the country with Islamic immigration and not dealing with the threats of Islam and not listening to people**".

Following the revelations of reportedly links with the EDL, Prime Minister, David Cameron, announced that right-wing groups (presumably including the EDL) in the UK would come under the scrutiny of the police. Cameron, who chaired a meeting of the National Security Council, promised to learn any lessons from the events in Oslo, to ensure the UK was '**more secure against horrific outrageous like this**'.

A Metropolitan Police liaison officer from the force's Domestic Extremist Unit was despatched to Norway. Police said they were following certain lines of investigation, to see if there were links between Breivik and the British far-right. A spokesman for the European Police Agency also announced it was setting up a task force to help investigate non-Islamist threats in Scandinavian countries. Spokesman Soeren Pedersen said the task force could be expanded to include more European nations. Pederson said there had been warnings that right-wing groups were getting more professional and more aggressive in the way they attracted people to their cause.

Lake released a statement denying that he knew Breivik and that he was his mentor. Lake claimed he had no interest in the Knights Templar movement (which was seemingly now being discussed as if it actually existed rather than just in the mind of Breivik) and hadn't become involved in '**political issues**' until the end of 2007. He condemned the actions of Breivik and claimed he lost three friends in the Norway attacks. Lake said he had only made one '**injudicious statement**' (referring to his infamous Final Solution post) which he had withdrawn, but he said it was being '**kept alive by leftist websites eager to cause damage to society**'. Lake said there were numerous '**false and fabricated stories**' about him in the media and modestly added that the people responsible should '**reflect on the effect this latent dishonesty has on the community discourse**'.

On Saturday 30 July, The Guardian ran a story on Lake '**EDL leader demanded debate on killing David Cameron and archbishop**'. Calling Lake a senior member of the EDL, the paper said that Breivik had closely monitored his *4freedoms* website and recanted Lake's Final Solution post. *The Guardian* claimed that users of the *4Freedoms* site had posted articles by a far-right blogger known as Fjordman who was extensively cited by Breivik in the 1,500-page manifesto he issued shortly before the mass killings. It also mentioned the interview Lake had given *TV 2 Nyhetene* where he had described the Islamic radicals who protested in the UK as '**seditious**' and said that he would be '**happy to execute people like that**'.

The paper also mentioned Paul Ray, claiming he was alarmed by Lake's comments, but it had become apparent as things had developed just how extreme the views of Lake were. Ray accused Lake of '**directing an extreme far-right movement in the UK**' and of playing an important role in linking the EDL to influential far-right communities online.

A number of people in the movement, especially those linked to *UKFD*, now felt it was time for Lake and others in the international counter-jihad network to leave the EDL. They had only seemed to have brought with them problems, and shifted the focus away from the EDL's founding ethos. The Jewish Division were however defiant. They issued a dictat which, referring to *UKFD* as a '**Nazi-like splinter group**', said the group did not represent the EDL nor the views of the majority of EDL supporters. The Jewish Division also implied that some members of *UKFD* weren't to be trusted. One in particular, who had opposed Lake and Moore from the start, was accused of being '**too clued up about "certain things" which we have observed, and this is not the behaviour of some "working class" guy from Birmingham, where he says he lives**'.

Lake released another statement on 31 July 2011, claiming that since the beginning of his involvement, there had been numerous false statements attributed to him and a variety of false claims and exaggerations. He alleged he had sent a legal warning to *Searchlight* regarding fourteen '**totally false statements they made about me**'. Lake said due to the current media attention, it was possible to correct some of the false information. He denied being a financier of the EDL and said he had '**merely given equipment worth a few hundred pounds**'. This obviously contradicted what he told Norwegian television news show *TV 2 Nyhetene* in April 2011, when he said, '**I have given some money to help some EDL things happen**'. Lake denied ever being part of the EDL management, he said he had only directed events at several demonstrations and given a few speeches. He said he was not currently involved with the EDL, and hadn't been for six months. He said there were also accusations that he was an upper class manipulator from the south, but said he was from the north, adding that his step father was a plumber. He said the allegations were from prejudiced people against people from different backgrounds and had been detrimental to the unity of the EDL. Like the Jewish Division, Lake accused the Birmingham activist linked to *UKFD* as being an '**SDS look-alike**' (Metropolitan Police Special Demonstration Squad). In a further post on the *4freedoms* site, Lake said that once the EDL located the SDS operatives, he hoped they knew what to do with the Birmingham activist: '**I'm not suggesting execution or anything, far be it for me to suggest what they should do**'.

Lake's statements were surprisingly followed by one from the EDL, expelling him from the movement. The EDL said that claims made by Lake which were recanted in *The Guardian* that he was an EDL leader or events director were simply not true. The group said Lake did have a role in the EDL during its early formation, but in reality had '**always jumped on the bandwagon of the EDL when in reality all he has ever done is bring shame on our movement with his 'Nazi Like' postings and his moribund rantings that would even make Himmler blush!**' The statement said that the fact of the matter was that '**Alan Lake does not speak for the EDL, he does not represent our membership and he certainly does not represent the thoughts of the EDL leadership in any way, shape, form or fashion. Again his comments on the killing of our Prime Minister MUST be rejected wholeheartedly. We distance ourselves from such rhetoric and we advise Alan Lake to move on, start up his own movement based on his murderous rhetoric and unrepentant hate. Alan Lake is no longer welcome at ANY EDL event**'.

One activist commenting on the official forum claimed: '**Alan Lake has been given the boot? Good. What a joke of a man he is. He must have known his time was running out because his latest absurd outburst of bull**** was to try and muddy good, loyal and trustworthy lads names with his lies. See ya Mr Lake. Last, and least, we have the Royal pain in the arse that is Roberta. Surely a statement is due out on her sometime soon? We've been told she has been given the boot, she says she hasn't. This situation needs sorting ASAP. She causes nothing but arguments and division**'.

The statement about Lake was followed by one regarding Moore: '**Roberta Moore and the Jewish Division of the English Defence League no longer represent our cause. They will not be welcome at any further EDL events or demonstrations. Their views are not those of the EDL and the EDL would like to make it clear that the murder of children is not something we support**'.

However, both of these statements were quickly withdrawn. Moore, posting on Lake's *4freedoms* site, said the people in charge of the Facebook site were '**true EDL**' adding that, '**they do not have the legal right to use the name they are using**'. There it was, the true reason why Moore had registered the EDL as a limited company. She now believed that she and Lake could not be kicked out of the movement because she had registered the name English Defence League.

The following day, the Support Group, headed by Hel Gower was unceremoniously closed down by the EDL leadership. In response the Angels who supported Gower formed their own group the Rebel Angels. It was proof for some supporters, that the Jewish Division, supported by Pamela Geller and Robert Spencer, had the leadership in their pockets. Many now said they would no longer attend EDL protests while the current situation existed.

It wasn't just the Jewish Division, there seemed to be a complete lack of direction from the EDL leadership, compounded by a lack of communication, which made them appear aloof from the core membership. The EDL finally released a statement entitled '**Standing Firm**' in which it said there had been a lot of speculation regarding its position on Israel, and the role the EDL Jewish Division was playing in determining its direction. However, the group said it did not believe it appropriate to single out any individuals involved in recent events, and believed it to be in everyone's interests that any further concerns were communicated privately. The EDL said it wished to make it clear it supported Israel's right to exist and to defend itself. The group said there was no reason why it could not continue to support Israel whilst still being fully committed to halting the advance of radical Islam in the UK. The statement claimed that England would always come first and the leadership would '**never risk the future of the EDL by pursuing an agenda that has little to do with the realities facing our country, and which would, quite rightly, do a great deal to jeopardise our cause**'.

The EDL said it would not allow the interests of a small minority override the concerns of the majority of its supporters, its focus was on England, it always had been and it always would be. Showing evidence of naivety or the influence of the pro-Zionists, the EDL then claimed there were parallels to be drawn between the radicalisation it claimed had infected the Palestinians and their supporters and radicalisation in British Mosques. The group claimed that in this respect, '**the people of England and the people of Israel have a great deal in common**'.

The statement continued with the '**Israel is the front line of the battle**' against '**Islam inspired terrorism**' (completely ignoring the reality that the Palestinian issue is primarily over land). The group said the battle against the global jihad was international and they had found they had '**friends in many distant lands, and that our goals often coincide**' and confirming it was retaining its pro-Zionist ethos claimed that the objective of the radicals was that '**Islam must come to dominate Judeo-Christian civilisation**' (this was obviously the new more subtle phrase which would be used attempt to link the fight against militant Islam to Israel). The group claimed the War on Terror was not simply aimed at defending the USA and her allies, but at defeating those who so despise the Judeo-Christian heritage that defines the Western World and that following 9/11 many Western nations had learned a great deal from Israel, a country it claimed had extensive experience of dealing with the realities of terrorism. This obviously ignored Britain's long history of fighting terrorism, including Jewish terrorists in British Mandate Palestine prior to the formation of the state of Israel, a burning unresolved issue in the minds of some EDL supporters.

The statement claimed that if Israel succumbed to '**the forces of radical Islam and the proponents of Sharia**' then the '**only working democracy in the Middle East**' would fall. The EDL claimed that the impact of such a thing would be felt across the world, and would '**massively embolden those who hate the freedoms we enjoy in the Western world. It is in all our interests that the nation on the front line of the battle against radical Islam should not fall**'.

However, the group claimed that its immediate concern would always be with the impact that radical Islam was having at home and its principle concern had always been representing the people that make up our membership, the people of England. Addressing the recent problems regarding Moore, but for some reason not naming her, the statement said the EDL refused to be drawn into alliances with individuals or organisations who '**in their laudable defence of Israel overstep the boundaries of what we believe to be legitimate and reasonable**'.

The group claimed that extremism could not be fought with extremism and the decision made by '**individuals within the EDL Jewish Division**' to ally themselves with the Jewish Task Force, an organisation whose leader, Victor Vancier, had been imprisoned on terrorism charges, was made without the authority of the EDL Leadership. The statement said the EDL had ensured that all ties with the JTF had been severed, as

'Israel itself has proscribed the JTF as a terrorist organisation, and Vancier has been recorded making incredibly offensive and inflammatory statements about black people, Christians, and homosexuals'. It claimed Vancier's comments could hardly be further from the objectives and beliefs of the EDL and it was 'hugely disappointing that in the fallout of this sorry episode a small number of Jewish Division members saw fit to make personal attacks on members of the EDL Support Group for criticising their decision to align themselves with known extremists'.

The group said that following the disagreement over the JTF, the leader of the EDL Jewish Division had decided to step down and leave both the Jewish Division and the EDL as their objectives were clearly not the same (Moore was clearly still involved in the administration of the Jewish Division Facebook page, she was also very vocal on *4freedoms* implying to Lake that he couldn't be expelled from the EDL as she believed that she owned the rights to the name). The EDL said they recognised the value of listening to people with different viewpoints, but that did not mean they were willing to turn a blind eye to other forms of extremism.

Referring to US pastor Terry Jones, the EDL said it did not invite Jones to speak at a demonstration because they believed it would be wrong to provide a platform to anyone who, like Victor Vancier of the JTF, had made incredibly offensive and intolerant statements about homosexuality. The group said that although there was a great deal of disagreement within the EDL about the situation in Israel, no EDL member, however critical of Israel, would justify any mistreatment of Jewish people, or their exclusion from the group. The EDL said the actions of a small minority should not be allowed to sully the reputation of the majority of the group's Jewish supporters, whose commitment to the objectives of the EDL was not in doubt. Obviously forgetting the shutdown of the old Internet forum the EDL claimed it 'would never think of censoring open debate by failing to permit criticism of Israel', but said it would continue to be 'vigilant against infiltration by those who hold antisemitic [sic] views'.

The group said that as well as representing a diverse range of viewpoints, it aimed to represent people of every ethnicity, every religion, every political persuasion and every social class. It claimed that radical Islam only discriminated between radical Muslims and everyone else, therefore and so should the EDL. The EDL said it could not fulfil that commitment if it favoured any one group of people over everyone else (presumably as it had with the LGBT and Jewish Divisions?) and it would continue to allow people to found specialist divisions that reflected their own religious or other views, but would not allow those groups to dictate what it is we believe, or why the EDL existed (again presumably as the LGBT and Jewish divisions had been allowed to do until now).

The EDL said it was 'incredibly disappointing that certain members of the 'wider counter-jihad' (presumably referring to Geller and Spencer) had taken their decision to distance from certain individuals as sheltering anti-Semites or Nazis, and said the accusation was as 'ridiculous as it is offensive'. The statement said that the accusation that the EDL subscribed to any views that could be regarded as fascist, racist or neo-Nazi was completely untrue and they were 'fed up with defending ourselves against these baseless accusations'.

The EDL claimed it wasn't the National Front or the BNP, and said that calling supporters Nazis because they dared to think the country is worth defending amounted to little more than shooting the messenger. The statement said that the more people critical of Islam, or of the government's approach to radical Islam, were condemned as Islamophobes, the more it encouraged ordinary Muslims into inaction. The group said that no one wanted British Muslims to be victimised because of the growing influence of the radicals within their communities, but they should at least feel the imperative to start taking serious action to expel the radicals and determine what needs to change to ensure peaceful integration rather than purposeful segregation and the hostility and misunderstanding that results.

The more the media, the government, and 'the so-called anti-fascists' claimed that the EDL was a Nazi organisation, the more they encouraged segregation, said the statement, because it encouraged the view that the concerns of ordinary people were born of prejudice and are not worth addressing. The EDL said that unprecedented success of the EDL as a street movement was not an indication that the English people had become less tolerant, it was, they claimed, proof that the government had increasingly started to demand that they tolerate the intolerable.

The statement said that the EDL existed to give a voice to ordinary people, who did not have people speaking for them. They were ordinary people, claimed the EDL, who saw the problems with Islam all too clearly, but had been let down by politicians. They were ordinary people who were constantly robbed of the opportunity to help safeguard their communities and their country. The EDL said a lot had changed since it was founded in 2009, but had stayed true to its founding principles, it was a non-violent, anti-racist and anti-Nazi national movement, dedicated to defeating a threat that the British Government was unwilling to address.

6–10 August 2011: England

While this book was being completed, riots broke out in a number of towns and cities across England. The disturbances followed a peaceful protest outside Tottenham Police Station calling for justice for a local man shot dead by police. Fires were started and shops looted, with police making 55 arrests.

Over the course of the next few days, riots and looting spread to other parts of London and also broke out in other major cities across England, resulting in millions of pounds worth of damage, thousands of arrests and five deaths. There was a definite sense among the public that the police were standing off. In the wake of this perceived police inactivity, people felt forced to defend themselves and their communities.

In Dalston, north-east London, Turkish and Kurdish vigilantes armed with sticks, bats and even a machete were followed by a *Guardian* reporter who described them as merely '**defending their businesses**'. The *Daily Mail* agreed, saying they were '**forced onto the streets to protect their shops**'. In Whitechapel, rioters were reportedly deterred by 1,500 Muslims who took to the streets. The *Daily Telegraph* claimed that along with Poles in Ealing who helped with a post-riot clean up, it was proof that '**Immigrants love this country more than we do**'. In Southall, west London, Sikhs took to the streets to defend their temple, some of them were carrying swords and hockey sticks, one man was pictured carrying an axe. They were described as '**defending their community**' by the *Daily Mail* and *Financial Times*. During a third night of violence in Birmingham, local Muslims gathered in the Winson Green area of the city. They were praised by the media as peaceful people protecting their community, even though there were reports they had armed themselves with bats and sticks. The *Telegraph* claimed they had '**shown themselves to be not just as law-abiding as the Anglo-Saxons, but far more inspiring**'.

In south London, over 300 English Millwall and Charlton supporters gathered in Eltham to defend their community from looting gangs. There were no reports of anyone being armed. They were joined by a handful of EDL, whose presence and the fact that patriotic songs were sung ensured the press condemned them as right-wing. In Enfield, north London, a large group of Tottenham Hotspur supporters, joined by local people who with the football hooligan presence on the streets finally felt safe to leave their homes, toured the area seeking to confront any looters. As in Eltham, they were only armed with their fists, however, the *Daily Telegraph* claimed there were '**ugly scenes and racial tension**'. A Sky News reporter desperately tried to intimate they were thugs just looking for trouble. There were various reports of EDL involvement, but this seems to have stemmed from a chant of '**England**' which was allegedly heard at one point.

Acting Metropolitan Police Commissioner Tim Godwin said he was worried that groups such as the EDL and BNP were trying to hijack the situation and cause more tension. Deputy Mayor of London, Kit Malthouse, condemned the people in Enfield as '**vigilantes**' and said it was '**deeply undesirable**' to see the EDL in the borough. The *Manchester Evening News* claimed that '**right-wing yobs**' were linked to a night of violence in Manchester and Salford, although the article provided no proof of this and GMP attributed the trouble to '**organised crime groups**'.

In an emergency meeting of Parliament, Prime Minister David Cameron set out plans to combat elements he referred to as '**broken and sick**'. Referring to claims the EDL were involved in vigilante action, Cameron said "**I described parts of our society as sick and there is none sicker than the EDL**". So after days of rioting and looting, millions of pounds worth of damage, deaths and injuries, the EDL, not the rioters, was singled out. Cameron said the riots and looting indicated a complete lack of responsibility, a lack of proper parenting, a lack of proper upbringing, a lack of ethics and morals. He was right of course, but who had abandoned morality and discipline? Yes, that's right his political peers. Of course, in matters of morality we should have our so-called betters in Parliament to take example from, except we don't.

Many still sitting on the benches of Westminster would know all about a complete lack of morality, the place is a moral vacuum. They are people who have helped themselves to thousands of pounds of tax-payers money by fraudulently claiming expenses and have also squandered billions on pointless schemes. We've also had cash-for-questions, cash-for-honours, cash-for-influence, passports or visas for favours, dodgy dossiers leading to illegal wars and thousands of British deaths. The list goes on and on. It's not just the fact they are dishonest either, they are by and large totally incompetent, frittering away billions of pounds of our money on hair-brained idealistic schemes such as Public Finance Initiatives or computer systems which never work, that is without considering the billions we have pumped into Europe or bailing out banks who aren't so keen to return the favour in lending to ordinary people whose money has kept them afloat.

Our Europhile middle class politicians have subsidised and dragged up the standard of living in other European countries, while our own has fallen. They know nothing of the real world, why would they? Most were born with a silver spoon in their mouth and have never known the dignity of manual labour. They are like spoiled children who don't know the value of money because most of them have never had to break sweat for it.

The riots, like the issue of militant Islam and the subsequent rise of the English Defence League, were about identity and alienation. The rioters are excluded from modern materialistic Britain and with unemployment so rife and immigration still virtually unchecked they wanted a part of it and took it. The riots, or rather the shopping with violence which took place, were a reaction to a lack of identity.

Traditional British culture has been abandoned, we now pursue a manufactured, egotistical, grasping culture and the riots were a subconscious attempt to identify with that. British values have also been purposely abandoned, along with education, discipline and morality and the riots were a reflection of that. But even so, the English were blamed because we are the ones they seek to destroy. Lack of identity is a problem which now affects all creeds in modern Britain and one which will cause an increasing number of events such as the riots over the next few years.

Summary

Following the initial outrage in Luton and an unsteady start, the EDL became the largest street movement Britain had seen in decades. The widespread media coverage the movement received, although wholly negative, rallied hundreds of disaffected British people to the cause. Someone had finally stood up to speak for them. Grinding the cities to a halt, subsequent demos in Manchester, Leeds and Stoke attracted the kind of numbers which made the authorities sit up and take notice. The counter-protest in Wootton Bassett also proved the group could mobilise effectively at short notice.

The rise in support was followed by a crack down by the authorities. The EDL was seemingly investigated for extremist links at the time of the Edinburgh demo, but none were apparently found as police attitudes to the group visibly mellowed following Lennon's release from custody. As a result, the EDL did start to conform to some extent, introducing its own stewards and engaging fully in liaison with the police prior to protests. Large peaceful demonstrations in London and Bolton followed, seeing big turnouts and large numbers of anti-fascists arrested. The far-left dominated anti-fascist movement was also totally unprepared for the EDL targeting its meetings and as a result, was virtually brought to its knees, in some cases forced to use anti-English racism to boost numbers in Wales and Scotland. In smashing the far-left, the EDL did what the British far-right had been unable to do and took their streets back from the communists.

Again as this book was being finalised, a petition organised by the far-left opposing a proposed EDL march in Tower Hamlets resulted in the Home Secretary announcing a ban on ALL marches in five London boroughs for 30 days. As well as preventing the EDL from marching, it has also cancelled an anti-fascist march on the same day, a far-left protest at an arms fair and potentially Gay Pride. The anti-fascists support of the establishment is akin to turkeys voting for Christmas and undoubtedly proves they are as reactionary as they accuse the EDL of being.

Numbers on demos steadily increased, Dudley, Aylesbury and Newcastle all attracted large numbers. The Dudley rooftop protest achieved national headlines and subsequent demonstrations across the country all achieved credible turnouts. The turnout for the '**Big One**' in Bradford was admittedly disappointing, but was followed by the poppy burning incident which forced more supporters onto the streets. Following the EDL demonstration in Amsterdam, the authorities, worried about foreign extremists (justifiably it would seem in the wake of the Norway atrocities), targeted the group again. Certain EDL members were handed harsh CRASBO restrictions, severely restricting their human rights. However, these orders have gone unchallenged, simply because as they did with terror legislation and suspected Muslim terrorists, the establishment has created a bogeyman to introduce draconian laws which will eventually be used on everyone.

Demonstrations in Preston and Nuneaton saw promising turnouts and were viewed as a success, if not for the fact the group staged two successful protests on one day, then for the statement by police beforehand that they did not consider the EDL an extremist organisation. The rapid rise of the EDL did have negative implications as it attracted people seeking to use the movement for their own agenda. The composition, structure and most importantly inexperience of the EDL left it vulnerable to infiltration, but ironically not by the contemporary far-right as many commentators would automatically presume. The Kahanists who entered the movement and the subsequent links to foreign extremists were hard to shake and have certainly damaged the movement.

In fact up until the Luton demonstration, numbers were rising steadily. That is when the famous '**air of legitimisation**' quote appeared in *The Guardian*, and the people standing in the shadows made their move for control of the EDL. How they achieved this and have maintained influence is open to question, but in response, the group stopped talking to its working class support, shifting to a 'hands across the water' international agenda that was overtly, and primarily, pro-Israel. The low turnouts at Harrow and the Israeli Embassy demonstrations illuminated how unpopular that agenda is with the majority of EDL supporters. The infamous London meeting followed, where the EDL, seemingly strongly influenced by Alan Lake and his entryist pro-Zionist Section 9 group, abandoned its working class roots and announced that the middle classes were joining the movement in their droves.

The shift towards Israel and middle class Pardonia alienated a lot of the EDL's core support; this was compounded further by the promotion of minority groups above the majority. This has resulted in a rapid decline in numbers on the streets and the formation of purist splinter group UKFD. However, even with an obvious loss of support, the EDL leadership, conforming to media and contemporary social requirements and having appeared to have moved on to greater things, didn't seem to care. After the EDL bizarrely claimed it was now a human rights organisation, it soon became apparent that the people now steering the movement cared little for its founding ethos. Some people were promoted into positions of power which they shouldn't have been anywhere near, not on merit, but because of their minority status or their vocal support for minority groups. Not only did the movement turn away from its founding ethos, it also started targeting other allied groups, such as Casuals United, organising spoiler demonstrations or briefing against UKFD, seemingly to rein in overall control of the resistance movement which was now evolving. In fact, control appeared more important to them than the cause.

When the issue finally came to a head, resulting in the resignation of Roberta Moore and the statement from Pamela Geller, the EDL was branded as being infiltrated by neo-Nazis. This was done because, as they have demonstrated throughout this book, the pro-Zionist lobby brands anyone who disagrees with it as anti-Semitic or neo-Nazi (while totally ignoring the supremacist nature of the Jewish Kahanist movement). These words are now employed to such an extent that they have little meaning anymore. In response to the accusation, instead of defending the movement and its loyal supporters, Stephen Lennon issued a statement stating that: '**Israel is a shining star of democracy. If Israel falls, we all fall. This is what our movement has been built on for two years**'.

It was ridiculous to even try and suggest that the EDL was built on Israel and resulted in a further fall in numbers and the leadership losing a lot of credibility with rank and file supporters. The EDL was built on the defence of British troops, it was built on defending working class communities against militant Islam and that evolved into opposing the corrupt political system which facilitates its existence. The EDL was built on defending English values, customs and the English way of life. It was certainly not founded to defend any foreign realm, to suggest such is nonsense and the sort of propaganda peddled by the foreign extremists.

As a result, many rank and file EDL supporters felt that the movement no longer represented what most of them signed up for. Many lost faith and stated they would no longer march under the EDL banner. The movement lost tried and tested activists, veterans of the streets, conquerors of the militant left, and replaced them with people high on promises but low on action. Although the EDL could undoubtedly still cause disruption and call on around 1000 hardcore activists (numbers at the Telford demo in August 2011 dipped to around a hundred) for high profile national demonstrations, only a year before it was pulling well over two thousand. If local demographic factors are disregarded, it is hard for anyone to dispute that since Luton, active support in the form of feet-on-the-street has fallen.

A lot of the EDL casual support is now also taken for granted. Two of the group's biggest turnouts, Stoke and Dudley, were both extensively leafleted beforehand. The continual hacking of the group's website and Facebook pages has also undoubtedly hindered the EDL in getting its message across. This has affected casual support, indicating a level of amateurism which could have been avoided and leaving the movement open to ridicule. The leaked merchandise list and the subsequent disappearance of the leadership and the supposed Support Group left some rank and file supporters who were named dangerously exposed and many more disillusioned. It was left to the rank and file support to defend their own people, which they did, but that also led to a further loss of leadership credibility.

The EDL undoubtedly has an image problem. The movement needs to mature, it needs to rid itself of the drink and drugs culture which, although only a reflection of society at large, hamstrings its progress. Some activists use demonstrations as an excuse to drink as much as possible and this is undoubtedly extremely counter-productive as it ensures a level of aggression on protests. The EDL also needs to evolve strategically and theoretically, but again, this is hampered by an intransient leadership and extremist outside influences. The whole issue of the non-integration into traditional Western society of some British Muslims is compounded by misunderstanding or ignorance of Islam or cultural traditions. A lot of the information bandied about by the EDL regarding Islam is from sources as extreme as the mujahideen it opposes. As English people, we need to find out for ourselves, view things with English eyes, the last thing we need are tutorials from foreign, or even home-grown, extremists.

The internal politics and infighting which has plagued the EDL for over a year has undoubtedly contributed to the fall in support. Although English regional identity has contributed, the infighting has been magnified by an intransient dictatorial leadership and an entrenched sub-leadership, both unelected. Mistakes have been made, but like we see in government, no one has paid the price. There are people in charge whose main concern, once their position is gained, is holding onto it, rather than furthering the aims of the EDL.

As a result, the EDL is in disarray, too many people want a slice of the action and control in some way. Of course, this is only a reflection of the narcissistic society we have allowed to develop, in which people aren't happy being a small anonymous cog in a big wheel, the Jeremy Kyle generation crave attention. Therefore, a multitude of small cliques have formed within the movement, this is proving counter-productive and many of these small groups are led by people who are solely active on the Internet, rather than on the streets, and only interested in self-promotion and their own agenda.

As working class English people, we are now second class citizens in our own land which our ancestors have slaved, fought and died for. We have been villainised, dumbed down, depoliticised and excluded from the democratic process. We face a two-tier system which discriminates against us, simply because the Europhile middle class establishment seek to subjugate and dilute our nationality and inherent patriotism for assimilation into the European super-state.

Whether the concerns of English people are addressed or not, or the problems within the EDL itself are tackled, something was awakened in the summer of 2009. It was something which had been repressed and the establishment believed had been conditioned out of the English people, our spirit of resistance. One by one we are waking up, however, our biggest enemy is still the apathy of our own people, they have been brainwashed into thinking they can no longer make a difference.

Their biggest mistake is turning us into the underdog. Now any further clampdown by the state will only add support to the English resistance movement. Take out one and ten will be spurred to take their place, jail one and ten more will be stirred into taking to the streets. We won't stop where we are, we will adapt, educate ourselves and our people. We will take this country back, if not for ourselves or for our betrayed generations, then for the future of our children.

We will reclaim our birthright, but will not do this by force of arms, as, contrary to popular belief, we are not stupid. We must take our lead from the American civil rights, or Indian independence movements, bearing arms will only play into the hands of the people who seek to subjugate us. ANY violence is counter-productive, we will only achieve our aims through the ballot box, but it can be done. Now is the time for the establishment to enter into dialogue with us, if not, they might find like their mate in Libya, by the time they realise they have to, it will be too late.

We are descendants of the people who built the biggest empire the world has ever seen, we have the blood of men who walked into sheets of steel on the Western Front without breaking step coursing through our veins. We are people who defied the might of Nazi Germany, the sons and daughters of people who worked all their lives so we could have the rights which are now denied us. The spirit of Peterloo and Jarrow burns deeply in our hearts and will never be extinguished.

There are some 'proper people' in this movement. Admittedly, they are people who would be frowned upon by polite society. They maybe haven't got the social graces, seem rough and ready, brutal or crude, but give me those people any day of the week. They are honest, salt of the earth types who would stand their ground for this country and their comrades no matter what the odds. I am proud to stand shoulder to shoulder with them.

We are the working class, we will never submit, the word surrender is not in our vocabulary and we are coming down the road. We stand defiant amidst the ruins of Rome. And Caesar's spirit, raging for revenge, with Ate by his side come hot from hell, shall in these confines with a monarch's voice, cry "**havoc!**" and let slip the working class.

No Surrender, not now, not ever. God save the Queen.